CREDIT
DERIVATIVES

TECHNIQUES TO MANAGE CREDIT RISK FOR FINANCIAL PROFESSIONALS

ERIK BANKS,
MORTON GLANTZ, AND PAUL SIEGEL

McGraw-Hill

New York   Chicago   San Francisco
Lisbon   London   Madrid   Mexico City
Milan   New Delhi   San Juan   Seoul
Singapore   Sydney   Toronto

1 2 3 4 5 6 7 8 9 0   DOC/DOC   0 9 8 7 6

ISBN-13 978-0-07-145314-1
ISBN-10 0-07-145314-8

This publication is designed to provide accurate and authoritative information in regard to
the subject matter covered. It is sold with the understanding that neither the author nor the
publisher is engaged in rendering legal, accounting, or other professional service. If legal
advice or other expert assistance is required, the services of a competent professional
person should be sought.

—From a Declaration of Principles jointly adopted by Committee
of the American Bar Association and a Committee of Publishers

McGraw-Hill books are available at special quantity discounts to use as premiums and
sales promotions, or for use in corporate training programs. For more information, please
write to the Director of Special Sales, McGraw-Hill Professional, Two Penn Plaza, New
York, NY 10121-2298. Or contact your local bookstore.

Library of Congress Cataloging-in-Publication Data
Banks, Erik.
  Credit derivaties : techniques to manage credit risk for financial professionals /
by Erik Banks, Morton Glantz, and Paul Siegel.
     p. cm.
  ISBN 0-07-145314-8 (hardcover : alk. paper)
  1. Credit derivatives. 2. Risk management. I. Glantz, Morton. II. Siegel, Paul.
III. Title.
  HG6024. A3B3615 2006

  332.64'57–dc22   2006006614

DEDICATION

This book is dedicated to our families and friends. We also want to pay homage to the Woody Allen axiom — to which we point all those wise souls who consider a career involved with credit derivatives — as it is good to be regularly reminded: "Money is better than poverty, if only for financial reasons."

CONTENTS

Acknowledgments   vii

Part 1

Credit Derivative Products and Applications   1

Chapter 1

An Introduction to Credit Derivatives   3

Chapter 2

Fundamental Credit Derivative Products   25

Chapter 3

Structured and Synthetic Credit Products   53

Chapter 4

An Overview of Credit Derivative Applications   97

Part 2

Quantitative Tools   121

Chapter 5

A Primer on Risk Modeling   123

Chapter 6

A Basic Credit Default Swap Model   163

Chapter 7

Modeling Credit Default Risk   183

Chapter 8

Portfolio Management of Default Risk   217

Chapter 9

Ancillary Credit Risk Tools and Techniques   255

Part 3

Regulatory, Control, and Legal Issues   283

Chapter 10

Credit Derivative Documentation   285

Chapter 11

Regulatory and Control Issues   301

Appendix

A Review of Commercial Credit Modeling Analytics   317

Answers to Chapter Exercises   323

Selected References   345

Index   349

ACKNOWLEDGMENTS

The authors greatly appreciate the efforts of Jeffrey Bohn, Ph.D. and Robert Kissell, who contributed important portions to this book. Jeff leads the Financial Strategies group at Shinsei Bank in Tokyo. Formerly, Jeff led Moody KMV's global research and credit strategies groups. He has published widely in the area of credit risk research. Jeff holds a BA with Honors in Economics from Brigham Young University and an MS in Finance from the University of California, Berkeley. He received his Ph.D. in Finance from the University of California, Berkeley. Robert Kissell is an expert in quantitative modeling and risk management. He holds a BS in Applied Math & Statistics, a MS in Business Management, a MS in Applied Math, and a Ph.D. in Economics.

PART 1

Credit Derivative Products and Applications

An Introduction to Credit Derivatives

The credit derivative market has emerged as one of the most dynamic and innovative sectors of the global financial system. Credit derivative contracts are financial instruments that transfer between two parties the risk and return characteristics of a credit-risky reference asset. These have become an integral part of the risk management and investment strategies of global investors and intermediaries. Though credit derivatives are relatively new compared to other derivatives—having been developed as recently as the mid-1990s—participation is already widespread and growth rates are impressive. Innovation and expansion show no signs of slowing, suggesting that the sector should continue to remain vital and vibrant. As we explore the credit derivative marketplace in this text, we shall examine the instruments from various different angles, including applications, valuation, and control; each provides an important perspective on the essential elements of the marketplace.

In order to create an appropriate framework for the material that follows in the balance of the book, we devote this chapter to a brief overview of the main credit derivative products. We also examine market growth drivers and discuss the general types of risks that characterize credit derivative contracts. We shall revisit each of these topics in greater detail throughout the text.

OVERVIEW OF PRODUCTS

Credit derivatives are contracts that generate an economic payoff based on the credit performance of a reference credit asset; performance may be determined by whether or not the reference credit defaults, and/or whether its credit spreads improve or deteriorate.

Credit default contracts pay off based on the occurrence of a predefined credit event related to a specific reference obligor; the event may be related to failure to pay, bankruptcy, restructuring, moratorium, or repudiation. If the event occurs, the credit guarantor (or protection seller, who is effectively "long" the credit) makes a payment to the beneficiary (protection buyer, who is "short" the credit) based on physical or cash settlement procedures. It is worth stressing at this early stage that clarity is important in defining the credit event underpinning a contract: if the contract is imprecise or allows for too much interpretation, one of the parties may dispute whether an event of default has actually occurred.[1]

Credit spread contracts pay off based on the creditworthiness of the reference asset; default is thus just one state in a continuum of creditworthiness. For instance, credit deterioration may occur as a result of weakness in the obligor's financial position, which leads to credit rating downgrades and a widening of the credit spread versus a risk-free benchmark; even if the obligor does not default on its obligations, the holder of the derivative will receive a payment related to the differential between the credit spread at trade date and maturity date. Credit deterioration can impact entire industries or sectors as a result of macro/exogenous events, suggesting that credit spread

---

1 For instance, interpretation issues are critical when the reference obligor undergoes a debt restructuring that impairs the value of the reference asset, but does not go into technical default. The occurrence of such an event may not be easy to verify and the description of the events in the agreement may be vague and require subjective judgments (i.e., whether the restructuring had a material adverse effect on the credit). If a materiality requirement is incorporated in the contract, two events must occur before a payment is triggered: (1) a credit event must occur, and (2) a significant change in the price of the reference security must take place. The logic behind a materiality requirement is that a "technical" default by the reference entity, which does not alter the value of the reference security, should not trigger payment under the contract. The most common materiality requirement relates to the reference asset's credit spread. If spread materiality is specified, then the spread between the reference security's yield and the interpolated swap rate must increase by some predetermined amount (e.g., 250 basis points) before the contract triggers a payment.

widening is a function of systematic, as well as idiosyncratic, forces. Of course, the opposite scenario can also occur: A reference credit's financial standing may improve, causing a spread tightening that benefits those holding long positions. In addition, systemic forces can create spread tightening across industries, sectors, and countries.

Credit derivatives have evolved considerably over the past decade, and the market now features a range of core default and spread products, along with certain "second generation" variations. The popularity of the main instruments allows them to act as direct competitors to traditional credit-based banking and insurance products. This is perhaps not surprising, because the sectors share certain similarities. For example, an issuer pays a bank a fee for a letter of credit or an insurer a premium for bond insurance to guarantee debt repayments on a particular issue or issuance program. The same can be done with certain credit derivative contracts.

For purposes of our introductory discussion, we review below the most common structures:

- Asset swaps
- Credit default swaps
- Credit spread forwards
- Total return swaps
- Basket swaps
- Credit spread options

These core products can be used to create other types of structured credit instruments, which we classify broadly as:

- Credit linked notes
- Synthetic collateralized debt obligations

To supplement our review in this chapter, we shall discuss each instrument in greater detail in Chapters 2 and 3.

Asset Swaps

An *asset swap* is a bilateral derivative contract that covers both default and deterioration (appreciation) scenarios. The asset swap, which is a package of a credit-risky bond and an interest rate or currency swap, has emerged as an integral component of the investor-driven capital markets over the past two decades. The contract is widely considered to be a building block of the credit derivative

FIGURE 1.1

Asset Swap Package: Synthetic FRN

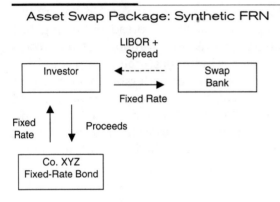

market, allowing investors to express a view or obtain protection on a credit reference from the long or short side. An investor may wish to invest in a specific credit-risky asset class. When the desired asset exists and the returns are favorable, the investor simply buys the asset by funding it through normal sources. However, if the precise features are not available, the asset can be created synthetically by repackaging a reference security with an interest rate or currency swap. For instance, if an investor seeks to invest in Company XYZ's bonds on a floating-rate basis, but XYZ has only issued fixed-rate bonds, the intermediary can sell the investor the fixed-rate bonds and attach a swap that converts the fixed-rate coupons into London Interbank Offered Rate (LIBOR) plus a spread; this creates a synthetic floating-rate note (FRN). The reverse structure can also be created.[2] The basic asset swap package is highlighted in Figure 1.1.

Variations on the asset swap theme emerged in the 1990s and have become increasingly common; the most prevalent include callable asset swaps, puttable asset swaps, asset swap switches, and asset swaptions, which we shall consider in greater detail in the next chapter.

---

2 Note that the same concept applies to asset swaps created with currency, rather than interest rate, swaps. In such cases the transaction also involves initial and final exchange of principal, as in any conventional currency swap. Asset swaps referencing basis flows (e.g., commercial paper (CP) versus LIBOR, EURIBOR versus EONIA) and nonstandard/amortizing/zero-coupon cash flows can also be created.

F I G U R E 1.2

Credit Default Swap

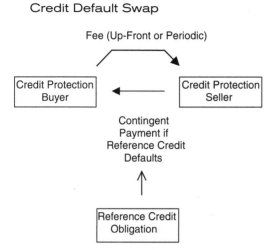

Credit Default Swaps

The credit default swap (CDS), the single most popular derivative instrument in the credit markets, is a unilateral contract covering default events. In a basic CDS the credit protection buyer pays the credit protection seller an up-front or periodic fee[3] in exchange for a compensatory payment that becomes due and payable if the reference credit defaults during the life of the contract; if no default occurs, the credit protection seller makes no payments and the contract terminates.[4] A CDS can be settled in cash or physical terms: under cash settlement the seller pays the buyer a sum equal to the notional amount times the postdefault price of the reference obligation (generally computed as an average of several market quotations); under physical settlement the buyer delivers the notional reference obligation and receives par value. The fundamental CDS structure is reflected in Figure 1.2.

The market also features a standard CDS index swap that merges elements of default swaps and collateralized debt obligation structuring technology. We shall discuss CDSs and index swaps in Chapter 2.

---

3 In fact, a quarterly payment of the fee, or premium, is the market standard.
4 This structure is equivalent to the buyer purchasing a digital credit put option, with a payout equal to 0 (if no default occurs) or a postdefault amount defined by market quotes (if default occurs); note that there is no continuum of payouts between the default/no-default scenarios as in the credit spread option.

FIGURE 1.3

Absolute Credit Spread Forward

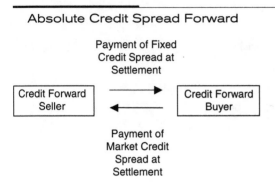

Credit Spread Forward

The credit spread forward, a bilateral contract covering default and deterioration (appreciation) scenarios, is simply a forward refer-encing risky credit spread in absolute or relative terms. The con-tract calls for the exchange of a single cash flow at a future time based on the differential between the credit spread contracted on trade date and the prevailing market spread at maturity (absolute), or the difference between two risky credit spreads (relative). For instance, in the absolute spread version the seller pays the buyer a fixed spread and receives a market spread compared to its risk-free benchmark; the fixed spread is set at trade date, and the evaluation versus the market spread occurs at transaction maturity. The buyer, by extension, agrees to pay the market spread over the risk-free benchmark in exchange for the fixed spread. In practice the pay-ments are netted into a single flow in one direction. The basic credit forward structure is illustrated in Figure 1.3.

Total Return Swaps

The total return swap (TRS) is a bilateral contract covering default and deterioration (appreciation) scenarios that transfers the eco-nomics of a credit reference between two parties.[5] The TRS receiver is entitled to the total return on the reference asset (appreciation plus coupons) in exchange for periodic floating payments (e.g., a LIBOR-based flow plus a spread); this is equivalent to creating a synthetic long position in the reference asset (indeed, the TRS is

---

5 Note that the TRS can be used in other asset classes as well; for instance, equity index TRSs, which function in the manner described in the text, are quite popular.

F I G U R E 1.4

Unfunded Total Return Swap

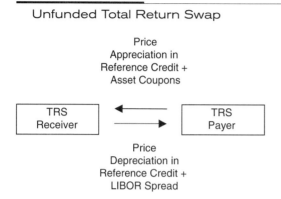

often considered a form of synthetic financing). The TRS payer, in turn, is entitled to any depreciation that occurs in the security, along with a LIBOR spread. When the TRS payer owns the underlying reference asset, it is effectively transferring the economic risk of the asset, thus creating a synthetic short position (or first loss credit protection).[6] However, because it still owns the position in such circumstances, it must continue to fund it through its own balance sheet sources.[7] If the price of the reference asset rises, the receiver benefits from the appreciation; if the price declines as a result of depreciation or default, the payer benefits. The TRS can be arranged on a funded or unfunded basis: A funded TRS requires the receiver to purchase a risk-free (or low-risk) floating-rate asset that yields the LIBOR stream payable to the TRS payer. In the unfunded TRS the receiver has no such asset, so the LIBOR stream must be sourced from cash flow; this means, of course, that the position in the TRS is highly leveraged. Figure 1.4 summarizes the flows of an unfunded TRS.

Basket Swaps

The basket swap is a unilateral contract covering multiple credit default events. The standard basket swap, created by pooling a number of reference credits into a single structure, generates

---

6 It is worth noting that in transferring the price appreciation/depreciation, the TRS mechanism transfers economic changes that are due to both interest rate movements and credit spread movements; the two are not separated, meaning that the vehicle is as much an interest rate risk tool as a credit risk tool.

7 In fact, the net profit to the TRS payer is the basis point spread over the funding cost times the notional amount of the transaction. Thus, if the payer receives LIBOR + 10bps from the receiver and can fund at LIBOR flat, they earn 10bps running on the notional of the transaction.

F I G U R E 1.5

Basket Default Swap

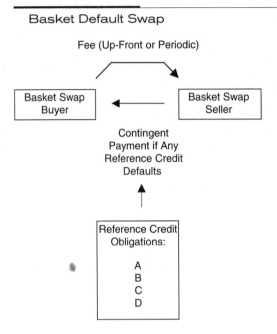

a payoff to the buyer if a credit defaults (but no payment if a reference credit deteriorates but does not default). If several credits in the basket default, the buyer receives a payout on each one; the basket thus functions as a portfolio of CDS swaps. As with any individual CDS, the credit buyer pays the seller a fee; however, the inclusion of multiple reference credits can lower the overall fee payable (though this depends ultimately on the construction of the basket and the correlation between the reference credits). Figure 1.5 highlights a standard basket swap.

Various other basket swap structures exist, including first (nth) to default baskets, senior baskets, and subordinated baskets; we explore these variations in Chapter 2.

Credit Spread Options

A credit spread option is a unilateral contract covering default or deterioration (appreciation). The standard option grants the buyer the right, but not the obligation, to obtain a compensatory payment from the seller if the spread of a reference credit widens beyond the strike level (for a put) or tightens inside the strike (for a call);

F I G U R E   1.6

Credit Spread Put Option

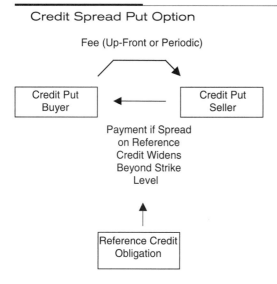

Fee (Up-Front or Periodic)

Credit Put Buyer

Credit Put Seller

Payment if Spread
on Reference
Credit Widens
Beyond Strike
Level

Reference Credit
Obligation

in exchange for this right, the buyer pays the seller an up-front premium. A put option gives the buyer the right to sell the spread at the strike, meaning a gain as the reference credit deteriorates and its spread widens out; in the extreme, a defaulting credit will feature a very wide credit spread, so the put provides a form of default protection. A call option, in contrast, gives the buyer the right to purchase the spread at the strike, meaning a gain as the reference credit improves and the spread tightens. The spread may be defined in terms of a floating-rate reference, such as LIBOR, or a fixed-rate risk-free benchmark, such as Treasuries. Figure 1.6 illustrates the flows of a credit spread put option.

The fundamental "building blocks" of the credit derivative market described above (which we summarize in Table 1.1) are used to create a series of synthetic assets, including credit-linked notes and synthetic/structured collateralized debt obligations, which we describe immediately below.

Credit-Linked Notes

Credit-linked notes (CLNs) are combinations of credit-risky assets and derivatives, or risk-free bonds and credit derivatives, and can be issued through highly rated host issuers or dedicated repackaging vehicles. The basic CLN is a package consisting of a fixed-rate

TABLE 1.1

Fundamental Credit Derivative Contracts

Contract	Type	Protection*
Asset swap	Bilateral	Default, deterioration
Credit default swap	Unilateral	Default
Credit spread forward	Bilateral	Default, deterioration
Total return swap	Bilateral	Default, deterioration
Basket swap	Unilateral	Default
Credit spread option	Unilateral	Default, deterioration

* Any contract providing protection against deterioration (e.g., spread widening) by extension provides the second party with exposure to appreciation (e.g., spread tightening).

bond or FRN and a simple or structured credit derivative, which allows investors to earn the returns on a credit-risky investment without having to own the underlying credit asset. The vanilla structure can be settled in cash or physical terms: if a credit event occurs, the note terminates and the investor receives a principal repayment reflecting the differential between the asset's pre- and postdefault value, or it delivers the reference asset and receives the market price. The repackaged bond is a securitized form of the asset swap described above, combining credit-risky securities with derivatives into a synthetic asset. The use of a trust or SPE to combine and repackage the bond and swap cash flows (rather than third-party host issuer) generally creates a more efficient and liquid structure. The basic CLN structure is illustrated in Figure 1.7.

FIGURE 1.7

Basic CLN

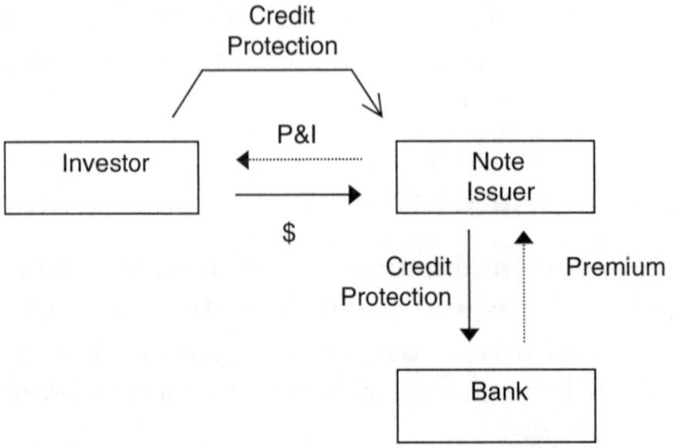

Structured and Synthetic
Collateralized Debt Obligations

The collateralized debt obligation (CDO) is an asset-backed mechanism that pools and securitizes corporate credit obligations, including credit-risky loans and bonds; though the CDO is not a credit derivative-based structure, its architecture has led to the development of derivative-based equivalents, as noted below. In creating a CDO, a bank sells a pool of credit-risky assets to an SPE or trust, which purchases the pool via the issuance of tranches of securities,[8] each with its own risk and return characteristics; in practice a portfolio manager, with relevant expertise, is appointed to manage the portfolio under the supervision of the trustee. The risk of the collateral pool depends primarily on credit quality and diversification: better credit quality and greater diversification reduce the specter of default risk (but lead to lower investor returns).

While the standard CDO is an asset-backed security based on balance sheet assets and funding, the same technologies have been used to create two credit derivative-based structures: the structured CDO and the synthetic CDO. In the structured CDO, a bank issues a CLN via an SPE that references individual credit assets in the target portfolio; the risk of the assets is transferred into the SPE, but the physical assets remain on the bank's balance sheet. In a standard synthetic CDO, a sponsoring bank issues CLNs to investors to finance a pool of high-quality collateral assets, which are used to secure a CDS between the sponsoring bank and the issuing SPE or trust; the CDS references the specific credits in the sponsoring bank's portfolio requiring protection. The SPE receives a fee for providing the default protection; this fee, combined with the principal and interest cash flows from the high-quality collateral pool, is paid to investors funding the CLNs. Variations and extensions include the single tranche synthetic CDO and the CDS index tranche, which we discuss in Chapter 3.

DRIVERS OF MARKET GROWTH

Credit derivatives have gained considerable popularity since their introduction several years ago. Participation has become increasingly

---

8 The actual tranche structure is a function of the pool and its characteristics, as well as
  the availability of different forms of enhancement, such as excess spread, subordination,
  and overcollateralization.

broad and global, with institutions from different economic sectors and regions using the contracts to achieve various end goals.

Financial institutions, including banks, investment banks, and securities firms, are still the single largest users of credit derivatives. This is logical, since financial institutions originate, trade, hedge, sell, and repackage credit risks; credit derivatives provide another tool by which to manage aspects of their core business. While financial institutions are vital market participants—and responsible for the majority of innovation and liquidity—they are not alone; other institutions play an important role in the market as well. Pension funds, hedge funds, investment funds, insurance companies, and corporations, for instance, use credit derivatives in order to hedge credit risk exposures or express a speculative/ arbitrage view on forward credit spreads or possible defaults. Indeed, the role of nonfinancial firms has been critical in building two-way flows, injecting liquidity, and increasing price transparency. We shall consider the role of financial and nonfinancial institutions with regard to credit derivative applications at greater length in Chapter 4. In this section, however, we summarize key drivers applicable across institutions.

Institutions can use credit derivative contracts in order to do the following:

- Separate/decompose credit risk from other forms of market risk or physical assets: this permits an institution to isolate the credit risk dimension of an asset explicitly, permitting a position to be taken or hedged without concern over other risk variables, and without needing to advise the issuer or owner of the asset.
- Optimize the risks and returns of a credit risk portfolio: this allows an institution to select from among all available instruments to generate the best possible returns on credit risk investment for a given level of risk; because credit derivatives are often more liquid than other credit assets, incremental returns can be generated for a given level of credit risk exposure.
- Hedge, reduce, or diversify credit risk portfolios: this permits an institution to again select from among all possible tools to hedge, diversify, or otherwise modify credit risk exposures in the most efficient and cost-effective manner possible; the cheapest possible

hedges can often be obtained in the credit derivative
market.

- Access new/restricted investment opportunities: this
  allows an institution to create synthetic assets or assets
  with synthetic maturities (including those to fill in term
  structure gaps), establish short positions where it may be
  difficult or impossible to do so, or invest in a marketplace
  that might otherwise be restricted from a regulatory
  perspective; ultimately, the creation of new investments
  can help optimize the investment risk/return profile.
- Establish speculative positions in one or more credit-risky
  assets: this allows an institution to express an outright view
  on credit spreads, credit default, credit volatility, or credit
  correlation directly; as the market expands, the ability to do
  so across an increasingly broad range of reference
  credits grows in tandem.
- Trade or position credit views on a forward basis: this
  allows an institution to crystallize a view on forward,
  rather than spot, credit spreads; because forward expectations may be quite different than current ones, the flexibility
  can create a more accurate portfolio.

Practical risk and investment management drivers such as
these have been instrumental in fueling market growth. They have
been aided by parallel efforts regarding standardization of documentation and clarification of legal terms and definitions. Growth
in electronic trading platforms that allow more flexible and transparent dealing of credit risks has also been an important driver;
because the market is an OTC forum, electronic conduits that promote pricing and dealing efficiencies have already helped build
volumes in "vanilla" default products.[9]

Market growth, driven by the factors noted above, is evidenced by the trend of industry volume statistics (Table 1.2).
Though compilation of credit derivative activities as a separate
subcategory of financial derivatives is a relatively recent initiative,
annual data released by the International Swap and Derivatives
Association (ISDA, the industry trade group) suggests that growth
has been rapid; indeed, OTC credit derivatives, though still much

---

9 For instance, electronic platforms such as Creditex allow registered participants to deal
  in an interactive, electronic environment.

T A B L E   1.2

OTC Derivative Market Statistics

$ Tln Notional	Credit	Credit (Annual Growth)	Interest Rate/ Currency	Equity
2005	17.3	105%	213.2	5.6
2004	8.4	123%	183.6	4.1
2003	3.8	66%	142.3	3.4
2002	2.1	37%	99.8	2.4
2001	0.9	45%	69.2	—

smaller in notional[10] market share terms than interest rate and currency derivatives, have already outpaced OTC equity derivatives.[11] The number of intermediaries and end-users involved in the marketplace has grown in tandem.

RISK PARAMETERS

While credit derivatives can serve as very effective risk and investment management tools, they also expose investors and intermediaries to credit risk, market risk, liquidity risk, legal risk, and operational risk. Because effective risk management is essential to the long-term success of any organization, institutions dealing in credit derivatives must consider, and ultimately control, all relevant risk parameters in a manner consistent with corporate imperatives and applicable regulations. And, though financial institutions comprise the single large share of the market, it is worth stressing that the risks described in this section are applicable to all corporate participants—financial as well as nonfinancial.

Credit Risk

Credit risk is defined as risk of loss due to a credit event that causes an obligor to become impaired or stop performing on its obligations. The credit risk of credit derivatives surfaces on two horizons: risk

---

10 The notional amount of a transaction or portfolio is simply a measure of volume transacted, and has no particular bearing on the amount of capital at risk.

11 Many institutions use the listed equity derivative markets to supplement their OTC activities.

of loss due to default or impairment of a reference credit asset, and risk of loss due to failure by the counterparty to a credit derivative contract. The first dimension of credit risk is present in every credit-risky reference asset and is, obviously, a key reason for the development of the sector. The second dimension, counterparty risk, exists when an intermediary or investor enters into a bilateral contract, (e.g., a credit forward or total return swap) or a unilateral contract where it is expecting its counterparty to perform should the contract gain value (e.g., a long CDS or long credit spread option).

Because a key goal of financial management is to maximize risk-adjusted rate of return for a given level of acceptable risk exposure, institutions with credit exposure must manage portfolio and transactional risks. Firms dealing in credit risks must ensure that they have a fundamental knowledge of credit risk; only then should they use credit derivatives to achieve risk reduction or investment goals.[12] Once the essential credit foundations have been established, an institution (and its regulator, where relevant), must ensure the availability of internal expertise in evaluating credit derivatives, the adequacy of relevant policies, including position limits, and the quality of the institution's information systems and internal controls.[13]

12 Indeed, some banking regulators have rightly indicated that banks should not enter into credit derivative transactions unless management has the ability to understand and manage the credit and other risks associated with these instruments safely.
13 While financial institutions have faced difficulties over the years for a multitude of reasons, the major cause of serious banking problems relates to lax credit standards for borrowers and counterparties, poor portfolio risk management, or inattention to changes in economic circumstances that can lead to deterioration in the credit standing of a bank's counterparties. The following three brief examples help illustrate the point: (1) The Comptroller of the Currency closed National State Bank, Metropolis, Illinois, in December 2000 when it found that the bank was critically undercapitalized, with less than 2 percent tangible equity capital to assets. Inadequate control of the credit and transaction risks and inadequate supervision by the board of directors resulted in significant credit losses. These losses, along with incremental provisions to absorb additional losses, depleted capital and threatened the bank's liquidity. The OCC determined that closure and FDIC intervention were necessary in order to protect the bank's insured depositors. (2) Monument National Bank, Ridgecrest, California, was closed in June 2000. The OCC used its receivership authority after finding that Monument National was critically undercapitalized. The bank never fully recovered from the poor credit administration practices and high volume of classified assets experienced in 1998. As a result, the bank incurred losses that depleted substantially all of its capital. (3) In January 1999, Victory State Bank was determined to be critically undercapitalized, causing the FDIC to take possession of the bank. Poor management, excessive insider compensation, operating losses, and a burdensome volume of problem assets plagued the bank. Unfortunately, many other examples of poor credit risk control exist; the misuse of credit derivatives can simply compound the problem.

When an institution acquires credit exposure through credit derivatives, its primary exposure is to the credit risk of the reference asset. Credit analysis of all relevant reference assets generating exposure should be performed, and limits should be developed to control overall exposure to borrowers, industries, geographic regions, and ratings classes—regardless of whether exposures are taken through cash instruments or credit derivatives.[14]

When an institution transfers credit risk through credit derivatives, its primary exposure is to counterparty performance; it will lose money only if the asset deteriorates and the counterparty is unable to fulfill its contractual obligations. Because the actual loss scenario relates to default of both the reference credit and the counterparty (an admittedly low probability event),[15] institutions should seek counterparties whose financial condition is not closely correlated with that of the reference credit. The financial strength of the counterparty is typically monitored throughout the life of the contract. In some cases, institutions may deem it appropriate to require collateral from certain lower-rated counterparties (or those to whom they have already extended substantial credit lines).

Market Risk

Market risk is defined as risk of loss due to adverse changes in market-driven variables, such as credit spreads, bond prices, interest rates, commodity or equity prices, or asset volatilities. Institutions dealing in credit derivatives face market risk exposures on various fronts, including changes in credit spreads, the basis, interest rate levels, and the shape of the yield curve; in some instances (e.g., basket structures) they may also be exposed to changes in credit correlations and credit volatilities. In order to control market-related losses, participants generally develop comprehensive hedging

---

14 For regulatory purposes, exposures acquired through credit derivatives are often treated as if they were letters of credit or other off-balance-sheet guarantees; we shall consider this point in more detail in Part 3.

15 The risk is akin to "two-name paper," it takes the default of two entities to generate a loss. Using the mathematics of joint probabilities, this transforms the risk into an exposure that is superior to that of either the reference entity or the counterparty.

policies,[16] limits, and systems to constrain and monitor market exposure.

Spread risk is the risk of loss attributable to the market performance of two related assets, such as a credit-risky asset and the risk-free bond that serves as a benchmark. As the spread widens due to credit deterioration or supply/demand imbalances, a long position in the risky bond generates losses while the short position gains; as it narrows due to credit improvement, the short position will lose while the long position gains. Not surprisingly, credit derivatives feature spread risk, exposing parties to potential gains/losses. *Basis risk* is the risk of loss arising from an imperfect price relationship between two underlying assets, or an asset and a hedge. For instance, an institution holding a loan position may seek to reduce its risk by entering into a credit derivative in which the reference credit is a widely traded bond of the same obligor. However, the risk, liquidity, and trading characteristics of the bond may be different from those of the loan; the end result may be a hedge that does not adequately compensate for any losses sustained on the loan.

Liquidity Risk

Liquidity risk is the risk of loss arising from an inability to obtain unsecured funding or liquidate/pledge assets in order to meet unexpected payments/obligations. Asset liquidity is of particular relevance to credit derivatives, as it can impact the marketability, and therefore value, of a contract. Asset liquidity risk can be measured by the size of the bid/ask spread; the less liquid or salable the instrument, the wider the bid/ask spread. Certain credit-risky assets and credit derivative contracts are considered to be quite illiquid, suggesting that any need to quickly liquidate or cover a position will come at a high cost—creating a loss. Credit derivatives

---

16 The unique characteristics of various default products makes it challenging for market makers to hedge contingent exposures. For example, institutions that sell default swaps will make infrequent payments because defaults are rare. Hence, the payoff profile for a default swap includes a large probability that default will not occur and a small probability that a default will occur with unknown consequences; the small probability event can be difficult to hedge and can contribute to losses if not handled accurately.

do not yet feature the liquidity of other financial derivatives due to unique structural features and/or potentially limited trade in certain underlying credit references (e.g., loan, private placements). Institutions dealing in credit derivatives must evaluate the level of liquidity risk inherent in specific transactions to minimize potential losses.

Legal Risk

Legal risk is the risk of loss arising from lack of proper legal documentation, or errors or ambiguity in defining key legal terms. Within the credit derivatives sector, legal disputes can arise over the definition of credit events or the validity of price-discovery mechanisms, as well as trade misrepresentations or unfair sales practices. While ISDA has produced standardized derivative documentation and improved transparency via credit event definitions (as we discuss in Chapter 10), difficulties can still arise.[17] Such problems tend not to become evident until reference entities have defaulted on their obligations and counterparties are called on to test the parameters of their legal documents. Institutions must also ensure that they (and their counterparties) have the legal and regulatory authority to participate in credit derivative transactions, and that any contemplated transactions adhere to relevant laws. In some cases institutions may not be authorized to enter into credit derivative contracts, acting outside of legal scope. Transactions that are arranged and executed outside the legal scope of an institution's activities may be considered *ultra vires*, and disallowed in the event of dispute. A counterparty believing it has a legitimate contract with an institution that is operating outside its approved authorities may thus find it has no legal recourse and may be forced to absorb any losses.

---

17 For instance, when U.S. company Conseco announced it would restructure $2.8 billion of debt, protection buyers viewed this as a "credit event" demanded recompense. Protection sellers argued that the restructuring should not qualify as a "credit event," as the company was not then in technical default. A similar event occurred with the restructuring by Marconi plc of its debt. Since the occurrence of those events, new ISDA definitions have clarified the parameters under which a corporate debt restructuring can trigger payment under a credit derivative; however, there is still no guarantee of conflict-free interpretation.

Operational Risk

Operational risk is the risk of loss arising from failures or errors in the external or internal technical, procedural, or control mechanisms surrounding the processing of business. Operational risk can span many fronts, including criminal/fraudulent behavior, personnel mismanagement, unauthorized activities, transaction processing errors, technological inadequacies, and external disasters. An institution's physical assets or technological infrastructure may be damaged or destroyed, prohibiting normal operation of business and leading to direct/indirect losses. Similarly, errors in, or collapse of, internal controls can lead to fraud or reputational losses.[18] Credit derivative processes may be at risk to the internal front- and back-office control failures that affect other businesses, and they may be vulnerable to external disruptions that threaten market activity. For instance, some institutions lack the proper infrastructure to handle credit derivative trading, from pricing and risk management to back-office processing. Legacy systems used to manage bond and swap transactions are often "updated" to accommodate credit derivative structures; such enhancements may not always be robust, meaning technical, data, valuation, and monitoring errors can surface and create losses.

The potentially large losses emanating from control failure have moved operational risk issues to the forefront in recent years, and regulators and institutions are more attuned to the need for effective operational risk management controls, including warning mechanisms, error tracking, internal audits, valuation checks, practical policies, and improved technology architecture and data recovery.

OUTLINE OF THE BOOK

In order to address the essential aspects of credit derivative products and the overall market, this book has been arranged in three distinct parts, each providing a specific focus. In Part 1, Credit Derivative Products and Applications, we continue with a discussion

---

18 For example, internal control failures, including lack of segregation between front-office trading and back-office processing, allowed traders in firms such as Barings, Daiwa Bank, Allied Irish, and National Australia Bank, among others, to manipulate position/risk reporting or trade in excess of authorized limits in order to generate false or inflated profits.

of the mechanics of various instruments and how they can be used to achieve particular goals:

- Chapter 2 begins our detailed discussion of credit derivatives by examining the mechanics and applications of a series of fundamental instruments, including asset swaps, credit default swaps, credit spread forwards, total return swaps, basket swaps, and credit spread options.
- Chapter 3 preserves the product focus by discussing how the basic credit derivative structures from Chapter 2 can be combined to create structured/synthetic assets, including credit-linked notes and synthetic collateralized debt obligations.
- Chapter 4 explores, in practical terms, how financial institutions, nonbank financial institutions, and corporations can use a range of credit derivative products to meet their investment and risk management goals.

In Part 2, Quantitative Tools, we adopt a more quantitative perspective by considering a range of tools and processes that can be used to quantify aspects of both credit risk and credit derivative risk. Analytics considered in the 5 chapters are an essential component of the market:

- Chapter 5 sets the stage with a primer on risk modeling, considering how accurate risk estimates can be obtained via models, and how risk models can be created in single or multifactor form.
- Chapter 6 considers credit default swap pricing by describing common valuation techniques and introducing a basic credit default swap pricing model that makes use of historical and market-implied default probabilities.
- Chapter 7 concentrates on modeling of credit default risk, defining the challenges involved in measuring default probabilities and introducing a practical approach to the issue. The chapter then develops the expected default frequency framework and illustrates how it can be used in measuring credit and default performance.

- Chapter 8, focused on portfolio management of default risk, considers a range of issues related to defaults, correlations, and valuations, and how these can be employed to manage and optimize the risk and return of credit portfolios.
- Chapter 9 introduces ancillary credit risk tools and techniques, examining how an institution can manage credit risk exposures through stochastic optimization and how it can employ ratings transitions as part of the credit portfolio management process.

In Part 3, Regulatory, Control, and Legal Environment, we consider essential documentary, capital, and control parameters surrounding credit derivative products.

- Chapter 10 commences our discussion by examining the nature and role of credit derivative documentation, with a particular focus on the ISDA Master Agreement framework and its application to the credit derivative market.
- Chapter 11 expands the control review by considering regulatory and risk issues of credit derivatives. Capital treatment of credit derivatives is compared and contrasted with standard balance sheet credit assets, and the supervisory view of minimum credit risk capital is considered. We also describe the general risk management framework and how it can be used to control aspects of credit risk and credit derivative exposure.

In order to reinforce understanding of key points, chapters contain a series of conceptual or practical exercises; the answer key is contained at the end of the text.

CHAPTER EXERCISES

1. Describe the difference between unilateral and bilateral credit derivative contracts and give an example of each one. Explain the impact of each one on intermediaries and end-users.
2. Explain how and why an investment fund might use credit derivative contracts.
3. Outline the types of risks a company might face and how they might be managed.

4. Explain why the ability to separate credit risk exposure from a credit-risky asset is an important driver of market growth.

5. Discuss why legal and operational risks must be considered as part of the overall risk management framework. Give two examples of each type of risk as related to credit derivatives.

CHAPTER 2

Fundamental Credit Derivative Products

INTRODUCTION

We noted in Chapter 1 that the global credit derivative market has expanded rapidly over the past decade in terms of both depth and breadth. The market has also grown in terms of product offerings and innovation. The fundamental "building blocks" that were originally introduced in the mid- to late-1990s have become relatively standard and liquid, and basic product construction and transaction procedures have become widely accepted. The "next generation" of credit derivatives, which creates additional risk/return opportunities for intermediaries and end-users, has started to appear and promises to extend market capabilities even further.

We divide our discussion of credit derivative products into two broad sectors: fundamental credit derivative instruments and structured/synthetic credit derivative instruments. Our focus in this chapter is on the essential credit derivative products introduced in Chapter 1, including asset swaps, credit default swaps, credit spread forwards, total return swaps, basket swaps, and credit spread options. We also consider certain innovations and extensions, including asset swap switches, asset swaptions, CDS index swaps, first to default baskets, senior baskets, and subordinated baskets. We will build on this base in the next chapter when we consider various structured and synthetic credit derivative assets.

ASSET SWAP STRUCTURES

The asset swap is often regarded as a pioneering, if somewhat limited, version of the modern credit derivative, enabling participants to trade the credit spreads of selected reference assets; the ability to trade credit spreads via an asset swap suggests that an institution can benefit from spread widening or tightening, just as it might with certain other types of credit derivatives. Asset swaps predate credit derivatives by nearly a decade and remain an integral, and relatively commoditized, element of the capital markets. In this section we consider standard asset swaps, callable and puttable asset swap packages, asset swap switches, and asset swaptions.

Asset Swaps

Investors routinely seek to deploy their capital in specific asset classes, currencies, or rates. If appropriate assets already exist in the marketplace, then an investor simply buys the desired asset by funding it through normal sources. However, if the precise characteristics are not available, then the asset can often be created synthetically by combining a host security with an interest rate or currency swap. Similarly, there are times when the asset swap structure can be used to capitalize on market inefficiencies, mispricings, and illiquidity. Both of these factors have proven important drivers of activity over the past two decades.

   The corporate capital markets feature an embedded quality differential that allows low-quality issuers to obtain a comparative advantage in the floating-rate markets and high-quality issuers to achieve a comparative advantage in the fixed-rate markets (and an absolute advantage in both markets). Depending on market conditions and the size of the quality differential, investors can therefore purchase high-rated fixed-rate bonds directly, or high-rated FRNs asset swapped into fixed rates; similarly, they can purchase lower-rated FRNs directly, or lower-rated fixed-rate bonds asset swapped into floating rates. For instance, if an investor seeks to invest in Company XYZ's bonds on a floating-rate basis, but XYZ has only issued fixed-rate liabilities, the intermediary can sell the investor the fixed-rate bonds and attach a swap that converts the fixed-rate coupons into LIBOR. In practice the swap flows are adjusted to provide investors with a synthetic investment trading at par with

F I G U R E   2.1

Asset Swap Packages

(a) Synthetic FRN Investment Package

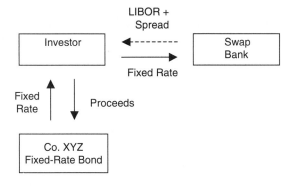

(b) Synthetic Fixed-Rate Investment Package

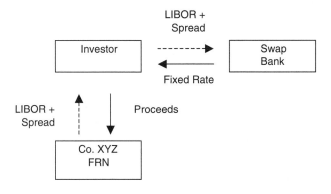

a stated yield.[1] Though no specific floating-rate XYZ asset actually exists, the intermediary synthesizes one by combining the fixed bond and the interest rate swap. The reverse transaction is also possible: if XYZ only features LIBOR-based liabilities and an investor seeks a fixed-rate return, the investor can buy the FRN and enter into an associated swap where it receives fixed and pays LIBOR plus a spread. The periodic flows on these fundamental asset swap packages (i.e., after the investor has purchased the asset from the swap bank and entered into the associated swap) are highlighted in Figures 2.1 (a) and (b). Note that the same concept

---

1 The adjustments may relate to premium/discount on the underlying asset, as well as any differences in accrued interest.

applies to asset swaps created with currency, rather than interest rate, swaps; in such cases the transaction also involves initial and final exchange of principal, as in any conventional currency swap. Asset swaps involving basis flows (e.g., CP versus LIBOR, EURIBOR versus EONIA) and nonstandard/amortizing/zero-coupon cash flows can also be created. Regardless of the specific structural details, the intent is to provide the investor with an opportunity to benefit from XYZ's credit spread levels and movements. Asset swaps are typically arranged on notional amounts ranging from $5 million to several hundred million, with maturities extending from approximately 1 year up to 10 years.

Asset swap activity is influenced by a number of factors, including the existence of arbitrage opportunities that permit the development of a synthetic investment at a higher yield, or restrictions that bar the creation of conventional fixed income supply (or which prohibit investors from acquiring certain classes of assets). The arbitrage differential between the asset yield and swap levels must be large enough to provide all parties with economic benefits. The differential is a function of supply/demand for fixed versus floating issues, asset liquidity, new issue supply, and, as noted above, the credit spread differentials between strong investment grade and weak investment grade/subinvestment grade issuers. For instance, an investor seeking to invest in LIBOR + x bp assets funded at LIBOR can do so on an outright basis, assuming it can find appropriate floating-rate assets and its funding levels are set at LIBOR (or sub-LIBOR). However, the investor may be able to take advantage of an arbitrage opportunity and use an asset swap to achieve the same goals. If fixed payments under the swap are less than the payments received from a fixed asset, then a LIBOR + x bp spread is created; if this spread is greater than the spread on a direct FRN purchase (funded at LIBOR flat or sub-LIBOR), then the asset swap arbitrage is effective. For example, if an investor can receive 5.5% on a three-year, fixed-rate bond and LIBOR + 15 bps on a three-year FRN, and can enter into a three-year pay fix/receive LIBOR at 5.25%, the net return on the synthetic asset is LIBOR + 25 bps, or 10 bps more than the direct purchase.

Callable and Puttable Asset Swaps

We can now extend our discussion to consider callable and puttable asset swap packages. A callable asset swap (also known as a remarketable asset swap) is similar to the asset swap package described above, except that the bank selling the package retains a call option on the underlying asset, allowing it to repurchase the asset at a given spread at some future time. The total package can therefore be regarded as a combination of a callable swap (itself a package of a swap and an option) and an underlying fixed or floating-rate bond. The option generally features a European or Bermudan exercise that is synchronized with the coupon dates of the asset. The strike spread is typically set equal to the spread at which the asset is placed with the investor; if the spread tightens during the life of the transaction (e.g., the price of the asset rises as a result of specific or general credit improvements), the bank calls the package away from the investor, delivering cash proceeds equal to the strike spread times invested principal. The bank can then sell the underlying asset in the marketplace at a profit, or enter into a new callable asset swap with a new investor at the tighter market spread; this process helps realize mark-to-market value arising from credit improvement. Naturally, if the spread widens instead of tightens, the swap bank will abandon the option and the investor will preserve its asset swap package until the contracted maturity date. In exchange for giving the bank the right to call away the package, the investor receives an incremental yield that represents the premium from selling the option. This synthetic structure gives both parties specific benefits: the bank preserves the ability, on an off-balance sheet basis, to efficiently crystallize value by liquidating or reselling the structure if asset spreads tighten, while the investor earns an incremental yield for granting the option. The callable asset swap structure (based on a fixed-rate bond) is summarized in Figures 2.2 (a) and (b).

A puttable asset swap functions in a similar way, except that the investor, rather than the bank, retains the option. Specifically, the investor acquires a package comprised of an asset (e.g., fixed-rate bond or FRN) and a puttable swap, where the put allows the investor to sell the asset swap package back to the bank at a predetermined strike spread. As with the callable structure above, the put option generally has a European or Bermudan exercise that is synchronized with the coupon dates of the asset (and, again, the strike spread is typically set equal to the investor's original purchase spread). If the spread widens during the life of the transaction (e.g., the price of the asset falls as a result of specific or general credit deterioration), the investor puts the package to the bank,

F I G U R E 2.2

Callable Asset Swap

(a) | Initial and Ongoing Flows Assuming No Exercise |

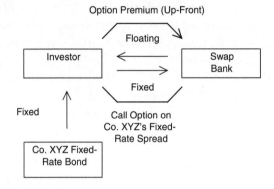

(b) | Terminal Flows Assuming Swap Bank Exercises |

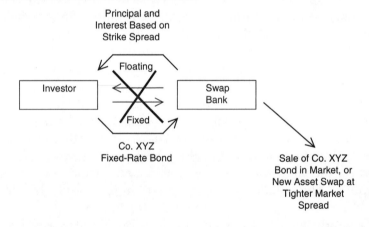

receiving principal and interest defined by the strike spread. The bank may then retain the asset in its portfolio, sell it in the market-place, or attempt to arrange a new asset swap structure with another investor at the new (albeit wider) spread level. Depending on carrying value, the bank may or may not post a mark-to-market loss. If the spread tightens, the investor will choose not to exercise the option, thus preserving its package until the contracted maturity date. The investor, in gaining the right to put the package back to the bank, pays an option premium in the form of an up-front payment or a lower yield on the asset swap coupon. As above, both parties obtain benefits through the synthetic structure: the bank receives incremental income from selling the put option (temporarily or permanently removing the underlying asset from its balance sheet), while the investor obtains de facto downside protection against spread widening on the underlying asset. Note that the puttable asset swap structure is also an essential element of callable bond investing, as investors must be assured that they can terminate the swap component of an asset swap strategy if the underlying bond is called back by the issuer; absent this feature, investors would be left with naked swap positions upon exercise of the bond call. The puttable asset swap structure (based on a fixed-rate bond) is summarized in Figures 2.3 (a) and (b).

Asset Swap Switches and Asset Swaptions

Asset swap switches involve the exchange of two different asset swap packages. Under the most basic version of this structure, an investor acquires an asset swap package from a bank or financial intermediary and simultaneously agrees to deliver the package and accept another one in return if the spread on the second package widens to a particular strike level; the credit references in the two asset swap packages are generally uncorrelated. By agreeing to switch assets, the investor receives an enhanced yield on its investment. For instance, an investor may own an asset swap package on credit reference ABC at LIBOR + 30 bps and agree with Bank D to exchange it for an asset swap package on reference XYZ, currently trading at LIBOR + 50 bps, if XYZ's trading spread widens to +70 bps. Bank D therefore has the right to put the XYZ package to the investor while simultaneously calling back the ABC package. In order for this transaction to function from an economic perspective, the investor and the bank must have different views on the current and future creditworthiness of ABC and XYZ. For instance, the investor must believe that XYZ represents good value at +70 bps, but is too expensive ("rich") at +50 bps. The bank is exposed to 20 bps of spread widening before it can trigger the swap, but effectively acquires default protection through the structure.

A more recent innovation in the sector is the synthetic lending facility, commonly known as an asset swaption. Under this synthetic contract, the investor earns an up-front or periodic fee for agreeing to purchase a security or a loan from an intermediary on a forward basis. This is equivalent to the investor selling, for premium, a

F I G U R E 2.3

Puttable Asset Swap

(a) Initial and Ongoing Flows Assuming No Exercise

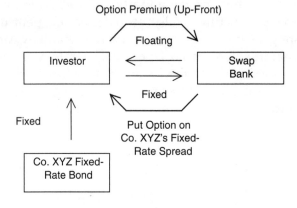

(b) Terminal Flows Assuming Investor Exercises

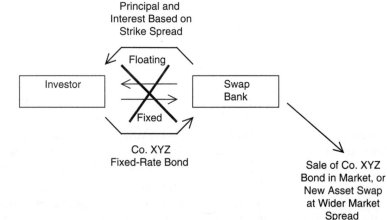

put option to the intermediary on a revolving credit line or note-underwriting program arranged for a third-party credit borrower/issuer and committing to participate in an unfunded revolver/note program until it is funded or terminated. If the intermediary exercises the option, the investor is obliged to purchase the reference asset on an outright or asset-swapped basis at the agreed strike level. Once this occurs, the investor has a long position in the borrower's credit risk.

CREDIT DEFAULT SWAPS

As indicated in Chapter 1, the credit default swap (CDS) has emerged as the single most popular credit derivative in the market. The CDS functions like an insurance policy, with the swap buyer paying the swap seller a premium to protect against losses resulting from a defined credit event such as bankruptcy, reorganization, moratorium, payment default, or repudiation. The swap purchaser (i.e., the beneficiary) "swaps" the credit risk with the provider of the swap (i.e., the insurer or guarantor), receiving a compensatory if the credit event is triggered. Because the transaction is unilateral (i.e., the purchaser expects the seller to perform if the credit event occurs), it does not take the form of a standard OTC swap contract, which is always bilateral. In fact, the CDS can more properly be considered a credit default put option,[2] giving the purchaser the economics of a long put position on a credit-risky bond price. If the defined credit event occurs, the CDS seller must either (a) accept delivery of the reference asset and pay par value (for an asset that is likely to be trading at a deep discount) through a process known as physical settlement, or (b) compensate the buyer for the difference between par and the postdefault price through a process known as cash, or financial, settlement. If cash settlement is used, the price discovery method must be stipulated in the contract document; price discovery generally involves obtaining quotes from multiple dealers and establishing an average after removing outliers. Though the CDS appears to be a form of insurance (i.e., payment of premium in exchange for indemnification that is contingent upon the occurrence of a named loss), it is distinct in two key respects: the swap is an OTC contract that is almost always documented via standard ISDA documentation rather than insurance forms; and, the contract can be arranged by a party that is not exposed to the underlying risk, meaning it need not be a contract of indemnification protecting an existing exposure. The latter feature, in particular, has generated significant two-way growth, as speculators and hedgers can participate without needing to demonstrate proof of insurability or proof of loss.

---

2 The reduced loss credit default put option is a variation on the theme, where the buyer of the option agrees to absorb a portion of a default in exchange for payment of a smaller premium. The first loss structure can be seen as a form of deductible.

T A B L E   2.1

Factors Affecting the Price of a Credit Default Swap

Factor	Pricing Impact
Time to maturity	The longer the maturity, the greater the likelihood of default, the higher the premium.
Probability reference credit will default	The higher the probability of default, the higher the premium.
Credit rating of CDS counterparty (as seller)	The lower the credit rating of the CDS counterparty, the lower the premium.
Correlation between CDS seller and reference credit	The higher the correlation between the seller and reference, the lower the premium.
Expected recovery rate	The higher the recovery rate, the lower the premium.

CDSs on major credit issuers have become extremely liquid over the past few years, to the point where end-users and dealers often prefer transacting in derivative contracts rather than physical reference assets; this is particularly true for institutions attempting to establish short positions in a reference credit, where it may be difficult to borrow and sell the physical security as a result of supply or regulatory issues. CDSs are also useful for institutions pursuing portfolio diversification and rebalancing efforts, as risk or investment exposures can be reshaped in an efficient and cost-effective manner.

The premium, or fee, payable on a CDS can be paid up-front or over the life of the transaction; in practice it is generally set as a basis point spread over LIBOR times the notional amount of the contract. The premium is a function of various factors, including time to maturity, probability of reference credit default, expected recovery rate given default, credit rating of the CDS counterparty, and possible correlation between the counterparty and the reference credit; these factors are summarized in Table 2.1.

CDSs are generally written for maturities ranging from six months to five years, with institutional trading size of $10–$50 million. Reference assets can be drawn from the high-grade, high-yield, and emerging market sectors; in practice, most activity and liquidity is found in the high-grade sector. Naturally, CDSs can be customized to meet the specific needs of the buyer. Let us consider an example of a U.S. bank that is concerned about pending

F I G U R E   2.4

Credit Default Swap on Tobacco Company Reference

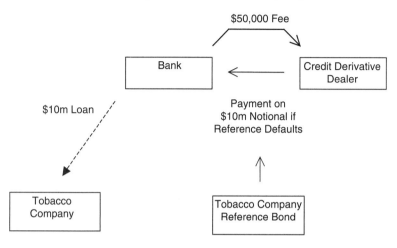

litigation that may result in a deterioration of the credit quality of one of its largest tobacco clients, to whom it has extended a $10 million loan. The bank is eager to reduce its default exposure to the tobacco firm, but does not want to sell its existing loan exposure (as it fears that any such action could damage the relationship). Accordingly, it enters into a five-year CDS with a credit derivative dealer for $10 million, sufficient to cover the credit risk on the loan; the reference under the transaction is the tobacco company's publicly traded 10-year bond. Importantly, the transaction is privately negotiated so that the bank's clients are unaware that the bank is hedging its exposure. The transaction fee for the CDS is 50 bp, or $50,000 per year. Figure 2.4 illustrates the flows of the CDS.

Under the terms of the agreement, the credit derivatives dealer makes a contingent payment to the bank equal to the difference between the market price and face value of the bond if a defined credit event occurs (e.g., bankruptcy, failure to pay). For example, if the tobacco company receives an adverse judgment that creates financial distress and it defaults on its bond (and other debt), the reference bond may drop to a price of 60. The dealer pays the bank 40 (the market-based recovery price), the difference between 60 and the bond's face value of 100; this amounts to $4 million in cash terms. This provides coverage for the bank's own $10 million loan to the company, which may also

F I G U R E 2.5

CDS Index Swap

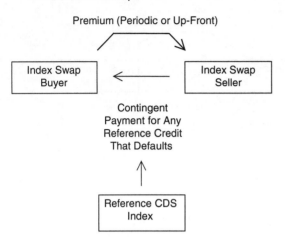

be worth approximately 60 postdefault.[3] Note that the bank is exposed to the credit risk of the tobacco company and the credit derivatives dealer as counterparty. While a simultaneous default by the dealer is unlikely, the correlation between the reference and dealer must be understood; if there is a high probability that a default by the reference credit might have a negative impact on the dealer's own financial standing, the bank will be less inclined to pursue the transaction, or will do so only by paying a lower premium.[4]

A recent entrant in the marketplace is the CDS index swap, a derivative contract covering a broad pool of credits that together comprise a standardized index. The buyer of an index swap pays the seller a premium in exchange for a compensatory payment if a credit event occurs within the index; if a credit event occurs, the reference asset is removed from the index and the contract continues based on the remaining reference assets, but on a reduced notional principal. The buyer is obliged to pay the same fixed premium on the remaining references. Figure 2.5 illustrates the index structure and cash flows.

---

3 In fact, the value may be slightly higher or lower, depending on asset valuation and priority of claims.

4 In practice this might occur if a weak financial institution is writing a great deal of unhedged contracts on weak reference credits; several defaults (and thus payouts) may be sufficient to trigger a default by the financial institution on its own liabilities.

CDS index swaps are becoming increasingly liquid because they rely on standardized indexes, which are comprised of the most liquid CDS references in the market (as determined by the largest credit derivative dealers). Previously disparate efforts led by Trac-X and iBoxx (with different dealers in support of each effort) have been consolidated into a single project administered by Dow Jones: These include the DJ CDX indexes for North America and emerging markets and the DJ iTraxx credit indexes for Europe and Asia. Each class is standardized with respect to index construction and maturities, and each class features a variety of sector and geographic subindexes (denominated in major currencies in order to avoid currency risk). The most active indexes are the North American high-grade index (CDX.NA.IG) and the European high-grade index (iTraxx Europe), each featuring 125 credit references. Though the indexes are considered high grade, the references are weighted heavily towards the lower end of the investment grade spectrum (e.g., 90% in A/BBB-rated entities). Each index remains static over its lifetime (apart from defaulting references, which are removed) and is rebalanced every six months in order to maintain a continuous supply of tradable references in both 5- and 10-year maturities. Liquidity of index contracts has led to a tightening of bid-offer spread for the major indexes (e.g., CDX.NA.IG swaps trade at a spread of 1–4 bps; the equivalent contract for a recognized physical bond index can be as wide as 40 bps). Index swaps can be traded in funded or unfunded form. Unfunded swaps are equivalent to multireference CDS basket swaps on the standard index of references; the protection buyer in this instance faces counterparty exposure risk. Funded swaps are a bond equivalent, where the protection buyer receives the pool of index references from the seller and pays a notional amount up-front. Because the structure is funded, the buyer faces no counterparty exposure.

Consider an example of a CDS index swap based on the iTraxx Europe, which is comprised of 125 of the most liquid investment grade CDSs in Europe.[5] Each day the 125 reference CDS prices are marked to market and a new fair price for the index is established. A firm that wishes to buy protection must pay the difference between the initial spread on the index and the current fair price (if the fair

---

5 All of the reference entities comprising the index have equal rating and can only be changed if a credit event occurs and the members of the index agree on a replacement or change. At the start of each index series (i.e., every six months), the spread for the index is established and remains constant throughout the series life.

price is above the initial index), or receive the difference (if the fair price spread is below the index). This payment is made whenever a participant enters or exits an index spread trade. Assume the initial iTraxx Europe index price is 35 bps, payable by the buyer quarterly for the life of the trade. If the fair price widens 1 month later to 55 bps, a protection buyer entering the trade must pay an up-front fee equivalent to the present value of the 20 bps for the life of the trade and then continue paying the fixed 35 bps every quarter. If one of the 125 reference entities in the index defaults, the protection seller pays the protection buyer € 1 million. The trade then continues at a premium of 35 bps on 124 credits and the lower notional amount.

CREDIT SPREAD FORWARDS

The credit spread forward is a forward contract on a risky credit spread that allows the purchase or sale of a credit spread at a forward price for settlement at some future date; credit spread forwards can be negotiated in absolute and relative versions. Under the absolute spread version, the seller agrees to pay the buyer a fixed credit spread and receive a market spread; the fixed spread is set at trade date and the evaluation against the market spread occurs at transaction maturity. The buyer, by extension, agrees to pay the market spread in exchange for the fixed spread; this structure is illustrated in Figure 2.6. For instance, if a bank agrees to pay a fixed 100 bps for the spread on Company ABC's reference bond and receive ABC's market spread, it will generate a gain as ABC's market spread widens beyond 100 bps (i.e., ABC's credit deteriorates) and

FIGURE 2.6

Absolute Credit Spread Forward

Payment of Fixed
Credit Spread at
Settlement

Credit Forward
Seller

Credit Forward
Buyer

Payment of
Market Credit
Spread at
Settlement

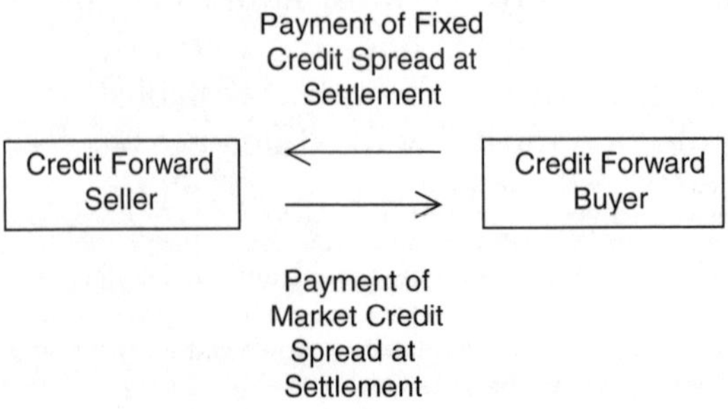

will post a loss as it tightens (i.e., improves); the bank's counter-party faces the opposite scenario. In the extreme, if ABC defaults the bank will receive a payment related to ABC's postdefault spread level. The payout on the forward is computed as the difference between the fixed and market spreads, times the duration of the reference asset,[6] times the notional of the transaction; the payment is thus net, adjusted by the duration to reflect the weighted average cash flows of the reference bond.

The relative spread version functions in a similar manner, except one party pays the spread over the risk-free benchmark on reference asset 1, while the second party pays the spread over the risk-free benchmark on reference asset 2; this essentially involves the spread differential between two credit-risky references and removes the risk-free benchmark from the equation. In practice asset swap spreads are often used as references in credit spread forwards, even though LIBOR is not strictly a risk-free benchmark rate. Like CDSs, forwards can be purchased/sold for periods of several months to several years, on dealing amounts ranging from $10 million to $100 million. While most forwards are structured for single periods, they can also be bundled into portfolios to create multiperiod swaps.

TOTAL RETURN SWAPS

The total return swap (TRS) is a bilateral contract that transfers the economics of a credit reference between two parties; the contract covers the entire spectrum of payoffs, from credit strengthening to credit deterioration and default. Under a standard transaction, the TRS receiver is entitled to the total return on the reference asset (appreciation plus coupons) in exchange for periodic floating payments (e.g., a LIBOR-based flow plus a spread); this is equivalent to creating a synthetic long position in the reference asset (indeed, the TRS is often considered a form of synthetic financing). The TRS payer, in turn, is entitled to any depreciation that occurs in the security, along with a LIBOR spread.[7] If the price of the reference

---

6 The credit spread duration, which measures the sensitivity of the security's price to a movement in spreads, captures the effects of price changes over the life of the security on a present value basis.

7 As noted, in transferring the price appreciation/depreciation, the TRS mechanism transfers economic changes that are due to interest rate movements and credit spread movements; the two are not separated, meaning that the vehicle is as much an interest rate risk tool as a credit risk tool.

asset rises as a result of credit improvement, the receiver benefits; if it declines as a result of depreciation or default, the payer benefits. Because the TRS payer often owns the underlying reference asset, it transfers the economic risk of the asset, creating a synthetic short position (or first loss credit protection); it must, of course, continue to fund the balance sheet position through its own sources.[8] The TRS can be arranged on a funded or unfunded basis. A funded TRS requires the TRS receiver to purchase a risk-free or low-risk floating-rate asset that yields the LIBOR stream payable to the TRS payer. The receiver holds no such asset in the unfunded TRS, so the LIBOR stream must be sourced from cash flow; this means that the TRS position is leveraged.

The standard TRS structure features dealing size that can grow to over $100 million and a maturity that can range from six months to approximately five years. Though valuation is generally transparent, challenges can arise when the underlying reference asset is illiquid and robust price quotes are difficult to obtain. The "total return" referenced under terms of the transaction includes all interest payments on the reference asset, plus an amount based on the change in the asset's market value. If a default occurs prior to maturity, the receiver compensates the payer through a net payment equal to the difference between the asset price on trade date and the asset price postdefault (cash settlement basis); alternatively, it can take delivery of the asset by paying par value (physical settlement basis). Figures 2.7 (a) and (b) summarize the flows of unfunded and funded TRSs.

Like the CDS buyer, the TRS payer can separate its economic exposure to a reference asset without having to sell it in the market, creating risk management and relationship management advantages. The receiver, in turn, can enjoy funding and investment benefits. Returning to the tobacco company introduced above, we can examine how an investor might benefit from a TRS position. Assume that a hedge fund believes the bond market has overreacted to the tobacco litigation risk, driving tobacco credit spreads to levels that are wider than warranted. The fund wants to crystallize this view and can do so by purchasing the tobacco company's

---

8 The net profit to the TRS payer is the basis point spread over the funding cost times the notional amount of the transaction. Thus, if the payer receives LIBOR + 10bps from the receiver and can fund at LIBOR flat, it earns 10bps running on the notional of the transaction.

F I G U R E 2.7

Total Return Swap

(a) Unfunded TRS

Price
Appreciation in
Reference Credit +
Asset Coupons

| TRS Receiver | ⟵ | TRS Payer |

⟶

Price
Depreciation in
Reference Credit +
LIBOR Spread

(b) Funded TRS

Price
Appreciation in
Reference Credit +
Asset Coupons

| TRS Receiver | ⟵ | TRS Payer |

⟶

LIBOR
Spread $

Price
Depreciation in
Reference Credit +
LIBOR Spread

Risk-Free/Low-Risk
Investment

bonds, arranging a credit spread forward, or entering into a TRS as a total return receiver. Because the fund wants to maximize the potential for returns (i.e., employ maximum leverage), it opts to use an unfunded $10 million TRS to express its view. We may also assume that the bank that has extended a loan to the tobacco company continues to be concerned about its exposure; instead of arranging a CDS, it can enter into a TRS with the hedge fund, offsetting its exposure to a potential decline in the value of the tobacco company's bond—creating a de facto hedge in the process. Though it does not have to pay an up-front premium as it did for the CDS protection, it is now liable for paying the total returns on the tobacco company's reference bond. The fund will benefit if the

F I G U R E 2.8

Total Return Swap on Tobacco Company Reference

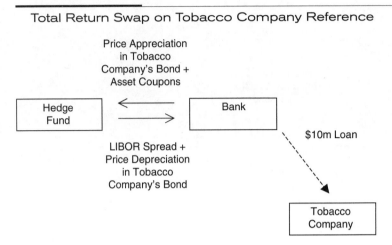

coupons and any price appreciation on the bond exceed the LIBOR spread it must pay; it remains at risk, of course, for any potential deterioration in the tobacco company's bond—including an event of default.[9] The bank will benefit if the tobacco company's credit deteriorates in the face of a negative legal judgment. Figure 2.8 summarizes the agreement between the bank and the hedge fund.

BASKET SWAP STRUCTURES

Basket swaps are credit derivatives that allow for the risk transfer of a pool of reference credits; this creates an efficient and cost-effective way of dealing with multiple credit exposures. Baskets effectively give institutions the chance to manage/hedge port-folios of reference credit risk exposures and investors an opportu-nity to earn premium from the creation of diversified portfolios of credit-risky assets. Though standard baskets are akin to miniport-folios of CDSs, the transactions are documented and executed as single trades, reducing administrative and control burdens. In addition, the act of combining discrete credits permits any benefi-cial effects of credit correlation to be reflected in the pricing; this can lead to a cheaper risk management solution (i.e., if the credits

---

9 Any negative bond portfolio returns unrelated to the tobacco company's credit risk would also be reflected in the hedge fund's payment (e.g., changing interest rates).

are uncorrelated). We consider several of the most common basket swap structures in this section, including the standard basket swap, first (*n*th) to default basket swap, senior basket swap, and subordinated basket swap.

Standard Basket Swaps

A standard basket swap, the most common of the synthetic credit portfolio structures, allows several reference credits to be combined into a single basket, providing the seller with a premium and the buyer with a compensatory payment if any of the credits defaults; if every credit in the basket defaults, the buyer receives a compensatory payment for each one. For instance, if the buyer specifies a basket of four reference credits of $10 million notional each, and three of the four default, it will receive a compensatory payment equal to the postdefault price of the defaulting credits times $10 million notional per credit. It is important to stress that a standard basket swap remains in force even after a credit has defaulted; indeed, the transaction terminates only on the stated maturity date. As each credit in the basket defaults and is removed, the standard basket swap transaction continues based on a reduced notional principal (but constant basis point premium). This "continuation" feature is distinct from the first-to-default baskets discussed immediately following. Note that although the basket buyer receives a payment for each default, it receives no payment if the reference credits deteriorate but do not default (e.g., credit spreads widen but the obligors remain current on their principal and interest payments); this reinforces the point that the basket swap is equal to a portfolio of CDSs (which are, themselves, binary default options).

There is considerable flexibility in assembling a reference basket: the structure can include 2 to 20+ obligations, industries can be identical or different, country exposure can be single or multiple source, and ratings can range from investment grade to subinvestment grade; maturities can range from six months to several years, and deal size can grow to several hundreds of millions of dollars. As with any individual CDS, the credit buyer pays the seller a fee; however, the inclusion of multiple reference credits can lower the overall fee payable—though this depends ultimately on the construction of the basket and the correlation between the reference credits. Credits that are very closely correlated do not receive the benefit

F I G U R E   2.9

Standard Basket Swap

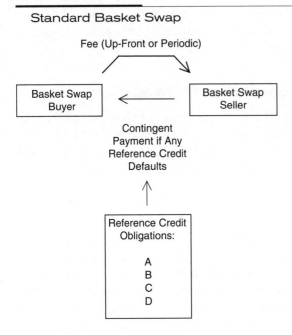

of a premium reduction, as no diversification is achieved; those that are less correlated (or, indeed, uncorrelated) can generate some degree of savings. Figure 2.9 highlights a standard basket swap.

First (*n*-th)-to-Default Basket Swaps

The first (or *n*-th)-to-default swap is a popular variation of the standard basket swap. The structure again begins with the creation of a portfolio of related or unrelated reference credits. In this instance, however, the buyer of the basket receives only a single compensatory payment when the first (or *n*-th) credit in the portfolio defaults; once the specified default event occurs, the structure unwinds and the seller faces no further liability—even if another default occurs. Assume, for instance, that a basket contains 10 reference credits and the buyer receives a payment based on the first credit to default. (Which of the 10 actually defaults is irrelevant—they are all considered equally.) Once the first default occurs, the buyer receives the notional amount of the basket times the postdefault price of the defaulting credit and, even though nine performing credits remain in the basket, the transaction terminates. Indeed,

F I G U R E   2.10

First-to-Default Basket Swap

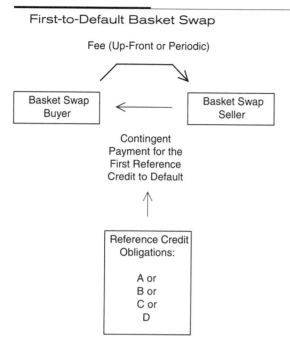

if a second default occurs one day after the first default, the seller is not obligated to make a compensatory payment. Though the first-to-default basket shares certain similarities with the standard basket swap, the fact that the payout is limited to a single default event means that the overall fee paid for the protection is much smaller. In some instances the structure is created to accommodate the second, third, fourth, or nth, credit to default; this means $(n - 1)$ defaults must occur among the reference obligations before the buyer receives a compensatory payment. Because this is obviously a much lower probability event, nth-to-default structures are considerably cheaper than standard basket swaps and first-to-default swaps. Figure 2.10 illustrates the flows of a first-to-default swap.

A first-to-default basket is similar to the standard collateralized debt obligation (CDO) we discuss in the next chapter. Specifically, the basket seller occupies a position similar to the investor in the equity/residual tranche (or subordinated tranche, depending on how the transaction is structured), bearing the first loss if default occurs. However, the basket seller has an off-balance sheet exposure while the CDO investor has a funded balance sheet investment; in addition, the basket features a narrower reference portfolio than the CDO.

Senior and Subordinated Basket Swaps

Senior and subordinated basket swaps represent two additional variations on the basket structure. As above, these basket swaps are customized credit portfolios that reference a number of credits. Their payment characteristics are, however, unique. In the senior basket swap the seller pays the buyer for any credits in the portfolio that default (and in that sense is identical to the standard basket swap), but will not do so until a minimum loss threshold has been reached. This creates a first-loss/deductible structure, suggesting that the seller holds a senior loss position while the buyer occupies the subordinated position. For instance, the reference portfolio might feature five credits at $10 million notional apiece and a first-loss level of $10 million. If all five credits default during the life of the transaction and the postdefault price for each is 40 (again, for simplicity), then the compensatory payment on a standard basket is $30 million. However, under the senior swap structure the buyer absorbs the first $10 million of losses as a form of deductible, meaning the compensatory payment nets to $20 million. Figure 2.11 summarizes the senior basket swap structure.

The subordinated basket swap is comprised of a customized portfolio of reference credits and provides a payout on every credit that defaults, from the instance of first dollar default; this indicates that the seller occupies the subordinated loss position and the buyer the senior loss position. However, the basket also features a cap, or aggregate limit, on the total amount of payout that can be made over the life of the contract. Thus, assuming a $25 million subordinated basket contract based on the same five-credits, $10 million basket noted above, the total payout to the buyer will be $25 million —even if all five credits default and the postdefault price on each is 40. Figure 2.12 illustrates the subordinated basket structure.

CREDIT SPREAD OPTIONS

The credit spread option is the last of the fundamental credit derivative products. The credit option grants the buyer the right, but not the obligation, to purchase (call) or sell (put) the credit spread of a reference credit at a particular strike level; in exchange for this

F I G U R E   2.11

Senior Basket Swap

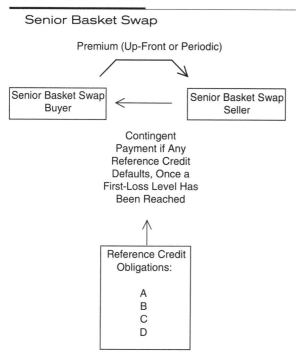

Premium (Up-Front or Periodic)

Senior Basket Swap Buyer

Senior Basket Swap Seller

Contingent
Payment if Any
Reference Credit
Defaults, Once a
First-Loss Level Has
Been Reached

Reference Credit
Obligations:

A
B
C
D

right, the buyer pays the seller an up-front premium payment.[10] Like other optionable contracts, the credit spread option is unilateral.

A put option on the credit spread gives the buyer the right to sell the spread at the strike, meaning a gain is generated as the reference credit deteriorates and its spread widens versus the risk-free benchmark; in the extreme, a defaulting credit will feature a very wide credit spread, so the credit spread put also provides default protection. A call option on the spread, in contrast, gives the buyer the right to purchase the spread at the strike, meaning a gain as the reference credit improves and the spread tightens. The spread may be defined in terms of a floating-rate reference, such as LIBOR, or a fixed-rate risk-free benchmark, such as Treasuries. For instance,

---

10 The credit spread option has its foundation in mortgage backed securities (MBS)/U.S. Treasury option strategies, with investors selling calls on MBS and buying calls on U.S. Treasuries in order to protect against a general widening of MBS spreads. This strategy ultimately expanded into other areas, such as spreads between Mexican government obligations and U.S. Treasuries, and has now become an established part of the credit derivative market.

F I G U R E 2.12

Subordinated Basket Swap

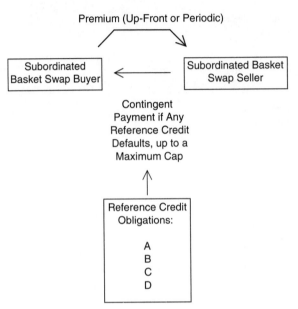

assume an investor purchases a credit spread put option at a strike spread of Treasuries +100 bps. If the reference credit is downgraded from A to BBB-, the spread on the bond may widen to T+200 bps; though the credit is not in default, the buyer is due the 100 bps spread over the strike spread (times the credit spread duration of the underlying bond reference, times the notional of the transaction). Accordingly, the spread option can be viewed as a conventional credit put that provides the buyer with a full continuum of payoffs.

Credit spread options can be used to capture relative value changes in spreads independent of interest rates, or to express a view on forward credit spreads[11] or the term structure of spreads. For instance, an investor believing an asset is overvalued but that

---

11 The forward credit spread can be computed by first determining the spot price of the risky bond and the associated risk-free benchmark; the forward prices of both instruments can then be computed and converted into forward yields, with the differential between the two yielding the forward spread. Forward credit spreads many not reflect investor expectations and are notoriously volatile.

FIGURE 2.13

Credit Spread Option

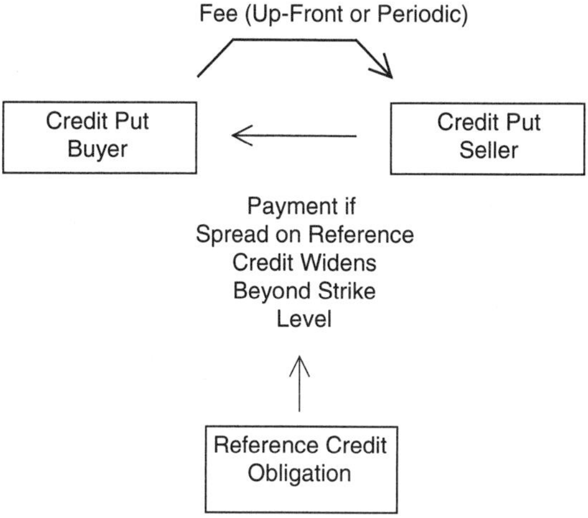

default is improbable can sell a credit spread put option on the asset, earning premium in the process. If the spread widens to the strike, the investor will have to purchase the asset from the option buyer, but may be comfortable doing so as its target spread level has been reached; in addition, it will have generated premium income to supplement the profit on the position.

Vanilla credit spread options are bought and sold on a range of reference credits, and can be structured with American or European exercise involving physical or cash settlement. Transaction maturities range from six months to five or more years, and dealing size ranges from $10 million to $100 million. Figure 2.13 highlights the cash-settled credit spread put structure.

Returning to our earlier example of the tobacco company, we illustrate how a bank might use a credit spread put to hedge a portion of its exposure on the $10 million loan. Assume the bank is still concerned about the results of pending litigation, which will be known within six months. Assume also that the public reference bond is trading at a spread of Treasuries +200 bps and has a duration of five-and-a-half years. Accordingly, the bank decides to purchase an at-the-money put option on $10 million for a premium of 60 bps. We can next imagine two scenarios: in six months' time the litigation is resolved in the tobacco company's favor, causing the spreads on the bond to tighten to +150 bps; although the bank's put option expires worthless, the specter of financial distress has been removed and the likelihood that the company will remain current on the $10 million loan is very favorable. The only sum the bank loses is the premium paid for the option. Under a second scenario the litigation result may be unfavorable, causing the spread on the bonds to widen to +400 bps as fears over possible financial distress mount. Though the bank now has increasing concerns about potential repayment on the loan, it has a partial hedge from the put option: the 200 bps widening over the strike, times the current duration of five years (six months have passed since the five-and-a-half duration at the start of the trade) yields a gain of $1 million, which can be used to offset any potential loss on the loan. Note that if the bank had been interested in a larger hedge, it could have arranged a notional amount of $20 million or more.

In addition to the standard structures noted above, exotic credit spread options, including knock-in and knockout options, are available. For instance, in a knockout credit spread put, the put is eliminated if the reference credit spread tightens by a certain number of basis points (i.e., it breaches the barrier). A knock-in put, in turn, becomes active once spreads widen to a certain level— meaning the put seller must take delivery of the asset at the wider spread level and the put buyer gains effective default protection. Because knock-ins and knockouts do not provide for a full spectrum of payouts, they are generally cheaper than standard spread options.

CHAPTER EXERCISES

1. Explain how the asset swap arbitrage works and provide an example using the following instruments/rates:
   5-year fixed bond rate of 6%
   5-year FRN yield of LIBOR + 35 bps
   5-year swap rate of 5.40%
2. Describe how a bank or investor can obtain default protection by using an asset swap switch.
3. In what way is a CDS different to a conventional OTC swap contract? Describe a more appropriate analogy from the financial markets.

4. Name three factors that drive the price of a CDS and describe how each one influences price levels.

5. Explain why an unfunded TRS is similar to a synthetic financing.

6. If an investor buys a 12-month credit spread call option on Company ABC's bond with a strike spread of 100 bps for a premium of 35 bps, what is the appropriate course of action if ABC's spread tightens to 50 bps? Widens to 150 bps? What is the breakeven level of the trade?

7. Assume the following reference credit portfolio:
   Credit 1: $10 million notional, postdefault price 40
   Credit 2: $10 million notional, postdefault price 30
   Credit 3: $10 million notional, postdefault price 50

   Given a $30 million structure, how much will an investor receive

   a. If Credit 2 defaults in a standard basket?
   b. If Credit 2 defaults in a first-to-default basket?
   c. If Credits 1 and 2 default in a first-to-default basket (in that order)?
   d. If Credit 3 defaults in a senior basket with a $5 million first-loss limit?
   e. If Credit 1 defaults in a senior basket with a $5 million first-loss limit?

CHAPTER 3

Structured and Synthetic Credit Products

INTRODUCTION

The fundamental instruments we described in the last chapter form the core of the credit derivatives market. Most daily activity occurs in CDSs, TRSs, basket swaps, and credit forwards and options, with intermediaries and end-users using the instruments regularly to implement their risk management and investment goals. The success of these instruments, coupled with the creativity of financial institutions and the specific requirements of end-users, has paved the way for further credit product development over the past few years.

In this chapter we consider the origins and applications of several structured and synthetic credit products, including credit-linked notes and repackaged bonds, structured and synthetic collateralized debt obligations (CDOs), single tranche CDOs, and index tranches. All of these instruments have grown to become part of the financial mainstream, lending further support and liquidity to the underlying credit derivative markets.

CREDIT-LINKED NOTES
Background and Market Drivers

Credit-linked notes (CLNs), which are structured debt securities that reference the financial performance of credit-risky issuers/borrowers (i.e., a form of funded credit derivatives), have emerged as one of the most important elements of the structured note marketplace. Though CLNs were originally developed as investment vehicles for institutions seeking specific credit exposures, they also serve as a tool for those seeking hedging, risk control, diversification, and liquidity access.[1] The first CLNs appeared in the early 1990s, but true growth came in subsequent phases, including the structured note cycle of the mid-1990s and the credit derivative expansion cycles of the late 1990s. Issuance and use remains strong through the millennium.

CLNs have proven popular with investors, issuers, and intermediaries for various reasons; in particular, the generic form of the security:

- Gives investors access to credit risk exposure in unique forms, with references, maturities, currencies, leverage, and coupon/principal payments customized to meet individual requirements; this includes providing access to markets that might otherwise be restricted (e.g., the leveraged loan market, which has traditionally been the domain of syndicate banks).

- Creates an efficient mechanism by which to purchase a desired reference asset and generates administrative savings when purchasing an entire portfolio of assets through a single transaction. For instance, investors purchasing a CLN need not enter into separate bond and credit derivative transactions, and need not use an ISDA agreement to confirm legal terms and conditions. In addition, because the investor does not arrange a derivative with a counterparty, it does not use any counterparty credit limits.

- Makes it possible to create synthetic, tradable credit references where none exist. For example, if investors are interested in acquiring five-year dollar-denominated fixed-rate debt of a particular BBB-rated firm, but the firm only features seven-year euro-denominated floating-rate debt, a customized CLN can be created by acquiring the seven-year

---

1 The CLN market has also been instrumental in restructuring other structured credit assets created in the mid- and late 1990s that encountered difficulties as a result of excess leverage.

FRN, shortening the maturity synthetically and converting the cash flows into fixed-rate dollars.[2]

- Transforms otherwise illiquid credit assets into more marketable form, which can add greatly to liquidity; this ultimately helps lower issuer funding costs and creates more attractive and secure opportunities for investors. For instance, if the market is not responsive to the BBB-rated company's seven-year FRN, the security will remain illiquid and trade at a spread that is wider than fair value might suggest. If, however, the transformation of the seven-year FRN into five-year fixed notes generates investor appeal, the synthetic bond will be more liquid and the company's trading spreads will tighten as a result.

- Offers tax and regulatory advantages that can benefit the investor and/or issuer. For instance, CLNs issued through offshore SPEs eliminate offshore investor withholding taxes, making the notes more economically appealing. They may also allow certain groups of investors to participate in the marketplace where they may be restricted from doing so, or where the cost of direct participation is prohibitively expensive.

- Allow participation in the credit markets by synthetically replicating existing assets that are in short supply and high demand. For instance, if a company has a ten-year benchmark bond that is in tremendous demand, embedding a CDS or TRS in a note can create a synthetic CLN that mimics the performance of the bond.

- Permit intermediaries or other users to transfer credit risk exposures (e.g., concentrations) that they wish to hedge or reduce. The CLN simply embeds default protection into the security.

General Structural Issues

The broad class of CLNs includes basic CLNs, repackaged (or synthetic) bonds, and credit portfolio securitizations; we focus our

---

2 An excessive amount of customization, e.g., creating an asset with an odd coupon payout profile, can drain liquidity from an issue. In addition, securities that are reissued strictly as private placements have a limited investor base (e.g., other qualified institutional buyers).

comments in the section below on basic CLNs and repackaged bonds, leaving the topic of credit portfolio securitizations (collateralized debt obligations) for the latter part of the chapter.

CLNs, which are combinations of credit-risky assets and derivatives, or risk-free bonds and credit derivatives, can be issued through highly rated host issuers or dedicated repackaging vehicles. Note that we can distinguish between standard CLNs, which function as pass-throughs by forwarding relevant cash flows from a risky asset to investors, and repackaged CLNs, which alter or restructure cash flows before passing them to investors; the latter approach is similar, in concept, to the asset swap structure described in Chapter 2. The payoff profile of all notes can be modified as to degree of leverage and principal protection; principal protected structures generally only function from an economic perspective on long-dated deals, because the actual risk/return parameters must be embedded in the coupon stream.

CLNs are available in various generic forms, including:

- Principal protected: The investor is only at risk for loss of coupons in the event that a defined credit risk event occurs.[3]

- Coupon increased: The investor's principal is at risk in unleveraged or leveraged form (up to the entire amount of principal).

- Coupon reduced: The investor receives full repayment of principal, and an extra payment in the event a defined credit risk event occurs; if no event occurs, the coupon is reduced.

- Step-up: The investor receives a larger coupon for each occurrence of a defined credit risk event.

Host issuers, generally AAA or AA corporate or supranational organizations, work with intermediaries to issue structured liabilities in exchange for a fee or reduced funding cost. Investors purchasing such securities thus face little default risk from the host

---

3 CLNs may be synchronized to credit events defined through the 2003 ISDA Credit Derivative definitions. The buyer of credit protection (i.e., the issuer) is generally the "notifying party" that triggers the credit event under a CLN or credit derivative. However, in some instances both parties (buyer and seller) can act as notifying parties. Apart from market-based credit spread movements associated with nondefaulting situations, the definitions are designed to cover bankruptcy, failure to pay, repudiation, moratorium, and restructuring.

issuer—coupon and principal-based returns are based solely on the external credit references incorporated into the payoff formula. While this type of structuring and issuance was very popular during the 1990s and still exists to some degree, activity has shifted in favor of the repackaging structure. Repackaging vehicles organized as bankruptcy-remote SPEs or trusts were originally introduced in the late 1980s, but gained greater popularity in the mid-1990s during the first cycle of structured note business. Most major financial institutions operate their own repackaging vehicles,[4] which serve to acquire assets, repackage cash flows, and issue notes to investors. Most vehicles are created for multiple issuance in order to improve cost efficiencies; indeed, once a vehicle is established, the costs of new note issuance are generally very modest, making the process economically viable for both intermediaries and investors. The securities that are ultimately placed by the repackager with investors can take the form of privately placed notes (SPE) or trust receipts (trust); each series features unique cash flow characteristics corresponding to the specific demands of investors. Notes and trust receipts are generally rated in order to increase marketability and liquidity; ratings are a function of both the underlying bond and the derivatives counterparty (which is typically a AAA/AA-rated financial institution). Note that CLNs are often structured with embedded leverage to magnify potential returns (and risks). Creating a credit derivative reference/portfolio with a notional size that is larger than note issue size typically does this. Some notes are structured with dynamic portfolios (reference credits, collateral, or both); this mechanism requires adherence to credit guidelines in order to preserve ratings.

A range of institutional investors seeking credit risk returns purchase CLNs, in either basic or repackaged form. Pension and investment funds, hedge funds, insurance companies, and other financial institutions are active buyers of CLNs. Some investors acquire a variety of notes, including those that are not principal protected or that are of lower credit quality; others face investment restrictions and are only permitted to purchase principal protected instruments or unleveraged structures.

---

4 For instance, Merrill Lynch uses the SIRES and STEERS vehicles, Citibank the TIERS vehicle, JP Morgan Chase the CRAVE vehicles, Barclays the ALTS vehicle, and so forth.

Basic CLNs

The basic CLN, which is a package of a low-risk bond or FRN and a simple or structured credit derivative, provides investors with the returns of a credit-risky investment without the need to own the underlying credit asset. In certain instances the host fixed-income vehicle may be a loan, rather than a bond or FRN, though this structure is less common. Securities may be issued through bank-sponsored vehicles or AAA-rated supranational/corporate issuers; MTNs and EMTNs of highly rated institutions have traditionally been popular issuance vehicles.[5] The "vanilla" CLN is generally issued at par with a payout calibrated to a defined credit event. Because payout is dependent on the credit event, the investor generally assumes the role of credit protection seller. In many instances the issuer acts as a pass-through conduit, selling the credit derivative it purchases from investors to the bank arranging the transaction. The vanilla structure can settle in cash or physical: if a credit event occurs, the note terminates and the investor receives as principal repayment the cash difference between the asset's value pre- and postdefault, or it delivers the reference asset and receives the postdefault market price. This basic structure is illustrated in Figure 3.1.

CLNs can be created using TRSs, credit spread options, credit spread forwards, or CDSs.

The TRS-linked CLN, which replicates the economic returns of a credit-risky asset by combining the TRS with a fixed or floating-rate host bond, provides the investor with the economic return of the reference asset in exchange for a LIBOR spread. For instance, an investor can purchase a CLN that pays LIBOR plus a spread based on a bank's credit. The spread is greater than might be obtained by purchasing the bank's liabilities directly, because the bank uses the CLN vehicle to receive the total return of an underlying risky asset, paying the spread in exchange; this structure is illustrated in Figure 3.2. Alternatively, the investor can receive the

---

5 Examination of the CLN structure suggests that risks must be considered on two levels: the performance obligation of the note issuer/asset repackager, and market/credit default elements of the reference obligor. The two dimensions can be considered separately, though in practice ratings agencies and sophisticated investors tend to view them jointly, on an expected loss basis. Note issuers/asset repackagers are generally sponsored by highly rated financial institutions, so the risk of nonperformance is quite small; that said, legal risks may exist that could lead to performance failures, so caution is necessary.

F I G U R E 3.1

Basic CLN

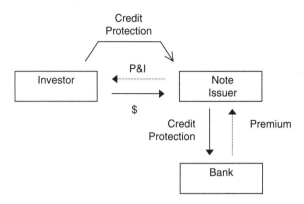

F I G U R E 3.2

TRS-based CLN

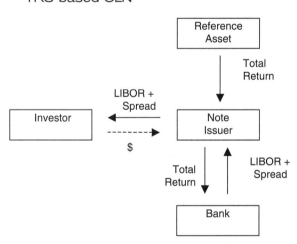

total return of a risky asset through the CLN vehicle. The bank pays the total return into the vehicle, allowing the investor to ultimately receive the economics of the risky reference asset. TRS-linked CLNs can also be based on an index or basket of credits rather than a single reference, which can provide a greater level of diversification. Banks often favor this structure, as it permits hedging of multiple credit references through creation of a synthetic short position, which can be cheaper and easier to manage.

The structures outlined above can be leveraged to increase risk/return profiles. Leverage is typically incorporated by making the notional value of the TRS greater than the face value on the reference bond. The note coupon is thus equal to (leverage factor * TRS margin) + LIBOR; if the leverage factor is large enough, a redemption floor is generally included in order to limit losses on the face value of the note (e.g., to avoid negative redemption value); the maximum an investor can lose is thus principal invested.[6]

The credit spread note, which embeds a credit spread call or put option (unilateral) or forward (bilateral) in a host security, creates an exposure to the spread movement of a reference asset without giving the investor direct ownership of the asset. An investor purchasing the note monetizes a view on expected versus implied forward credit spreads. Thus, if the note is created using a call option, the investor anticipates a tightening of spreads; if a put option is used, then a widening of spreads is expected. In exchange for purchasing a put or call through the note, the investor pays a premium through a lower coupon yield. A note created using a forward rather than an option features bilateral flows. If the investor expects a tightening (long the forward) and the reference spread tightens, principal redemption increases, and if the reference spread widens principal redemption decreases. The credit spread in a note is always defined as the yield to maturity of the reference security, less the yield of the risk-free benchmark; this allows the interest rate risk of the position to be eliminated. As with the TRS-based note above, leverage can be added by increasing the notional value of the derivative; alternatively, creating an off-market spread can enhance yield. The note can also be based on a basket of credits rather than a single reference, and can also include maturity mismatching (as discussed below).

The credit default CLN, which packages a host bond with a CDS, is similar in both form and function to the credit spread note, but generates a payoff that relates only to default of the reference asset (while CLNs referencing the default of a single reference asset are most common, they can also be created using basket swaps, or first-to-default basket swaps). The default note allows an end-user to invest in default risk (through the sale of the CDS) and an issuer, such as a financial intermediary, to hedge default risk (through the

---

6 In fact, such an "extreme" risk profile is relatively unusual; most structures have some
  degree of principal protection (e.g., 50–90%).

F I G U R E 3.3

Default-based CLN

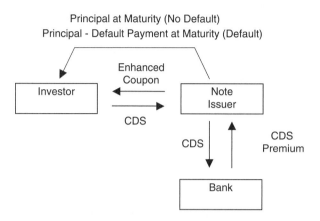

purchase of the CDS). Notes issued by corporate rather than finan-cial institutions generally include back-to-back swaps between the corporate issuer and the bank in order to transfer the CDS. Under the standard structure, the note provides the investor with an enhanced yield based on the value of the CDS being sold, along with par redemption at maturity if no default occurs, or par redemption less a default payment if an event occurs. The default event can be defined specifically or generally, though the move towards greater standards of definition typically means that bank-ruptcy, restructuring, cross default, failure to pay, repudiation, or moratorium are often specified. The default payment is calculated as a set percentage of recovery or the change in the reference asset price between issue date and default date; it may thus be a fixed amount or an ex-post market-determined amount. Figure 3.3 summarizes the default-based CLN structure.

The CLN market features a number of variations on the basic structures noted above. For instance, a CLN may include a knock-out feature, which pays the investor a lower return if the reference asset trades above or below a particular spread. This, of course, is simply a package of a bond, a credit forward (providing payout within a range), and two digital options (creating the upper- and lower-range boundaries). Thus a note might pay principal redemption of 120% of face value if the reference spread trades between 75 and 100 bps, but only 100% if it trades below 75 or above 100 bps. The enhanced return that is generated when the spread is in the range is created through the investors' sale of the two digital options. Assuming that the bond is issued through a company rather than an SPE or asset repackager, the note issuer, which buys the digital options from the investor, immediately sells them to a dealer in order to lower its all-in cost of funds.

The callable credit default note is an extension on the standard default CLN. This structure, which is a package of an FRN, CDS, and issuer call option, functions just as a default note but gives the issuer the right to call the note back at regular intervals (generally every quarter or semiannual interest payment date). If the bond is not called, the coupon payment steps up to a higher predefined margin over LIBOR. Through this structure the issuer determines on each call date whether or not to preserve the default protection; if the note is not called, it may indicate that the reference credit is deteriorating, meaning that the cost of protection via the higher coupon is easily justified. A further variation is the principal guaranteed credit default note, which allows the investor to participate in the credit risk exposure without placing principal at risk; this can be structured as a risk-free bond and a call option on the credit reference. Another extension is a default CLN linked both to the credit performance of the asset and continued convertibility in a local marketplace. This structure, which is often applied to local currency emerging market bond investments where capital controls present an additional dimension of risk, features a coupon/principal payout that is a function of default and restricted convertibility. If either event occurs, principal redemption is adjusted.

Repackaged Bonds

Repackaged bonds represent the second main component of the overall CLN market and have proven popular because of their flexible payout characteristics.

The repackaged (or synthetic) bond is essentially a securitized form of the asset swap we described in the last chapter packaging credit-risky securities with derivatives into a synthetic bond.[7]

---

7 Issuers generally regard the use of a single bond, rather than a bond and swap package, as convenient and efficient. Such convenience generally commands a premium, with the SPE charging the investor a slight premium for mechanically arranging the package.

F I G U R E 3.4

Repackaged Bond Flows

Trust Receipts with
Customized
Coupons/Principal

| Investors | ← — — | Repackaging Vehicle (SPE) |

$

Derivatives $ Coupons and Principal

| Bank | | Reference Assets |

Issuance via an SPE, rather than corporate or supranational conduits, creates greater flexibility and cost savings (e.g., no third-
party issuer permission or compensation is required). In order to
structure a repackaged bond, a bank determines investor demands
and then acquires relevant credit-risky assets in the primary or secondary markets (primarily those that it believes are trading cheap
to theoretical value, including illiquid, distressed, or out-of-favor
securities). The bank then sells the assets to the SPE/trust, which
enters into one or more derivatives with the bank to alter the cash
flows to a profile required by investors. The new cash flows are
repackaged into notes/trust receipts, which are placed with
investors; the proceeds from the note issuance are used to refund
the initial purchase of assets. The resulting synthetic notes give
investors access to customized credit-linked asset returns.
Repackaging may be based on new or seasoned assets: primary
market transactions involve repackaging of newly issued bonds,
while secondary market transactions center on repackaging outstanding bonds or reverse engineering structured notes/CLNs
notes back into "vanilla" form. Figure 3.4 illustrates the basic
repackaging process.

Repackaging trades are often used to create relative value
opportunities. For instance, this approach has been used in emerging market countries that have floated bonds under the Brady

program.[8] The repackaging vehicle purchases Brady bonds of a target country, attaches a currency swap related to the target country's currency, and passes the combined flows to investors via a note; after accounting for the value of the Brady principal and interest protection, the yield on the package provides a relative value pickup versus straight local currency sovereign issuance.

Repackaging vehicles are also used for maturity shortening trades, a very popular strategy that allows investors to create an optimal investment horizon by decoupling the maturity of the reference from a desired maturity. Under this structure the repackaging vehicle purchases a medium- or long-dated credit asset and arranges a credit derivative transaction (e.g., TRS, CDS) with a bank, synchronized to the investor's preferred horizon. For instance, in a TRS version of the trade, the investor receives periodic coupons from the security until trade maturity, at which time the asset, which may still have several years remaining until maturity, is sold in the secondary market. If the asset has gained in value, the investor receives principal plus the gain; if it has depreciated, the repackaging vehicle withholds the differential from the principal redemption. Another variation provides investors with a return based on a leveraged portfolio of reference credits: The repackaging vehicle issues notes to investors and uses the proceeds to purchase high-grade assets, then arranges a TRS with a bank based on the desired portfolio of reference credits, receiving the total return in exchange for paying the coupon flow on the asset pool. The vehicle forwards the total return on the reference assets received from the bank through a structured coupon; in order to leverage the returns, the notional of the TRS is larger than the face value of the bonds. At maturity the notes pay off a principal amount that is linked to the value of the reference assets in the TRS; any appreciation is paid in the form of enhanced redemption, while any depreciation results in discounted redemption (up to some defined floor level). This repackaged leveraged TRS note is depicted in Figure 3.5.

---

8 The Brady program is a debt restructuring framework where sovereign nations with rescheduled bank loans and their creditor banks originally agreed to swap the outstanding troubled loans for a new series of dollar-based bonds backed by rolling coupon guarantees and a U.S. Treasury zero coupon bond covering principal redemption in order to create a liquid obligation; banks exchanging their loans accepted a discount for a higher-yield bond, or preserved par but accepted a lower coupon. The Brady programs were extended to countries such as Mexico, Brazil, Argentina, Poland, Venezuela, and others, and have proven very successful.

F I G U R E   3.5

Leveraged TRS Bond on Portfolio of Reference Credits

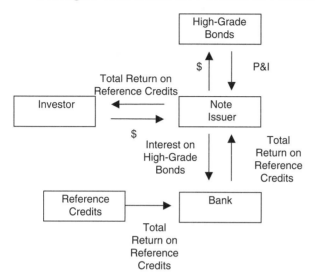

Like basic CLNs, repackaged notes can also be used to manage convertibility risk. For instance, an SPE can purchase a sovereign nation's local currency obligations and issue dollar-denominated notes to investors in exchange (which pay dollar coupons and principal through a foreign exchange swap arranged between the SPE and a bank). The SPE then arranges a separate note with a bank where final redemption is based on the onset of a convertibility event; if a defined event occurs, the bank receives a lower redemption amount (i.e., it bears the convertibility risk) and the investor receives the full redemption amount (i.e., it receives the benefit of convertibility protection). Note that the investor continues to bear the sovereign nation's default risk, as payout depends only on the convertibility event.

Synthetic bonds are a further extension of the class and are typically used to replicate an issuer's existing bond. Though synthetic bonds are similar to asset repackagings arranged through an SPE, they feature several key differences: The structures are arranged by banks that are seeking to hedge risks, rather than investors seeking return opportunities (meaning the deals are often much larger in size); and, the transactions are generally launched in the public, rather than private placement, markets, allowing a certain level of liquidity to build. For instance, a bank may issue a $100 million synthetic bond on reference credit ABC through a repackaging SPE or trust; the investor purchases the note and the SPE uses the proceeds to buy a high-grade asset, such as U.S. Treasuries. The bank, through a TRS with the SPE, pays the investor the total return on the ABC bond and receives the return on the underlying U.S. Treasuries; the investor thus receives principal and interest on the $100 million ABC credit as long as no default occurs. In the event of a default by ABC, the bank pays investors a discounted redemption price (via the SPE) based on market quotes, de facto hedging any exposure it might have to ABC through its other dealings. Investors face various dimensions of risk through the synthetic bond: default risk on ABC's credit, counterparty risk on the bank supplying the TRS flow through the SPE, and default risk on the underlying notes representing the SPE's obligations.

STRUCTURED AND SYNTHETIC COLLATERALIZED DEBT OBLIGATIONS

Background and Market Drivers

The second major class of assets based on the credit derivative market involves structured and synthetic CDOs. Before considering credit derivative-based versions of the CDO, it is important to gain an understanding of the general CDO mechanism; accordingly, the first part of our discussion in this section is devoted to a detailed review of balance sheet CDOs. With that background in place, the evolution towards credit derivative-based CDOs becomes clearer and more logical.

The CDO, a mechanism that pools, securitizes, and redistributes corporate credit obligations, is a relatively new addition to the world of structured assets, with the first transaction having been introduced in the early 1990s. Despite this relatively short history, the CDO has been instrumental in transforming intermediary and investor perceptions of credit risk investment and risk management, and growth through the early part of the millennium has been rapid. The market for CDOs is based primarily on U.S. and European asset pools and investors. The most significant transactions originated through the early part of the millennium have come via large international financial institutions, with the resulting securities placed through their global institutional investor networks. While U.S. and U.K. banks were pioneers in the original balance sheet CDO structure, they have since been joined by Swiss, German, Dutch, and French banking and asset management institutions. CDO structures are not yet prevalent in other countries, primarily as a result of inadequate securitization laws, and/or insufficient pools of local credit risk (i.e., too small or concentrated to be used in the development of a CDO).

In the section below we consider the main forms of CDOs, which can be viewed along multiple axes:

- Product axis: collateralized loan obligations (CLOs) and collateralized bond obligations (CBOs)
- Motivation axis: balance-sheet CDOs (risk transfer) and arbitrage CDOs (profit)
- Cash flow axis: cash flow CDOs and market value CDOs
- Structure axis: cash CDOs (funded, asset-based) and structured/synthetic CDOs (partially funded or unfunded, credit derivative-based)

Figure 3.6 summarizes these general CDO classes.

F I G U R E 3.6

General CDO Classes

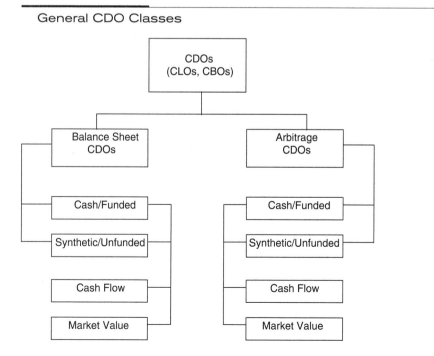

CDOs are arranged for specific risk/financial management reasons, or to capitalize on market opportunities. For instance, a CDO:

- Provides investors with professionally managed credit risk portfolio securities with a desired risk/return profile.
- Allows credit originators to shift the physical and/or risk dimensions of their credit portfolios. The balance sheet CDO, for instance, allows the sponsoring institution to reduce its credit exposure to a series of borrowers.
- Optimizes capital and balance sheet usage. By arranging a CDO, the sponsor gains financial flexibility: the transfer of credit-risky assets to end-investors allows it to lower its credit reserves and internal/regulatory capital allocations and decrease its balance sheet footings. Though capital treatment varies, a bank transferring credit-risky assets into a CDO may only face an 8% capital charge on the unleveraged amount of the transaction, or 100% on any new liability it retains (e.g., the small residual tranche); by some estimates this represents a 50% + savings in regulatory capital.
- Permits new credit originations. For instance, if a sponsor is comfortable with its level of reserves and capital allocations, it can generate new business to replace transferred business.
- Allows access to new sources of capital (i.e., capital markets investors, rather than traditional wholesale or retail depositors) and crystallization of term funding.
- Gives intermediaries an opportunity to take advantage of market opportunities. The arbitrage CDO, for instance, is driven by a sponsor's desire to capitalize on perceived discrepancies between the fair and theoretical value of credit-risky assets, and to lock in a profit margin by acquiring the assets and funding them via the issuance of securities.

While risk management and arbitrage motivations have been key CDO market drivers over the past decade, arbitrage-related opportunities have gathered momentum in recent years. Indeed, as financial institutions have become adept at using credit derivatives to manage their exposure levels, some of the original risk/capital motivations have begun to subside. Still, CDOs cannot always be arranged at will. For instance, an environment featuring very tight credit spreads may not be conducive to risk transfer or arbitrage transactions, as the spread available to investors may be insufficient (unless the collateral pools are comprised solely of very high yielding, and thus risky, assets).[9]

Investors may choose to invest in CDOs if they are seeking repackaged credit risk managed by professional portfolio managers—in a specific form that matches preferred risk/return profiles. This is an especially important factor for investments based on higher-yielding assets, where a diversified, professionally managed portfolio of assets may be considered preferable to investment in single-obligor exposures. Senior CDO tranches are often placed with high-grade asset buyers (e.g., funds restricted to AAA/AA risks that are primarily interested in capital preservation). Subordinated tranches, in turn, are sold to sophisticated institutional investors (e.g., insurers and hedge funds that are eager to assume subordinated risk in exchange for a yield pickup of 10–50 bps); residual/equity tranches are generally retained by the sponsor and/or portfolio manager, and may also be placed with hedge funds. (Because the residual/equity tranche is the riskiest component of any CDO, it features the greatest amount of exposure to the true skills of the portfolio manager.) Investors have discovered that CDOs can offer good value relative to similarly rated corporate bonds; this appears to hold true across a variety of market cycles. CDOs generally offer yield pickups of 50–60 bps over comparable corporate bonds, and feature less default risk as a result of the diversified nature of the collateral portfolios; however, CDOs are generally less liquid.

General Structural Issues

CDOs can be structured in various ways, each one designed to achieve particular investor/intermediary goals or take advantage of specific market opportunities. The standard CDO, which has an average life ranging from 5 to 15 years, involves a sponsoring institution (generally a large bank), a portfolio manager, end-investors,

---

9 In such instances there may be greater activity in investor-driven, single tranche synthetic CDOs. Because the deals are entirely synthetic, no cash purchases are required, and because only one tranche is placed with one institutional investor, the degree of acceptable enhancement can be established in advance. Indeed, the investor often has significant input into the selection of the portfolio manager and the initial portfolio.

and asset issuers (bonds) or borrowers (loans). The sponsor establishes an SPE or trust in a tax-friendly jurisdiction[10] that purchases the pool of credit assets through the issuance of tranches of securities, each with its own risk and return characteristics; in practice the credit assets are warehoused by the sponsor and are sold to the SPE/trust once the liabilities have been issued and good funds are available. The SPE/trust also engages a trustee, custodian, paying/settlement agent, and a portfolio manager to manage the operational dimensions of the deal.

A typical CDO pool may include several dozen to several hundred obligors/issuers from different industries. An experienced portfolio manager is appointed to manage the portfolio[11] under the supervision of the trustee; the portfolio manager must adhere to the investment parameters set forth in the indenture and prospectus, as well as any additional guidelines imposed by the rating agencies. The risk of the collateral pool depends primarily on credit quality and diversification: better credit quality leads to lower default risk but lower returns; greater diversification reduces the variability of losses but again generates lower returns. Note that the portfolio manager often retains a portion of the residual/equity first-loss tranche,[12] and thus has incentives that are properly aligned with a goal of maximizing earnings while taking prudent risks. The sponsor and portfolio manager work to construct the portfolio. The process passes through various distinct stages: in the ramp-up phase, or the accumulation period prior to deal closing date, the sponsor and portfolio manager assemble or purchase a portfolio of assets; in the reinvestment phase, principal from maturing or amortizing assets is used to acquire new credit assets (not every CDO features a reinvestment phase); in the winddown phase, principal from maturing assets is returned to investors, creating a note redemption effect.

---

10 The tax-haven locale is essential in order to reduce friction costs and maximize returns; the downside may be relative lack of transparency on certain reporting/regulatory issues.
11 The portfolio manager performs a crucial role in constructing and managing the collateral pool. Accordingly, it is essential for a manager's experience and past performance record to be thoroughly vetted. A proper alignment of economic interests can be a considerable help in the process, ensuring that the risks contained within the fund also drive the portfolio manager's own economic outcome.
12 This share may increase to a maximum of 49% in order not to breach nonconsolidation accounting rules; the balance of the equity is then distributed to hedge funds and other institutional investors, with the CDO's sponsor also retaining a portion.

A standard CDO, which can be created in public or private placement form, may feature one or more senior tranches (AAA/AA-rated), one or more subordinated tranches (BBB- to B-rated), and a residual or equity tranche (unrated),[13] all backed by the pool of credit assets.[14] Indeed, this structure can be viewed in standard balance sheet form, as noted in Figure 3.7.[15] The more rated debt tranches a deal has, the less residual/equity it requires; this can lead to lower returns but a more secure structure.

---

13 The market value of the equity tranche can be viewed as the mark-to-market value of the asset portfolio less all outstanding liabilities/obligations, including senior/subordinated notes issued, other borrowings, and service fees.

14 Note that some transactions also feature participating coupon notes (PCNs), which are subordinated debt/equity hybrids that pay coupons and a percentage component of any equity returns. Though the PCN structure dates back to the mid-1990s, deals did not actively feature such tranches until the early years of the millennium. Part of the motivation for renewed and increased use is that many equity CDO investors have already allocated their capital in support of existing transactions, making it difficult for sponsors to sell the equity risk to traditional buyers. The PCN has thus surfaced as a mechanism to broaden the base of investors. The earliest iterations combined CDO equity and a zero coupon bond in a trust, which was explicitly rated with respect to the zero coupon principal guarantee. After encountering certain tax/regulatory difficulties, the next version combined notes and equity from the same deal through internal structuring (and not via a trust). Investors in the PCN receive an investment-grade tranche with a below-market coupon, and an additional equity-related cash flow. Some PCNs are rated on the basis of principal only or principal and below-market coupon. If an investor requires an A-rated security for principal and coupon, then the PCN can be tailor-made to accommodate that requirement (e.g., perhaps 90% debt, 10% equity component). If it needs the A rating only for the principal, the percentage split can be shifted (e.g., 60% debt, 40% equity). If default rates are lower than expected, the PCN outperforms the conventional rated tranche, and vice versa, as a result of the "equity kicker." Other transactions include a "PIK-able" feature, allowing for payment-in-kind if current coupons cannot be serviced with cash. Some CDOs permit the trustee to halt current coupons to investors under certain circumstances (though sometimes these can be interpreted very broadly, e.g., the current coupon may be halted even if a sufficient amount of cash exists to service the notes); in exchange, the par value of the tranche is increased by an amount equal to the suspended coupon. This is precisely equal to the PIK structure that is commonly used in the high-yield markets. The PIK CDO allows the portfolio manager to conserve cash or redirect it to pay down the principal on senior tranches in order to avoid any violation of overcollateralization or interest coverage tests (any breach of which would create a deleveraging). In fact, the more stringent the tests, the more likely it is that cash flows from the deal will be diverted, and the greater the likelihood that subordinated tranches will become PIK-able. Investors need to approach PIK CDOs with caution, as they may be unaware of the fact that tranches that they purchase are "deferrable" in this manner; indeed, the rating agencies may not award an A-rating to a PIK-able tranche.

15 Although the equity tranche serves the same purpose as common equity (e.g., first-loss capital), it is actually issued as a form of debt security in the CDO structure.

F I G U R E   3.7

The General CDO Balance Sheet

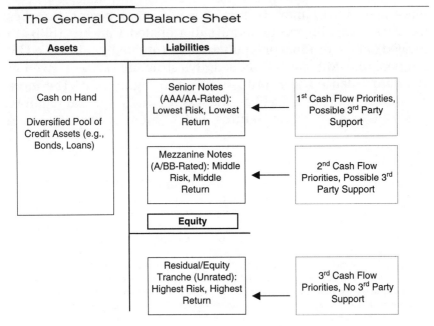

For instance, a high-grade CDO, with lower default probabilities in the asset pool, requires a smaller residual/equity tranche than a high-yield CDO (i.e., 3–5% versus 8–10%, respectively); by extension, the larger the equity tranche, the smaller the resulting AAA/AA-rated tranches. CDOs generally feature a predominance of high-rated tranches in order to take advantage of cheaper funding levels.

Tranching and Cash Flows

The actual tranching structure of a CDO and the amount of subordination and equity depends ultimately on the size of the profit spread; this is true of all CDOs, not simply the arbitrage CDOs considered below. The portfolio of credit assets, financed by a combination of debt tranches, must yield enough to service the debt obligations and provide an adequate return to the equity investors. The primary factor is whether the available returns are sufficient to attract the right combination of investors. If the available returns appear to match investor expectations, then the CDO's structural features can be refined and stress-tested to determine performance under a range of plausible and implausible scenarios.[16] If the returns appear to fall short under plausible scenarios, the CDO must generally be abandoned. The modeling process must also incorporate the effect of fees (up-front (which are generally 1–3%) and annual (0.50–1%)), funding costs (based on a range of forward curve stresses),[17] delayed portfolio ramp-up, and default and recovery scenarios; for CDOs created with structured finance assets such as mortgage-backed securities, prepayment effects must also be evaluated. Only after completing these exercises will it become clear whether the CDO can be profitably structured and whether the cash flows generated by the securitized pool will be sufficient, under all realistic scenarios, to service noteholder obligations. When the modeling scenarios suggest that debt obligations can be successfully serviced and the equity tranche will generate a return of 15–20%, then a successful transaction may be at hand. The sponsor can then adjust the details of the tranches, leverage, and asset pool to optimize risk and maximize returns. Naturally, a CDO that appears to "work" based on overly generous assumptions may actually fail to provide the intended returns.

Cash flows are distributed in sequence based on seniority; the deal prospectus typically contains information on the structural "tests" that are performed to ensure proper cash flow coverage, as discussed below. A CDO in compliance with its tests typically pays cash flows as follows: fees/expenses of the CDO SPE (typically 25 bps up-front, and 25 bps after satisfying the structural tests

---

16 In practice, a hypothetical portfolio of assets is run through the sponsor's model to compute potential returns. Different model variables can then be added (e.g., changing portfolio credit quality, diversification, concentrations, interest rates, and so forth). For instance, increasing the credit quality of the portfolio means reducing the specter of default risk, which means lowering overcollateralization and reducing the equity tranche needed to support the overall structure. Because equity returns are greater (though more variable) than senior/subordinated returns, the cost to the sponsor declines. The opposite is also true. Alternatively, the model can be run with more subordinated tranching and less equity, thereby increasing deal leverage; while greater leverage can lead to greater returns, it can also magnify default-induced losses and must be subjected to tighter overcollateralization and interest coverage tests (any violation of which will cause a more rapid deleveraging).

17 Funding costs are vital in determining the amount of subordination; the higher the interest costs, the lower the level of subordination, as junior tranches are more expensive than AAA tranches. That said, too little subordination can impact AAA participation: AAA investors tend to focus heavily on the amount of subordination that exists in a deal as their first-loss protection; if they consider that it is too small, they may be reluctant to participate or may demand a greater risk premium.

below)[18], interest to senior tranches, interest to subordinated tranches, interest to equity tranche, principal to senior and subordinated tranches until retired, and then principal to equity tranche. However, if tests reveal a cash flow shortfall, the payment stream is redirected in favor of the senior-most tranches.

Returns on subordinated tranches can be examined on a relative value basis versus corporate bonds, though they encompass a different set of risks; default risk differences, in particular, must be considered closely (e.g., a BBB-rated pool of default risk versus a BBB-rated single obligor default risk). A more logical relative value comparison can be made against a corporate bond index comprised of similarly rated obligors (e.g., a BBB corporate index). Historical and estimated default experience between the two asset pools can be analyzed to determine whether the CDO's subordinated tranche appears cheap or rich to the BBB corporate bond index. The residual/equity tranche, which protects the senior and subordinated tranches that rank above it, has the potential of providing attractive returns if the pool performs well; the equity can thus be viewed as a leveraged position in the collateral pool's default performance.[19] Importantly, it occupies the first-loss position and is thus at considerable risk; violation of any of the structural tests can seriously impair the value of the instrument. Equity investors only receive cash flows after the CDO's fees have been paid and the senior/subordinated tranches have been serviced. If the tests fail, it is very difficult for the equity to later generate a meaningful return, as the structure will already have delevered by a certain amount. Note that equity investors tend to receive a disproportionate amount of their cash flows in the early part of a deal (e.g., before any credits in the pool have defaulted), meaning that seasoned equity tends to sell at a discount to the flotation price.[20] The potential value of the equity tranche can be analyzed through standard internal rate of return (IRR) scenarios, including scenarios where defaults shift

---

18 The split fees are increasingly common and used to align the portfolio manager's interests with those of other investors. By subordinating half of the fees, the manager has incentives to manage the portfolio more closely.

19 The CDO equity can also benefit from credit spread tightening versus LIBOR if the interest rate risk is hedged versus floating coupons. The equity also benefits from a high-spread environment, as investors will receive excess coupons over the amount needed to service the senior/subordinated tranches.

20 The value of the CDO equity that has experienced no defaults also declines over time as cash flows are returned as interest or amortized principal.

IRRs from positive to negative. For instance, with 0% defaults (an unrealistic scenario), the IRR of the equity may exceed 25%; with 2% defaults (an unlikely, but possible, scenario), the IRR may drop to 0%; in practice a well-managed CDO, with default experience near historical averages for a pool of a given set of characteristics, can generate an IRR of 15–20%. More sophisticated analyses, including those performed via simulations, allow potential equity investors to examine the distribution of equity returns and establish confidence levels across a range of default and recovery experience.

The portfolio manager is generally required to sell defaulted assets in the pool within one year, and may also be required to mark the position at the lower of the postdefault market price or 30%. The underlying assets comprising the pool generally have finally maturities that are less than, or equal to, the maturities of the securities. In practice, the actual average life of pool assets tends to be shorter than the maximum life, meaning that a given deal may have a higher yield to maturity than is otherwise apparent.[21] As noted in the ratings section below, the sponsoring institution or portfolio manager attempts to structure and maintain a properly diversified asset pool, avoiding undue concentrations by obligor, industry, country, or ratings class. CDOs actively use swaps, caps, floors, and collars to transform cash flows from fixed into floating, or to hedge any interest rate or basis risk between the asset pool flows and the securities. Because hedges are rarely perfect, most CDOs feature a certain amount of outright overexposure or underexposure to market factors at any point in time. Transactions generally require about six months of lead-time to structure and arrange (depending on portfolio complexity and asset liquidity), and are heavily influenced by market conditions. For instance, if funding spreads are too high, or credit spreads too wide or too tight, the economic rationale for pursuing a transaction may not be compelling. Figure 3.8 illustrates the general CDO structure.

As noted above, a CDO must undergo certain tests to confirm the investor payment sequence (e.g., the "waterfall"). Consider a CDO comprised of three tranches, Class 1 (AAA-rated), Class 2 (BBB-rated), and Class 3 (BB-rated). In order for principal

---

21 Note that although the collateral pool may contain callable securities, in practice these are unlikely to cause a deal's average life to vary by more than 12 months; the effects of this optionality are thus limited.

FIGURE 3.8

General CDO Structure

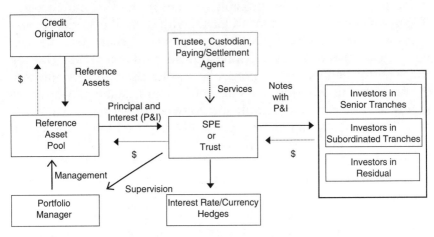

and interest to flow from one class to the next, overcollateralization/ interest coverage tests must be performed and successfully passed.[22] The process begins with an interest income flow, which, after being used to cover fees, is used to pay Class 1 interest. Then the Class 1 test is performed: if the test results are positive (e.g., the asset/interest coverage ratios are adequate), Class 2 interest is paid; if the test results are negative, Class 1 principal, rather than Class 2 interest, is paid—by using excess interest to pay Class 1 principal, the senior-most investors are protected. The paydown of senior investors is equal to early amortization of the structure, which creates a deleveraging effect. Assuming the test is passed, however, the waterfall structure then moves to a Class 2 test: if the test is passed, Class 3 interest is paid, and any remaining cash flow is allocated to the residual; if the test fails, additional Class 1 principal is paid, and then Class 2 principal is paid. The structure thus continues for each payment period. Assuming that interest flows are successfully applied, the same process applies to the distribution of principal. The payment sequence of interim and final cash flows on a standard CDO that remains current on its tests is summarized in Figure 3.9.

---

22 It is increasingly common for CDOs to feature separate overcollateralization and interest coverage test levels for each class of notes.

F I G U R E 3.9

CDO Interim and Final Cash Flows

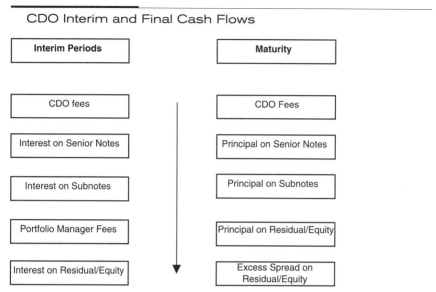

The overcollateralization and interest coverage tests are used to evaluate the allocation of principal and interest via the waterfall structure.

The overcollateralization test is given as follows:

Principal value of collateral portfolio/(Principal for a tranche + Principal for all tranches ranking senior)

The results of the overcollateralization are compared to established guidelines and overcollateralization triggers. If the computed figure is greater than the trigger, the test is successfully passed and the waterfall structure remains intact; if it is less than the trigger, the flows are redirected in the manner described above. Multiple defaults within the pool, which subtract from the principal value of the collateral pool, may cause a test to fail. Typical overcollateralization ratios at a BBB-rated level might range from 102–105% for high-grade asset pools, and 105–115% for high-yield asset pools. CDOs that use a greater amount of collateral selling at a discount to par have a greater level of implied overcollateralization, allowing for a lower equity requirement. Thus, deals created during severe market downturns or corrections (e.g., 1997, 1998, 2000) can feature substantial overcollateralization buffers. The reverse is also true: a widespread, systemic spread-widening event that occurs after a CDO has been created can lower the principal value of the collateral pool by enough to create test failure—even though no defaults occur.

The second major test, interest coverage, is computed as:

Interest on collateral portfolio/(Interest for a tranche
+ Interest for all tranches ranking senior)

Again, the results of the computation are compared to guidelines and explicit coverage triggers. A successful result leads to a continuation of the waterfall, an unsuccessful result leads to cash flow redirection. Typical interest coverage at the BBB-rated level might range from 100–105% for high-grade asset pools, and 110–120% for high-yield asset pools.

As noted, if the overcollateralization and/or interest coverage tests fail, the structure begins to de-lever, with principal and interest receipts from existing pool assets redirected to the senior-most tranches. The equity investors absorb the majority of this redirection. The process of deleveraging and redirecting cash flows continues until the proper coverage levels are regained, at which point the CDO can resume its normal operations. The smaller the difference between the actual and trigger levels, the greater the structural leverage in the CDO, and the greater the risks and returns to the equity investors and subordinated tranche investors. CDOs constructed with an average asset pool rating of BBB will feature a smaller difference between the actual/trigger levels on the two tests than one comprised of BB or B assets because the volatility of default rates is much smaller.

Supplemental quality tests may also be used. These tests relate primarily to portfolio construction, diversification, concentration, expected default, and loss given default (e.g., 1 less the recovery rate). Portfolio assets are decomposed by industry group to determine the actual level of diversification in the pool, given an assumed correlation between industry groups. Cross-industry diversification is generally regarded as a favorable characteristic of the asset pool. Pools with more diversification require less equity and can support more leverage; those with less diversification require more equity. Maximum allowable concentrations per obligor are also computed; in most cases these cannot exceed more than 2% of a given pool. Expected defaults based on estimated default probabilities are applied to the entire portfolio based on historical data (adjusted for possible anomalies). Defaults are value-weighted across the target portfolios to create a time-dependent, cumulative probability of default. Recovery rates are generally taken as a historic constant based on seniority; loss given default, in turn, is defined as (1 – recovery rate). Expected loss within the portfolio is thus a summation of (loss given default * probability of default) for each asset. For instance, if asset 1 in the pool ($10 million notional) has a 5% probability of default and a 40% recovery rate, the expected loss is 3%, or $300,000. The same computation is then applied to the next asset, and so forth. Default correlation features in the portfolio calculation. A portfolio with low default correlation has a high probability of experiencing only a few losses, but virtually no probability of sustaining zero losses. A portfolio featuring high default correlation, in contrast, functions more as a single credit/obligor: either many credits default, or no credits default. As default correlation increases, the probability of large losses grows and the probability that the CDO's senior tranches will be exposed to default-related losses increases in tandem; this means that even AAA/AA investors will demand a greater return.

CDOs often allow for a certain amount of asset substitution if particular references in the collateral pool show signs of deterioration. Such substitutions, which may be capped at 5 or 10 per year, are designed to avoid an event of default (which would permanently damage CDO value) rather than promote opportunistic trading.[23] If an asset is removed from the portfolio, it must be replaced by another asset in order not to deleverage the structure. If a capital loss is sustained in liquidating a troubled asset, the losses are generally reflected through the tranche coupon. Certain CDOs are structured so that the sponsor can call them at par after a blackout period; however, a "prepayment penalty" may be levied to discourage exercise of the call.[24]

---

23 There are, however, instances when substitution is allowed if certain assets have increased in value by a significant amount, in order to help crystallize reserves that can be used to protect investors.

24 A transaction may be called if it is performing well or poorly: if it is performing well, the sponsor is generally required to pay a call premium equal to some percentage of the annual coupon, and if it is performing poorly the sponsor may not have to pay any such premium (in which case the call functions as a deal "clean up" mechanism). Some CDOs grant the equity holders the right to call the deal after the lockout period under certain predefined circumstances (generally performance related). CDOs may also feature refinancing options that allow the portfolio manager to refinance the structure while leaving the asset pool intact. This occurs when the value of the liabilities has risen and it is unwise to sell the collateral (e.g., it is illiquid, or worth more if held to maturity); such refinancings are, however, relatively uncommon. Early termination is also possible, though only if the CDOs covenants are breached, the senior tranches fail to receive cash flows, the issuer of the CDO declares bankruptcy, or the portfolio manager/team departs.

A secondary market in CDOs has developed over the past decade, primarily for senior, and certain subordinated, tranches; equity tranches have very limited resalability. However, because the market is still relatively new and each CDO has somewhat unique structural features, liquidity is not deep, and pricing inefficiencies exist. Hedge funds have emerged as aggressive players in the CDO market, and some have been successful in capitalizing on price discrepancies. Their ability to model CDOs and derive certain theoretical values that may be different to market values allows them to purchase "cheap" CDOs in the secondary market and/or to sell "rich" ones. Most price support and market-making activity comes from the underwriter initially responsible for issuing the CDO on behalf of the sponsor; this is logical, as the underwriter (generally one of the major investment banks) is likely to be intimately familiar with the structure and its cash flows. Valuation becomes more transparent once a CDO exits the primary offering stage, as the portfolio backing a particular deal becomes widely known;[25] this allows potential secondary investors to analyze the deal on its merits. Secondary investors buying seasoned CDOs must pay particular attention to an issue's overcollateralization and interest coverage tests, and whether the pool contains any concentrations of "borderline" securities that may trigger defaults at a future time horizon.

CLOs: High Grade and High Yield While the generic CDO template is relatively straightforward, and quite comparable to the securitization technologies used in the MBS and ABS market, specific details related to the construction of a CLO tend to be complicated, as loans are not always easily transferable from the original borrower into a collateral pool. In addition, loans can take many forms, including direct loans, participations/subparticipations in drawn or undrawn commitments, revolvers, leveraged leases, project finance loans, and distressed loans.[26] A CLO may be arranged using loan participation agreements (sale without the knowledge/agreement of the borrower), meaning if the seller

---

25 The offering memorandum and trustee reports reflect the structure and current holdings of a CDO; this information also includes overcollateralization and interest coverage test levels.

26 That said, a CLO comprised of an excessive amount of unfunded commitments or revolvers may not work, as cash flow uncertainties may simply be too great.

becomes insolvent, the SPE or trust is unlikely to have any direct recourse to the borrower. Alternatively, it may be arranged through the assignment process, which provides for a full assignment of the seller's rights, thus linking the SPE or trust with the borrower; this, however, is a more time-consuming method, as it requires prior notification and/or approval by the borrower. The difficulties associated with easily transferring loans are at least one reason why banks have begun using structured and synthetic CDOs more actively.

CLOs may be based on high-grade or high-yield loans; though high-grade conduits are easier to structure and sell, they offer lower returns. High-yield CLOs, which feature more attractive returns to compensate for the added default and liquidity risks, are more difficult to structure, as sourcing a sufficient amount of suitable loans can be challenging; indeed, deals originally intended as pure high-yield CLOs may become broader high-yield CDOs through the inclusion of high-yield bonds. In addition, it may be difficult identifying a portfolio manager with suitable high-yield experience, as well as investors interested in acquiring the residual tranche of the deal.

CBOs: High-Grade, High-Yield, Emerging-Market, Structured Finance
CBOs can be collateralized by pools of high-grade, high-yield, emerging-market, convertible, distressed, or structured finance bonds; on rare occasions asset pools may contain a mix of bonds from each sector, though this demands considerable portfolio management expertise and very specific investor needs. While most assets in CBO pools tend to feature fixed coupons, floating-rate notes may also be used; this requires the SPE to arrange additional hedges to reduce or eliminate interest rate risk. Because bonds are easily traded/transferred among investors (unless they are structured as private placements), a CBO can generally be assembled more rapidly than a CLO. In addition, creating a security interest in the pool of bearer bonds for the holders of the securities is a well-established process that has been widely used in the MBS and ABS markets for several decades.

CBOs often use inefficiently priced illiquid securities that can be held in the collateral pool until maturity; high-yield bonds, emerging-market bonds, private placements, and other structured notes/bonds tend to feature prominently in CBOs. In fact, emerging market CBOs have become a popular component of the market;

T A B L E   3.1

CLO and CBO Collateral Assets

CLO Assets	CBO Assets
Senior, secured bank loans	High-grade bonds
Senior, unsecured bank loans	High-yield bonds
Mezzanine loans	Emerging market bonds
Funded/unfunded revolving credit lines	Convertible bonds
Leveraged leases	Structured finance bonds (ABS, MBS, CMO)
Project finance loans	Distressed bonds
High-yield loans	
Distressed loans	

though emerging market borrowers have a significant amount of loans outstanding, bonds tend to be the asset of choice for collateral pools as default experience is often much better.[27] Structured finance CDOs, comprised of other structured assets, tend to feature better credit quality than high-yield CDOs, but also feature longer maturity tails and, on occasion, a degree of prepayment risk.[28] Some portfolio managers include callable bonds in their collateral pools; because these securities are generally callable at a premium equal to a certain percentage of par or the current coupon, returns to CBO investors can improve by a commensurate amount.

Table 3.1 summarizes assets that are commonly used as collateral in CBOs and CLOs. Many of these assets also serve as references for structured and synthetic CLOs and CBOs.

---

27 For instance, emerging market borrowers have a long history of defaulting on, or renegotiating, their external loans as well as their domestic (local currency) bonds; many, however, have avoided similar actions on their external bonds, as they prefer not to threaten their ability to access the international capital markets at future points in time (renegotiating terms with investors holding bearer bonds is also largely impractical). Consider that at the turn of the millennium emerging market borrowers featured a combined default rate of nearly 12%, with only 2.5% centered in external bonds. Default/restructuring actions can, in fact, be selective, meaning certain debt obligations may be damaged and others not.

28 Because most structured finance CDOs feature less than one-third of their pools in residential MBS, negative convexity and prepayment risks are much smaller than in standard MBS or CMO structures.

Ratings

Rating agencies are generally contacted once legal structure and investment strategies have been developed in order to obtain detailed guidance on portfolio construction, overcollateralization, and interest coverage. CDOs are typically rated through an analysis of various factors, including credit risk, market risk, legal risk, cash flow timing, expected credit losses, credit enhancements, portfolio manager experience, operational complexity, and use of third-party support (e.g., monoline insurer guarantees, bank letters of credit).[29] Each one of these factors may be subjected to certain stress tests to determine how the structure will perform under adverse conditions. The rating agencies often require CDOs to adhere to certain standards, including minimum pool diversification, maximum asset maturities, minimum weighted average pool asset ratings, minimum overcollateralization (e.g., asset principal greater than securities issued), and minimum interest coverage; they assign specific scores to many of these attributes, which influence ratings of various tranches within a CDO. Rating agencies generally also require deals with a greater amount of leverage to use higher-quality asset pools and adhere to stricter overcollateralization and interest coverage tests. Conversely, those with less leverage can comfortably accept lower quality assets.[30]

Diversification is an especially critical factor, particularly for structures that may be subjected to industry- or countrywide difficulties. For instance, the rating agencies tend to follow a conservative approach in considering diversification attributes of emerging-market CDOs; they often group emerging-market assets into broad groups and give only partial benefit to cross-country diversification in order to avoid damage that might arise from

---

29 Consider, for instance, the process used by one major rating agency in evaluating a CDO: the parameters of the hypothetical portfolio are evaluated by examining aggregate and individual industry scores; the weighted average probability of default is then determined by computing the expected loss of each credit in the portfolio; a stress factor is then applied to the weighted average probability of default on the entire portfolio; weighted average recovery rates are then applied, and a cash flow model is then used to determine investor losses under particular scenarios. The resulting expected loss of a senior or subordinated note is then mapped to a default table to obtain an equivalency rating.

30 In certain unusual cases, the equity tranche (which is generally unrated), may be rated investment grade if deal leverage is low (e.g., sub-8x) and the credit quality of the pool is high (e.g., average BBB or better).

contagion effects. Borrowers within a single emerging market are given no diversification benefit.[31]

Most CDOs rely on internal/external enhancement in order to achieve a particular minimum rating level for the highest-rated tranches within the overall structure. It is common to create standard senior/subordinated tranching in order to redirect cash flows to the senior (AAA or AA-rated) tranches; alternatively, the structure may feature fast-pay/slow-pay tranches (with accelerated cash flows directed to the highest rated securities). A CDO can also be enhanced using excess spread that accumulates in a reserve account, or a third-party guarantee from a highly rated monoline insurer or financial institution. CDOs that feature lower diversification scores (e.g., emerging-market or high-yield CDOs) must be created using higher structural standards in order to achieve the same ratings level as a well-diversified, high-grade transaction; this typically means more overcollateralization, greater subordination, and/or a greater amount of equity (e.g., the equity tranche of an emerging market deal may be as high as 20%, while that of a high-yield deal may be 8–10%, and that of a high-grade deal only 2–4%).

While most early CDOs had limited/no right of asset substitution, that has changed with market evolution and introduction of new CDO structures. Right of substitution has expanded, making it more difficult for the rating agencies to monitor and enforce minimum standards. This is likely to remain a challenge as greater "flexibility" is built into new transactions.

The rating agencies generally require the trustee to compile and report regularly on the target CDO's portfolio, diversification, defaults, overcollateralization and interest coverage tests, excess spread account, asset turnover, and portfolio manager performance in order to ensure adherence to required parameters and thresholds.

Cash Flow CDOs and Market Value CDOs

A CDO can be created as a cash flow structure or a market value structure. The cash flow CDO relies primarily on principal and interest cash flows from the securitized portfolio to service outstanding notes, while the market value CDO depends on both

---

31 For instance, borrowers in a non-Latin American region are assumed to have a default correlation of approximately 30%, those in Latin America a default correlation of 60%, and individual borrowers within a country a default correlation of 100%.

principal and interest streams and active management (e.g., maturing assets, properly timed sales creating capital gains) to generate debt service. Most of the balance sheet CDOs described below are structured in cash flow form, while arbitrage CDOs may take either cash flow or market value form.

Under the cash flow structure, the sponsor and portfolio manager design the collateral pool of loans or bonds so that the assets generate sufficient principal and interest to pay investors periodic coupons, along with principal at maturity. Pool cash flows thus drive investor cash flows. Under the market value structure the pool is subject to a daily or weekly mark-to-market evaluation and overcollateralization testing. If the market value of the portfolio times the advance rate[32] falls below outstanding debt, a portion of the pool[33] is sold in the market and the proceeds are used to redeem investor notes in order to preserve the appropriate level of overcollateralization. If the market value stays above the trigger level, the notes remain outstanding. Market value structures also allow for tests of the equity/residual tranche; if a minimum level of equity is not maintained (i.e., an amount sufficient to protect the senior and subordinated tranches), the senior noteholders can elect to accumulate their payments.

While most CBOs and CLOs are structured using the cash flow method, certain CBOs based on distressed securities use the market value approach, suggesting that turnover within the collateral pool may be more active. The market value structure is more flexible; the portfolio manager can enjoy considerable discretion in

---

32 The advance rate reflects the discount, or "haircut," on the value of the asset pool required by the rating agencies; thus, an 80% advance rate implies a 20% discount, a 70% advance rate a 30% discount, and so forth. Haircuts on high-yield bonds are approximately 5%, distressed bank loans 10%+, and so forth. Advance rates are critical to the success of a market value CDO; if they are set too high, investors may not be adequately protected, and if they are set too low, the economics of the structure may not function properly. The advance rate is a direct function of price volatility and liquidity of the asset—the greater the volatility and the lower the liquidity, the larger the discount and the smaller the resulting advance rate. Each asset in the pool features an advance rate that is related to the target rating, based on the structure of the deal and the composite of the portfolio. The advance rate also increases with portfolio diversification, at a level that depends on the correlation between pool assets (correlation may be measured under normal or stressed conditions, depending on the specifics of the collateral pool); thus, the lower the correlation, the greater the diversification benefits, and the greater the advance rate.

33 In practice the amount of collateral that needs to be liquidated is computed as deficit/(1 − advance rate).

buying/selling securities within the portfolio (e.g., up to 20% of the portfolio per year), though it must still adhere to operating parameters related to diversification, overcollateralization, and credit quality. In fact, portfolio managers do not always have complete flexibility to trade in and out of positions in the portfolio. The goal of the market value structure is to maximize total returns while minimizing price volatility; sharp and sudden declines in asset value can be dangerous for market value structures, sometimes even triggering note redemption. Repayment of liabilities under the market value structure occurs when assets are sold rather than when they mature. As such, they are not well suited for collateral pools that feature unpredictable cash flows, or those with assets maturing well after the final maturity of the CDO; both of these can expose the structure to significant losses if assets need to be liquidated early.

Balance Sheet and Arbitrage CDOs

Balance sheet CDOs were originally developed by sponsoring banks attempting to optimize their balance sheets, capital, and risk exposures by transferring portions of their loan (and eventually bond) portfolios to third-party investors. Like other securitizations, balance sheet CDOs, involve the creation of an SPE (for a single issue of securities) or a master trust (for multiple issues), which buys a pool of credit-risky assets from the transaction sponsor or credit originator. The asset purchase is funded through the issuance of multiple tranches of securities, which are placed with investors; the sponsoring institution often retains the equity. A typical balance sheet deal is likely to feature senior notes comprising 90–95% of total deal size, subordinated notes (both strong and weak investment grade) of up to 8%, and an equity tranche of approximately 2%.

Arbitrage CDOs have grown more rapidly than balance sheet CDOs over the past few years, as sponsors and investors seek to capitalize on market opportunities.[34] If a bank identifies in the secondary market credit assets that it perceives to be cheap to theoretical value, it can purchase and repackage them in an SPE or trust to

---

34 While a cash flow arbitrage CDO functions in a manner similar to a balance sheet CDO (except for the goal of profit generation rather than risk transfer), a market value arbitrage CDO functions like an actively traded investment or hedge fund.

lock-in value. By doing so it crystallizes the spread differential between the cash outflows (funding) and the cash inflows (principal and interest), and is guaranteed an attractive return as long as default performance within the portfolio does not outpace default-related assumptions used in constructing the CDO. Arbitrage CDOs, which are leveraged from 8–12 times, may include high-grade bonds, high-yield bonds, and emerging-market bonds; sponsors increasingly use loans in their arbitrage structures as well, which has been made possible by growing secondary liquidity in certain types of high-grade bank loans. (It does not apply uniformly, however, as the transfer of many loans must still occur on a case-by-case basis between the borrower and originator/seller, as noted above.)

The economics of the arbitrage CDO are ultimately driven by the returns payable on the equity tranche. The net flows on the structure can be separated into inflows and outflows: interest inflows include interest from collateral assets and any swaps that might be used to convert tranches into floating rates; interest outflows include interest payable to the senior and subordinated tranches and any swaps used in the structure; outflows also include fees payable to the trustee and portfolio manager. The net balance remaining is the amount payable (if any) to the equity investors; this varies based on defaults, asset callability, spread performance on assets that are sold during the period, swap hedges, and fees. If the arbitrage CDO has been structured correctly, the tranche equity may generate returns of up to 30%.

Structured and Synthetic CDOs

Cash-funded CLOs and CBOs, which rely on true sale transfers, represent the core of the CDO market and remain popular to the present time. The structured and synthetic CDO sector, which returns our focus to the credit derivative marketplace, developed several years after the first funded CDOs were introduced as a logical extension of the asset class. Structured and synthetic CDOs rely on derivative replication transfer, rather than true sale transfer, to achieve the risk transfer and investment goals outlined above.

For purposes of this discussion, we define a structured CDO as any structure that relies on CLNs for risk transfer, and a synthetic CDO as one that uses only credit derivatives to achieve the same results. As noted earlier in the chapter, a CLN is simply a combination of a bond and a credit derivative and is thus one step "removed" from a pure synthetic derivative structure.[35] Structured and synthetic CDOs ultimately convey the risks/returns of the collateral pool without transferring legal ownership into an SPE or trust.

In the structured CDO the sponsor, via an SPE, issues a CLN that references individual loans in the target portfolio; the CLN transfers the risk of the loans into the SPE but not the physical assets, which remain in the sponsor's possession. Investors in structured CDOs purchase tranches of rated securities that are backed by a pro-rata share in CLNs (meaning they have no recourse back to the originating bank). Principal and interest from the CLNs are paid to investors; the CLN sources its principal and interest flows from the pool of reference loans or bonds. If an obligor from the reference portfolio defaults, the SPE bears the initial loss of principal and interest, which is transferred to the investors. In common with other CLNs, the defaulting note is effectively redeemed at a fixed recovery rate percentage, or at a dealer-quoted postdefault price.

Standard diversification techniques are employed in the structuring process, so that the portfolio of CLNs references a pool that has maximum exposures by obligor, industry, country, and rating. The final maturity of any CLN reference asset must always be shorter than the maximum maturity on any CLN or funding tranche. Minimum levels of overcollateralization are typically used, just as in a conventional CDO; thus, a pool of $105 million of loans or bonds might be needed to secure $100 million of CLNs. This provides first-loss protection that can help boost a deal's ratings. Because there is no separation between the underlying reference obligations in the portfolio of the sponsoring bank, the structure depends on the sponsoring bank's performance; accordingly, the highest rating of the best tranche in the CDO cannot exceed the sponsoring bank's rating. Some structures incorporate early amortization triggers to protect investors in case reference asset loss experience accelerates; this results in an unwinding of the

---

35 A CDS embedded in a CLN that is used for a structured or synthetic CDO allows for payments to the protection buyer if a credit event occurs; such credit events generally include bankruptcy, restructuring, moratorium, repudiation, failure to pay, and/or acceleration of obligations. Note that ISDA's restructuring definition was revised to encompass instances where multiple-bank lenders exist and two-thirds of the lenders agree to the restructuring.

F I G U R E   3.10

Structured CDO

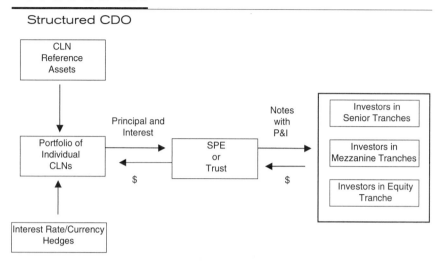

entire structure. In some instances the structured CDO also allows for dynamic replacement (e.g., pool assets can be retired or new credits extended), indicating the CLNs are redeemable and reissuable on a quarterly or semiannual basis. Each CLN represents a single pool obligation, facilitating the management process.

Structured CDOs feature a number of important advantages over balance sheet structures: they avoid the security interest and transfer issues that characterize standard balance sheet CDOs and simplify the hedging process by allowing currency and interest rate hedges to be embedded within each individual note (rather than requiring them to be managed discretely through the issuing SPE or trust). One notable disadvantage, however, is that the sponsor retains the reference assets on their balance sheet, which inflates total footings. Figure 3.10 highlights the basic structured CDO.

The synthetic CDO serves as an extension of the structured CDO. The first synthetic CDO, JP Morgan's 1997 BISTRO transaction, demonstrated that it was possible to use CDSs to transfer credit risk in the CDO structure, reducing the need for funding via the SPE/trust.[36] Under the standard synthetic CDO, which has

---

36 Through the pioneering BISTRO deal, which transferred the credit default risk on $9.7 billion of loans, JP Morgan retained the residual ($32 million), subordinated investors accepted the next layer of risk ($237 million), senior investors the third layer of risk ($470 million), and JP Morgan the remaining excess layer of risk.

since become widely used,[37] a sponsoring bank issues CLNs to investors to finance a pool of high-quality collateral assets, which are used to secure a CDS between the sponsoring bank and the issuing SPE or trust; the CDS references the specific credits in the sponsoring bank's portfolio requiring protection. The SPE receives a fee for providing the default protection; this fee, combined with the principal and interest cash flows from the high-quality collateral pool, are paid to investors funding the CLNs (again, via multiple tranches). The extent to which a synthetic CDO employs credit derivatives dictates the degree of required cash funding; in the extreme, a 100% unfunded synthetic CDO relies on complete use of credit derivatives to transfer risk to investors.

Synthetic CDOs, like conventional and structured transactions, feature senior/subordinated tranching that allocates losses in sequence; the cash flow stream is preserved while coverage tests remain in order. The sponsor generally retains the first-loss equity tranche in a synthetic CDO. In order for the sponsor to gain capital relief, it must limit the amount of default exposure it retains through the first-loss tranche; this generally means that the portfolio is structured with high-grade, rather than high-yield, credit assets. In order for a synthetic structure to work properly, the derivatives counterparty on the CDSs must have payment priority over investors in the CDO's tranches.

Synthetic CDOs can be created with static or dynamic reference pools; though static pools still account for more than two-thirds of the synthetic market, investor interest in dynamic pools has been on the rise (creating additional challenges for the rating agencies, as noted earlier). Investors in static transactions have full

---

37 For instance, after the BISTRO deal, UBS (via Warburg) created Eisberg Finance and CSFB created Triangle II to transfer portions of their own credit portfolios. Citibank applied the same technologies to the European market by structuring the € 4 billion C-Star structure in 1999: the bank retained the 1% first loss tranche, arranged a CDS with C-Star, which issued CLNs to collateralize the transaction; Citibank then arranged uncollateralized CDSs with high-grade banks directly. The end result was a shift in the credit risk to a variety of investors and counterparties. The same synthetic securitization technologies have been applied to repackaging of mortgage loan risk, letters of credit, and underwriting commitments. For instance, rather than using standard private-label pass-through technologies, certain banks have used the synthetic CDO mechanism to shift the risk, though not the balance sheet impact, of portions of their mortgage loan portfolios. Each of these transactions must, of course, be viewed as pure risk transfer rather than funding.

knowledge of the underlying pool, while those in dynamic pools are aware only of the general ratings parameters, rather than specific obligors, of the pool. Because static pools feature less "active management" than dynamic structures, they feature lower fees. Synthetic arbitrage CDOs remain the fastest-growing sector of the CDO market, far outpacing activity in traditional balance sheet structures; more than 70% of new deal flow occurring since the millennium has been in the form of synthetic arbitrage transactions. The appeal lies in the fact that deals can be assembled much more rapidly, ramp-up periods are shorter,[38] and structures can be customized more precisely.

Partially funded synthetic CDOs, where the SPE issues only 5–15% of the notional amount of the credit risk being transferred via the default swaps, have become quite popular, as they are funding- and capital-efficient. Such deals function just as any fully funded cash, structured, or synthetic CDO, except that the SPE or trust issues fewer notes and thus holds less high-grade collateral.[39] The senior-most risk position of the deal, which exists above the senior funded position, remains unfunded; this so-called "super senior" tranche is characterized by only a small probability that losses will exceed the funded component of the transaction. In some cases the risk of the super senior tranche is transferred via a separate CDS. A typical partially funded CDO might be comprised of 80–90% unfunded super senior tranches, 5–10% funded AAA tranches, and 5–10% mezzanine and equity tranches. Because the super senior tranche remains unfunded, the sponsor can generate significant cost savings. For instance, if a bank funds at LIBOR + 50 bps, a super senior CDS costs 10 bps, and reinvestment in high-quality assets yields LIBOR flat, then the sponsor saves 40 bps running. In addition, the super senior tranche generally receives very favorable capital treatment (e.g., 20% risk weighting).

Synthetic CDOs, like structured CDOs, preserve assets on the sponsor's balance sheet, though credit risk is clearly transferred.

---

38 A synthetic transaction can ramp-up and close in a matter of days, rather than the weeks or months required for conventional CDOs. Even CDOs that make use of warehouse facilities, where up to 75% of assets are purchased prior to settlement and the residual investor bears the spread/default risk, can only shorten ramp-up periods by a few weeks.

39 The SPE must retain enough liquidity to fund the physical delivery or cash settlement of any underlying assets that default.

Though synthetics do not generate funding, neither do they require
the full amount of securities to be placed with investors; for
instance, a fully funded balance sheet CDO involving $5 billion of
credit risk assets requires $5 billion of tranches to be placed in the
market—a considerable distribution task. However, the synthetic
CDO may only require placement of $400 million of securities (a far
easier task), which is sufficient for the sponsor to acquire the collateral needed to secure the CDS covering the $5 billion credit risk
portfolio. Synthetic CDOs also give the portfolio manager greater
flexibility; the asset portfolio may ultimately include a combination
of physical assets and CDSs, while the liability portion may include
securities and CDSs. Synthetic short credit positions can also be
arranged, making certain CDOs look similar to hedge funds.

Synthetic CDOs have proven appealing to investors, who gain
exposure to high-grade credit risk portfolios at an incremental
yield pickup over standard bond portfolios (we have noted that
CDSs are often cheaper than cash bonds/loans), and face none of
the prepayment or extension risk characteristic of other ABS. That
said, some price opacity exists because synthetics are based on
OTC derivatives that are impacted by liquidity, model, and hedging risks; the "true value" of a synthetic CDO trading on a secondary basis may be challenging to determine. The market for
synthetic structures is constantly evolving. For instance, some
deals of the millennium have featured participating tranches,
which are subordinated tranches that are granted a percentage participation in the equity returns normally allocated to the residual.
Some CDOs also feature payment-in-kind tranches, which are triggered when default experience is on the rise (e.g., an issuer can
suspend the current coupon and pay-in-kind with an additional
allocation of the PIK tranche).

Table 3.2 summarizes certain key characteristics between a
standard cash CDO, a structured CDO, and a synthetic CDO.

Variation 1: Single Tranche Synthetic CDOs   The single tranche
CDO, created in both physical and synthetic form (though the latter has become dominant), emerged at the turn of the millennium
as an effective way of using CDO technology to customize individual tranches for investors. Rather than create a full capital structure
(from senior to equity), the single tranche CDO contains only a single portion of the loss distribution and is tailored to an investor's
specific requirements. The investor specifies the underlying

TABLE 3.2

CDO Characteristics

Feature	Cash CDO	Structured CDO	Synthetic CDO
Transfer Mechanism	Assignment, sale, participation	CLN	Credit default swaps
Funding	Yes (via sales)	Yes (via CLN)	No/partial
Capital Impact	Risk capital reduced by amount of transfer	Risk capital reduced if CLN acts as hedge	Risk capital reduced in swap acts as hedge
Balance Sheet Impact	Transfer assets off balance sheet	No transfer of assets off balance sheet	No transfer of assets off balance sheet

reference portfolio (which may include dozens to hundreds of reference credits) as well as the attachment point and the cap (which define the subordination and the size of the tranche, e.g., 3–5%); the sponsoring bank retains the balance of the capital structure. The investor may also specify whether the portfolio is to be static or dynamic (though even when dynamic it is only "lightly" managed). Through the single tranche structure the bank sponsor essentially buys a tranche of credit protection on the bid side of the market on each credit in the portfolio; it can use that hedge to offset its own portfolio exposure, or it can sell on the offer side and lock in a spread. If a reference defaults the sponsor is protected, though the revenue it earns declines once the defaulted credit is removed.

For example, a bank might create, on behalf of its client, a $30 million mezzanine tranche based on a $1 billion notional portfolio of 100 reference CDSs ($10 million each). The tranche might attach at a loss level of 5% and detach (or cap out) at 8%, meaning that the investor bears losses of up to $30 million once the first $50 million of losses has occurred. If we assume for simplicity that recovery on defaulted assets is 0, the investor will not begin to suffer losses until the sixth credit in the reference portfolio defaults. Thereafter, it will suffer losses until the cap level is reached. In exchange for accepting credit risk at the mezzanine level, the investor might earn a coupon of L + 200 bps.

Variation 2: CDS Index Tranches   A CDS index tranche, which acts as a hybrid of a CDS and a single tranche CDO, is a derivative contract covering a specific segment (or "loss width") of the CDS index default loss distribution; this means that each tranche reacts differently to the credit risk correlation of the references comprising the index. Although the CDS index tranche is similar to the single tranche synthetic CDO, it features two key differences: the CDS index tranche references a standard pool of credits that is always the same, while the CDO tranche references a customized, deal-specific pool; and, the index tranche features a standard "loss width" (e.g., the equity tranche is always the first 3% of losses), while the CDO tranche "loss width" varies by deal. These standard features have helped the index tranche product build a greater mass of liquidity, leading to attractive pricing (e.g., bid-offer spreads on senior tranches trade at 1 to 2 bps, mezzanine tranches at 5 to 10 bps and equity tranches from 15 to 70 bps, depending on market conditions).

In practice, the investor in the equity tranche (who is synthetically long the index of credits and is thus the protection seller) pays its counterparty an amount equal to the losses from the default (e.g., par - postdefault price) up to a maximum of 3% of the index. The mezzanine, senior, and super senior tranches likewise bear loss levels of their own, as noted in Tables 3.3 and 3.4, which depict the Dow Jones CDX North America and Europe/Japan indexes.

In exchange for bearing the risk of loss, investors (as protection sellers) receive a quarterly premium payment from the protection buyers equal to the basis point premium times the

T A B L E   3.3

Index Tranches: Dow Jones CDX North America

Tranche	Default "loss width"
Equity	First 3% of index default losses
Mezzanine	3–7% of index default losses
Senior	7–10% of index default losses
Senior	10–15% of index default losses
Senior	15–30% of index default losses

T A B L E   3.4

Index Tranches: iTraxx Europe and iTraxx Japan

Tranche	Default "loss width"
Equity	First 3% of index default losses
Mezzanine	3–6% of index default losses
Senior	6–9% of index default losses
Senior	9–12% of index default losses
Senior	12–22% of index default losses

outstanding notional of the tranche; the outstanding notional, in turn, is the original notional less any losses impacting that tranche. Mezzanine and senior tranche investors receive only a quarterly premium spread. Equity tranche investors receive a quarterly premium spread plus an up-front payment equal to some percentage of the original notional amount of the contract; this additional payment is a reflection of the higher degree of risk the equity investors bear.

Variation 3: CDOs-Squared   The CDO-squared, as the name suggests, is a CDO of a CDO, or a repackaging of other single-tranche CDOs (it can be likened to a collateralized mortgage obligation from the mortgage market, which is simply a repackaging of pools of structured mortgage assets). A CDO squared is characterized by a "parent" tranche and a series of "children" tranches; the latter reference pools of credits, some of which may contain some of the same references. Like other single-tranche CDOs, each child tranche has an attachment and detachment point, e.g., 5%–10%, which defines the loss level and magnitude. Similarly, the parent tranche features its own attachment/detachments (e.g., 10%–20%). Thus, a reference pool of $1 billion (100 credits, $10 million each) might be used for 8 child tranches of 5%–10% ($50 million loss layer), suggesting the total notional is $400 million. The parent, in turn, would feature a loss layer of $40 million (10–20% of $400 million). Arrangers do not always sell the child tranches to external investors; they may simply serve as components of internal deals.

CHAPTER EXERCISES

1. Describe four factors that drive CLN issuance and why each one is important.

2. Consider a $100 million structured CLN on a reference credit trading at T+100 bps, that pays 110% redemption when the spread is between T+90 bps and T+110 bps, and a reduced redemption of 1% for each basis point below T+90 bps or above T+110 bps. What will the dollar redemption value amount to if the reference credit trades at T+85 bps? At T+91 bps?

3. Describe the principal differences between standard CLNs and repackaged bonds.

4. Describe how a TRS CLN can be structured to provide an investor with leveraged returns.

5. Explain how an investor seeking a three-year Brazilian corporate credit exposure can use the CLN market to obtain its desired risk/return profile when the market only features five-year corporate bonds.

6. What minimum factors is a rating agency likely to require in a rated CDO?

7. Explain how the two most common CDO "waterfall" tests work. Given an overcollateralization trigger of 105%, will the test pass or fail if the value of the collateral is 105, the principal for a tranche is 50, and the principal of all tranches ranking senior is 55? What if the value of the collateral is 115?

8. Distinguish the key features of cash, structured, and synthetic CDOs.

9. Describe three ways in which CDS index tranches can be used to achieve specific risk or investment management goals.

An Overview of Credit Derivative Applications

INTRODUCTION

In the last two chapters we described the mechanics of the main products of the credit derivative market and noted, through various simple examples, how CDSs, TRSs, basket swaps, CLNs, and synthetic CDOs can be used to achieve certain end goals. We extend our discussion in this chapter to consider in greater detail how financial, nonbank financial, and corporate institutions might employ credit derivatives to meet their specific needs. Firms in all three sectors may act at any time as *providers* of risk capacity (e.g., sellers of credit risk protection), in order to express a view on the financial condition and outlook of specific reference credits, or as *users* of risk capacity (e.g., buyers of credit risk protection), in order to hedge or protect their exposures. Before introducing these practical applications we frame our discussion by reviewing market drivers and the specific requirements/goals of participants.

REQUIREMENTS AND GOALS OF PARTICIPANTS

We know that growth in the credit derivatives market over the past decade has been rapid and broad, driven by need, opportunity, and innovation. That said, acceptance and use of credit derivatives has not been completely universal—particularly among corporate end-users. Industry surveys and anecdotal evidence suggest that some corporate institutions are hesitant to deal in credit derivatives because they are insufficiently prepared, from a management perspective, to deal with the products; they lack clear guidance on accounting issues and/or capital treatment; they have difficulty obtaining reliable pricing quotes for second-or third-tier reference credits; they face challenges related to valuation and modeling; and/or they are constrained by governance issues, lacking the necessary internal, board-level, or regulatory approvals to proceed. Firms impacted by these types of problems may not be prepared to deal in credit derivatives for several more years—though ultimately all of these challenges appear surmountable. In fact, participants in the credit derivative market are grappling with many of the same issues that impacted the interest rate, currency, and equity derivative markets in the early 1980s and 1990s. All three have since become vital risk and investment management conduits, suggesting that the outlook for broader corporate involvement in credit derivatives is positive.

Institutions may elect to participate in the credit derivative market if they can adequately meet their transactional requirements and end goals. Minimum transactional requirements that users expect to satisfy include:

- Transparency in pricing and dealing terms; ongoing knowledge of risks and upside/downside scenarios.
- Efficiency in arranging and concluding transactions on a timely basis; use of electronic conduits wherever possible.
- Ability to tap into a sufficient base of dealing liquidity.
- Clarity regarding definitions of credit events and payouts, leaving no room for subjectivity or interpretation.
- Suitability of products in terms of a stated risk/return profile (which may be mandated by a firm's board of directors or external regulators).

If these minimum requirements can be met, the likelihood of successfully achieving end goals improves. Reverting to our discussion from Chapter 1, key goals may include:

- Access to credit products, references, and markets in a manner that serves to enhance enterprise value.
- Creation of effective hedges that allow a credit spread or default exposure to be properly isolated and eliminated, reduced, diversified, or otherwise mitigated.

- Optimization of all significant corporate resources, including capital, funding, and balance sheet.
- Construction of attractive and innovative investment/ speculation opportunities in the credit risk sector, including optimal credit risk portfolios that maximize return for a given level of market, credit, and liquidity risk.

The marketplace can already help many participants meet some or all of these requirements and goals. For instance, credit derivatives improve loan/bond price transparency and risk liquidity. Prior to the advent of credit derivatives, loan and bond pricing suffered from a significant degree of opacity: credit spread margins on many deals were not necessarily self-evident, making it difficult for intermediaries, borrowers, and investors to properly gauge risk and return. Expanding market breadth and depth, based on growing two-way market quotations on many large corporate and sovereign credits, have increased price transparency, allowing investors and intermediaries to more clearly discern the value of credit risk. This transparency, in turn, has attracted additional participants and liquidity, in a self-fulfilling cycle. Market flexibility and product customization have also improved; while an investor purchasing a standard loan participation or bond is restricted to the specific characteristics of the reference instrument, an investor arranging a customized credit derivative can define precisely the specific parameters it wants to trade, including reference instrument, face amount, maturity, spread or default conditions, rating downgrade triggers, and so forth. More work remains to be done, of course, particularly with regard to education, modeling of default risk, and standardization of legal terms. Ultimately, if these transactional requirements and end-goals can be successfully met, there is every expectation that the market will continue to expand—much as the core interest rate, currency, and equity derivative markets have done over the past three decades.

With these basic concepts in mind, let us now consider how financial institutions, nonbank financial institutions, and corporations can employ credit derivatives to meet the end-goals summarized above.

PRACTICAL APPLICATIONS

Credit derivatives can be applied to meet the needs of both financial and nonfinancial firms. An analysis of practical applications suggests that financial institutions, investment funds, insurance companies, and corporations can, at any time, be risk capacity providers (e.g., sellers of default/spread risk) and risk capacity users (e.g., buyers of default/spread risk); the market does not necessarily appear to be permanently skewed in one direction within a given sector or industry. For instance, a bank may sell default risk in order to create a more diversified loan portfolio, or buy default risk in order to hedge a concentration; a corporation may sell default risk in order to express a view on a particular reference credit within its treasury trading portfolio, or it may buy default risk to protect against credit exposure in its receivables portfolio. Ultimately, institutions from different industries that are able to deal on both sides of the market add greatly to depth and breadth.

The market is already flexible enough to allow for the development of very unique applications; indeed, standard hedging or positioning of default/spread risk has already become a "commoditized" trade, and increasingly sophisticated applications are becoming the norm. For instance, we noted in Chapter 3 that an institution can decouple the term of the reference asset from a desired investment horizon, creating a synthetic maturity that coincides with a specific investment need. Such "maturity shortening" can be done through direct products or via a CLN. Alternatively, a firm can position a credit risk exposure for a future horizon. If a bank or investor wishes to establish a long or short position in a credit risk to start 12 or 18 months hence, it can structure a forward-starting CDS, TRS, or spread option. An institution can also define with precision the parameters of a transaction, allowing it to create potential value based on its own market expectations. For example, contracts can be designed with broad credit event definitions (e.g., any event of default, restructuring, moratorium, downgrade, repudiation) or very narrow ones (e.g., only a default on domestic currency liabilities).

Financial Institutions

Financial institutions have become the single largest participants in the credit derivative market, using the contracts to reduce/hedge exposures, diversify portfolios, and optimize capital usage. A bank can originate and hold loans/bonds to maturity or act as a risk-driven originator, trader, repackager, and distributor of credit products. Indeed, conventional, static "buy-and-hold" banking has fundamentally shifted into a dynamic "manage and trade risk" process as a result of credit derivatives (supported by related credit analytics, such as those described in Part 2). For instance, when a bank approves a large loan exposure it must decide whether to: preserve the loan on its balance sheet, assigning a loss provision based on expected losses and a capital allocation based on unexpected losses; sell the loan, in part or whole, thereby removing the obligation from the balance sheet and releasing associated loan loss provisions/capital allocations (but absorbing the costs associated with negotiating the sale); or eliminate the credit risk, partially or totally, by using a credit derivative. The optimal strategy is likely to be determined by the bank's risk-adjusted calculations and its operating imperatives; it may also be influenced by operational requirements. For example, loan sales involve significant administrative and legal costs/duties and often require borrower consent prior to transfer; such loan sales are also very evident to market players, who may be able to track the source and path of credit exposures. Credit derivatives, in contrast, are invisible to borrowers. No administrative or legal approvals need to be completed, as only the credit exposure, rather than the credit asset, is transferred through the contract. Credit derivatives separate client relationships from the risk decision, allowing banks to manage portfolio concentrations while preserving client relationships and goodwill.

Application 1: Generating an Adequate Return in the Loan Business

A midsized bank has a high cost of funding that makes it difficult for it to generate an adequate return on equity through traditional lending to high-grade borrowers. While it is reluctant to embark on a new policy of high-risk lending, it realizes that it must originate or purchase a greater amount of credits in the weak investment-grade/subinvestment-grade sector in order to boost returns. To accomplish this, it can pursue various strategies in the credit derivative market: (1) it can sell a series of CDSs on a range of diversified, higher-yielding counterparties, which generates a risk premium and requires no funding; (2) it can sell a series of credit spread put options on credit references it believes will reflect credit improvement, and a series of credit spread call options on credit references it believes may weaken—collecting premium income in the process; (3) it can originate a series of high-yield loans to various new clients, and purchase a basket swap from another bank counterparty to protect against the specter of default. This strategy will work only if the return on the high-yield loans is greater than the cost of the premium on the basket swap and the cost of funding on the loans. Each one of these strategies involves risks:

1. Default risk in strategy
2. A reversal of credit spread tightening/widening in strategy
3. Counterparty default in strategy

Nevertheless, the bank believes these risks are acceptable and will help it achieve its goal of boosting returns on its core business.

Application 2: Managing Large Deal Exposures and Dynamic Credit Exposures

Investment banks are active in underwriting large bond deals for clients on a fully committed basis. They routinely agree to purchase bonds from issuers and place them through their distribution networks, bearing full price risk; any difficulty placing the bonds on a primary basis may lead an investment bank to hold the securities on its own balance sheet after syndicate has broken, or may require an immediate discount in price in order to make the yield more attractive to investors. An investment bank may be presented with an opportunity to place a $1 billion, 10-year bond issue for a BBB-rated credit at approximately $T + 200$ bps. While the bank may feel reasonably comfortable placing $500 million at a spread of 200 bps, it may be concerned about distributing the full amount quickly, within the quoted spread; its particular concern centers on its potential inability to place the bonds for a period of up to several weeks, during which time the company's credit spreads may widen by 10 to 50 bps (e.g., a $500 million remaining balance, 50 bp widening and an 8-year duration on the 10-year bond leads to a $20 million loss). However, as a result of competitive pressures the bank feels obliged to bid to place the bonds at no more than $T + 210$. It may be willing to do so by purchasing a credit spread put option that provides a de facto hedge on spread widening. If the company's credit spread widens before it can place the full amount of the deal, its gain on the put option will serve to offset any mark-to-market loss it takes in revaluing the remaining bonds held on its balance sheet. If the company's credit spread tightens, the bank will let the option expire unexercised, but it should be able to sell the remainder of its bond position at its mark or better. However, in order to reduce the cost of this protective strategy, it may decide to purchase an option that is 10–20 bps out-of-the-money, on a notional amount of $500 million (being relatively confident of its ability to place the other $500 million directly with its end clients or by forming a syndicate of other investment banks).

The same investment bank may also be engaged in very large counterparty derivative transactions with dynamic credit exposure profiles. While derivative analytics provide good estimates of the potential maximum credit exposure the bank might face over the life of any given transaction, a sharper than expected market move on an underlying reference (as might occur during periods of extreme market turmoil), along with downgrades within the universe of its largest counterparties, may create concerns. To mitigate this potential risk, the bank identifies the five largest counterparty credit exposures it is most concerned about and discovers that they are all rated in the A to BBB– category. It then examines the credit thresholds of each, and the maximum amount it is able to extend on an unsecured basis through its risk governance process. To deal with any exposures above those amounts (arising from an unexpected market movement) as well as any credit downgrades, the bank arranges with another bank for the purchase of a series of knock-in default swaps, one for each reference, that become effective when two conditions are met: a reference credit is downgraded below a BBB– threshold and the mark-to-market exposure exceeds the predetermined threshold (which varies by reference, e.g., $10 million to $100 million). By creating individual CDSs that are contingent on the occurrence of both events, the investment bank is able to create a cheaper risk protection mechanism that guards against very low probability "disaster" events.

Case Study: Using Credit Derivatives to Manage a Concentrated Loan Portfolio

Financial institutions protect against credit exposure concentrations in their loan portfolios in various ways. A bank may set internal single obligor limits (or may be required to do so by regulators), as well as limits by industry, sector, country, collateral, and ratings. Banks must continuously reposition their loan portfolios to maximize returns while adhering to the prudent risk constraints created by exposure limits. This is not an easy task because portfolios are constantly in motion.

Consider the case of a small, midwestern bank located in the U.S. farm belt that has the bulk of its loan portfolio extended to agricultural concerns in the region. The loan portfolio is heavily exposed to the local economy, agricultural prices, and climatic changes; when these variables are favorable, agricultural borrowers are able to service their loans, but when they become unfavorable, loan delinquencies and defaults rise. Because the bank is small, it does not have a loan origination team capable of marketing loans outside the farm belt region. Accordingly, it is very difficult for the bank to run a balanced portfolio and avoid breaching concentration limits. It may also be exceedingly difficult for the bank to earn a sufficient return on its loans to compensate for the additional risk it runs in holding a concentrated agricultural portfolio.

How can the bank solve this problem?

Strategy 1: The bank can participate in loans arranged by other banks that deal in nonagricultural lending. Through loan syndications and outright loan purchases, the bank can reposition its portfolio by adding credit exposures that are not correlated with the agricultural sector. This strategy requires the bank to develop relationships with nonagricultural lenders and expertise in evaluating nonagricultural loans originated by other banks. In addition, any loans the bank assumes through this strategy will be funded through the balance sheet, inflating total footings and requiring the allocation of loan loss reserves and capital. However, if the margins on the loans are sufficiently attractive, the strategy may prove optimal. Figure 4.1 summarizes this option.

Strategy 2: The bank can enter into credit derivative transactions (including CDSs, basket swaps, TRSs, forwards) that transfer to other counterparties the risk of a certain percentage of its agricultural portfolio (e.g., 20–30% of its total outstandings). This is equivalent to hedging a portion of the portfolio by establishing synthetic short positions against the existing long credit positions. By entering into these derivatives, the bank assumes the counterparty credit risk of a series of other institutions, including other banks and intermediaries whose credit performance is not linked to the same variables as borrowers in the agricultural sector. This strategy, highlighted in Figure 4.2, requires the bank to establish appropriate reserve/capital allocations for each credit derivative counterparty.

Strategy 3: The bank can enter into a series of credit derivative transactions where it accepts from other counterparties a certain

F I G U R E 4.1

Credit Rebalancing Strategy 1

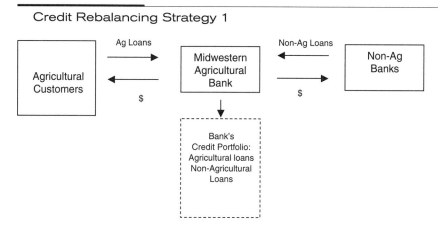

F I G U R E 4.2

Credit Rebalancing Strategy 2

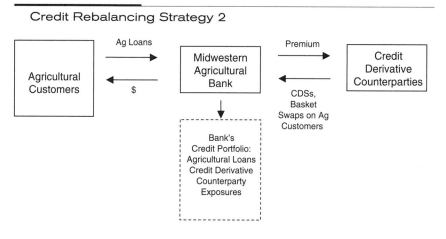

amount of credit exposure from reference assets that are not corre-lated with the agricultural sector, earning premium income in the process. This is equivalent to expanding its credit portfolio by estab-lishing synthetic long positions that help balance the concentrations in its existing agricultural loan portfolio. By entering into contracts such as basket swaps and CDSs, the bank accepts the credit risk of the reference obligors. Figure 4.3 illustrates this strategy.

F I G U R E 4.3

Credit Rebalancing Strategy 3

Strategy 4: Finally, the bank may choose to fuse strategies 1 and 2. It may commit to accepting large shares in new loans outside of the agricultural sector, and then "hedge down" through credit derivatives, portions of each newly approved facility, reducing credit exposure and altering capital allocations associated with specific exposures. This leaves the portfolio with a combination of new nonagricultural loans and counterparty credit derivative exposures, as noted in Figure 4.4.

F I G U R E 4.4

Credit Rebalancing Strategy 4

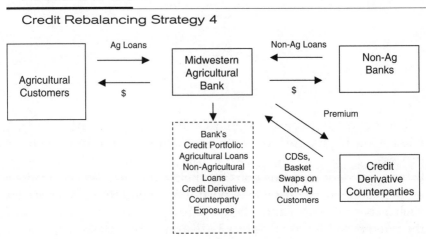

This simple case illustrates that credit derivatives can be used in various ways to help a bank, or any other originator of credit, deal with a concentrated portfolio of credit risk.

Nonbank Financial Institutions

We define the nonbank financial institution sector to include hedge funds, mutual funds, pension funds, insurance companies and reinsurance companies. Firms in this sector have already become significant users of credit derivatives, providing significant liquidity. In most instances involvement by funds is centered on the long side, i.e., establishing long credit risk positions based on single or multiple reference assets. Depending on the nature of a fund, its investment mandate, and the ability to take risk, these positions may be simple relative value or yield enhancement transactions, or they may be speculative leveraged transactions. In some cases funds may also use the credit derivative market to hedge a credit risk position subject to default, or protect against credit deterioration; this relates particularly to credit exposures that a fund may have with derivative counterparties. Insurers and reinsurers are active on both sides of the market. They are exposed to credit risks in the normal course of business (e.g., writing credit guarantees) and may thus seek to hedge or rebalance their portfolios using credit derivatives; they may also seek to introduce relative value credit derivative strategies into their investment portfolios in order to enhance returns.

Application 1: Creating a Credit Derivative Index Opportunity

A pension fund is bullish on European high-grade credits and wishes to enhance its income stream by monetizing this view. Accordingly, it decides to sell an index swap contract that references the Dow Jones iTraxx European High Grade index (covering 125 European CDS references, €1 million apiece). At the start of the six-month index period, the fund will receive an up-front premium equal to the market-offered basis point quote for the index, times a notional of €125 million; assuming the index is currently quoted at 50 bps, the fund will earn an up-front premium of €625,000. If the credits in the index remain current on their obligations during the six-month trade life, the pension fund will be able to preserve the full amount of the premium; however, if one of the credits defaults, the fund will be required to pay €1 million (and receive the defaulted obligation from the buyer in exchange, which will be worth some amount less than €1 million). Through this CDS index swap mechanism, the fund can express its view on the pool of European credits without having to bear the administrative and operational burden of individual security or CDS transactions.

Application 2: Maximizing Credit Returns while Adhering to Investment Guidelines

A pension fund is permitted to invest in credit-risky assets in physical or derivative form, but must adhere to certain minimum rating thresholds (e.g., no credit exposure below BBB− equivalent). The fund manager wishes to maximize the fund's returns within established risk parameters and examines the marketplace for opportunities. An A-rated security can be purchased to yield T+10 bps, while a BB+ security of the same maturity yields T+150 bps. A CDS with an AA-rated counterparty referencing the BB+ security costs 120 bps running. Accordingly, the fund manager can purchase the BB+ security and the CDS from the AA-rated bank, earning a yield pickup of 20 bps (gross of funding costs), while still adhering to its operating parameters.

Application 3: Creating a Relative Value Trade through Recovery Rate Assumptions

A hedge fund examines the quoted market prices on a BB+ rated entity (80 bps) and, through its proprietary analytics, determines that the implied probability of default is 3% and the expected recovery rate assuming default is 40%. It concurs with the default probability assessment but is convinced, after analyzing the reference entity's balance sheet, that the recovery rate should be at least 50%—that is, creditors will receive more in bankruptcy than the market expects. In order to monetize this view, it finds a bank that is willing to purchase the CDS based on a fixed recovery rate of 50%. If the credit is trading at 80 bps based on a 40% recovery rate, then the bank should be willing to pay up to 100 bps for the hedge fund's CDS (e.g., 80 bps $*$ 50/40). If the hedge fund and bank can agree on terms between 80 and 100 bps, both will improve their relative positions based on their views of recovery rates.

Application 4: Reducing the Risk on an Insurance Credit Guarantee

A monoline insurance company is active in writing credit performance guarantees for various industrial companies, receiving premiums in exchange for indemnifying named beneficiaries should the reference companies fail to perform on their contractual obligations. The insurer runs a diversified portfolio of such single reference credit guarantees, managing its exposures by limiting concentrations by obligor, industry, country, and ratings class. As a result of a new business opportunity, the insurer is in a position to write a $500 million, one-year credit guarantee covering Company JKL's performance; JKL pays a premium for this guarantee, and Bank ABC, a lender to JKL, is the named beneficiary. The insurer believes the business opportunity is attractive and that the premium is large enough to meet its internal hurdle rates, but the exposure is well above its standard maximum exposure of $200 million per obligor. Rather than refuse the business as a result of internal risk constraints, the insurer determines it will use various solutions. It can first cede up to $200 million of risk through a treaty reinsurance agreement that it has in place with a syndicate of reinsurers; because the exposure conforms to the parameters of the treaty, each syndicate member will absorb a pro rata share of the $200 million. That leaves the insurer with $300 million of default exposure, which is $100 million more than its capacity. Accordingly, it purchases a $100 million CDS on the reference credit from an AAA-rated counterparty at an economically reasonable premium. However, because the insurance company is not authorized to purchase the derivative directly as a result of regulatory restrictions, it must arrange the transaction through its Bermuda Class B transformer insurance subsidiary. The Bermuda subsidiary purchases the $100 million CDS from the AAA-rated bank, and writes a reinsurance contract with the same terms to the insurer. Through the combination of internal risk capacity, the reinsurance market, and the CDS market, the insurer is able to absorb the full $500 million credit commitment. Figure 4.5 summarizes this multileg transaction.

F I G U R E   4.5

Insurance Credit Guarantee Hedging

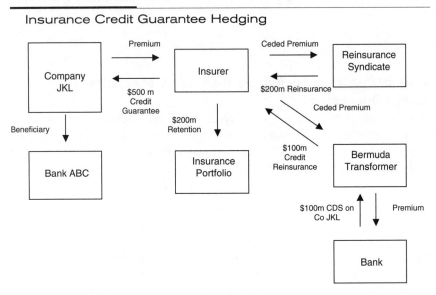

Application 5: Creating Arbitrage Returns
With Convertible Bonds

A hedge fund is interested in exploiting potential arbitrage opportunities in the convertible bond and credit markets, focusing on
generating value from the fixed-income component of the security. It first identifies a five-year FRN floated by a BBB-rated corporate issuer (Company LMN), which trades at a current spread
of LIBOR + 75 bps. It then identifies LMN's convertible bond, also
with five years to maturity that features an embedded equity
option that is approximately 10% out-of-the-money. The fund
buys the convertible and strips out the equity component by selling
an identical OTC equity option to a bank, receiving premium in
exchange. It then enters into an asset swap with a AAA bank,
exchanging the convertible's fixed coupon into a floating coupon
stream. The asset swap generates an all-in synthetic floating rate
return of L + 85 bps, which is 10 bps better than LMN's conventional FRN. In addition, the sale of the equity option nets the fund
10 bps more than the theoretical value of the equity option
embedded in the convertible. While it gains an arbitrage pickup
of 10 bps on the FRN and 10 bps on the equity option, it remains

exposed to LMN's BBB default risk. The fund next decides to replace LMN's BBB default risk with the credit risk of a AA-rated bank, from whom it buys a CDS referencing LMN's credit (at a cost of 15 bps running). The combination of these transactions allows the hedge fund to create a synthetic credit risk exposure to the AA-rated bank that is 5 bps better than the bank's traded obligations.

Application 6: Developing a Synthetic Syndicated Loan Portfolio

A pension fund believes that the syndicated loan market offers good value relative to the FRN market and is interested in creating a diversified portfolio of 15 loans ($10 million each) comprised of obligors from different industries and ratings classes. The fund can attempt to buy each $10 million participation in the primary or secondary markets but lacks the access required to purchase the entire portfolio at attractive economic levels. Instead, it works with a bank to develop a TRS basket structure in unleveraged (rather than leveraged) form. Under this mechanism the fund becomes the total return receiver on the $150 million basket, paying the bank a LIBOR plus spread in exchange; the fund thus benefits from coupons and any spread tightening, and remains exposed to any spread widening and/or defaults. In order to adhere to its investment and operating parameters, the fund needs to construct the TRS basket in funded form; accordingly, it places the $150 million notional amount into a risk-free money market/Treasury bill equivalent. Figure 4.6 summarizes this example.

Application 7: Monetizing a View of Forward Credit Spreads

An investment fund operating in a tight credit spread environment is interested in enhancing current returns on a reference credit's 10-year bond. Based on an examination of market fundamentals, the fund believes that credit spreads over the next three years will reflect some widening, while the term structure will reflect some steepening. In order to monetize this widening/steepening view, the fund decides to sell a three-year credit spread forward on the reference credit's 10-year bond. The forward spread on the reference credit is 50 bps, but in order to crystallize value, the deal is structured with a forward spread of 60 bps (e.g., the forward

F I G U R E   4.6

Synthetic Syndicated Loan Portfolio

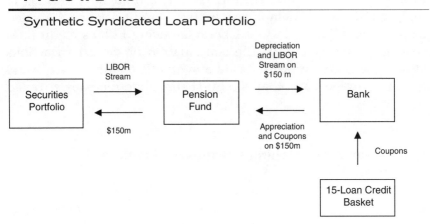

is in-the-money). The fund will benefit if spreads on the reference credit widen above 60 bps, and will lose if they tighten below 60 bps.

Case Study: Using Credit Spread Options to Capitalize on a Troubled Industry

Company ABC, rated BBB–, is involved in the production of small- and midsized aircraft and derives the bulk of its revenues from sales or leases to regional airline operators. After turmoil in the global airline industry resulting from economic slowdowns and high jet fuel prices, several of ABC's tentative orders for aircraft delivery are canceled. The cancellations, which represent an esti- mated 40% of the current year's order book and revenues (and 20% of next year's), place financial strains on the company. ABC's stock price falls and the credit spreads on its sole five-year bond widen from T+250 bps to T+350 bps.

An investment manager, who remains cautious on the airline industry but continues to see reasonably solid financial fundamen- tals in ABC's balance sheet and cash flows, believes that an oppor- tunity exists to capitalize on the company's recent credit weakness. Though the manager is reasonably bullish on the credit, it must still avoid direct exposure to ABC's default risk, as a "disaster" scenario could strike. It has several options to choose from:

Strategy 1: It can purchase the public bond at the current spread of T+350 bps, but will only be able to source a small block of $10 million. While the purchase of the bond gives it exposure to the spread tightening it believes will occur, it exposes the fund to default risk; though the fund manager believes default by ABC is very improbable, the loss of any more airline orders could increase the specter of financial distress. In addition, it will have to fund the position at its own funding costs of LIBOR + 100 bps.

Strategy 2: It can enter into a $50 million TRS, where it receives the total return and pays a bank counterparty LIBOR plus a spread. While this will give it exposure to the spread tightening it desires, and can be constructed on an unfunded basis, the fund remains exposed to ABC's default risk. Figure 4.7 highlights this option.

Strategy 3: It can purchase a $50 million call option on ABC's credit spread, as noted in Figure 4.8. This will again give the fund its desired exposure to a possible tightening in ABC's spreads, but will not involve the assumption of any default risk. The option will, however, entail the payment of an up-front premium. However, the fund can purchase a call that is slightly out-of-the-money, which will reduce its all-in premium cost.

The fund decides to take a view on ABC's credit spread by purchasing a 12-month, $50 million call option with a strike spread of T+400 bps at a cost of 80 bps. Its maximum loss on the transaction is limited to the premium paid, or $400,000. Its gain will be equal to:

$$(\text{Strike spread} - \text{market spread at settlement}) * \text{CS duration} * \text{notional}$$

Let's consider three different scenarios at maturity, in 12 months.

FIGURE 4.7

Total Return Swap on ABC

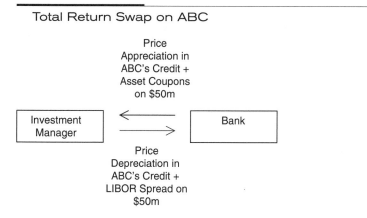

FIGURE 4.8

Credit Spread Call Option on ABC

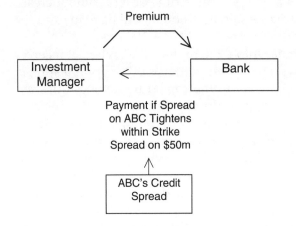

Scenario 1: ABC's credit improves as it secures several new airline orders. Though the rating agencies preserve the company's rating at BBB–, the firm's stock price rallies and the spread on the five-year bond (now with four years to maturity) tightens from T+350 bps to T+200 bps. The fund's net gain, assuming a credit spread duration of 3, is:

$$(.04 - .02) * 3 * \$50 \text{ million} = \$3 \text{ million,}$$
$$\text{less } \$400,000 \text{ premium} = \$2.6 \text{ million}$$

Scenario 2: ABC's credit remains unchanged as no new airline orders come through and no existing orders are cancelled. The bond trades in a relatively narrow range during the year, ending at T+375 bps. The fund's option expires unexercised, leading to a net loss of $400,000 on premium paid.

Scenario 3: ABC receives more negative news during the year, as several more airline orders are canceled. The firm goes through a period of financial distress, which culminates in default on the outstanding bonds. The fund is not exposed to the default event, however, and its sole loss on the transaction is again limited to the premium paid for the call option, or $400,000.

Corporations

Corporations are exposed to credit risks in the normal course of business, including those generated by accounts receivable financing, vendor/supplier financing, contract prepayments, single/ concentrated supplier arrangements, and financial transactions/ derivatives. Credit derivatives can be applied to mitigate any concentrated or troubled exposures in these areas. Corporations may also operate treasury centers that are responsible for managing excess cash/capital. Such treasury operations often manage portfolios of credit obligations and may choose to create or diversify portfolios through credit derivatives; they may also use credit derivatives to lock in future funding levels.

Application 1: Hedging Default Risk of a Single Source Supplier

A major automaker purchases all of its tires from a single, subinvestment-grade tire manufacturer. Though the auto company pays for the tires on a delayed basis (e.g., after the tires have been delivered each month), and is thus not directly exposed to the tire manufacturer's credit on a payment basis (e.g., at no time does it prepay for tire inventory), it is concerned that if the tire manufacturer continues to experience financial deterioration, its operations could be impacted. Specifically, the automaker fears that if the tire company enters a period of extreme financial distress and is forced to declare bankruptcy, it will take several weeks or months to develop a production relationship with another tire manufacturer; any such delays could idle production lines, costing the auto firm millions of dollars in lost revenues. To protect against a possible financial loss arising from the bankruptcy of the tire manufacturer, the auto company purchases from a bank a CDS referencing the tire manufacturer's credit, which will provide a compensatory payment equal to the estimated amount of lost revenues should a default occur. The CDS remains in place until the auto manufacturer is able to negotiate a "backup" agreement with another tire supplier.

Application 2: Hedging Default Risk of Accounts Receivable Financing

Company XYZ has a policy of offering 90 and 180-day accounts receivable financing to its customer base, which is largely concentrated in a single industry. As a result of competitive pressures, XYZ finds that it is extending a larger amount of credit to its customers than it wants; in addition, the customer base at large is experiencing fundamental credit weakness that may ultimately cause late payments—or even defaults. Because XYZ is, itself, an industrial company, it has no way of originating credit in other economic sectors in order to diversify its overall portfolio. Accordingly, it decides to use credit derivatives to protect against possible defaults within the customer base. Working with a credit derivatives dealer, it develops a basket swap that includes its top 20 receivables obligors and provides for a fixed payout (e.g., a fixed recovery rate structure) in the event any one of the obligors defaults during the term of the transaction. The basket swap is set with rolling 90-day terms to coincide with its standard cycle of receivables due dates; the notional amounts of the basket swap are readjusted every 90 days to reflect the dynamic nature of the credit extension process. Though the basket swap includes 20 obligors, XYZ does not receive a correlation-driven discount in the premium pricing, as all of the firms are based in the same industry and are thus susceptible to the same pressures. Nevertheless, the basket swap protection allows XYZ to continue offering receivables financing to its customer base so that it can remain competitive and keep its overall risks under control.

Application 3: Locking in a Forward Funding Requirement

Corporation QRS, which is an active borrower in the public credit markets, has determined that it will need to raise $250 million of five-year fixed-rate funds in one year to fund a new capital investment project. It can currently raise five years' funds at T+50 bps, the narrowest funding spread it has enjoyed in recent years. QRS's treasury team is concerned that the cyclically tight credit spreads will reverse by the time the funding is required in one year, and that its resulting financing costs will be 10–30 bps higher. The team considers a number of alternatives to address this problem.

Strategy 1: It can issue the $250 million of five-year bonds in the current market and invest the proceeds for one year in short-term paper. While this locks in the current funding spread, it inflates the company's balance sheet for one year. In addition, when the funds are needed in one year's time, the remaining term on the bond will be only four years, leaving the company with a refinancing requirement of one year when the bond matures. To circumvent this problem QRS could issue a six-year bond today, but the odd maturity (e.g., nonbenchmark) may be perceived by investors as undesirable and might require a liquidity premium.

Strategy 2: QRS can enter into a one-year, $250 million credit spread forward on its own reference, based on today's implied forward spread; it can then issue the five-year bond in one year's time. If the credit spread increases in one year, QRS generates an economic gain on the forward that offsets the higher funding spread it will face in the market. If the credit spread tightens, QRS loses on the forward but benefits from a tighter funding spread in the market. If properly constructed the two should offset each other. Importantly, the credit spread forward is off balance sheet and does not impact the firm's total footings. Though QRS will face the credit exposure of a bank counterparty on the forward, it will not have to make any payment for the contract as it is a bilateral obligation. The actual effectiveness of the structure will, of course, be based on changes in the spread and the absolute interest rate level; the interest rate component can be locked in separately through futures or forward rate agreements.

Based on these alternatives, the QRS treasury team opts to use the credit spread forward to lock in its forward funding requirements.

Application 4: Protecting a Global Company's Sovereign Risk Exposure

A global engineering firm that develops capital infrastructure in various nations around the world has an opportunity to invest $300 million of capital resources in a new project in an emerging nation that is currently experiencing economic instability and political uncertainty. After thoroughly analyzing the macro and micro fundamentals of the country, the company determines that the investment project will be highly profitable over the long term, and that the prospects for long-term growth and stability are favorable. The company's primary concerns center on the 24-month horizon, when the country's government will need to make critical decisions regarding financial and political policies. This could create a period of instability. Though the engineering firm can attempt to delay any decision for the next 24 months, it is likely to lose the project to a competitor. Accordingly, the company's management attempts to protect against the possibility that sovereign actions will jeopardize its capital investment over the next two years. It investigates the possibility of obtaining political risk insurance from a special insurer to cover specific events related to asset expropriation and nationalization. However, because the nature of the political risk cover is extremely precise (e.g., indemnification for a defined sovereign event) the policy is very expensive and reduces the economics of the project below the firm's hurdle rate.

Rather than abandon the project or assume an excessive amount of sovereign risk, the firm next explores the use of a credit derivative as a proxy. The company realizes that it cannot specifically cover the expropriation risk associated with the project, but knows that it can purchase a credit spread put option covering the country itself. If a sovereign event were to happen, such as nationalization, there is a strong likelihood that the credit spreads on the country's public bond issues would widen significantly. This would provide a compensatory payment under the put, helping reduce some of the losses associated with any asset expropriation. Because there exists a considerable amount of basis risk, the price is much cheaper than the political risk insurance policy. The company also analyzes the use of a CDS, but determines that an event of nationalization or expropriation that occurs while the country remains current on its debt will not trigger a payment under the contract. It also considers establishing a short position in the country's traded bonds, but fears suffering capital losses from nonsovereign events, such as rate movements. As a result, the engineering company decides to proceed by purchasing a two-year out-of-the-money credit spread put option on the country's reference debt, recognizing that it still bears basis risk between an event of nationalization and spread widening.[1]

Corporate use of credit derivatives to hedge or protect exposure to other corporations is not, of course, theoretical. The spectacular credit defaults of the millennium suggest the risk of problems is all too real and the need for some form of protection is advisable. Consider, for instance, that certain companies dealing with Enron,

---

[1] A company may also be exposed to convertibility risk, which arises if the sovereign places capital controls on repatriation of hard currency. This can occur in an emerging market that is suffering from extreme capital imbalances and hard currency reserve depletion, and bars institutions from converting local currency into hard currency for onward remittance to the home country. An active market has developed for pricing and transferring convertibility risk between counterparties, some based on the CLNs/repackaged bonds described in Chapter 3.

WorldCom, Mirant, and Marconi, among others, as suppliers or customers used credit default contracts to protect their firms against potential losses; they received compensatory payments from protection sellers when the reference companies actually defaulted. Many others, unfortunately, did not and sustained losses.

CHAPTER EXERCISES

1. What minimum transactional requirements and end goals must be satisfied in order to increase participation in the credit derivative market?

2. Discuss how a fund might protect itself from concentrated credit risks using a combination of TRSs, CDSs, and credit spread options.

3. Describe three ways in which a bank can use credit derivatives to improve/diversify its loan portfolio.

4. Assume a company has a $200 million dollar portfolio of accounts receivable (180-day maximum maturity) extended to a diverse base of institutional customers. Describe two credit derivative strategies that the company can employ to protect against defaults in the portfolio.

5. Assume a pension fund is attempting to capitalize on potential deterioration of a reference credit. To do so it decides to purchase a 12-month €10 million notional credit spread put with a strike spread of EURIBOR + 120, for 30 bps of up-front premium. The put references a company's 10-year bond (current duration of 7 years). What will the fund's gross and net payouts be in 1 year (when the duration of the reference bond is 6 years) if the reference spread widens to 160 bps? If it tightens to 100 bps? What is the breakeven spread level?

PART 2

Quantitative Tools

A Primer on Risk Modeling

By Robert Kissell[1]

INTRODUCTION

As we have seen, credit derivatives are contracts that transfer an asset's risk and return from one counterparty to another without transferring ownership of the underlying asset. For those protecting against credit downgrades or defaults, risk refers to the asset's potential decrease in value. Having accurate risk estimates provides counterparties with meaningful representations of potential gains or losses. Portfolio managers most commonly assess risk over a specified period of time such as yearly, monthly, weekly, daily, or even for shorter periods such as by hour or minute.

Managers use risk estimates to determine the likelihood that portfolio asset values will be higher or lower than some specified value at some future date. Risk statistics provide valuable insight into a portfolio's risk decomposition, which, in turn, provides insight into hedging schemes that improve risk management and ultimately provide greater certainty surrounding future portfolio values.

It is essential that credit derivative specialists have accurate volatility and covariance forecasts to make proper risk decisions. First, accurate volatility (variance) estimates are important for analyzing credit and equity risk exposures, performing value-at-risk analysis, and pricing derivatives. Second, accurate covariance estimates are needed to obtain total portfolio risk and uncover hedging opportunities. Inaccurate estimates are counterproductive to bankers, likely leading to unacceptable levels of risk exposure, inappropriate management decisions, inaccurate hedging schemes, and eventually higher levels of losses.

In this chapter we seek to formalize our understanding of risk with a degree of mathematical rigor. We begin by noting that the value of a CDS written on a particular firm is primarily driven by the probability of that firm's default and the recovery in the event of default. The typical firm has a default probability of approximately 2% in any given year.[2] Many of the more recent CDS contracts define a specific recovery amount, eliminating much of the uncertainty regarding the sum that will be recovered upon default. Consequently, the bulk of estimation effort should be focused on producing accurate default probabilities, which, of course, means surveying the risk landscape in quantitative language.

MODEL DEFINITIONS

We begin by providing a brief background and definitions for some of the more important risk measures. These include price returns, volatility, covariance, and correlation.

Price Return

$$r_{it} = \ln(p_{it} / p_{i,t-1}) = \ln(p_{it}) - \ln(p_{i,t-1}) \qquad (5.1)$$

where r_{it} denotes the change from asset i in period t and p_{it} is the actual price or value of asset i in period t. Returns have a log normal distribution, therefore, returns are measured using the natural log rather than percentage change.

---

2 As noted in Chapter 7, "The variation across firms, however, can be quite large. In particular, the range of possible default probabilities (typically 2 basis points to 2,000 basis points) is much larger than the range of possible recoveries (typically 30 percent to 70 percent). Viewed from a different perspective, a completely incorrect estimate of recovery may only be off by a factor of 2, whereas a completely incorrect estimate of default probability may be off by a factor of 1,000."

Average Return

$$\bar{r}_i = 1/n \sum r_{it} = 1/n \cdot (\ln(p_{it}) - \ln(p_{i0})) \tag{5.2}$$

Variance

Price volatility σ_i provides a measure of dispersion surrounding expected future returns. It is also used to compute the likelihood that an asset will decrease in value. Volatility is most commonly described as the standard deviation of price returns; for convenience we will use the variance expression. Volatility is simply the square root of variance.

$$\sigma_i^2 = \frac{1}{n-1} \sum_{t=1}^{n} (r_{it} - \bar{r}_i)^2 \tag{5.3}$$

Covariance

The covariance of returns σ_{ij} describes the comovement of prices in the market. Positive covariance indicates that the assets trend together while negative covariance indicates assets trend in the opposite direction.

$$\sigma_{ij} = \frac{1}{n-1} \sum_{t=1}^{n} (r_{it} - \bar{r}_i)(r_{jt} - \bar{r}_j) \tag{5.4}$$

Correlation

$$\rho_{ij} = \frac{\sigma_{ij}}{\sigma_i \sigma_j} \tag{5.5}$$

The correlation of prices returns ρ_{ij} for two instruments i and j is simply the covariance of returns divided by the standard deviation of each instrument. This normalization process defines the correlation coefficient to be between one and negative one. That is, $-1 \leq \rho_{xy} \leq 1$. Assets with correlation of $\rho_{ij} = 1$ move perfectly with one another, assets with a correlation of $\rho_{ij} = -1$ move perfectly but in the opposite direction of one another, and assets with a correlation of $\rho_{ij} = 0$ do not trend together.

Portfolio Return

The expected return for a portfolio of assets, $\bar{r}_p$ is calculated as the weighted average of individual asset average returns:

$$\bar{r}_p = \sum_{i=1}^{n} w_i \bar{r}_i \tag{5.6}$$

where w_i is the dollar weight of the ith instrument.

Portfolio Variance

The variance for a portfolio of loans and/or other financial instruments σ_p^2 is defined as follows:

$$\sigma_p^2 = \sum_{i=1}^{n} \sum_{j=1}^{n} w_i w_j \sigma_{ij} \tag{5.7}$$

where $\sigma_{ii} = \sigma_i^2$ is the variance of the ith instrument and σ_{ij} is the covariance of returns between the ith and j^{th} instrument.

In matrix notation, portfolio returns $\bar{r}_p$ and portfolio risk σ_p^2 can be written as follows:

$$\bar{r}_p = w'\bar{r} \tag{5.8}$$

$$\sigma_p^2 = w'Cw \tag{5.9}$$

where,

$$\bar{r}' = (\bar{r}_1 \quad \bar{r}_2 \quad \cdots \quad \bar{r}_n)$$

$$w' = (w_1 \quad w_2 \quad \cdots \quad w_n)$$

and,

$$C = \begin{pmatrix} \sigma_1^2 & \sigma_{12} & \cdots & \sigma_{1n} \\ \sigma_{21} & \sigma_2^2 & \cdots & \sigma_{2n} \\ \vdots & \vdots & \ddots & \vdots \\ \sigma_{n1} & \sigma_{n2} & \cdots & \sigma_n^2 \end{pmatrix} \tag{5.10}$$

By definition, the covariance matrix C is symmetric (e.g., $C = C'$) with variance as the diagonal entry and covariance as the off-diagonals entries. In risk management it is important that C be semipositive definite.[3] That is, for any $x \in \Re^n$ we have $x'Cx \geq 0$. If a vector x with $x'Cx < 0$ exists, then the portfolio x would have negative variance (which is meaningless). Accordingly, we assume that C is always semipositive definite.

ACCURATE RISK ESTIMATES

Risk estimates such as volatility and covariance are used through all areas of finance and in all markets (equity, credit, derivatives, currency, commodities). For example, portfolio optimization, option pricing, value-at-risk, credit default probabilities, and optimal portfolio liquidation strategies, are all heavily dependent on variance and/or covariance estimates. A brief example of usage of variance and covariance is provided below.

Portfolio Optimization

Markowitz (1952) provided the industry with a means to construct optimal portfolios that maximize expected return for a specified level of risk. Because the formulation is dependent on the covariance matrix of returns C, inaccurate volatility and covariance estimates will lead to suboptimal portfolios. This is shown as follows:

$$\underset{w}{Max} \quad w'r - \lambda \cdot w'Cw$$

$$s.t. \quad \sum w = 1$$

where w is the optimal portfolio weights, r is a vector of expected returns, and C is the covariance matrix of returns.

Option Pricing Models

The Black-Scholes (1971) option pricing model is the most famous derivatives pricing model and provides the price premium for a call option. It is highly dependent on volatility, as shown in the model formulation:

$$C = S \cdot N(d_1) - X \cdot e^{-r_f T} \cdot N(d_2)$$

---

3 It is often stated in the literature that C must be strictly positive definite (i.e., $x'Cx \geq 0$). But as we have seen it is possible to construct riskless portfolios of instruments (i.e., a stock and its option). In these situations, the expected return must equal the risk-free rate, otherwise the no arbitrage condition would be violated. That is, $x'r = r_f$ and $x'Cx = 0$.

where,

$$d_1 = \frac{\ln(S/X) + (r_f + \sigma^2/2)T}{\sigma\sqrt{T}}$$

$$d_2 = d_1 - \sigma\sqrt{T}$$

and,

C = Call Price
X = Strike Price
S = Stock Price
$N(d)$ = probability that actual return will be less than d
r_f = risk free rate of return
T = future time period

The price premium for a put option P is also dependent on volatility. This is best demonstrated through the call-put parity relationship:

$$C + \frac{X}{(1+r_f)^T} = S + P$$

and solving for P we have,

$$P = C + \frac{X}{(1+r_f)^T} - S$$

Credit Risk

Credit risk is defined as the potential loss that may occur if an obligor is not able to make its contractual payment. This includes the possibility that an issuer is unable to fulfill its bond payments (interest and premium) and/or the possibility that a corporation is not able to repay its loan. In either case, the lender assumes the risk that they may not receive some or all of the money owed.

Credit risk is comprised of three main components: probability of default, recovery rate, and credit risk exposure. The probability of default is the likelihood that the obligor will default on its obligations to the lender. The recovery rate is the amount of the loan the lender is likely to recover if the obligor defaults. The credit exposure is the amount of the loan the lender is likely to lose if the obligor defaults. Credit risk exposure, however, is often stated as the replacement cost minus the recovery rate.

Credit managers are very concerned with the expected credit default loss (*EDL*) of an investment. Knowledge of this quantity allows better fiduciary investment decisions and better insight into proper hedging schemes (such as portfolio swaps) to further reduce risk. The process to compute *EDL* is as follows:

1. Estimate the probability of default θ. For a new corporation it is possible to gain insight into the likelihood of default by analyzing similar companies in the specific industry, market penetration, potential for growth, etc.
2. Compute expected credit exposure (*ECE*) as follows:

$$ECE = \int_{-\infty}^{\infty} \max(x,0) \cdot f(x)dx$$

where x is the estimated replacement value with distribution $f(x)$. Then, if $x \sim N(x, \sigma)$ the *ECE* is as follows:

$$ECE = \sigma \cdot \frac{1}{\sqrt{2\pi}}$$

3. Compute expected credit loss (*EDL*) as follows:

$$EDL = ECE \cdot \frac{\theta}{2}$$

Again, if $x \sim N(x, \sigma^2)$ the expected default loss is:

$$EDL = \sigma \cdot \frac{1}{\sqrt{2\pi}} \cdot \frac{\theta}{2}$$

Notice the dependency of *EDL* on the volatility of replacement cost.

Value-at-Risk

The value-at-risk (VaR) is a summary statistic that quantifies the potential loss (most typically resulting from market risk) corresponding to a specified probability α level or alternatively a $(1 - \alpha)$ confidence level where $0 \le \alpha \le 1$. Suppose an asset's expected return r is $r \sim N(\bar{r}, \sigma^2)$. The value-at-risk V^* associated with a probability of α is the value V^* that satisfies the following:

$$\alpha = \int_{-\infty}^{V^*} \frac{1}{\sqrt{2\pi\sigma}} \exp\left\{-\frac{(r-\bar{r})^2}{2\sigma}\right\}$$

Many companies (e.g., banks, brokers, institutions) place limits on the total value at risk at any one time in order to protect investors from potentially adverse market conditions. Inaccurate volatility estimates would lead to misleading VaR estimates and could result in extraordinary losses for investors.

Notice the large dependency of each of these financial models on accurate variance and covariance estimates. It is obvious from this formulation that inaccurate estimates can result in improper execution, higher costs, and ultimately lower returns. Accurate risk estimates are essential for proper investment analysis and risk management in numerous areas of finance. The remainder of the chapter will present various techniques to estimate volatility and covariance for application across all areas.

Forecasting Volatility

In this section we consider four alternative volatility estimation models: historical moving average, exponential weighted moving average, ARCH, and GARCH models.

First, it is important to mention that in practice, a short-term forward forecast of $\bar{r}$ is rarely known and incorrect estimates of expected return can have dramatic effects on volatility estimate. Hence, it is often assumed that $\bar{r} = 0$. For example, for short-term volatility estimates such as a day or less it is often impossible to distinguish between expected price movement and random noise ex-post. Furthermore, in many cases (short term) the analyst is more interested in potential change from the current price rather than the potential change from a trend. Therefore, variance and covariance are commonly written as follows:

$$\sigma_i^2 = \frac{1}{T-1}\sum_{t=1}^{T} r_t^2$$

$$\sigma_{ij} = \frac{1}{T-1}\sum_{t=1}^{T} r_{it} r_{jt}$$

Historical Moving Average

The historical moving average (HMA) is an unbiased volatility estimate dependent on the previous n-observations. Each successive day produces a forecast based on the most recent n-observations. HMA applies equal weights to all data points and assumes returns are independent and identically distributed. The unbiased estimate of variance $\hat{\sigma}^2$ at time t is:

$$\hat{\sigma}_t^2 = \frac{1}{T-1}\sum_{i=1}^{T} r_{t-i}^2 \qquad (5.11)$$

The advantage of the HMA technique is that volatility estimates are straightforward and easy to calculate. But it assumes that variance is constant. Therefore, in situations of time-varying variance and volatility clustering, the HMA technique would tend to provide erroneous estimates. Figure 5.1 illustrates this process.

Exponential Weighted Moving Average

The exponential weighted moving average (EWMA) is a volatility estimation technique similar to the HMA but does not place equal weights on all observations. In EWMA, weights are applied to historical observations following an exponential smoothing

F I G U R E 5.1

Daily Price Returns for S&P 500. Evidence of Volatility Clustering and Time Varying Volatility

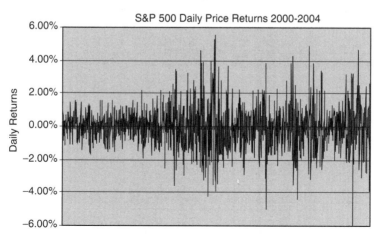

process so that they decrease geometrically in time. For example, an EWMA estimate using T-periods of data is calculated as follows:

$$\hat{\sigma}_t^2 = \sum_{i=1}^{T} w_i r_{t-i}^2 = w_1 r_{t-1}^2 + w_2 r_{t-2}^2 + \ldots w_n r_{t-T}^2 \tag{5.12}$$

where the weights of each observation are determined using an exponential smoothing parameter λ in the following manner:

$$w_i = \lambda^{i-1} \Big/ \sum_{i=1}^{T} \lambda^{i-1} \text{ for } 0 < \lambda < 1.$$

The EWMA places more emphasis on the most recent data and less emphasis on older data. The belief is that the more recent data points provide greater explanatory power than the older data points, and are thus better able to detect structural shifts in volatility and volatility clustering.

If we allow the historical period to grow infinitely large (e.g., $n\to\infty$), the EWMA assumes interesting properties. First, the weight applied to each observation simplifies to $w_i = (1 - \lambda)\lambda^{i-1}$ because the denominator simplifies to $1/1 + \lambda$, hence, $w_i = \lambda^{i-1}/(1/1 + \lambda) = (1 + \lambda)\lambda^{i-1}$.

We thus have:

$$\sum_{i=1}^{T} \lambda^{i-1} = 1 + \lambda + \lambda^2 + \lambda^T = \frac{1-\lambda^T}{1+\lambda}$$

$$\lim_{T\to\infty} \frac{1-\lambda^T}{1+\lambda} = \frac{1}{1+\lambda}$$

Then, the EWMA can be written as:

$$\hat{\sigma}_t^2 = \sum_{i=1}^{\infty} (1-\lambda)\lambda^{i-1} r_{t-i}^2$$

or as,

$$\hat{\sigma}_t^2 = (1-\lambda)r_{t-1}^2 + \sum_{j=2}^{\infty} (1-\lambda)\lambda^{j-1} r_{t-j}^2$$

Now, because $\hat{\sigma}_{t-1}^2$ can be rewritten as:

$$\hat{\sigma}_{t-1}^2 = \sum_{i=1}^{\infty} (1-\lambda)\lambda^{i-1} r_{t-1-i}^2 = \sum_{i=2}^{\infty} (1-\lambda)\frac{1}{\lambda}\lambda^{i-1} r_{t-i}^2$$

we have,

$$\lambda\hat{\sigma}_{t-1}^2 = \sum_{i=2}^{\infty}(1-\lambda)\lambda^{i-1}r_{t-i}^2$$

and finally,

$$\hat{\sigma}_t^2 = (1-\lambda)r_{t-1}^2 + \lambda\hat{\sigma}_{t-1}^2 \tag{5.13}$$

An appealing aspect of the infinite time horizon EWMA volatility estimate is that any subsequent asset/equity volatility forecast only depends on the previous day's observation (squared return) r_{t-1}^2 and the previous day's forecast value $\hat{\sigma}_{t-1}^2$. We do not continuously need to update credit risk forecasts using streams of historical data. The smoothing parameter λ used in the computation of the EWMA is found through maximum likelihood estimation (MLE) as follows:

$$\underset{\lambda}{Min} \sum_{i=0}^{T}(r_{t-i}^2 - \sigma_{t-i}^2)^2 \tag{5.14}$$

where $\hat{\sigma}_{t-1}^2$ is defined according to (5.13).

ARCH

The autoregressive conditional heteroscedasticity (ARCH) model is a nonstochastic process used to forecast volatility (Engle (1982) first introduced the measure). ARCH models incorporate previous volatility forecasts to estimate future volatility (autoregressive) and allow variance to be time varying (heteroskedasticity). That is, volatility is not constant across all periods. These models work best when:

1. Returns are serially correlated.
2. Returns exhibit leptokurtosis (fat tails and peaked means).
3. Evidence of volatility clustering exists.

The ARCH(p) model captures the conditional heteroscedasticity of price returns using returns over the previous p-periods. It is formulated as follows:

$$\hat{\sigma}_t^2 = \omega + \alpha_1 r_{t-1}^2 + \alpha_2 r_{t-2}^2 + \cdots + \alpha_p r_{t-p}^2$$

$$\hat{\sigma}_t^2 = \omega + \sum_{i=1}^{p}\alpha_i r_{t-i}^2 \tag{5.15}$$

with $\omega > 0, \alpha_1, \alpha_2, \ldots, \alpha_p \geq 0$

The simplest and most common form of the these models is the ARCH(1) written as follows:

$$\hat{\sigma}_t^2 = \omega + \alpha r_{t-1}^2$$
$$\omega > 0, \text{and} \, \alpha \geq 0$$

(5.16)

In this formulation only the previous day's return and parameters ω and α are needed to forecast future period variance. ARCH parameters are estimated via OLS regression.

GARCH

The GARCH model is a generalized form of the ARCH model, originally introduced by Bollerslev (1986). This technique forecasts volatility based on the previous p observations of returns and the previous q volatility forecasts. It is formulated as follows:

$$\hat{\sigma}_t^2 = \omega + \alpha_1 r_1^2 + \cdots + \alpha_p r_p^2 + b_1 \sigma_{t-1}^2 + \cdots + b_q \sigma_{t-q}^2$$
$$\hat{\sigma}_t^2 = \omega + \sum_{i=1}^{p} \alpha_i r_{t-i}^2 + \sum_{j=1}^{q} b_j \hat{\sigma}_{j-1}^2$$

with, $\omega > 0$, and $\alpha_1,\ldots,\alpha_p,b_1,\ldots,b_q \geq 0$ to ensure positive variance estimates.

The simplest of the GARCH models is the GARCH(1,1) model written as follows:

$$\hat{\sigma}_t^2 = \omega + \alpha r_{t-1}^2 + b \hat{\sigma}_{t-1}^2$$
$$\omega > 0, \quad \alpha, b \geq 0, \quad \text{and} \quad \alpha + b \leq 1$$

In this formulation, all one needs to forecast variance is the previous day's excess return, and the previous day's forecast (along with constant). It has been found that even in this simplified form of GARCH(1,1) the results have been very favorable.

The parameters of the GARCH model are determined through MLE. For example, if $r_1, r_2, \ldots, r_n$ are the returns over some period of time and we assume that each r_t is normally distributed with mean 0 and variance $\hat{\sigma}^2$ then the likelihood (probability) of observing those exact returns is:

$$L(\sigma^2 | r_1, r_2, \ldots r_n) = \prod_{t=1}^{n} f(r_t)$$

T A B L E   5.1

Volatility Forecasting Models

Volatility Model	Formula	Parameters	Calculation
Historical Moving Average	$\hat{\sigma}_t^2 = \dfrac{1}{T-1}\sum_{i=1}^{T} r_{t-i}^2$	n/a	By Definition
Exponential Weighted Moving Average	$\hat{\sigma}_t^2 = (1-\lambda)r_{t-1}^2 + \lambda\hat{\sigma}_{t-1}^2$	λ	MLE
ARCH(1)	$\hat{\sigma}_t^2 = \omega + \alpha\, r_{t-1}^2$	$\omega > 0, \alpha \geq 0$	OLS
GARCH(1,1)	$\hat{\sigma}_t^2 = \omega + \alpha\, r_{t-1}^2 + b\hat{\sigma}_{t-1}^2$	$\omega > 0, \alpha, b \geq 0$ $\alpha + b \leq 0$	MLE

where each r_t has pdf:

$$f(r_t) = \frac{1}{\sqrt{2\pi\sigma_t^2}}\exp\left(-\frac{r_t^2}{2\sigma_t}\right)$$

The estimated parameters ω, α, and β, are thus found by maximizing L above. But this is identical to maximizing $ln(L)$ or equivalently by minimizing $-ln(L)$. The log-likelihood transformation of L is as follows:

$$\ln(L) = -\frac{n}{2}\ln(2\pi) - \ln(\sigma_t^2) - \frac{1}{2}\sum_{i=1}^{n}\frac{r_i^2}{\sigma_i^2} \qquad (5.17)$$

Table 5.1 summarizes the key volatility forecasting models.

Forecasting Covariance

As shown above the covariance matrix is symmetric with variance in the diagonal entries and covariance in the off-diagonal entries. An n x n covariance matrix C will have $1/2 \cdot (n^2 - n) + n = (n^2 + n)/2$ unique parameters.

Estimation of these parameters requires a sufficient number of data points to ensure statistical significance. First, there needs to be at least as many data points (observations) as there are independent variables in order to solve a system of equations. For example, consider a deterministic system of n-equations and m-unknowns. In order to determine a solution for each unknown we need to have $n \geq m$. If $n < m$ then the set of equations is underdetermined meaning no unique solution exists. The solution of each entry in the covariance matrix is further amplified because we are not solving for a deterministic set of equations. We are seeking to estimate the value of each parameter rather than solve for its exact value. A general rule of thumb is that there needs to be at least 20 observations for each parameter to have statistically meaningful results.

Recall C_{nxn} for an n-asset portfolio. There are $(n^2 + n)/2$ unique parameters to estimate which requires at least $T \geq 20 \cdot (n^2 + n)/2 = 10 \cdot (n^2 + n)$ observations. Since there are n data observations for each period (one for each asset) the number of historical periods required for statistically significant estimates is determined as follows:

$$n \cdot T \geq 10 \cdot (n^2 + n)$$

$$T \geq 10(n + 1)$$

Therefore, a portfolio of 10 assets will consist of 55 unique parameters $((10^2 + 10)/2 = 55)$ and would require 1,100 data observations $(20 \cdot 55 = 1100)$ to produce a statistically significant estimate. Using daily returns, this will require at least 110 days of data $(T \geq 10(10 + 1) = 110)$. Following the same process we determine that the covariance matrix for a 25 asset would consist of 625 unique parameters and require at least 260 days of observations.

To show how quickly our data requirement explodes, consider three equity portfolios: S&P 500, Russell 2000, and Wilshire 5000. The S&P 500 covariance matrix consists of 125,250 unique parameters requiring more than 5,010 days of observations (over 20 years of data). The Russell 2000 covariance matrix has more than 2 million unique parameters and needs 80 years of daily observations. Finally, the Wilshire 5000 covariance matrix consists of more than 12 million unique parameters requiring more than 200 years of daily observations. Table 5.2 highlights the relationship between assets and days of data, while Figures 5.2 and 5.3 illustrate the process graphically.

T A B L E 5.2

Relationship between Assets and Days of Data

Number of Assets	Number of Parameters	Required Days	Number of Years
10	55	110	<1
25	325	260	1
50	1,275	510	2
100	5,050	1,010	4
500	125,250	5,010	20
1,000	500,500	10,010	40
2,000	2,001,000	20,010	80
3,000	4,501,500	30,010	120
5,000	12,502,500	50,010	200

There is not enough reliable data available to devise accurate risk estimates for portfolio of assets, and considering any changes in business plans, company reorganization, mergers and acquisitions, bankruptcies, start-ups, shifts in fiscal or monetary policy, change in economic conditions, and so on, constructing accurate risk estimates for even small portfolios using historical data proves ineffective.

F I G U R E 5.2

Number of Unique Parameters of Covariance Matrix as Function of Number of Assets

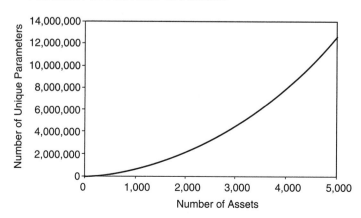

F I G U R E 5.3

Number of Years of Data Required for Significant Estimate
of Covariance Parameters

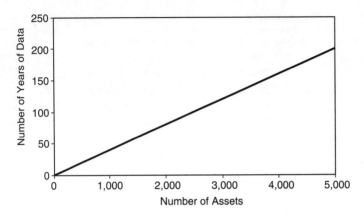

RISK MODELS

We must turn to risk models in order to overcome data limitation
problems associated with covariance matrix estimation. These
models are built on the assumption that asset returns can be
explained by a linear combination of factors (e.g., index returns,
macroeconomic indicators, company characteristics, trading statistics, etc.). For example, a general multifactor model has the form:

$$r_{it} = \alpha_i + b_{i1}f_{1t} + b_{i2}f_{2t} + \cdots + b_{im}f_{mt} + e_{it} \tag{5.18}$$

where, r_{it} is the return for asset i at time t, α_i is the asset specific
expected return unrelated to the specified factors, b_{ik} is the sensitivity
of asset i to factor k, f_{kt} is the value of the factor k at time t, and e_{it} is
asset specific random noise at time t with mean zero and variance
σ_{it}^2, i.e., $e_{it}\ iid \sim (0,\sigma_{ei}^2)$.

The estimated parameters $\hat{b}_{ik}$ are computed via ordinary least
squares (OLS) regression analysis. But this requires the model to
satisfy the set of assumptions listed below (Kennedy, 1998). If any
of these assumptions are violated, the estimated parameters $\hat{b}_{ik}$ are
not guaranteed to be significant and analysts cannot be certain that
the parameters correctly describe the relationship. In these cases,
analysts will need to make appropriate adjustments to determine
significant estimates.

Assumptions:

1. $E(e_{it}) = 0$
2. $Cov(e_i, f_k) = E((e_i - \bar{e}_i)(f_k - \bar{f}_k)) = E(e_i(f_k - \bar{f}_k)) = 0$
3. $Cov(f_k, f_l) = E(f_k - \bar{f}_k)(f_l - \bar{f}_l) = 0$
4. $E(e_{it}e_{it-j}) = 0$
5. $E(e_{it}e_{kt}) = 0$

Assumption one refers to the error term having a mean of zero. Assumption two refers to constant variance, i.e., no heteroscadisticity. Assumption three states the error term is uncorrelated with each factor. Assumption four states that each factor is independent of one another, in other words, there is no multicollinearity present in the model. This means that there is no factor that can be written as a linear combination of another factor. Assumption five states that in a properly specified model where all return is accountable return, e_{it} is random noise across all time periods and across all assets.

Following, we compute the variance of factors as follows:

6. $Var(e_{it}) = \sigma_{ei}^2$
7. $Var(f_k) = E(f_k - \bar{f}_k)^2 = \sigma_{ki}^2$

The multifactor model can be used to compute the following risk statistics. This is illustrated following the approach of Elton & Gruber (1995). An alternative formulation can be found in Bodie, Kane, and Marcus (2005).

Expected Return

$$E(r_i) = \bar{r}_i = \alpha_i + b_{i1}\bar{f}_1 + b_{i2}\bar{f}_2$$

Variance

$$
\begin{aligned}
Var(r_i) = \bar{\sigma}^2(r_i) &= E(r_i - \bar{r})^2 \\
&= E(\alpha_i + b_{i1}f_1 + b_{i2}f_2 + e_i - \alpha_i - b_{i1}\bar{f}_1 - b_{i2}\bar{f}_2)^2 \\
&= E(b_{i1}f_1 + b_{i2}f_2 + e_i - b_{i1}\bar{f}_1 - b_{i2}\bar{f}_2)^2 \\
&= E(b_{i1}(f_1 - \bar{f}_1) + b_{i2}(f_2 - \bar{f}_2) + e_i)^2 \\
&= E\{b_{i1}^2(f_1 - \bar{f}_1)^2 + b_{i2}^2(f_2 - \bar{f}_2)^2 + 2b_{i1}b_{i2}(f_1 - \bar{f}_1)(f_2 - \bar{f}_2) \\
&\quad + 2b_{i1}(f_1 - \bar{f}_1)e_i + 2b_{i2}(f_2 - \bar{f}_2)e_i + e_i^2\} \\
&= b_{i1}^2E((f_1 - \bar{f}_1)^2) + b_{i2}^2E((f_2 - \bar{f}_2)^2) + 2b_{i1}b_{i2}E((f_1 - \bar{f}_1)(f_2 - \bar{f}_2)) \\
&\quad + 2b_{i1}E((f_1 - \bar{f}_1)e_i) + 2b_{i2}E((f_2 - \bar{f}_2)e_i) + E(e_i^2)
\end{aligned}
$$

by assumption 2,

$$E(e_i(f_k - \bar{f}_k)) = 0$$

by assumption 3,

$$E((f_k - \bar{f}_k)(f_l - \bar{f}_l)) = 0$$

by assumption 6,

$$E(e_i^2) = \sigma_{ei}^2$$

by assumption 7,

$$E((f_k - \bar{f}_k)^2) = \sigma_{fk}^2$$

Therefore, we have,

$$\bar{\sigma}^2(r_i) = b_{i1}^2 \sigma_{f1}^2 + b_{i2}^2 \sigma_{f2}^2 + 2b_{i1}b_{i2} \cdot 0 + 2b_{i1} \cdot 0 + 2b_{i2} \cdot 0 + \sigma_{ei}^2$$
$$= b_{i1}^2 \sigma_{f1}^2 + b_{i2}^2 \sigma_{f2}^2 + \sigma_{ei}^2$$

In general, for a k-factor model we have,

$$\bar{\sigma}_i^2 = \sum_{l=1}^{k} b_{il}^2 \sigma_{fl}^2 + \sigma_{ei}^2$$

Covariance

Now consider the following two factor model for assets i and j:

$$r_{it} = \alpha_i + b_{i1}f_{1t} + b_{i2}f_{2t} + e_{it}$$
$$r_{jt} = \alpha_j + b_{j1}f_{1t} + b_{j2}f_{2t} + e_{jt}$$

Then, the covariance of returns is computed as follows:

$$Cov(r_i, r_j) = \bar{\sigma}_{ij}$$
$$= E(r_i - \bar{r}_i)(r_j - \bar{r}_j)$$
$$= E(\alpha_i + b_{i1}f_1 + b_{i2}f_2 + e_i - \alpha_i - b_{i1}\bar{f}_1 - b_{i2}\bar{f}_2)$$
$$\quad (\alpha_j + b_{j1}f_1 + b_{j2}f_2 + e_j - \alpha_j - b_{j1}\bar{f}_1 - b_{j2}\bar{f}_2)$$
$$= E(b_{i1}f_1 - b_{i1}\bar{f}_1 + b_{i2}f_2 - b_{i2}\bar{f}_2 + e_i)$$
$$\quad (b_{j1}f_1 - b_{j1}\bar{f}_1 + b_{j2}f_2 - b_{j2}\bar{f}_2 + e_j)$$

$$= E(b_{i1}(f_1 - \bar{f}_1) + b_{i2}(f_2 - \bar{f}_2) + e_i)$$
$$(b_{j1}(f_1 - \bar{f}_1) + b_{j2}(f_2 - \bar{f}_2) + e_j)$$
$$= E\{b_{i1}b_{j1}(f_1 - \bar{f}_1)^2 + b_{i1}b_{j2}(f_1 - \bar{f}_1)(f_2 - \bar{f}_2) + b_{i1}(f_1 - \bar{f}_1)e_i$$
$$\quad + b_{i2}b_{j1}(f_1 - \bar{f}_1)(f_2 - \bar{f}_2) + b_{i2}b_{j2}(f_2 - \bar{f}_2)^2 + b_{i2}(f_2 - \bar{f}_2)e_j$$
$$\quad + b_{j1}(f_1 - \bar{f}_1)e_i + b_{j2}(f_2 - \bar{f}_2)e_i + e_i e_j\}$$
$$= b_{i1}b_{j1}E(f_1 - \bar{f}_1)^2 + b_{i1}b_{j2}E((f_1 - \bar{f}_1)(f_2 - \bar{f}_2))$$
$$\quad + b_{i1}E((f_1 - \bar{f}_1)e_i) + b_{i2}b_{j1}E((f_1 - \bar{f}_1)(f_2 - \bar{f}_2))$$
$$\quad + b_{i2}b_{j2}E(f_2 - \bar{f}_2)^2 + b_{i2}E((f_2 - \bar{f}_2)e_j)$$
$$\quad + b_{j1}E((f_1 - \bar{f}_1)e_i) + b_{j2}E((f_2 - \bar{f}_2)e_i) + E(e_i e_j)$$

by assumption 3,

$$E(f_k - \bar{f}_k)(f_l - \bar{f}_l) = 0$$

by assumption 2,

$$E((e_i - \bar{e}_i)(f_k - \bar{f}_k)) = E(e_i(f_k - \bar{f}_k)) = 0$$

by assumption 5,

$$E(e_{ij}e_{kj}) = 0$$

by assumption 6,

$$Var(e_{it}) = \sigma_{ei}^2$$

by assumption 7,

$$Var(f_k) = E(f_k - \bar{f}_k)^2 = \sigma_{ki}^2$$

Therefore,

$$\bar{\sigma}_{ij} = b_{i1}b_{j1}\sigma_{f1}^2 + b_{i1}b_{j2} \cdot 0 + b_{i1} \cdot 0 + b_{i2}b_{j1} \cdot 0 + b_{i2}b_{j2}\sigma_{f2}^2$$
$$\quad + b_{i2} \cdot 0 + b_{j1} \cdot 0 + b_{j2} \cdot 0 + 0$$
$$= b_{i1}b_{j1}\sigma_{f1}^2 + b_{i2}b_{j2}\sigma_{f2}^2$$

In general, for a k-factor model we have,

$$\bar{\sigma}_{ij} = \sum_{l=1}^{k} b_{il} b_{jl} \sigma_{fl}^2$$

Correlation

The correlation ρ_{ij} between two assets is defined as

$$\rho_{ij} = \frac{E(r_i - \bar{r}_i)(r_j - \bar{r}_j)}{\sqrt{Var(r_i) \cdot Var(r_j)}} = \frac{\sigma_{ij}}{\sqrt{\sigma_i^2 \sigma_j^2}}$$

Using the two-factor model from above, the correlation of asset returns is as follows:

$$\rho_{ij} = \frac{b_{i1} b_{j1} \sigma_{f1}^2 + b_{i2} b_{j2} \sigma_{f2}^2}{\sqrt{(b_{i1}^2 \sigma_{f1}^2 + b_{i2}^2 \sigma_{f2}^2 + \sigma_{ei}^2)(b_{j1}^2 \sigma_{f1}^2 + b_{j2}^2 \sigma_{f2}^2 + \sigma_{ej}^2)}}$$

For a general k-factor model we have:

$$\rho_{ij} = \frac{\sum_{l=1}^{k} b_{il} b_{jl} \sigma_{fl}^2}{\sqrt{\left(\sum_{l=1}^{k} b_{il}^2 \sigma_{fl}^2 + \sigma_{ei}^2\right)\left(\sum_{l=1}^{k} b_{jl}^2 \sigma_{fl}^2 + \sigma_{ej}^2\right)}}$$

Portfolio managers often find it useful to examine returns in excess of the risk-free rate to determine what is driving overall performance. By arbitrage pricing theory we expect asset-specific return α_i to be equal to the risk-free rate of return r_f, otherwise, it would be possible to enter an arbitrage position and earn in excess of the risk-free rate without any incremental risk. Therefore, it is appropriate to define $\alpha_i = r_f$ for all assets.

Risk managers, however, have slightly different needs with regard to these models. The goal is to develop accurate portfolio risk estimates and this requires accurate variance and covariance estimates. To simplify these calculations, it is appropriate to formulate the multifactor model as an excess return model, i.e., returns in excess of the historical average return. This formulation is as follows:

1. Start with equation 5.18:

$$r_{it} = \alpha_i + b_{i1}f_{1t} + b_{i2}f_{2t} + \cdots + b_{im}f_{mt} + e_{it}$$

2. Compute $E(r_{it})$:

$$E(r_{it}) = E(\alpha_i + b_{i1}f_{1t} + b_{i2}f_{2t} + \cdots + b_{im}f_{mt} + e_{it})$$
$$= \alpha_i + b_{i1}\overline{f_1} + b_{i2}\overline{f_2} + \cdots + b_{im}\overline{f_m}$$

3. Subtract $E(r_{it})$ from both sides:

$$r_{it} - E(r_{it}) = \alpha_i + b_{i1}f_{1t} + b_{i2}f_{2t} + \cdots + b_{im}f_{mt} + e_{it} - E(r_{it})$$
$$= \alpha_i + b_{i1}f_{1t} + b_{i2}f_{2t} + \cdots + b_{im}f_{mt} + e_{it}$$
$$- (\alpha_i + b_{i1}\overline{f_1} + b_{i2}\overline{f_2} + \cdots + b_{im}\overline{f_m})$$
$$= \alpha_i + b_{i1}f_{1t} + b_{i2}f_{2t} + \cdots + b_{im}f_{mt} + e_{it} - \alpha_i$$
$$- b_{i1}\overline{f_1} - b_{i2}\overline{f_2} - \cdots - b_{im}\overline{f_m}$$
$$= b_{i1}f_{1t} - b_{i1}\overline{f_1} + b_{i2}f_{2t} - b_{i2}\overline{f_2} + \cdots + b_{im}f_{mt}$$
$$- b_{im}\overline{f} + e_{it}$$
$$r_{it} - \overline{r_i} = b_{i1}(f_{1t} - \overline{f_1}) + b_{i2}(f_{2t} - \overline{f_2})$$
$$+ \cdots + b_{im}(f_{2t} - \overline{f_2}) + e_{it}$$

4. The general multifactor model is then simplified as follows:

$$r_{it}^* = b_{i1}f_{1t}^* + b_{i2}f_{2t}^* + \cdots + b_{im}f_{mt}^* + e_{it}$$

where, $r_{it}^* = (r_{it} - \overline{r_i})$ and $f_{kt}^* = (f_{kt} - \overline{f_k})$. Following we have, $E(r_{it}^*) = 0$ and $E(f_{kt}^*) = 0$. Therefore, the assumptions simplify to:

$$Cov(e_i, f_k) = E((e_i - \overline{e_i})(f_k - \overline{f_k})) = E(e_i f_k^*) = 0$$
$$Cov(f_k, f_l) = E(f_k - \overline{f_k})(f_l - \overline{f_l}) = E(f_k^* f_l^*) = 0$$

This transformation preserves the value of each parameter b_{ik}. In other words, reformulating the model in this manner does not change the parameters of the equation.

Equation (5.18) can now be rewritten in matrix notation as follows:

$$r_i = Fb_i + e_i \tag{5.19}$$

where,

$$r_i = \begin{bmatrix} r_{i1}^* \\ \vdots \\ r_{it}^* \\ \vdots \\ r_{in}^* \end{bmatrix} \quad F = \begin{bmatrix} f_{11}^* & f_{21}^* & \cdots & f_{k1}^* \\ \vdots & \vdots & \ddots & \vdots \\ f_{1t}^* & f_{2t}^* & \cdots & f_{kt}^* \\ \vdots & \vdots & \ddots & \vdots \\ f_{1n}^* & f_{2n}^* & \cdots & f_{kn}^* \end{bmatrix} \quad b_i = \begin{bmatrix} b_{i1} \\ b_{i2} \\ \vdots \\ b_{ik} \end{bmatrix} \quad e_i = \begin{bmatrix} e_{i1} \\ \vdots \\ e_{it} \\ \vdots \\ e_{in} \end{bmatrix}$$

and r_i is a column vector of returns for asset i, F is a matrix of factor returns, b is a vector of sensitivities to those factors, and e is a vector of random noise. From this point forward we define r and f to be excess price and factor returns respectively, unless otherwise specified.

The model parameters $\hat{b}_{ik}$ can then be estimated as follows:

$$\hat{b}_k = (F'F)^{-1}F'r_i$$

and standard error:

$$\hat{\sigma}^2(\hat{b}_k) = \left(\frac{1}{n-2} e_i^T e_i \right) \cdot (F'F)^{-1}$$

A direct and intended consequence of working with excess returns is that it simplifies our risk calculations. For example, consider two column vectors of excess returns r_i and r_j (i.e., mean zero). Variance and Covariance is calculated as follows:

$$Var(r_i) = E((r_i - \bar{r_i})'(r_i - \bar{r_i})) = E(r_i'r_i) \tag{5.20}$$

$$Cov(r_i, r_j) = E((r_i - \overline{r_i})'(r_i - \overline{r_j})) = E(r_i'r_j) = E(r_j'r_i) \qquad (5.21)$$

The multifactor model can be used to estimate the covariance matrix. Suppose the portfolio consists of n-stocks and the linear relationship is described using k-factors. Then, we can estimate the sample covariance matrix as follows:

Let R be a matrix of excess returns where r_{it} represents the return of asset i at time k. That is:

$$R = \begin{bmatrix} r_{11} & r_{21} & \cdots & r_{n1} \\ \vdots & \vdots & \ddots & \vdots \\ r_{1t} & r_{2t} & \cdots & r_{nt} \\ \vdots & \vdots & \ddots & \vdots \\ r_{1T} & r_{2T} & \cdots & r_{nT} \end{bmatrix}$$

Then, the covariance matrix C calculated by definition is as follows:

$$C = E[R'R] = \begin{pmatrix} E(r_1'r_1) & E(r_1'r_2) & \cdots & E(r_1'r_n) \\ E(r_2'r_1) & E(r_2'r_2) & \cdots & E(r_2'r_n) \\ \vdots & \vdots & \ddots & \vdots \\ E(r_n'r_1) & E(r_n'r_2) & \cdots & E(r_n'r_n) \end{pmatrix} = \begin{pmatrix} \sigma_1^2 & \sigma_{12} & \cdots & \sigma_{1n} \\ \sigma_{21} & \sigma_2^2 & \cdots & \sigma_{2n} \\ \vdots & \vdots & \ddots & \vdots \\ \sigma_{n1} & \sigma_{n2} & \cdots & \sigma_n^2 \end{pmatrix}$$

We are able to compute the covariance matrix C can also be estimated directly from the multifactor model as follows.

Let, B represent the matrix of sensitivities where b_{ik} is the sensitivity of asset i to factor k, and ε represents the matrix of random noise (i.e., the portion of the returns not explained by the factors) where e_{it} is the unexplained returns of asset i in period t. That is

$$B = \begin{bmatrix} b_{11} & b_{21} & \cdots & b_{n1} \\ b_{12} & b_{22} & \cdots & b_{n2} \\ \vdots & \vdots & \ddots & \vdots \\ b_{1k} & b_{2k} & \cdots & b_{nk} \end{bmatrix} \quad \varepsilon = \begin{bmatrix} e_{11} & e_{21} & \cdots & e_{n1} \\ \vdots & \vdots & \ddots & \vdots \\ e_{1t} & e_{2t} & \cdots & e_{nt} \\ \vdots & \vdots & \ddots & \vdots \\ e_{1T} & e_{2T} & \cdots & e_{nT} \end{bmatrix}$$

Then, C is estimated as follows:

$$R = FB + \varepsilon$$
$$E[R'R] = E[(FB + \varepsilon)'(FB + \varepsilon)]$$
$$= E[B'F'FB + B'F'\varepsilon + \varepsilon'FB + \varepsilon'\varepsilon]$$
$$= B'E(F'F)B + B'E(F'\varepsilon) + E(\varepsilon'F)\,B + E(\varepsilon'\varepsilon)$$
$$= B'\Omega B + \Lambda \qquad\qquad\qquad\qquad (5.22)$$

where,

$$\Omega = \begin{pmatrix} \sigma_{f1}^2 & 0 & \cdots & 0 \\ 0 & \sigma_{f2}^2 & \cdots & \vdots \\ \vdots & \vdots & \ddots & \vdots \\ 0 & \cdots & & \sigma_{fk}^2 \end{pmatrix} \quad \Lambda = \begin{pmatrix} \sigma_{e1}^2 & 0 & 0 & \cdots & 0 \\ 0 & \sigma_{e2}^2 & 0 & \cdots & 0 \\ 0 & 0 & \sigma_{e3}^2 & \cdots & 0 \\ \vdots & \vdots & \vdots & \ddots & \vdots \\ 0 & 0 & 0 & \cdots & \sigma_{en}^2 \end{pmatrix}$$

because,

$$E(F'\varepsilon) = 0$$
$$E(\varepsilon'F) = 0$$

Therefore, the covariance matrix C for a portfolio of stock can be estimated using the parameters of the multifactor model as follows:

$$C = B'\Omega B + \Lambda \qquad\qquad\qquad\qquad (5.23)$$

Here, $B'\Omega B$ represents the systematic or market risk and Λ represents stock specific or idiosyncratic risk.

In many cases, the factors of the model are constructed to have zero mean and variance one, that is, $f_{kt} \sim (0,1)$. In these instances we have $\Omega = I$ so estimation of C simplifies to:

$$C = B'\Omega B + \Lambda$$
$$C = B'BIB + \Lambda \qquad\qquad\qquad\qquad (5.24)$$
$$C = B'B + \Lambda$$

Very often risk managers on both the equity and banking side are more interested in estimates of correlation rather than covariance. Recall,

$$\rho_{ij} = \begin{cases} \dfrac{\sigma_{ij}}{\sigma_i \sigma_j} & i \neq j \\[2mm] 1 & i = j \end{cases}$$

Therefore, the portfolio correlation matrix Φ is written as:

$$\Phi = \begin{pmatrix} 1 & \rho_{12} & \cdots & \rho_{1n} \\ \rho_{21} & 1 & \cdots & \rho_{2n} \\ \vdots & \vdots & \ddots & \vdots \\ \rho_{1n} & \rho_{2n} & \cdots & 1 \end{pmatrix} = \begin{pmatrix} 1 & \dfrac{\sigma_{12}}{\sigma_1 \sigma_2} & \cdots & \dfrac{\sigma_{1n}}{\sigma_1 \sigma_n} \\ \dfrac{\sigma_{21}}{\sigma_1 \sigma_2} & 1 & \cdots & \dfrac{\sigma_{2n}}{\sigma_1 \sigma_n} \\ \vdots & \vdots & \ddots & \vdots \\ \dfrac{\sigma_{1n}}{\sigma_1 \sigma_n} & \dfrac{\sigma_1^2}{\sigma_1 \sigma_1} & \cdots & 1 \end{pmatrix}$$

The correlation matrix can be calculated directly from the covariance C as follows:

$$\Phi = D_c^{-1/2} C D_c^{-1/2} \tag{5.25}$$

where, D_c is the diagonal matrix of C. That is.

$$D_C = \begin{pmatrix} \sigma_1^2 & 0 & \cdots & 0 \\ 0 & \sigma_2^2 & \cdots & 0 \\ \vdots & \vdots & \ddots & \vdots \\ 0 & 0 & \cdots & \sigma_n^2 \end{pmatrix} \quad D_C^{-1/2} = \begin{pmatrix} 1/\sigma_1 & 0 & \cdots & 0 \\ 0 & 1/\sigma_2 & \cdots & 0 \\ \vdots & \vdots & \ddots & \vdots \\ 0 & 0 & \cdots & 1/\sigma_n \end{pmatrix}$$

Parameter Reduction

In a k-factor model there are $n \cdot k$ unique parameters $\hat{b}_{ik}$ (one for each stock). Using our rule of thumb for 20 data observations for each parameter, we only need $20 \cdot n \cdot k$ total data points. Because there are n observations per period, we only need $T = 20 \cdot k$ historical periods for statistically significant sensitivity estimates. Compare this to the historical sample calculation technique where $T = 10 \cdot (n + 1)$ historical periods. It is easy to see that the sample periods for the risk modeling approach are only dependent on the number of model factors k (regardless of the number of stocks), whereas the sample calculation technique is dependent on the number of assets n – leading to the limited data problem.

Risk Decomposition

Multifactor risk models offer insight into an asset's return behavior and both systematic (the quantity explained by the model) and idiosyncratic risk (stock specific or risk quantity not explained by the model). That is:

Portfolio Variance = Systematic + Idiosyncratic

Following the multifactor formulation we decompose risk as follows:

$$C = \underbrace{B'\Omega B}_{\text{Systematic}} + \underbrace{\Lambda}_{\text{Idiosyncratic}}$$

Decomposition of risk into systematic and idiosyncratic risk provides the foundation to estimate the covariance of price movement between any two stock groups without the data limitations encountered above. We accomplish this by measuring how stock prices change in relationship to the index. Decomposition is essential when we forecast correlation portfolio risk.

CONSTRUCTING MULTIFACTOR MODELS

The multifactor model is a risk-return model based on the underlying assumption that a set of factors, such as market movement (index returns), macroeconomic factors, or stock specific factors (cross-sectional), explains excess returns. We examine the derivation of the covariance matrix C using each of these methodologies below.

Single-Index Model

The simplest of all multifactor models is the single index model that formulates a relationship between stock returns and market movement. In most situations, the S&P 500 index or some other broad market index is used as a proxy for the whole market.

In matrix notation, the single factor model has the general form:

$$r_i = Rb_i + e_i \qquad (5.26)$$

where,

$$r_i = \begin{bmatrix} r_{i1} \\ r_{i2} \\ \vdots \\ r_{iT} \end{bmatrix}, \quad R_m = \begin{bmatrix} R_{m1} \\ R_{m2} \\ \vdots \\ R_{mT} \end{bmatrix}, \quad e_i = \begin{bmatrix} e_{i1} \\ e_{i2} \\ \vdots \\ e_{iT} \end{bmatrix}$$

r_i = column vector of stock excess returns for stock i
R_m = column vector of excess market returns
e_i = column vector of random noise for stock i
b_i = stock return sensitivity to market returns

The estimated value of b_i is the traditional stock beta. It provides insight into the stock's sensitivity to the market. A stock with $b_i > 0$ will move in the same direction as the market, a stock with $b_i < 0$ will move in the opposite direction of the market, and a stock with $b_i = 0$ will not have any relationship with the market. A beta of $b_i > |1|$ indicates the stock will fluctuate more than the market, a beta of $b_i < |1|$ indicates the stock will fluctuate less than the market, and beta of $b_i = |1|$ indicates the stock will fluctuate with the market on average.

Multi-Index Models

The index-based multifactor model is an extension of the single index model, capturing the commonality of price returns due to the market, sector, and industry group. Because there has been sufficient empirical evidence in the literature to highlight the correlation between residual returns and sector returns as well as residual returns and industry grouping returns, it seems a natural extension to incorporate these factors into the risk model. It is essential, however, that we only incorporate the uncorrelated excess returns of the sector and industry group.

Each stock or company is classified into an economic sector and further into an industry group based on business practice.

Then, the multi-index model will have the general form (Elton & Gruber, 1995):

$$r_{it} = b_i R_{mt} + b_k \tilde{S}_{kt} + b_l \tilde{I}_{lt} + e_{it}$$

Excess sector return unrelated to the market index returns $\tilde{S}_t$ is determined as follows:

$$S_t = \hat{\alpha}_0 + \hat{\alpha}_1 R_{mt} + d_{st}$$

and $\tilde{S}_t$ is:

$$\tilde{S}_t = d_{st} = S_t - \hat{\alpha}_0 - \hat{\alpha}_1 R_{mt}$$

The next step is to determine the excess industry group returns $\tilde{I}_t$ unrelated to the market index and corresponding sector index. This is estimated as follows:

$$I_{lt} = \hat{\gamma}_0 + \hat{\gamma}_1 R_{mt} + \hat{\gamma}_2 \tilde{S}_t + c_{lt}$$

and $\tilde{I}_t$ is:

$$\tilde{I}_{lt} = c_{lt} = I_{lt} - \hat{\gamma}_0 - \hat{\gamma}_1 R_{mt} - \hat{\gamma}_2 \tilde{S}_t$$

A stock specific multi-index model is formulated as follows:

$$r_{it} = R_{mt} b_{iRm} + \tilde{S}_{kt} b_{ik} + \tilde{I}_{\ell t} b_{i\ell} \tag{5.27}$$

or, in matrix notation, as:

$$r_i = f_i b_i + e_i$$

where, f_i is a matrix of column vectors $f_i = [R_m \ \tilde{S}_i \ \tilde{I}_i]$ with R_m the vector of market returns, $\tilde{S}_i$ the vector of uncorrelated excess returns for the sector corresponding to i and $\tilde{I}_i$ the vector of uncorrelated excess returns for the industry corresponding to i. The sensitivities to these factors are computed as follows:

$$\hat{b}_i = (f f)^{-1} f' r_i$$

A generalized portfolio multi-index model formulated in matrix notation is:

$$R = FB + \varepsilon$$

where,

$$R = \begin{bmatrix} r_{11} & r_{21} & \cdots & r_{n1} \\ r_{12} & r_{22} & \cdots & r_{n2} \\ \vdots & \vdots & \ddots & \vdots \\ r_{1T} & r_{2T} & \cdots & r_{nT} \end{bmatrix} \quad F = \begin{bmatrix} R_{m1} & \tilde{S}_{11} & \cdots & \tilde{S}_{k1} & \tilde{I}_{11} & \cdots & \tilde{I}_{\ell 1} \\ R_{m2} & \tilde{S}_{12} & \cdots & \tilde{S}_{k2} & \tilde{I}_{12} & \cdots & \tilde{I}_{\ell 2} \\ \vdots & \vdots & & \vdots & \vdots & \vdots & \vdots \\ R_{mT} & \tilde{S}_{1T} & \cdots & \tilde{S}_{kT} & \tilde{I}_{1T} & \cdots & \tilde{I}_{\ell T} \end{bmatrix}$$

$$B = \begin{bmatrix} b_{11}^* & b_{21}^* & \cdots & b_{n1}^* \\ b_{12}^* & b_{22}^* & \cdots & b_{n2}^* \\ \vdots & \vdots & \ddots & \vdots \\ b_{1k}^* & b_{2k}^* & \cdots & b_{nk}^* \end{bmatrix} \quad \varepsilon = \begin{bmatrix} e_{11} & e_{21} & \cdots & e_{n1} \\ \vdots & \vdots & \ddots & \vdots \\ e_{1t} & e_{2t} & \cdots & e_{nt} \\ \vdots & \vdots & \ddots & \vdots \\ e_{1T} & e_{2T} & \cdots & e_{nT} \end{bmatrix}$$

where, $b_{ik}^* = \begin{cases} b_{ik} & \text{if } i \in S_j \text{ or } i \in I_j \\ 0 & \text{o.w.} \end{cases}$

Macroeconomic Factor Models

A macroeconomic multifactor model attempts to explain stock returns and risk through a set of macroeconomic variables that are common to all stocks (e.g., inflation, industrial production). This approach suggests potential explanatory variables of stock returns and risk (they are incorporated and highly scrutinized in many pricing models). For example, in the most basic of all stock pricing models, the growth dividend model, assumptions center on expected growth rate, interest rates, and inflation. Thus changes to any variable influences security prices. The appeal of macroeconomic data lies in the intuitiveness of the data. All macroeconomic variables are readily measurable and have real economic meaning. For example, if there is a measured decrease in industrial production, and an increase in unemployment and inflation, it is likely that the economy as a whole has begun to slow down. These models provide good insight into future growth of the economy and expected returns of stock. Stocks are expected to increase less rapidly in a slowing economy and more rapidly in an increasing economy.

However, these models are often quite sensitive to specified macroeconomic variables, and thus any measurement error can easily produce poor results. Further, a significant amount of data comes from government sources along with the inevitable time lag; the data may be suspect. Therefore, while these models offer some insight into the likely direction of the economy, they do not sufficiently capture the most accurate correlation structure of price movement across stocks—vital information in helping us develop our short-term covariance matrix. Finally, macroeconomic models may not do a good job capturing the covariance of price movement across stocks in "new economies" or a "shifting structure." For example, many practitioners have been using macroeconomic variables to model returns of technology and "e-commerce" companies identical to those used to model strong industrials and blue chips of earlier years.

Ross, Roll, and Chen (1986) identified the following four macroeconomic factors as having significant explanatory power. These are unanticipated changes in the following:

- Inflation
- Industrial production
- The yield between high-grade and low-grade corporate bonds
- The yield between long-term government bonds and t-bills (slope of the term structure)

Other macroeconomic factors that have been incorporated into these models include changes in interest rates, growth rates, GDP, capital investment, unemployment, oil prices, housing starts, exchange rates, and so on. The parameters are typically determined via regression analysis using monthly data over a five-year period, e.g., 60 observations.

A macroeconomic multifactor model is a time series model similar to the multi-index model but uses real economic indicators. Furthermore, it is often assumed that these factors are uncorrelated and analysts do not make any adjustment for correlation across returns. An m-factor model has form:

$$r_{it} = f_{1t}b_{i1} + f_{2t}b_{i2} + \cdots + f_{mt}b_{im} + e_{it} \qquad (5.28)$$

and can be written in matrix notation as follows:

$$r_i = Fb_i + e_i$$

where,

$$r_i = \begin{bmatrix} r_{i1} \\ r_{i2} \\ \vdots \\ r_{in} \end{bmatrix}, \quad F = \begin{bmatrix} f_{11} & f_{21} & \cdots & f_{m1} \\ f_{12} & f_{22} & \cdots & f_{m2} \\ \vdots & \vdots & \ddots & \vdots \\ f_{1n} & f_{2n} & \cdots & f_{mn} \end{bmatrix}, \quad e_i = \begin{bmatrix} e_{i1} \\ e_{i2} \\ \vdots \\ e_{in} \end{bmatrix}, \quad b_i = \begin{bmatrix} b_{i1} \\ b_{i2} \\ \vdots \\ b_{im} \end{bmatrix}$$

Cross-Sectional Multifactor Model

Cross-sectional multifactor models determine the relationship between stock return and risk and a set of variables specific to each company rather than through factors common across all stocks. Cross-sectional models specify factors based on fundamental and technical data. The fundamental data consists of the company characteristics, and the technical data (also called market driven) consists of observations of trading activity for the stock in the market. Because of the reliance on fundamental data, many authors use the term "fundamental model" instead of cross-sectional model. The rationale behind the cross-sectional models is similar to the rationale behind the macroeconomic model. That is, because managers and decision makers incorporate fundamental and technical analysis into their stock selection process, it is only reasonable that these factors provide insight into risk and return of those stocks. French and Fama (1992) reported that the market, size, and book/value factors have considerable explanatory power. However, the exact measure of these variables remains a topic of much discussion.

While many may find it intuitive to incorporate cross-sectional data into multifactor models because it is based on the analytical techniques performed for pricing and selecting stocks, these models have several limitations. First, data requirements are cumbersome, requiring analysts to develop models using company-specific data (each firm requires its own set of factors). Second, it is often difficult to find a consistent set of robust factors across stocks that provide strong enough explanatory power. Ross and Roll had difficulty determining a set of factors that provided more explanatory power than the macroeconomic models without introducing excessive multicollinearity into the data. The parameters are typically determined via regression analysis using company specific monthly data over a five-year period, e.g., 60 observations.

For consistency across stocks the parameter loadings are typically normalized as follows:

$$x_{kl}^* = \frac{x_{kl} - E(x_k)}{\sigma(x_k)}$$

A cross-sectional risk model works in the opposite manner of the other factor models we mentioned. Here, rather than estimate the sensitivities to the factors, we estimate (construct) the factors from a set of stock-specific data called factor loadings. In other words, a cross-sectional model derives a set of common factors in each time period based on stock specific data. Rather than estimate factor sensitivities for each stock and factor, we estimate each of our k factors in each time period (e.g., daily or monthly) from normalized stock data.

The cross-sectional model is written as:

$$r_{it} = x_{i1}^* f_{1t} + x_{i2}^* f_{2t} + \cdots + x_{ik}^* f_{kt} + e_{it} \tag{5.29}$$

and can be written in matrix notation as follows:

$$r_i = x_i F + e_i \tag{5.30}$$

where,

$$r_i = \begin{bmatrix} r_{i1} \\ r_{i2} \\ \vdots \\ r_{iT} \end{bmatrix}, \quad F = \begin{bmatrix} f_{11} & f_{21} & \cdots & f_{k1} \\ f_{12} & f_{22} & \cdots & f_{k2} \\ \vdots & \vdots & \ddots & \vdots \\ f_{1T} & f_{2T} & \cdots & f_{kT} \end{bmatrix}, \quad e_i = \begin{bmatrix} e_{i1} \\ e_{i2} \\ \vdots \\ e_{iT} \end{bmatrix}, \quad x_i' = \begin{bmatrix} x_{i1}^* \\ x_{i2}^* \\ \vdots \\ x_{ik}^* \end{bmatrix}$$

Companies such as Barra combine various types of data (market, fundamental, and index returns) in derivation of the risk model.

Principal Component Analysis

Principal component analysis (also referred to a statistical factor model or implicit factor model) is the multifactor modeling approach that most closely resembles the original work of Ross and Roll (1984) in arbitrage pricing theory (APT). In principal component analysis (PCA), both the explanatory factors and sensitivities (or factor loadings) are unknown in advance. They are not readily observed in the marketplace but are derived directly from historical data. The statistical multifactor model differs from the previously mentioned models in that they estimate both the factors ($f_k's$) and the sensitivity loadings ($b_{ik}'s$) from a series of historical returns. This model does not make any prior assumptions regarding the explanatory factors or force any preconceived structure into the model. This approach is in contrast to the explicit modeling approaches where analysts must specify either the explanatory factors or sensitivities (factor loading). Analysts begin with either a set of specified factors and estimate sensitivities to those factors (i.e., index models and macroeconomic factor model) or begin with the factor loadings and estimate the set of explanatory factors (cross-sectional model).

The advantage of PCA is that it provides risk managers with a process to uncover accurate covariance and correlation relationships of returns without making any assumptions regarding what is driving the returns. The disadvantage of PCA is that it does not provide portfolio managers with information necessary to understand what is driving returns because the statistical factors do not have any real-world meaning. But to the extent that analysts are only interested in uncovering covariance and correlation relationships for risk management purposes, PCA has proven to be a viable alternative to the traditional explicit modeling approaches. The approach behind PCA can best be explained as follows:

Any independent series of data can be modeled as a linear combination of orthogonal factors. For a series of n asset returns r_{nx1} there is a set of orthogonal factors f_{nxn} and sensitivities B_{nx1} that satisfy the following relationship:

$$
\begin{bmatrix} r_1 \\ r_2 \\ \vdots \\ r_n \end{bmatrix} = \begin{bmatrix} f_{11} & f_{21} & \cdots & f_{n1} \\ f_{12} & f_{22} & \cdots & f_{n2} \\ \vdots & \vdots & \ddots & \vdots \\ f_{1n} & f_{2n} & \cdots & f_{nn} \end{bmatrix} \begin{bmatrix} \beta_1 \\ \beta_2 \\ \vdots \\ \beta_n \end{bmatrix} \tag{5.31}
$$

For a series of multiple asset returns, this relationship can be written as follows:

$$
\begin{bmatrix} r_{11} & r_{21} & \cdots & r_{m1} \\ r_{12} & r_{22} & \cdots & r_{m2} \\ \vdots & \vdots & \ddots & \vdots \\ r_{1n} & r_{2n} & \cdots & r_{mn} \end{bmatrix} = \begin{bmatrix} f_{11} & f_{21} & \cdots & f_{n1} \\ f_{12} & f_{22} & \cdots & f_{n2} \\ \vdots & \vdots & \ddots & \vdots \\ f_{1n} & f_{2n} & \cdots & f_{nn} \end{bmatrix} \begin{bmatrix} \beta_{11} & \beta_{21} & \cdots & \beta_{m1} \\ \beta_{12} & \beta_{22} & \cdots & \beta_{m2} \\ \vdots & \vdots & \ddots & \vdots \\ \beta_{1n} & \beta_{2n} & \cdots & \beta_{mn} \end{bmatrix} \tag{5.32}
$$

or in matrix notation as:

$$R = F\beta + \varepsilon \tag{5.33}$$

Then, the covariance matrix of returns is calculated as follows:

$$E[R'R] = E[(F\beta + \varepsilon)'(F\beta + \varepsilon)]$$
$$C = \beta'E\,[F'F\,]\beta + \Lambda$$
$$C = \beta'I\beta + \Lambda \tag{5.34}$$
$$C = \beta'\beta + \Lambda$$

We next compute the historical sample covariance matrix C by definition. This matrix can then be factored via eigenvalue-eigenvector decomposition as follows:

$$C = VDV' \tag{5.35}$$

where, D is the diagonal matrix of eigenvalues sorted from largest to smallest and V is the corresponding matrix of eigenvectors. That is,

$$D = \begin{bmatrix} \lambda_1 & 0 & \cdots & 0 \\ 0 & \lambda_2 & \cdots & 0 \\ \vdots & \vdots & \ddots & \vdots \\ 0 & 0 & \cdots & \lambda_n \end{bmatrix} \tag{5.36}$$

where $\lambda_1 > \lambda_2 > \ldots > \lambda_n$ and V is a matrix of eigenvalues where column k is the eigenvector that corresponds to λ_k. Because D is a diagonal matrix we have $D = D^{1/2}D^{1/2}$ and $D = D'$. Then, our covariance matrix C can be written as:

$$C = VD^{1/2}\,D^{1/2}V'$$
$$= VD^{1/2}\,D^{1/2}V'$$
$$= VD^{1/2}\,(VD^{1/2})' \tag{5.37}$$

Now relating the covariance decomposition in terms of the linear factor relationship we have:

$$\beta'\beta = VD^{1/2}(VD^{1/2})' \tag{5.38}$$

which yields:

$$\beta = (VD^{1/2})' \tag{5.39}$$

Now substituting $\beta = (VD^{1/2})'$ into the linear model we have:

$$R = F\beta = F(VD^{1/2})'$$
$$R = FD^{1/2}V' \tag{5.40}$$

The expression $FD^{1/2}$ is referred to as the principal components of the matrix. The factor matrix, hence, is computed as follows:

$$R = FD^{1/2}V'$$
$$R(D^{1/2}V')'(D^{1/2}V'(D^{1/2}V')')^{-1} = FD^{1/2}V'(D^{1/2}V')'(D^{1/2}V'(D^{1/2}V')')^{-1} \tag{5.41}$$
$$R(D^{1/2}V')'(D^{1/2}V'(D^{1/2}V')')^{-1} = FI$$
$$F = R(D^{1/2}V')'(D^{1/2}V'(D^{1/2}V')')^{-1}$$

This, however, does not address the limited data problem described above. Fortunately, PCA offers a process to overcome this problem. It can be shown from the relationship above that the return for asset i on day t can be determined via the following:

$$r_{it} = f_{1t}\sqrt{\lambda_1}v_{11} + f_{2t}\sqrt{\lambda_2}v_{21} + \cdots + f_{nt}\sqrt{\lambda_n}v_{n1} = \sum_{k=1}^{n} f_{kt}\sqrt{\lambda_k}v_{k1} \tag{5.42}$$

In matrix notation this is written as:

$$r_{it} = \begin{bmatrix} f_{1t} & f_{2t} & \cdots & f_{nt} \end{bmatrix} \begin{bmatrix} \sqrt{\lambda_1} & 0 & \cdots & 0 \\ 0 & \sqrt{\lambda_2} & \cdots & 0 \\ \vdots & \vdots & \ddots & \vdots \\ 0 & 0 & \cdots & \sqrt{\lambda_n} \end{bmatrix} \begin{bmatrix} v_{11} \\ v_{21} \\ \vdots \\ v_{n1} \end{bmatrix} \tag{5.43}$$

Now consider a row vector of asset returns $r_t = (r_{1t}\, r_{2t} \ldots r_{nt})$ and corresponding factor returns $f_t = (f_{1t}\, f_{2t} \ldots f_{nt})$. The expected return and covariance are given as:

$$E[r_t] = f_t D^{1/2}V'$$
$$E[r_t r_t'] = E\left[(f_t D^{1/2}V')(f_t D^{1/2}V')' \right]$$
$$= E\left[f_t D^{1/2}V'VD^{1/2'} f' \right]$$
$$= E\left[f_t D^{1/2}D^{1/2} f_t' \right]$$
$$= E\left[f_t D f_t' \right] \tag{5.44}$$

and after working through the algebra we have:

$$E[r_t r_t'] = E[\lambda_1 f_{1t}^2 + \lambda_2 f_{2t}^2 + \cdots + \lambda_n f_{nt}^2]$$
$$= \lambda_1 E[f_{1t}^2] + \lambda_2 E[f_{2t}^2] + \cdots + \lambda_n E[f_{nt}^2]$$
$$= \lambda_1 + \lambda_2 + \cdots + \lambda_n \tag{5.45}$$

Therefore, the total variance of r_t is $\sigma^2(r_t) = \lambda_1 + \lambda_2 + \cdots + \lambda_n$ and each eigenvalue explains exactly the $\lambda_k/\Sigma\lambda$ percentage of the total variance. Because we constructed D from largest to smallest value, we can plot the decrease in predictive power of each factor. This is shown in Figure 5.4.

It is possible to construct the covariance matrix C in terms of a smaller number of principal components and not suffer spurious relationships caused by the limited data problem. As long as $20 \cdot n \cdot k \leq n \cdot T$ there are sufficient data observations to determine statistically significant factor sensitivities (and ultimately principal components). This is accomplished as follows:

Suppose that through PCA of the entire historical covariance matrix it is found that first k eigenvalues explain a sufficient quantity of variance and $20 \cdot n \cdot k \leq n \cdot T$ holds. Then we can rewrite the covariance decomposition as follows:

$$C = UGU' + WHW' \tag{5.46}$$

FIGURE 5.4

Explanatory Power of Eigenvalues

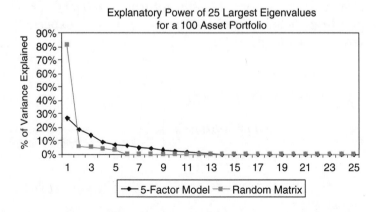

where G_{kxk} is the diagonal matrix containing the more predictive k eigenvalues, U_{nxk} is the matrix of corresponding eigenvectors, $H_{n-k \, x \, n-k}$ is the diagonal matrix of the least predictive n-k eigenvalues, and $W_{n \, x \, n-k}$ is the corresponding matrix of eigenvectors. Here, UGU' is the explainable or systematic risk of C and WHW' is the unexplainable or idiosyncratic risk of C, and any covariance in the off-diagonals of WHW' is assumed to be by change and not statistically different from zero. It is often referred in financial literature as the error matrix.

Next, we revisit the multi-factor formulation of returns $R = F\beta + \varepsilon$ where C is computed as follows:

$$C = B^t B + \Lambda \qquad (5.47)$$

where $B^t B$ is the explainable risk and Λ is the unexplainable risk. Then we can equate 5.46 to 5.47 as follows:

$$UGU' + WHW' = \beta'\beta + \Lambda \qquad (5.48)$$

Because we are interested in systematic risk we have,

$$UGU' = \beta'\beta$$
$$UG^{1/2}G^{1/2}U' = \beta'\beta \qquad (5.49)$$
$$\rightarrow \beta = G^{1/2}U'$$

Hence, the covariance matrix via principal component analysis is computed as follows:

$$C = \beta'\beta$$
$$= UG^{1/2}G^{1/2}U' \qquad (5.50)$$

Risk managers can therefore construct a covariance matrix using historical returns and need only maintain a matrix of PCA sensitivities β and idiosyncratic risk Λ.

Deriving a Short-Term Covariance Matrix

The covariance matrix derived from the multi-factor model approach provides estimates of average volatility over a historical time horizon. Recall from above that quite often asset variance exhibits heteroscadisticity and is time-varying. In these instances, the covariance matrix may not be a good enough estimate of short-term volatility, which is most important for risk managers and derivatives traders. For these purposes, it would be appropriate to adjust the historical covariance for short-term volatility. That is, we use estimated asset volatility and historical correlation. Kissell & Glantz (2003) provide a detailed description of the coupling principal component analysis with a GARCH volatility model to estimate a short-term covariance matrix.

Estimated covariance can be written as $\hat{\sigma}_{xy} = \rho_{xy}\hat{\sigma}_x\hat{\sigma}_y$. Therefore, a short-term covariance matrix $\hat{C}$ can be computed from Φ above as follows:

$$\hat{C} = \begin{pmatrix} \hat{\sigma}_1^2 & \rho_{12}\hat{\sigma}_1\hat{\sigma}_2 & \cdots & \rho_{1n}\hat{\sigma}_1\hat{\sigma}_n \\ \rho_{21}\hat{\sigma}_2\hat{\sigma}_1 & \sigma_2^2 & \cdots & \rho_{2n}\hat{\sigma}_2\hat{\sigma}_n \\ \vdots & \vdots & \ddots & \vdots \\ \rho_{1n}\hat{\sigma}_n\hat{\sigma}_1 & \rho_{2n}\hat{\sigma}_n\hat{\sigma}_2 & \cdots & \sigma_n^2 \end{pmatrix}$$

$$= \begin{pmatrix} \hat{\sigma}_1 & 0 & \cdots & 0 \\ 0 & \hat{\sigma}_2 & \cdots & 0 \\ \vdots & \vdots & \ddots & \vdots \\ 0 & 0 & \cdots & \hat{\sigma}_n \end{pmatrix} \begin{pmatrix} 1 & \rho_{12} & \cdots & \rho_{1n} \\ \rho_{21} & 1 & \cdots & \rho_{2n} \\ \vdots & \vdots & \ddots & \vdots \\ \rho_{n2} & \rho_{2n} & \cdots & 1 \end{pmatrix} \begin{pmatrix} \hat{\sigma}_1 & 0 & \cdots & 0 \\ 0 & \hat{\sigma}_2 & \cdots & 0 \\ \vdots & \vdots & \ddots & \vdots \\ 0 & 0 & \cdots & \hat{\sigma}_n \end{pmatrix} \quad (5.51)$$

or more simply as,

$$\hat{C} = \hat{D}\Phi\hat{D} \quad (5.52)$$

where D is a diagonal matrix of forecasted short-term volatility.

Finally, a short-term covariance estimate $\hat{C}$ can be derived from a multifactor model and adjusting for short-term volatility as follows:

$$\hat{C} = \hat{D}\Phi\hat{D} = \hat{D}(D^{-1/2}(B'\Omega B + \Lambda)D^{-1/2})\hat{D} \quad (5.53)$$

CHAPTER EXERCISES

1. Describe the relationship between covariance and correlation. If 2 reference credits have a default correlation coefficient of +0.7, do we expect the likelihood of both defaulting to be greater or lesser than if the default correlation is −0.7?

2. What is the main challenge an institution might face in attempting to estimate covariances? What alternatives exist?

3. Explain the steps involved in computing expected credit losses.

4. Describe the differences between systematic and idiosyncratic risks.

5. What result does a macroeconomic factor model attempt to produce? What advantages and disadvantages characterize this approach?

6. In what ways is a cross-sectional model different from other multifactor models?

A Basic Credit Default Swap Model

INTRODUCTION

Calculating the price of default risk and, by extension, the value of credit derivative instruments is a complex task that relies on various assumptions about mathematical models and market behavior. We have noted in the last chapter some of the essential tools required for financial modeling. In this chapter we review basic approaches to modeling default swaps and introduce a model to demonstrate practical application. Although the model, which uses historical and implied default probabilities to generate a pricing estimate, is simplified, it provides an intuitive guide to considering the evaluation of default risk. Chapters that follow propose alternative approaches.

PRACTICAL PRICING CONSIDERATIONS

We begin our discussion on practical pricing issues by considering a basic example related to the valuation of a CDS. Assume Bank X is scheduled to receive a payment of $650,000 from Company A one year from now. Because Bank X is concerned about Company A's credit quality, it wants to buy credit protection from Dealer Y. Dealer Y estimates there is a 2.5% probability that Company A will default in the next year, and therefore a 2.5% chance that it will have to make a payment to Bank X; it also estimates that recoveries in the event of default will equal 30% of face value, or $195,000.

There is thus a 2.5% probability that Dealer Y will be required to pay Bank X $455,000 ($650,000 − $195,000); Y therefore estimates that the fair value of the CDS is $11,375 ($455,000 * 2.5%).

These calculations are easy to perform but rely on assumptions that may or may not represent market realities. For instance, in order to derive a realistic value of the CDS's expected value, we must determine whether the assumed default probability (2.5%) and recovery rate (30%) are reasonably accurate, and whether there is any meaningful joint default probability between the reference credit (Company A) and the protection seller (Dealer Y). Slight variations in these factors can be enough to change the value by a reasonable amount. For instance, if the default probability increases to 3.5% and the recovery rate declines to 20%, the fair value rises by nearly $7,000, to $18,200. Participants in the credit derivative market must ultimately establish their own comfort levels regarding these types of assumptions, and then implement a model that is consistent with that view. As in all modeling exercises, a balance may be required between analytical tractability and precision.

The two key inputs in the example above are default probabilities and recovery rates. Default probabilities are the single most important input into any credit derivative pricing model. Proxies can be obtained from various sources, including historical rating agency data, factor models, and market prices. Default probabilities from rating agencies such as Moody's, S&P's, and FitchIBCA are widely used; these provide useful and convenient estimates of default as they are built atop historical data and current financial analysis; they are not, however, market variables and are not available for all companies quoted in the credit derivative market. In addition, rating actions can sometimes lag current events (reacting to, rather than anticipating, financial difficulties) and may therefore not be the most accurate reflection of current default probabilities. Default probabilities can also be obtained by examining the default levels implied by market-traded contracts, or the relation of equity prices to a firm's capital structure. These, too, have benefits and shortcomings of their own, as noted below. Recovery rates are vital to default modeling as well. These can again be sourced from the rating agencies, which compile statistics related to recoveries by region and seniority class. Such estimates, however, are relatively static and may be insufficiently granular. Other approaches are more dynamic, making use of stochastically determined recovery rates. Valuation must also take into account the probability that the reference credit and default protection seller will default at the same time, e.g., when the protection buyer's contract has value. Some approaches assign a nil or low probability to this joint occurrence, essentially assuming a lack of correlation between default by the reference entity and the CDS protection seller. This is often regarded as a reasonable working assumption, as CDS sellers are generally of investment-grade quality. However, any assumptions to the contrary require that the model be adjusted to reflect the possibility that the protection seller may default when the reference credit defaults (i.e., when the derivative contract is in-the-money to the buyer).

GENERAL REVIEW OF PRICING APPROACHES

Credit derivative valuation is still largely a combination of historical and market-based processes, and fair value estimates can vary by some degree. Ultimately, however, those active in the market do not require complete precision; reasonable estimates of value are often sufficient. Various types of models are used to estimate default contract values, including:

- Option-based models
- Ratings-based models
- Credit spread models
- Expected default frequency models
- Replication models

These may be supplemented by a review of traded market references, primarily as a benchmarking mechanism.

Option-Based Models

The seminal work by Merton (1974) and Black and Scholes (1973) forms the basis of option-based, or structural, credit derivative pricing models. Such "Merton-style" models determine default probabilities from measures of firm value. For instance, it is assumed that creditors possess contingent claims on an obligor's assets, and seniority and bankruptcy rules determine the order in which creditors are repaid. Loan values are obtained by modeling the dynamics of an obligor's underlying value and default events, and default probabilities are derived through specified default triggers (i.e., a state of insolvency, where asset value is less than liability value). In fact, corporate liabilities can be viewed as combinations of options, meaning that the Black Scholes formula can be employed; in particular, the option pricing formula determines the discount applicable to a corporate bond attributable to the possibility of default. Others have proposed alterations to this basic framework to deal with the specific details of different forms of debt.[1]

To circumvent some of the problems encountered in complex structural-form modeling, reduced-form, or intensity-based, modeling has also developed. Using default probabilities, recovery rates, and risk-free interest rates,[2] the framework suggests that default probabilities and recovery rates jointly determine risky yield spreads over a risk-free interest rate benchmark. Default intensity can be derived from transition matrixes, either deterministically or stochastically; the first method relies on data from rating agencies, with matrixes reflecting macroeconomic cycles and industrial performance,[3] while the second method requires specification of the default process (e.g., deterministic, Gaussian, or mean reverting).[4]

---

1 For instance, Ingersoll (1987) proposed extensions to the basic model, allowing for coupon-bearing bonds, subordinated bonds, convertibles, and stochastic interest rates. Brennan and Schwartz (1980), Leland (1994), Leland and Toft (1996), Hull and White (1995), and Longstaff and Schwartz (1995) have also added to the body of academic work.

2 The first issue to overcome in reduced form models is risk-free modeling of interest rates. Equilibrium models and the no-arbitrage models represent two broad families of models. In the first family, we mention models by Vasicek and Cox, Ingersoll, Ross (CIR). The second family of models, the no-arbitrage class, includes those by Ho and Lee and Hull and White. Within the no-arbitrage model sector we also have two factor models such as Heath, Jarrow, and Morton (HJM) and the LIBOR Market Model. These models can be adapted to incorporate default features while keeping the same structure and type of solutions.

3 Jarrow, Lando and Turnbull (1997) is an example of this approach to modeling.

4 The first model to consider stochastic default intensities was proposed by Madan and Unal (1998). Duffie (1999) models interest rates and intensities of default as CIR two-factor processes, allowing for correlation between the processes. Houweling and Vorst (2002) have implemented a simplified model in the spirit of Duffie and Singleton (1999); they also provide a detailed analysis of the implications of choosing between treasury, swap, and repo rates. Finally, a model proposed by Hull and White (2000) simplifies the specification of the variables of the reduced-type model framework. They consider default intensities, interest rates, and recovery rates to be independent and rely on default probability densities rather than the default intensity directly.

Ratings-Based Default Probability Models

Ratings-based default probability models rely on published ratings and default loss data to estimate a reference credit's probability of default; this data may be supplemented by assumptions about recovery rates. Some models base recovery rates on fixed percentages related to industry or obligor credit ratings or level of seniority/subordination, while others employ stochastic processes. A general advantage of ratings-based default probability pricing models is that they are not overly data intensive, relying primarily on aggregate statistics. Such generalizations can, however, limit their ability to introduce specific details about a particular issuer, and may therefore not be sufficiently precise.

Credit Spread Models

Credit spread models track an issuer's credit spreads by maturity and time to establish a term-structure of credit risk. Credit spreads assume that the risk premium over a risk-free benchmark is attributable primarily to default risk. The reference issuer owns an implied (put) option to default, the value of which is contained in the credit spread. Once the term structure is established, it can be used to estimate the issuer's default probability over a specific term. One of the advantages of this approach is that it permits use of issuer-specific data, suggesting a greater degree of precision. However, factors apart from pure default can affect the value of the credit spread (e.g., asset liquidity, investor sentiment, industry or competitor difficulties) and a full-term structure of credit spreads is not typically available for most issuers (e.g., a company might only feature three tranches of public debt, requiring interpolation to create a more meaningful term structure).

Expected Default Frequency Models

The expected default frequency (EDF) model, such as the one developed by Moody's KMV (which we discuss at greater length in the next chapter), is based on the assumption that a company defaults when its liabilities exceed the real value of its assets; this is akin to the Merton-style trigger condition. Equity prices are used as a proxy indicator of default probabilities; however, multiple factors can influence equity prices, suggesting that default probabilities may be skewed unless adjustments are made.

Replication (Cost of Funds) Models

Replication/cost-of-funds models use credit derivative hedging costs to generate a pricing baseline. The dealer, using the default probability method of its choice, determines default ratings related to assets it needs to hedge (e.g., if a dealer uses a TRS, the spread (margin) required on the swap is used as the base). When hedges are constructed, the blend of hedge costs and the dealer's required return establish the price of the credit derivative contract. Problems with this method arise when robust hedges are not available or costs associated with constructing hedges are excessive.

Traded Market References

When the credit derivative market ultimately becomes more liquid, market default instruments should provide supplemental valuation/benchmarking points. In a process analogous to the extraction of implied volatilities from the vanilla options market, the price of simple default instruments may provide a market estimate of the perceived or implied likelihood of default.

Most public bonds and widely syndicated loans enjoy a recognized market with readily available quotations, suggesting some ability to obtain market-based default information. However, an active, transparent market does not exist for all loans or privately placed debt issues at all times. In addition, comparables may not always be perfect—events of default may differ along with terms, tenors, and credit structures (senior versus subordinated, secured versus unsecured). Due caution is therefore necessary. The same is true for credit derivatives; while market quotes exist for many references, the lack of a specific quote for a given maturity/structure means pricing must be driven by an examination of related instruments and the general credit profile of the reference entity. Ultimately, traded market references must be viewed as a pricing supplement rather than substitute. End-users relying solely on quotations from dealers or calculation agents active in the credit derivative market are relying on the valuation models of third parties. This is hardly satisfactory from a control perspective. From a strict governance viewpoint, using traded market references from the marketplace at large must be regarded as ancillary information.

A BASIC CREDIT DEFAULT SWAP MODEL

Valuing credit derivatives is a complex process that requires that certain assumptions be made prior to implementation; indeed, selection of any of the approaches summarized above implies that an institution is making assumptions about which valuation process/drivers it believes are most suitable. Model specification is thus an involved project. However, the essence of a credit derivative pricing process can be simplified in order to illustrate the salient points. Our goal in this section is to introduce a basic CDS model to demonstrate the development of a workable framework. Though the model is based on generalizations, it provides a starting point related to default probability and recovery rates and how these can impact credit derivative prices.

We know that a standard CDS provides the protection buyer with a compensatory payment if a reference asset is impacted by a credit event. CDS pricing is typically based on a reference asset's credit spread over a floating-rate benchmark (e.g., LIBOR or EURIBOR); the spread reflects the market's assessment of default probability, when default might occur, and what amount is likely to be recovered on the outstanding debt after the company's assets have been liquidated.

The pricing approach can be considered in two ways:

- Establishing the current probability that the reference credit will default during the chosen exposure period; the default probability will vary by tenor, i.e., the longer the tenor, the greater the default probability.
- Hypothesizing that the market price of the CDS reflects the true price of the reference entity's credit and that the default probability implied in this price is correct.

An estimate of the recovery rate is required in either case. If we find that the credit derivative market is truly arbitrage free, however, the two approaches should yield the same result.

Sources for Probabilities of Default and Recovery Rates

As we have noted, the rating agencies compile historical data on defaults and recovery rates. It is important to stress, once again, that the data is in macro form, so it does not relate to individual

T A B L E 6.1

Standard and Poor's Default Rates

%	Yr1	2	3	4	5	6	7	8	9	10
AAA	0.00	0.00	0.03	0.06	0.10	0.18	0.26	0.40	0.45	0.51
AA	0.01	0.04	0.09	0.16	0.25	0.37	0.53	0.63	0.70	0.79
A	0.04	0.11	0.19	0.32	0.49	0.65	0.83	1.01	1.21	1.41
BBB	0.22	0.50	0.79	1.30	1.80	2.29	2.73	3.10	3.39	3.68
BB	0.98	2.97	5.35	7.44	9.22	11.11	12.27	13.35	14.29	15.00
B	5.30	11.28	15.88	19.10	21.44	23.20	24.77	26.01	26.99	27.88
CCC	21.94	29.25	34.37	38.24	42.13	43.62	44.40	44.82	45.74	46.53
InvG	0.08	0.19	0.31	0.51	0.72	0.95	1.17	1.37	1.54	1.71
SpecG	4.14	8.34	11.93	14.67	16.84	18.64	19.98	21.09	22.05	22.85

Source: Standard and Poor's

credits (individually rated credits can, of course, be evaluated using their own ratings). Tables 6.1 and 6.2 provide illustrative data on S&P's default probabilities and Moody's weighted average recovery rates (European sample). The information in the two tables can be used to help construct the basic model.

For our purposes we extract a set of probabilities for a BBB borrower and incorporate them into Table 6.3, along with standard discount factors for a yield curve in order to generate the present value of future cash flows that comprise today's fair price. Table 6.3 also includes the probability of survival, which we define as (1 − probability of default); this means that the probability of survival and the probability of default should equal 1 for any single

T A B L E 6.2

Moody's European Recovery Rates

Secured bank loans	47.6%
Senior secured bonds	48.3%
Senior unsecured bonds	18.2%
Senior subordinated bonds	24.3%
Subordinated bonds	7.8%

Source: Moody's Investors Services

T A B L E 6.3

Yield Curve and BBB Default and Survival Probabilities

Period	Years	Futures/Swap Prices	Discount Factors	Probability of Default	Probability of Survival
1	0.5	2.81	0.9861	0.0022	0.9978
2	1	3.16	0.9694	0.0050	0.9928
3	1.5	3.41	0.9505	0.0079	0.9849
4	2	3.71	0.9289	0.0130	0.9719
5	2.5	3.99	0.9054	0.0180	0.9539
6	3	4.31	0.8789	0.0229	0.9310
7	3.5	4.66	0.8493	0.0273	0.9037
8	4	5.01	0.8175	0.0310	0.8727
9	4.5	5.16	0.7916	0.0339	0.8388
10	5	5.31	0.7652	0.0368	0.8020

period. Thus, a 10% probability of default implies a 90% probability of survival, a 20% probability of default implies an 80% probability of survival, and so on. However, as we develop default and survival probabilities for multiple periods, we must take account of a cumulative effect. The S&P probability statistics in the table reflect cumulative default rates, which increase as time passes; this means that the probability of survival decreases with time. For instance, in period 1 survival is simply (1 − probability of default in period 1), or 0.0022—yielding a survival probability of 0.9978. The probability of survival in period 2 is 0.9978 − 0.0050, or 0.9928. This process is repeated for all survival probabilities up to period 10 (year 5).

Determining Probability of Default from Market Spreads

In order to develop the pricing model we need to determine the credit spread over the risk-free rate for a risky bond. The spread compensates the investor for accepting the probability that the credit may default; the higher the perceived probability of default, the higher the compensation demanded by the investor and the higher the resulting spread. We can extract this implied probability of default from the quoted market spread.

The future value (FV) of a continuously compounded return on a risk-free investment over time can be expressed as:

$$e^{\,rate * time}$$

where e is the natural logarithm.

For example, the FV of $1 invested for 5 years at a continuously compounded rate of 5% is:

$$= \exp[(0.05*5)] = \$1.284025$$

The present value (PV) of a cash flow can be computed by using the negative exponential. For instance, the PV of $1 to be received in 5 years at a 5% continuously compounded rate is:

$$= \exp[(-0.05*5)] = \$0.778801$$

We know that the return for a risky bond must also include the credit spread, so we expand the equation as follows:

$$e^{\,(rate + spread) * time}$$

Assuming that the credit spread over the risk-free rate for this bond is 50 bps, the FV is:

$$= \exp[(0.05 + 0.0050) * 5)] = \$1.316531$$

If the spread of 50 bps truly compensates the investor for accepting the associated probability of default, then the return on the risk-free bond should equal the return on the risky bond, adjusted for the probability of default (PD), in a no-arbitrage market. We can express this as follows:

$$e^{\,rate * time} = e^{\,(rate + spread) * time} * (1 - PD) \qquad (6.1)$$

If this equation holds true, then we can rearrange terms and solve for the probability of default, PD:

$$PD = (1 - e^{\,(-spread * time)}) \qquad (6.2)$$

Using our previous example, the cumulative 3-year probability of default for a reference with a credit spread of 50 bps is:

$$PD = (1 - e^{\,(-0.005 * 3)}) = 1.49\%$$

This calculation can be performed for all maturity combinations. For example, the cumulative default probability in year 2 (using 50 bps) is 0.995%. Similarly, the default probability from year

2 to 3 is the difference between the two cumulative probabilities: $1.49\% - 0.995\% = 0.495\%$.

When calculating these figures we must remember that there is a term structure of credit spreads. For most reference credits, the further out in time we go, the greater the probability of default and the greater the credit spread; the term structure is said to be positive. There is, however, one exception to this rule: CCC-rated credits tend to feature a negative term structure, as there is a perception that while such credits may default in the near term, they may actually survive for the long term if they overcome short-term difficulties (such as a liquidity crisis). Table 6.4 illustrates this phenomenon.

We have described how the probability of default can be determined, but our calculations have not yet considered recovery rates. We therefore return to our original equation and consider how recoveries can impact value.

Probability of Default and Recoveries

When a credit defaults, we know that there is a strong likelihood that creditors will receive some recovery value after the defaulting company's assets are liquidated; only in the most severe insolvencies, based on extreme asset overvaluation, might recoveries be close to zero. Our original equation above assumes no recoveries, meaning that any capital invested would be completely lost in the

T A B L E 6.4

Credit Interest Rate Term Structure

Yr	Risk-Free Rate	AAA Rates	AAA Spread	A Rates	A Spread	CCC Rates	CCC Spread
1	2.80	3.05	0.25	3.25	0.45	10.55	7.75
2	3.15	3.45	0.30	3.70	0.55	9.50	6.35
3	3.40	3.75	0.35	4.05	0.65	9.00	5.60
4	3.70	4.10	0.40	4.45	0.75	8.20	4.50
5	3.98	4.43	0.45	4.73	0.75	7.90	3.92
6	4.30	4.80	0.50	5.15	0.85	7.70	3.40
7	4.65	5.20	0.55	5.55	0.90	7.50	2.85
8	5.00	5.60	0.60	6.00	1.00	7.40	2.40
9	5.15	5.80	0.65	6.25	1.10	7.30	2.15
10	5.30	6.00	0.70	6.55	1.25	7.20	1.90

event of default; this assumption must therefore be adjusted to reflect greater market consistency. By incorporating the recovery rate RR, any loss can be described as (1 – RR). The adjusted formula indicates that the probability of default is the PV of the credit spread extended to reflect recoveries.

$$PD = \frac{(1 - e^{(-spread * time)})}{1 - RR} \tag{6.3}$$

We illustrate how this formula works by using a 3-year spread of 50 bps and an assumed recovery rate of 50%.

$$PD = \frac{(1 - e^{(-0.0050*3)})}{1 - 0.50} = 2.98\%$$

The formula generates an adjusted 3-year cumulative probability of default of 2.98%, higher than the 1.49% calculated earlier when recoveries were assumed to be zero. Note that if we had used a credit spread of 25 basis points and a recovery rate of 50%, we would again have generated a 1.49% probability of default. Thus, if using a 50% recovery rate still requires a 50 bp spread to compensate for the default risk, it follows that the probability of default must be higher. This simple example shows the close relationship between market credit spreads, default probabilities, and recovery rates.

Default and Survival Probabilities

We noted earlier that the probabilities of survival and default for a particular period must always equal 1. There is, however, a conditional aspect in credit derivatives pricing that must be considered. The probability of default in some future period exists only if the credit has not defaulted by the end of the previous period. This means that the probability of survival up to a particular future point *plus* the sum of the probability of defaults to that point must equal 1. We extend Table 6.3 by including a total for the probability of default column; this yields the results in Table 6.5. Looking at the 10-year period we note that if we sum the default probabilities we obtain a total of 0.1980. Adding this to the 10-year probability of survival (0.8020) yields a total of 1. The probability of survival to a specific point is a key factor in assessing the value of the CDS premium.

T A B L E   6.5

Yield Curve and BBB Default and Survival Probabilities

Period	Years	Futures/Swap Prices	Discount Factors	Probability of Default	Probability of Survival
1	0.5	2.81	0.9861	0.0022	0.9978
2	1	3.16	0.9694	0.0050	0.9928
3	1.5	3.41	0.9505	0.0079	0.9849
4	2	3.71	0.9289	0.0130	0.9719
5	2.5	3.99	0.9054	0.0180	0.9539
6	3	4.31	08789	0.0229	0.9310
7	3.5	4.66	0.8493	0.0273	0.9037
8	4	5.01	0.8175	0.0310	0.8727
9	4.5	5.16	0.7916	0.0339	0.8388
10	5	5.31	0.7652	0.0368	0.8020
				Total = 0.1980	

Present Value of the CDS Premiums

Our next step is to calculate the present value of the CDS premium stream to assess whether compensation for default risk is adequate.

The PV of the spread for the first period is given as:

= CDS Spread * Discount Factor * Probability of Survival
to end of period 1 * (actual days/basis for period 1).

We are attempting to determine the PV of the CDS spread which, when calculated, will be the same for all periods in a given maturity. The discount factor is simply the zero coupon interest rate required to bring the future cash flow to today's value. The probability of survival is applied to the future period, as this indicates the probability of actually receiving the premium in the future. The day count for the period in question is applied to adjust the value. To simplify this process we assume that each semiannual period is exactly half a year (i.e., 0.5 years instead of actual/basis); the formula can, of course, be made more general.

Returning to our continuing example, the first period yields:

PV of CDS Payment, period 1
= CDS Spread * 0.9861 * 0.9978 * 0.5

The same calculation for period two is:

PV of CDS payment, period 2
= CDS Spread * 0.9694 * 0.9928 * 0.5

We can repeat this process for all 10 periods. Using S to denote the CDS spread and P to denote a single period, the sum of the PVs of all of the CDS spread payments is:

$$PV_{spread} = S \sum_{P=1} DF_P * PS_P * 0.5 \qquad (6.4)$$

This produces the PV of all of the CDS spreads received or paid during the life of the transaction, assuming no default, and represents the denominator in the CDS pricing formula described below.

We next consider how to evaluate the PV of the cash flow stream assuming that default occurs.

Present Value of a Default Payment

If a default occurs at the beginning or end of a period, the CDS protection seller is only entitled to the CDS premiums up to that point. However, the seller of protection is entitled to receive the recovery value of the underlying asset. We can capture the PV of default payments in period 1 as:

PV of Default Payment
= (1 – Recovery) * Discount Factor for period 1
* Probability of Default in Period 1.

Assuming default and a recovery rate of 30%, the PV of the loss in period 1 is thus:

PV of Default Payment = (1 – 0.30) * 0.9861 * 0.0022

Using the discount factor and probability of default for period 2 yields:

PV of Default Payment = (1 – 0.30) * 0.9694 * 0.0050

Summing these gives us the PV of the possible default payments. Using RR as the assumed recovery rate, we can summarize the process as:

$$PV_{default} = (1 - RR) \sum_{P=1} DF_P * PD_P \qquad (6.5)$$

This equation forms the numerator in the total pricing equation below.

Calculating the CDS Spread Premium

We now have an equation that computes the PV of the CDS spread premiums and an equation that gives us the PV of any possible default payment. The value of a CDS at inception is based on equal pay/receive flows between the two counterparties; this is consistent with standard swap convention. The two equations developed above should, therefore, be equal to one another if the transaction is priced fairly:

$$PV_{spread} = PV_{default}, \text{ or}$$

$$S\sum_{P=1} DF_P * PS_P * 0.5 = (1 - RR)\sum_{P=1} DF_P * PD_P \qquad (6.6)$$

This equation can now be simplified and rearranged in order to solve for the CDS spread S:

$$S = \frac{(1 - RR)\sum_{P=1} DF_P * PD_P}{\sum_{P=1} DF_P * PS_P * 0.5} \qquad (6.7)$$

The calculation can be performed for each period. We can then add the PVs to determine the CDS premium for this transaction; the results are given in Table 6.6.

The formula we have developed gives us calculated CDS premiums for different maturities. Given the parameters and assumptions, a 6-month CDS would feature a premium of 0.31%, while a 5-year CDS would command a premium of 2.83%. Let's examine the 2-year (4-period) CDS price in more detail:

First, the period 4 (year 2) denominator is calculated:

= (0.9289 * 0.9719 * 0.5) + 1.441233
  (the sum of the calculations to period 3) = 1.892614

Next, the period 4 numerator is computed:

= ((1 − 0.30) * 0.9719 * 0.0130) + 0.010167
  (the sum of the calculations to period 3) = 0.018620

T A B L E 6.6

Complete CDS Premium Pricing

Period	Years	Futures/ Swap Prices	Discount Factors	Probability of Default	Probability of Survival	Denominator (eq 6.4)	Numerator (eq 6.5)	CDS Price
1	0.5	2.81	0.9861	0.0022	0.9978	0.491988	0.001519	0.0031
2	1	3.16	0.9694	0.0050	0.9928	0.973182	0.004911	0.0050
3	1.5	3.41	0.9505	0.0079	0.9849	1.441233	0.010167	0.0071
4	2	3.71	0.9289	0.0130	0.9719	1.892614	0.018620	0.0098
5	2.5	3.99	0.9054	0.0180	0.9539	2.324460	0.030029	0.0129
6	3	4.31	08789	0.0229	0.9310	2.733591	0.044117	0.0161
7	3.5	4.66	0.8493	0.0273	0.9037	3.117340	0.060347	0.0194
8	4	5.01	0.8175	0.0310	0.8727	3.474051	0.078087	0.0225
9	4.5	5.16	0.7916	0.0339	0.8388	3.806048	0.096871	0.0255
10	5	5.31	0.7652	0.0368	0.8020	4.112904	0.116584	0.0283

Finally, the CDS premium S is obtained:

$$= 0.018620/1.892614 = 0.98\%$$

This corresponds to the result contained in the table.

Other Considerations

The process described above gives us a straightforward way of calculating CDS premiums from default probabilities. The calculation relies heavily on data input, and we have already discussed the difficulty of accurately forecasting default probabilities and recovery rates; these are sensitive assumptions that can impact significantly on model accuracy. The CDS premiums quoted in the market reflect assumptions, and the bid-offer spread for a particular entity and maturity reflects the market's current evaluation of the assumptions. It is possible, of course, to use market CDS prices and adjust the probabilities to reflect the market's actual CDS premiums; doing so assumes that the recovery rate used by the market is the same as the one used in the model.

An institution believing that its proprietary assessments of recovery rates and default probabilities are more accurate than those contained in the market can take a position based on that belief. Higher expected recovery rates or lower default probabilities would encourage the institution to sell protection at a higher market rate than might otherwise be justifiable. Similarly, an assessment that the market has underestimated the probability of default or overestimated the recovery rate would encourage the purchase of protection at the lower market rate.[5]

To reiterate, any method used to price a CDS premium is only as good as the assessment of the probability of default over a specific period and the accuracy of the recovery rate. Most efforts by market makers to improve their pricing process concentrate on refining these two factors.

---

5 Commercial products such as CreditMetrics and CreditRisk supply market participants with a ready-made application to manage the pricing factors discussed above. However, it appears that the application of products such as these has been somewhat limited and that the main driver of CDS premiums is still derived from the pricing of bonds in the capital markets.

Period	Years	Futures/ Swap Prices	Discount Factors	Probability of Default	Probability of Survival	Denominator	Numerator	CDS Price
1	0.5	2.81	0.9861			0.491642	0.001716	0.0035
2	1	3.16	0.9694			0.971916	0.005322	0.0055
3	1.5	3.41	0.9505			1.437638	0.011538	0.0080
4	2	3.71	0.9289			1.885861	0.019842	0.0105
5	2.5	3.99	0.9054			2.313134	0.031413	0.0136
6	3	4.31	08789			2.717827	0.043490	0.0160
7	3.5	4.66	0.8493			3.094867	0.060305	0.0195
8	4	5.01	0.8175			3.436945	0.085320	0.0248
9	4.5	5.16	0.7916			3.744046	0.114293	0.0305
10	5	5.31	0.7652			4.012601	0.148269	0.0370

CHAPTER EXERCISES

1. Using the framework developed above, and assuming both a recovery rate of 40% and the same interest rate structure for both the market and the model, establish the probabilities of default and survival from the market CDS prices shown below.

Recovery rate = 40%.

Period	Years	Market Rates
1	0.5	0.0035
2	1	0.0055
3	1.5	0.0080
4	2	0.0105
5	2.5	0.0136
6	3	0.0160
7	3.5	0.0195
8	4	0.0248
9	4.5	0.0305
10	5	0.0370

2. If the recovery rate were 45% rather than 40%, would an institution buy or sell protection at the CDS prices indicated above? Why?
3. Why should a traded market reference approach to modeling not be regarded as a sufficient form of pricing?
4. Why is the term structure of credit spreads not always upward sloping?
5. Given a 75 bp credit spread, a 4% risk-free rate, and a 3-year time horizon, what is the future value of $1 on a continuously compounded basis? What is the implied probability of default assuming the same market data?

Modeling Credit Default Risk

By Jeffrey Bohn[1]

INTRODUCTION

The value of a credit default swap (CDS) written on a particular firm is primarily driven by the probability of that firm's default and the recovery in the event of that firm's default. Default is a deceptively rare event. The typical firm has a default probability of approximately 2% in any given year. The variation across firms, however, can be quite large. In particular, the range of possible default probabilities (typically 2 basis points to 2,000 basis points) is much larger than the range of possible recoveries (typically 30% to 70%). Viewed from a different perspective, a completely incorrect estimate of recovery may only be off by a factor of 2, whereas a completely incorrect estimate of default probability may be off by a factor of 1,000. Many of the more recent CDS contracts define a specific recovery amount eliminating most of the uncertainty in what will be recovered upon the underlying defaulting. Consequently, the bulk of estimation effort should be focused on producing accurate default probabilities.

Given the increasing liquidity in various credit markets, a number of approaches have become feasible for estimating default probability. This chapter outlines one approach using equity prices for the firm on which a CDS is written. This method relies on a structural model relating equity value to the underlying asset value of the firm issuing the equity. In this way, an independent estimate of a firm's default probability can be compared to the spreads observed in the CDS market. Because the default probability estimated from the equity market is an actual probability (sometimes called a physical probability), it can be used in conjunction with a valuation model describing CDS spreads to determine an implicit market price of credit risk reflected in the CDS market.

A CDS spread can be considered a function of the actual default probability adjusted by the market price of credit risk (i.e., the risk premium demanded by investors to compensate for the uncertainty associated with the CDS cash flows) and the expected recovery given default (also adjusted by a risk premium if the expected recovery is uncertain). We call these adjusted values risk neutral (see Bohn, 2000 for more detail on risk-neutral probabilities in the context of structural credit risk modeling). This chapter describes how to estimate and use default probabilities estimated from the equity market.

MEASURING DEFAULT PROBABILITY: THE PROBLEM

Three main elements determine the default probability of a firm:

- Value of Assets: the *market value* of the firm's assets. This is a measure of the present value of the future free cash flows produced by the firm's assets discounted back at the appropriate discount rate. This measures the firm's prospects and incorporates relevant information about the firm's industry and the economy.
- Asset Risk: the *uncertainty or risk* of the asset value. This is a measure of the firm's business and industry risk. The value of the firm's assets is an estimate and is thus uncertain. As a result, the value of the firm's assets should always be understood in the context of the firm's business or asset risk.
- Leverage: the extent of the firm's contractual liabilities. Whereas the relevant measure of the firm's assets is always its market value, the book value of liabilities relative to the market value of assets is the pertinent measure of the firm's leverage, because that is the amount the firm must repay.

F I G U R E   7.1

Winstar Communications

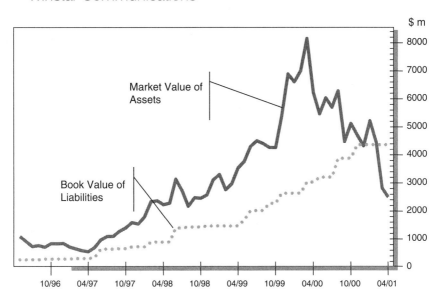

For example, Figure 7.1 illustrates the evolution of the asset value and book liabilities of Winstar Communications, a New York Telephone company that filed for Chapter 11 bankruptcy protection in April 2001.

The default risk of the firm increases as the value of the assets approaches the book value of the liabilities, until finally the firm defaults when the market value of the assets is insufficient to repay the firm's liabilities.

Research at MKMV[2] has demonstrated that, in general, firms do not default when their asset value reaches the book value of

---

2 Moody's KMV (MKMV), a wholly owned subsidiary of Moody's Corporation, is the world's leading provider of quantitative credit risk analysis tools to lenders, investors, and corporations. MKMV's tools provide current default probabilities, recovery estimates, valuations, and correlations, and are widely used to assess portfolio risk/return. Serving over 2,000 clients in 80 countries, including most of the world's 100 largest financial institutions, MKMV maintains the largest database of corporate defaults in the world. In addition to its San Francisco headquarters, MKMV has offices around the world to serve its global customer base. MKMV research publications are available at www.moodyskmv.com.

their total liabilities. While some firms certainly default at this point, many continue to trade and service their debts. The long-term nature of some of their liabilities provides these firms with some breathing space. We have found that the default point, the asset value at which the firm will default, generally lies somewhere between total liabilities and current, or short-term, liabilities.

The relevant net worth of a firm is therefore the market value of the firm's assets minus the firm's default point:

$$\begin{bmatrix} \text{Market Value} \\ \text{of Assets} \end{bmatrix} - \begin{bmatrix} \text{Default} \\ \text{Point} \end{bmatrix}$$

A firm will default when its market net worth reaches zero.

Like the firm's asset value, the market measure of net worth must be considered in the context of the firm's business risk. For example, firms in the food and beverage industries can afford higher levels of leverage (lower market net worth) than high-technology businesses because their businesses, and consequently their asset values, are more stable and less uncertain.

For example, Figure 7.2 shows the evolution of asset values and default points for Compaq Computer and Anheuser-Busch. Figure 7.3 shows the corresponding evolution of the annual default probabilities. The default probabilities shown in this figure are the one-year default rates, the probability that the firm will default in the ensuing year, and are displayed on a logarithmic scale.

The effect of the relative business risks of the two firms is clear from a comparison of the two figures. For instance, as of April 2001, the relative market values, default points, asset risks, and resulting default probabilities for Compaq and Anheuser-Busch are given in Table 7.1.

The asset risk is measured by the asset volatility, the standard deviation of the annual percentage change in the asset value. For example, Anheuser-Busch's business risk is 21%, which means that a one-standard-deviation move in their asset value will add (or remove) $9 billion from its asset value of $44.1 billion. In contrast, a one-standard-deviation move in the asset value of Compaq Computer will add or remove $16.5 billion from its asset value of $42.3 billion. The difference in their default probabilities is thus driven by the difference in the risks of their businesses, not their respective asset values or leverages.

F I G U R E   7.2

Compaq Computer and Anheuser-Busch: Asset Values
and Default Points

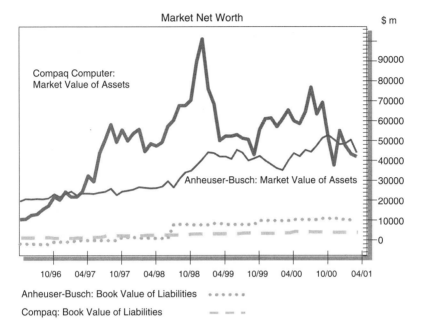

Anheuser-Busch: Book Value of Liabilities   • • • • • •

Compaq: Book Value of Liabilities   ▬ ▬ ▬

As you would expect, asset volatility is related to the size and nature of the firm's business. For example, Figure 7.4 shows the asset volatility for several industries and asset sizes.

Asset volatility is related to, but different from, equity volatility. A firm's leverage has the effect of magnifying its underlying asset volatility. As a result, industries with low asset volatility (for example, banking) tend to take on larger amounts of leverage, while industries with high asset volatility (for example, computer software) tend to take on less. Intuitively, a lender will be less likely to facilitate high levels of leverage for a company whose asset value is expected to move around to a great extent. As a consequence of these compensatory differences in leverage, equity volatility is far less differentiated by industry and asset size than is asset volatility.

Asset value, business risk, and leverage can be combined into a single measure of default risk that compares the market net worth to the size of a one-standard-deviation move in the asset

FIGURE 7.3

Compaq Computer and Anheuser-Busch: Annual Default
Probabilities

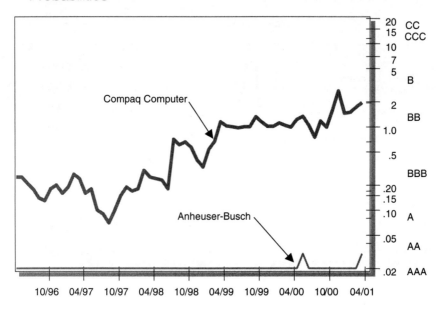

value. We refer to this ratio as the *distance-to-default*, which is conceptually calculated[3] as follows:

$$\begin{bmatrix} \text{Distance} \\ \text{to Default} \end{bmatrix} = \frac{\begin{bmatrix} \text{Market Value} \\ \text{of Assets} \end{bmatrix} - \begin{bmatrix} \text{Default} \\ \text{Point} \end{bmatrix}}{\begin{bmatrix} \text{Market Value} \\ \text{of Assets} \end{bmatrix}\begin{bmatrix} \text{Asset} \\ \text{Volatility} \end{bmatrix}}$$

For example, in April 2001 Anheuser-Busch was approximately 4.2
standard deviations away from default while, in contrast, Compaq

---

3 The actual formula is slightly different, with the Market Value of Assets (*A*) and Default
Point (*X*) transformed by the natural logarithm and only asset volatility (*σ*) as a percentage in the denominator. The firm's expected growth rate (*μ*) and dividends (*δ*) also enter
the actual formula as well as the square root of the time (*T*) over which the distance-to-
default is being calculated: $DD = \dfrac{\ln A_0 + \left(\mu - \dfrac{1}{2}\sigma^2\right)T - \delta - \ln X}{\sigma\sqrt{T}}$.

TABLE 7.1

Anheuser-Busch and Compaq Computer Statistics

	Anheuser-Busch	Compaq Computer
Market Value of Assets ($ billion)	44.1	42.3
Default Point	5.3	12.2
Market Net Worth ($ billion)	38.8	30.1
Asset Volatility	21%	39%
Default Probability (per annum)	.03%	1.97%

Computer was only 1.8 standard deviations away from default. That is, it would take a 4.2 standard deviation move in the asset value of Anheuser-Busch before it will default while only a 1.8 standard deviation move is required in Compaq's asset value to result in its default.

The distance-to-default measure combines three key credit issues: the value of the firm's assets, its business and industry risk, and its leverage. Moreover, the distance-to-default also incorporates, via the asset value and volatility, the effects of industry, geography, and firm size.

FIGURE 7.4

Asset Volatility Across Industries and Asset Sizes

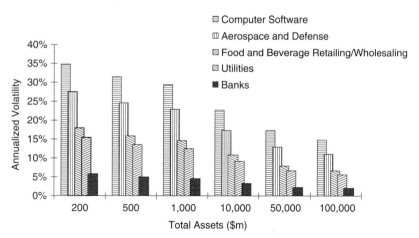

The default probability can be computed directly from the distance-to-default if the probability distribution of the assets is known, or, equivalently, if the default rate for a given level of distance-to-default is known.

MEASURING DEFAULT PROBABILITY: A PRACTICAL APPROACH

There are three basic types of information available that are relevant to the default probability of a firm: financial statements, market prices of the firm's debt and equity, and subjective appraisals of the firm's prospects and risk. Financial statements, by their nature, are inherently backward looking. They are reports of the past. Prices, by their nature, are inherently forward looking. Investors form debt and equity prices as they anticipate the firm's future. In determining the market prices, investors use, among many other things, subjective appraisals of the firm's prospects and risk, financial statements, and other market prices. This information is combined using their own analysis and synthesis, and results in their willingness to buy and sell the debt and equity securities of the firm. Market prices are the result of the combined willingness of many investors to buy and sell, and thus prices embody the synthesized views and forecasts of many investors.

The most effective default measurement, therefore, derives from models that use both market prices and financial statements. There is no assertion here that markets are perfectly efficient in this synthesis. We assert only that, in general, it is difficult to do a better job than the markets. That is, in general, it is very difficult to consistently beat the market. Consequently, where available, we want to use market prices in the determination of default risk because prices add considerably to the predictive power of the estimates.

Vasicek and Kealhofer have extended the Black-Scholes-Merton framework to produce a model of default probability known as the Vasicek-Kealhofer (VK) model. This model assumes the firm's equity is a perpetual option, with the default point acting as the absorbing barrier for the firm's asset value. When the asset value hits the default point, the firm is assumed to default. Multiple classes of liabilities are modeled: short-term liabilities, long-term liabilities, convertible debt, preferred equity, and common equity. When the firm's asset value becomes very large, the convertible securities are assumed to convert and dilute the existing equity. In addition, cash payouts such as dividends are explicitly used in the VK model. A default database is used to derive an empirical distribution relating the distance-to-default to a default probability. In this way, the relationship between asset value and liabilities can be captured without resorting to a substantially more complex model characterizing a firm's liability process.

MKMV has implemented the VK model to calculate an Expected Default Frequency™ (EDF™) credit measure, which is the probability of default during the forthcoming year, or years, for firms with publicly traded equity. (This model can also be modified to produce EDF values for firms without publicly traded equity.) The EDF value requires equity prices and certain items from financial statements as inputs. EDF credit measures can be viewed and analyzed within the context of a software product called CreditEdge™ (CE). On a daily basis, CE calculates EDF values for years 1 through 5 allowing the user to see a term structure of EDF values. MKMV's EDF credit measure assumes that *default* is defined as the nonpayment of any scheduled payment, interest, or principal. A more recent extension to CE called CreditEdge Plus facilitates analysis across multiple markets. A probability of default estimated from the equity market can be compared (in the context of a sophisticated valuation model) to the spreads observed in the CDS and corporate bond markets. In this way, users of CE Plus can determine how the different markets are reflecting a particular firm's default probability, expected recovery in the event of default, and the risk premium implicit in the market. These tools highlight the strength of structural models of default risk in that multiple market views on the same firm can be reconciled in the context of an economically meaningful model framework. The remainder of this section describes the procedure used by MKMV to determine a public firm's probability of default.

There are essentially three steps in the determination of the default probability of a firm:

- Estimate asset value and volatility: In this step, the asset value and asset volatility of the firm is estimated from the market value and volatility of equity, and the book value of liabilities.
- Calculate the distance-to-default: The distance-to-default (DD) is calculated from the asset value and asset volatility

(estimated in the first step), and the book value of liabilities.

- Calculate the default probability: The default probability is determined directly from the distance-to-default and the default rate for given levels of distance-to-default.

Estimate Asset Value and Volatility

If the market price of equity is available, the market value and volatility of assets can be determined directly using an options-pricing-based approach, which recognizes equity as a call option on the underlying assets of the firm. For example, consider a simplified case where there is only one class of debt and one class of equity, as in Figure 7.5.

The limited liability feature of equity means that the equity holders have the right, but not the obligation, to pay off the debt holders and take over the remaining assets of the firm. That is, the holders of the other liabilities of the firm essentially own the firm until those liabilities are paid off in full by the equity holders. Thus, in the simplest case, equity is the same as a call option on the firm's assets with a strike price equal to the book value of the firm's liabilities.

The VK model uses this option nature of equity to derive the underlying asset value and asset volatility implied by the market value, volatility of equity, and the book value of liabilities. This process is similar in spirit to the procedure used by option traders in the determination of the implied volatility of an option from the observed option price.

FIGURE 7.5

Simplified Balance Sheet

Assets	Liabilities
100	80
	Equity
	20

FIGURE 7.6

VK Model and the Option Framework

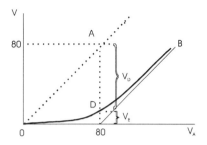

For example, assume that the firm is actually a type of levered mutual fund or unit trust. The assets of the firm are equity securities and thus can be valued at any time by observing their market prices. Further, assume that our little firm is to be wound up after five years and that we can ignore the time value of money (discounting adds little to our understanding of the relationships and serves only to complicate the picture). That is, in five years time, the assets will be sold and the proceeds divided between the debt and equity holders.

Initially, assume that we are interested in determining the market value of the equity from the market value of the assets. This is the reverse of the problem we face in practice, but provides a simpler perspective to initially understand the basic option relationships; Figure 7.6 illustrates this issue. To be specific, assume that we initially invest $20 in the firm and borrow a further $80 from a bank. The proceeds, $100, are invested in equities. At the end of five years, what is the value of the equity? For example, if the market value of the assets at the end of year five is $60, then the value of the equity will be zero. If the value of the assets is $110, then the value of the equity will be $30, and so on. Thus, in Figure 7.6, the lines from $0 to $80 and from $80 to point B represent the market value of the equity as a function of the asset value at the end of year five.

Assume now that we are interested in valuing our equity prior to the final winding up of the firm. For example, assume that three years have passed since the firm was started and that there are two years remaining before we wind the firm up. Further, we have marked the equities in our portfolio (not to be confused with the equity position in the structure that holds the equity securities; imagine that this firm is holding a mutual fund) to market and their value is determined to be $80. What is the value of the firm's equity? Not zero. It is actually something greater than zero because it is the value of the assets two years hence that really matters, and there is still a chance that the asset value will be greater than $80 in two years time. In Figure 7.6, the value of the equity with two years to go is represented by the curve joining $0 and point B.

The higher the volatility of the assets, the greater the chance of high asset values after two years. For example, if we were dissatisfied with our fund's performance after three years because it has lost $20 in value, dropping from $100 to $80, we may be tempted to invest in higher-potential, higher-risk equities. If we do, what is the effect on the firm's equity value? It increases. The more volatile assets have higher probabilities of high values, and consequently, higher payouts for the equity. Of course, there are accompanying higher probabilities of lower asset values, because volatility works both ways, but with limited liability, very low asset values do not affect the equity value. At the end of the five years, it makes no difference to the equity if the final asset value is $79 or $9; its payout is the same, 0.

Assuming we did sell our existing equity securities and replaced them with the same total value of higher-potential, higher-risk equity securities, where did the increase in the firm's equity value come from? It did not come from an increase in the asset value. We simply sold our original portfolio for $80 and purchased a new portfolio of higher-risk equities for $80. There was no value created there. The value, of course, came from the bank holding our firm's debt. In Figure 7.6, the value of the firm can be divided between the debt and equity holders along the line joining the points $80 and A, where the line 0 to A plots the asset value against itself. Thus, the only way the value of equity can increase while the asset value remains constant is to take the value from the market value of the debt. This should make sense. When we reinvested the firm's assets in higher-risk equities, we increased the default risk of the debt and consequently reduced this debt's market value.

The value of debt and equity are thus intimately entwined. They are both really derivative securities on the underlying assets of the firm. We can exploit the option nature of equity to relate the market value of equity and the book value of debt to determine the implied market value of the underlying assets. That is, we solve the reverse of the problem described in our simple example. We observe the market value of the equity and solve backwards for the market value of assets. See Figure 7.7.

F I G U R E   7.7

Market Value of Equity and Assets

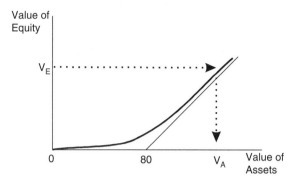

In practice, we need to take account of the more complex capital structures and circumstances that exist in real life. For example, we need to consider the various terms and nature of debt (for example, long- and short-term debt, and convertible instruments), the perpetuity nature of equity, the time value of money, and of course, we have to solve for the volatility of the assets at the same time. Thus, in practice, we solve[4] the following two relationships simultaneously:

$$
\begin{bmatrix} \text{Equity} \\ \text{Value} \end{bmatrix}
= OptionFunction \left(\begin{bmatrix} \text{Asset} \\ \text{Value} \end{bmatrix}, \begin{bmatrix} \text{Asset} \\ \text{Volatility} \end{bmatrix}, \begin{bmatrix} \text{Capital} \\ \text{Structure} \end{bmatrix}, \begin{bmatrix} \text{Interest} \\ \text{Rate} \end{bmatrix} \right)
$$

$$
\begin{bmatrix} \text{Equity} \\ \text{Volatility} \end{bmatrix}
= OptionFunction \left(\begin{bmatrix} \text{Asset} \\ \text{Value} \end{bmatrix}, \begin{bmatrix} \text{Asset} \\ \text{Volatility} \end{bmatrix}, \begin{bmatrix} \text{Capital} \\ \text{Structure} \end{bmatrix}, \begin{bmatrix} \text{Interest} \\ \text{Rate} \end{bmatrix} \right)
$$

---

4 For the more technically inclined: Simply inverting this system of equations and solving for the two unknown variables (asset value and asset volatility) is typically not possible in practice. Instead, the two unknown variables are determined by iteratively searching for quantities that make the equations hold for each date in a time series of equity returns. This iterative solution technique also allows for simple and straightforward implementation of robust estimation techniques that makes it easier to control for the influence of outliers. This estimation framework significantly improves the default predictive power of the EDF credit measure produced at MKMV. For more details on how EDF credit measures are estimated, please refer to the research papers available at www.moodyskmv.com.

Asset value and volatility are the only unknown quantities in these relationships and thus the two equations can be *solved* to determine the values implied by the current equity value, volatility, and capital structure.

Calculate the Distance to Default

There are six variables that determine the default probability of a firm over some horizon, from now until time H (see Figure 7.8):

- The current asset value.
- The distribution of the asset value at time H.
- The volatility of the future assets value at time H.
- The level of the default point, the book value of the liabilities.
- The expected rate of growth in the asset value over the horizon.
- The length of the horizon, H.

The first four variables, asset value, future asset distribution, asset volatility, and the level of the default point are the critical variables. The expected growth in the asset value has little default discriminating power and the analyst defines the length of the horizon.

If the value of the assets falls below the default point, the firm defaults. Therefore, the probability of default is the probability that

FIGURE 7.8

Distance to Default

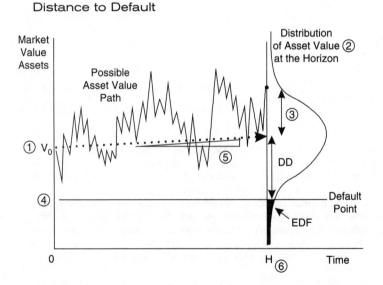

the asset value will fall below the default point. This is the shaded area (EDF value) below the default point[5] in Figure 7.8. Figure 7.8 also illustrates the causative relationship and trade-off among the variables. This causative specification provides analysts with a powerful and reliable framework in which they can ask what-if questions regarding the model's various inputs and examine the effects of any proposed capital restructuring. For example, analysts can examine the effect of a large decrease in the stock price or the effects of an acquisition or merger.

If the future distribution of the distance to default were known, the default probability (Expected Default Frequency, or EDF value) would simply be the likelihood that the final asset value was below the default point (the shaded area in Figure 7.8). However, in practice, the distribution of the distance to default is difficult to measure. Moreover, the usual assumptions of normal or lognormal distributions cannot be used. For default measurement, the likelihood of large adverse changes in the relationship of asset value to the firm's default point is critical to the accurate determination of the default probability. These changes may come about from changes in asset value or changes in the firm's leverage. In fact, changes in asset value and changes in firm leverage may be highly correlated. Consequently, MKMV first measures the distance to default as the number of standard deviations the asset value is away from default and then uses empirical data to determine the corresponding default probability. As discussed in a previous section, the distance to default is conceptually calculated[6] as:

$$
\begin{bmatrix} \text{Distance} \\ \text{to Default} \end{bmatrix} = \frac{\begin{bmatrix} \text{Market Value} \\ \text{of Assets} \end{bmatrix} - \begin{bmatrix} \text{Default} \\ \text{Point} \end{bmatrix}}{\begin{bmatrix} \text{Market Value} \\ \text{of Assets} \end{bmatrix}\begin{bmatrix} \text{Asset} \\ \text{Volatility} \end{bmatrix}}
$$

and is marked as DD in Figure 7.8.

---

5 Strictly speaking, the shaded area in Figure 7.8 is the default probability if we assume that the default point is not an absorbing barrier. In other words, a firm whose asset value falls through the default point before the time horizon date H can still recover and end up above the default point by time H. In practice, MKMV uses an absorbing barrier model that more realistically models default as being possible at any time. The default probability calculated out of an absorbing barrier model will be higher than the default probability characterized in Figure 7.8.

6 Refer to the previous footnote associated with distance to default for discussion of the actual formula.

Calculate the Default Probability

One method for obtaining the relationship between distance to default and default probability requires data on historical default and bankruptcy frequencies. MKMV maintains a database that includes over 100,000 company-years of data and over 7,000 incidents of default or bankruptcy. From this data, a lookup or frequency table can be generated, which relates the likelihood of default to various levels of distance-to-default.

For example, assume that one is interested in determining the default probability over the next year for a firm that is seven standard deviations away from default. To determine this EDF value, one would query the default history for the proportion of the firms that were seven standard deviations away from default that defaulted over the next year. The answer from the MKMV data is about five basis points (bp), 0.05%, or an equivalent rating of AA.

MKMV has tested the relationship between distance to default and default frequency for industry, size, time, and other effects and has found that the relationship is typically constant across all of these variables. This is not to say that there are no differences in default rates across industry, time, and size, but only that it appears that these differences are captured by the distance-to-default measure. MKMV's studies of international default rates are continuing, but the preliminary results of these studies (as well as studies completed by some MKMV clients) indicate that the relationship is also invariant across most countries and regions.

In summary, there are three steps required to calculate an EDF credit measure: (1) estimate the current market value and volatility of the firm's assets, (2) determine how far the firm is from default (i.e., determine its distance to default), and (3) transform the distance to default into a probability. For example, consider Philip Morris Companies Inc., which, at the end of April 2001, had a one-year EDF value of 25 bp, close to the median EDF value of firms with an A rating. Table 7.2 illustrates the relevant values and calculations for the EDF credit measure.

A CLOSER LOOK AT CALCULATING EDF CREDIT MEASURES

Merton's general derivative pricing model was the genesis for understanding the link between the market value of the firm's assets and the market value of its equity. It is possible to use the

T A B L E 7.2

Philip Morris Companies Statistics

Variable	Value	Notes
Market value of equity	$ 110.688 billion	(Share Price) X (Shares Outstanding)
Book liabilities	$ 64.062 billion	Balance sheet
Market value of assets	$ 170.558 billion	Option-pricing model
Asset volatility	21%	Option-pricing model
Default point	$ 47.499 billion	Liabilities payable within one year
Distance to default	3.5	Ratio: $\dfrac{72-37}{72\times 10\%}$
		(In this example we ignore the growth in the asset value between now and the end of the year.)
EDF (one year)	25 bp	Empirical mapping between distance to default and default frequency

Black-Scholes (BS) option-pricing model, as a special case of Merton's model to illustrate some of the technical details of estimating EDF values. The BS model is too restrictive to use in practice but is widely understood and provides a useful framework to review the issues involved. As explained before, MKMV actually implements the VK model to calculate MKMV's EDF credit measure. This section works an example of the calculation of an EDF value using the BS option-pricing model. The section also discusses some of the important issues that arise in practice and, where necessary, highlights the limitations of the BS model in this context.

Equity has the residual claim on the assets after all other obligations have been met. It also has limited liability. A call option on the underlying assets has the same properties. The holder of a call option on the assets has a claim on the assets after meeting the strike price of the option. In this case, the strike of the call option is equal to the book value of the firm's liabilities. If the value of the assets is insufficient to meet the liabilities of the firm, then the shareholders, holders of the call option, will not exercise their option and will leave the firm to its creditors.

One can exploit the option nature of equity to derive the market value and volatility of the firm's underlying assets implied by the equity's market value. In particular, one can solve backwards from the option price and option price volatility for the implied asset value and asset volatility.

To introduce the notation, recall that the BS model posits that the market value of the firm's underlying assets follows the following stochastic process:

$$dV_A = \mu V_A dt + \sigma_A V_A dz \tag{7.1}$$

where

V_A, dV_A	are the firm's asset value and change in asset value,
μ, σ_A	are the firm's asset value drift rate and volatility, and
dz	is a Wiener process.

The BS model allows only two types of liabilities, a single class of debt and a single class of equity. If X is the book value of the debt that is due at time T, then the market value of the equity and the market value of the assets are related by the following expression:

$$V_E = V_A N(d1) - e^{-rT} X N(d2) \tag{7.2}$$

where

V_E is the market value of the firm's equity,

$$d1 = \frac{\ln\left(V_A / X\right) + \left(r + \frac{\sigma_A^2}{2}\right)T}{\sigma_A \sqrt{T}},$$

$d2 = d1 - \sigma_A \sqrt{T}$, and

r is the risk-free interest rate.

It is straightforward to show that equity and asset volatility are related by the following expression:

$$\sigma_E = \frac{V_A}{V_E} \Delta \sigma_A \tag{7.3}$$

where

σ_E	is the volatility of the firm's equity, and
Δ	is the hedge ratio, $N(d1)$, from (7.2).

Consider the example of a firm with a market capitalization of $3 billion, an equity volatility of 40% per annum and total liabilities of $10 billion. The asset value and volatility implied by the equity value, equity volatility, and liabilities are calculated by solving the call price and volatility equations, (7.2) and (7.3), simultaneously. In this case,[7] the implied market value of the firm's assets is $12.511 billion, and the implied asset volatility is 9.6%.

In practice, it is important to use a more general option-pricing relationship as characterized by the VK model that allows for a more detailed specification of the liabilities and that models equity as perpetuity. MKMV's EDF credit measure currently incorporates five classes of liabilities: short-term, long-term, convertible, preferred equity, and common equity.

The model linking equity and asset volatility given by (7.3) holds only instantaneously. In practice, the market leverage moves around far too much for (7.3) to provide reasonable results. Worse yet, the model biases the probabilities in precisely the wrong direction. For example, if the market leverage is decreasing quickly then (7.3) will tend to overestimate the asset volatility, and thus the default probability will be overstated as the firm's credit risk improves. Conversely, if the market leverage is increasing rapidly then (7.3) will underestimate the asset volatility, and thus the default probability will be understated as the firm's credit risk deteriorates. The net result is that default probabilities calculated in this manner provide little discriminatory power.

Instead of using the instantaneous relationship given by (7.3), MKMV's EDF credit measure is produced using a more complex iterative procedure to solve for the asset volatility. The procedure uses an initial guess of the volatility to determine the asset value and to de-lever the equity returns. The volatility of the resulting asset returns is used as the input to the next iteration of the procedure that in turn determines a new set of asset values and hence a new series of asset returns. The procedure continues in this manner until it converges. This usually takes no more than a handful of iterations if a reasonable starting point is used. In addition, the asset volatility derived above is combined in a Bayesian manner with country, industry, and size averages to produce a more predictive estimate of the firm's asset volatility.

---

7 All liabilities are assumed to be due in one year, $T = 1$, and the interest rate r is assumed to be 5%.

The probability of default is the probability that the market value of the firm's assets will be less than the book value of the firm's liabilities by the time the debt matures. That is:

$$p_t = \Pr[V_A^t \le X_t \mid V_A^0 = V_A] = \Pr[\ln V_A^t \le \ln X_t \mid V_A^0 = V_A] \quad (7.4)$$

where

P_t is the probability of default by time t

V_A^t is the market value of the firm's assets at time t, and

X_t is the book value of the firm's liabilities due at time t.

The change in the value of the firm's assets is described by (7.1) and thus the value at time t, V_A^t, given that the value at time 0 is V_A, is:

$$\ln V_A^t = \ln V_A + \left(\mu - \frac{\sigma_A^2}{2}\right)t + \sigma_A \sqrt{t}\varepsilon \quad (7.5)$$

where

μ is the expected return on the firm's asset, and

ε is the random component of the firm's return.

The relationship given by equation (7.5) describes the evolution in the asset value path that is shown in Figure 7.8. Combining (7.4) and (7.5), we can write the probability of default as:

$$p_t = \Pr\left[\ln V_A + \left(\mu - \frac{\sigma_A^2}{2}\right)t + \sigma_A \sqrt{t}\,\varepsilon \le \ln X_t\right], \quad (7.6)$$

and after rearranging:

$$p_t = \Pr\left[-\frac{\ln \dfrac{V_A}{X_t} + \left(\mu - \dfrac{\sigma_A^2}{2}\right)t}{\sigma_A \sqrt{t}} \ge \varepsilon\right] \quad (7.7)$$

The BS model assumes that the random component of the firm's asset returns is normally distributed, $\varepsilon \sim N(0,1)$ and as a result, we can define the default probability in terms of the cumulative normal distribution:

$$p_t = N\left[-\frac{\ln \dfrac{V_A}{X_t} + \left(\mu - \dfrac{\sigma_A^2}{2}\right)t}{\sigma_A \sqrt{t}}\right], \quad (7.8)$$

Recall that the distance to default is simply the number of standard deviations that the firm is away from default and thus in the BS world is given by:

$$DD = \frac{\ln \dfrac{V_A}{X_t} + \left(\mu - \dfrac{\sigma_A^2}{2}\right)t}{\sigma_A \sqrt{t}} \qquad (7.9)$$

Continuing with our example, assume that the expected return on the assets, μ, is equal to 7% and that we are interested in calculating the one-year default probability. The distance to default, DD, in this case[8] is 2.8, and the corresponding default probability from (7.8) is 25 bp.

In practice, we need to adjust the distance to default to include not only the increases in the asset value given by the rate but also adjust for any cash outflows to service debt, dividends, and so on. In addition, the normal distribution is a very poor choice to define the probability of default. There are several reasons for this, but the most important is the fact that the default point is in reality also a random variable. That is, we have assumed that the default point is described by the firm's liabilities and amortization schedule. Of course, we know that this is not true. In particular, firms will often adjust their liabilities as they near default. It is common to observe the liabilities of commercial and industrial firms increase as they near default, while the liabilities of financial institutions often decrease as they approach default. The difference is usually just a reflection of the liquidity in the firm's assets and thus their ability to adjust their leverage as they encounter difficulties.

Unfortunately, ex ante we are unable to specify the behavior of the liabilities and thus the uncertainty in the adjustments in the liabilities must be captured elsewhere. We include this uncertainty in the mapping of distance to default to the EDF credit measure. The resulting empirical distribution of default rates has much wider tails than the normal distribution. For example, a distance to default of four, four standard deviations, maps to a default rate of around 100 bp. The equivalent probability from the normal distribution is essentially zero.

---

8 The distance to default is calculated by equation (7.9), $DD = \dfrac{\ln \dfrac{12.5116}{10} + \left(0.05 - \dfrac{0.0092}{2}\right)}{0.0961}$.

CALCULATING LONG-TERM EDF CREDIT MEASURES

The extension of the model to longer terms is straightforward. This extension is particularly important for calculating a default probability to understand the value of a credit default swap given that most credit default swaps have a maturity of five years. The default point, asset volatility, and expected asset value are calculated as before except they take into account the longer horizon. For example, suppose one is interested in calculating the EDF value for a five-year horizon. Over the five years, one can expect that the default point will increase as a result of the amortization of long-term debt. This is a conservative assumption that all long-term debt is refinanced short term. One could just as easily model the asset value decreasing as the debt is paid down, but in practice, debt is usually refinanced. In any case, it really does not matter whether the assets go down by the amount of the amortization or the default point increases by the same amount—the net effect on the default point is the same.

In addition to the default point changing, as one extends the horizon the future expected asset value is increasing, as is the uncertainty regarding its actual future value. The expected asset value increases at the expected growth rate and the total asset volatility increases proportionally with the square root of time.[9]

The distance to default is therefore calculated using the relevant five-year asset value, asset volatility, and default point. The scaling of the default probability again uses the empirical default distribution mapping five-year distance to defaults with the cumulative default probability to five years. That is, the mapping answers the question, what proportion of firms with this five-year distance to default actually default within five years. The answer to this question is the five-year cumulative default probability. EDF values are annual default probabilities and the five-year EDF value is calculated as the equivalent average annual default probability.[10] For example, suppose the five-year cumulative probability is 250 bp, then the five-year (annualized) EDF value is 51 bp.

---

9 The asset variance is additive and therefore increases linearly with time. The asset volatility is the square root of the variance and therefore increases with the square root of time.

10 The EDF credit measure is calculated from the cumulative default probability using survival rates. For example, the five-year cumulative probability of default and the five-year EDF value are related by the following expression: $1 - CEDF_5 = (1 - EDF_5)^5$. The probability of not defaulting within five years, $1 - CEDF_5$, and the average annual probability of not defaulting, $1 - EDF_5$.

TESTING THE DEFAULT MEASURE'S PERFORMANCE

Determining the performance of a default measure is both a theoretical and an empirical problem. For example, what exactly do we mean by performance or predictive power? In practice, we can only hope to estimate probabilities of default. That is, we will not be able to definitively classify firms into "will default" and "will not default" categories. As a result, in assessing the performance of a model, we face the task of assessing its ability to discriminate between different levels of default risk.

In the context of analyzing CDS, performance of a particular model relates to the objectives of the analysis. If we are concerned only about risk management, then standard policies such as never selling protection on a firm with an EDF value greater than 2%, around a B rating, may be sufficient. Alternatively, we may determine that we always buy protection on a firm whose EDF value exceeds 2%. We can test these rules by looking at actual default history and determining the discriminatory power of the EDF model. Thus, one measure of a model's performance is the trade-off between the defaulting firms on which we avoided selling protection and the proportion of firms we exclude. This trade-off is commonly called the power curve of a model.

The next level of CDS analysis concerns the relative value of a particular contract. In this case, we combine the EDF credit measure with a CDS pricing model to determine some measure of fundamental or intrinsic value as implied by the equity-based default measure. Given the limited availability of data and the fact that a CDS price is a function of more than just the EDF credit measure (market risk premium, expected recovery in the event of default, and liquidity are a few examples of other factors driving CDS value), it is difficult to do performance analysis on the EDF value alone in this context. Moreover, the fact that an equity-based CDS price diverges from an existing CDS price is not necessarily reflective of a model problem if the implied price and the actual price later converge. Questions then arise regarding the proper time horizon for analysis and the criteria for labeling a model as "successful."[11]

For the purposes of this discussion, we will focus on the discriminatory power of the EDF value as a measure of its usefulness. The reader is encouraged to look at other research in the area of

_____

11 MKMV continues to research this area.

relative value analysis to understand the subtleties involved in that level of testing.

First-time observers of this type of model often question its validity by making claims about the lack of market efficiency. The efficiency of a market usually refers to the degree to which the current price reflects all the relevant information about a firm's value. While the EDF model does not require that the price reflects all the relevant information about a firm to be effective, available evidence suggests that it is difficult to consistently beat the market. For example, over 90% of managed funds were unable to outperform the market in 1998. That is, it is difficult to pick stocks consistently and difficult to know when the market is under- or overvaluing a firm. The market reflects a summary of many investors' forecasts, and it is unusual if any one individual's, or committee's, forecast is better. The strength of the model depends not on the market's efficiency per se, but rather on the extent to which the market meaningfully coordinates available information about a firm. That said, a more efficient equity market does produce better EDF estimates. The examples and power curve testing that follows indicate that the EDF model does, in fact, effectively coordinate relevant information regarding a firm's credit risk. Consequently, we believe that the best source of information regarding the value of a firm is the market.

The market, however, can be caught by surprise. For instance, Koninklijke KPN NV, a Norwegian telephone company depicted in Figure 7.9, caught the market and rating agencies by surprise, although some credit analysts undoubtedly worried that it was

F I G U R E   7.9

Koninklijke KPN NV

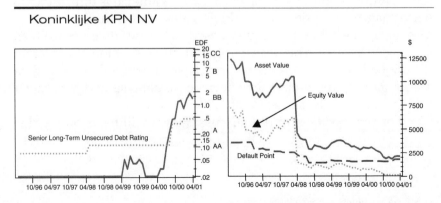

FIGURE 7.10

Mercury Finance

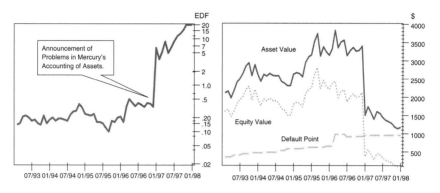

overvalued. Fraud is often the cause of extremely large and sudden changes in credit quality. For example, as Figure 7.10 demonstrates, it is not hard to spot when the announcement regarding the improprieties in the reporting of Mercury Finance's assets was made.

However, most of the time the market will be well aware of problems or opportunities, and this information will be fairly reflected in the EDF value, as in the examples of Owens Corning and W.R. Grace in Figure 7.11. Owens Corning, an American Construction Materials company, failed in November 2000. The equity value of WR Grace, a U.S. Chemical Products company, dropped significantly in May 1998; the company failed in October 2000.

Before looking at aggregate performance results, consider the examples in the financial industry presented in Figure 7.12. Financial institutions are notoriously difficult to model, so the early warning from this kind of model supports the claim that the equity market is meaningful in sorting through publicly available information. In each case, the EDF credit measure began deteriorating several months before the actual default. Notice also that the examples come from a number of countries, not just the United States, demonstrating that this kind of model can be applied to non-U.S. firm analysis as well. In particular, Yamaichi Securities defaulted during November 1997 and Reliance Group Holdings, the property and casualty insurance company, has been in default on its payment obligations since November 2000. Finova Group Inc., the financial services company, filed for Chapter 11 protection in March 2001. United Companies Financial Group, the mortgage banker and Loan Company, filed for bankruptcy in March 1999.

FIGURE 7.11

WR Grace and Owens Corning

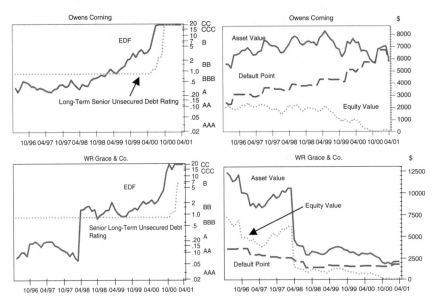

Let's now turn to aggregate performance analysis of the EDF credit measure. In Figure 7.13, we plot the power curves for EDF credit measures and the senior unsecured debt rating from a major rating agency. The cutoff points for the population are plotted along the horizontal axis and the proportion of defaults excluded at each cutoff point is plotted on the vertical axis. If we rank all firms by their EDF credit measures and impose a cutoff at the bottom 10%, then we avoid selling protection on 73% of the defaulting firms. That is, by not selling protection on the bottom 10% as ranked by the EDF credit measure, we can avoid 73% of all defaulting firms. At a cutoff of 30%, we are able to avoid selling protection on 97% of defaulting firms and of course, if we do not sell protection on any firm, a cutoff of 100%, we avoid all the defaulting firms. Thus, for a given cutoff, the larger the proportion of defaults that are excluded, the more powerful is the model's ability to discriminate high-default-risk firms from low-default-risk firms.

The overall default rate, and thus the default probability of firms, varies considerably over time. Figure 7.14 plots the default history for the United States from 1973 through 2001. The chart

F I G U R E   7.12

Yamaichi Securities, Reliance Group, Finova Group, United Companies Financial

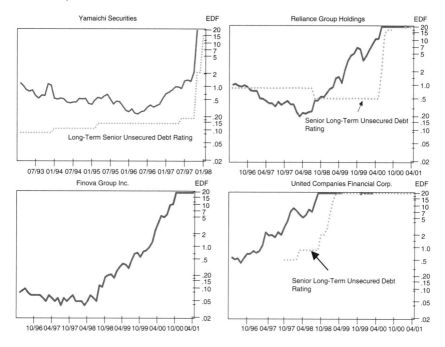

shows that, as a general rule of thumb, we can expect the default rate to double or triple between the high and low of the credit cycle. Thus, an effective measure of default risk cannot average default rates over time; instead, it must reflect the changes in default risk over time. Because MKMV's EDF credit measure incorporates asset values based on information from the equity market, it naturally reflects the credit cycle in a forward-looking manner. For example, Figure 7.15 shows the median EDF value for U.S.A, BBB, BB, and B-rated firms from April 1996 through April 2001, and Figure 7.16 shows the EDF value quartiles for financial institutions in Korea and Thailand from February 1993 through January 1997.

At the individual firm level, the model's ability to reflect the current credit risk of a firm can be assessed by observing the change in the EDF value of a firm as it approaches default. Figure 7.17 plots the medians and quartiles of the EDF values for five years prior to the dates of default for rated companies.

F I G U R E   7.13

EDF Credit Measures and Senior Unsecured Debt

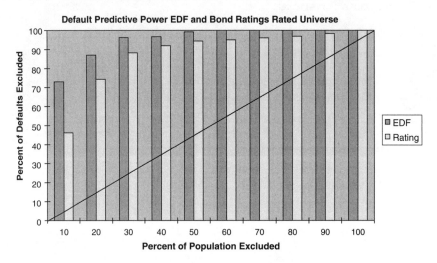

F I G U R E   7.14

U.S. Default History, 1973–2001

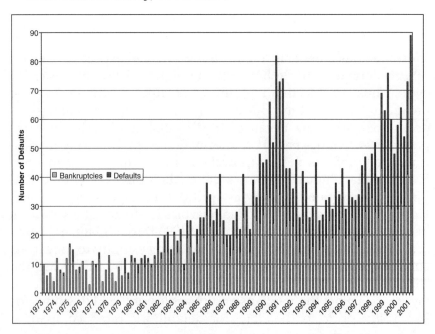

F I G U R E   7.15

Median EDF Values, 1996–2001

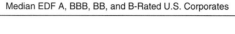

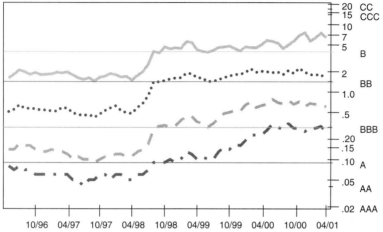

F I G U R E   7.16

EDF Value Quartiles, 1993–1997

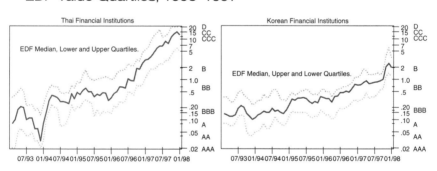

Default dates are aligned to the right such that the time moving to the left indicates years prior to default. EDF values are plotted along the vertical axis. The level of EDF values is sloping upward, towards increasing levels of default risk, as the date of default draws closer. Moreover, the slope increases as the date of default approaches.

Five years prior to default, the median EDF value of defaulting companies is approximately 1%, around BB. One year prior to

FIGURE 7.17

EDF Values, Median and Quartiles

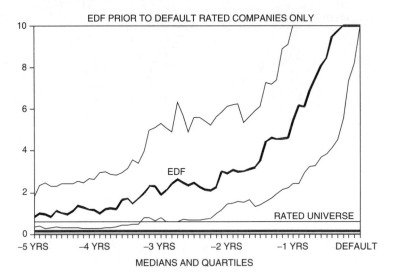

default the median has increased to over 6%. During the time of this sample, the median EDF value for all rated companies, both default and nondefault, was around 0.16%. (The median and percentiles for the rated universe are the straight lines running parallel to the horizontal axis at the bottom of the chart.) Two years prior to default, the lower quartile of EDF values (the riskiest 25%) of the defaulting firms breaks through the upper quartile of the rated universe (the safest 25% as measured by the rating agency). Thus, two full years prior to default, 75% of the defaulting firms had EDF values in the bottom quartile of the universe.

There is no single measure of performance for default measures such as MKMV's EDF credit measure. Performance must be measured along several dimensions including discrimination power, ability to adjust to the credit cycle, and the ability to quickly reflect any deterioration in credit quality. The EDF value generated from the equity market and financial statement information of a firm does all of these things well. The dynamics of the EDF credit measure come mostly from the dynamics of the equity value. It is simply very hard to hold the equity price of a firm up as it heads towards default. The ability to discriminate between high and low default risks comes from the distance-to-default ratio. This key ratio compares the firm's net worth to its volatility and thus embodies all of the key elements of default risk. Moreover, because the net worth is based on values from the equity market, it is both a timely and superior estimate of the firm's value.

USING AN EDF IN CDS ANALYSIS

The discussion thus far has focused on the equity market as the source of information for calculating default probabilities. Some researchers prefer to focus only on the credit markets (e.g., bonds, loans, and CDS) to parameterize models for analyzing CDS. In principle, one should make use of as much good data and as many effective modeling techniques as possible. Research done at MKMV has convinced us that the equity markets continue to be the best and most reliable source of data for constructing credit models. Continual problems with data quality and data availability make the credit markets less appealing for parameterizing robust and reliable credit models. The recent explosion in the size and liquidity of the CDS market and the availability of better bond data through a variety of marketwide initiatives have finally made it possible to use credit market data in a more effective way.

For the particular application of analyzing CDS, a default probability such as an EDF credit measure calculated from equity data can prove quite useful, regardless of the quality of available CDS data. If the pricing for a specific CDS is questionable, the equity-based EDF credit measure can be used to develop an objective view of the CDS's intrinsic value. If the pricing for a large number of CDS is reliable and readily available, these data can be combined with the equity-based EDF data to determine estimates of the credit market risk premium as well as recovery expectations. The key benefit derives from the fact that it is a "clean" estimate of the underlying firm's default probability. A CDS spread reflects the underlying firm's risk neutral expected loss.

Expected loss (*EL*) is defined as follows:

$$EL = LGD * EDF \qquad (7.10)$$

with *LGD* defined as the loss given default (1 – expected recovery) and *EDF* as the probability of default for the underlying firm over the one-year life of the CDS contract.

For determining the CDS premium paid for one year of protection, we need to convert the actual EL into a risk-neutral EL.[12] This conversion requires an estimate of the CDS's market price of risk, or the risk premium investors demand to take a unit of CDS risk. The simple formula for our one-year CDS contract can be written as follows:

$$S = e^{-r}(LGD^Q \times EDF^Q) \qquad (7.11)$$

with r equal to the risk-free rate, and the Q superscripts indicative of the LGD and EDF being transformed to their risk-neutral quantities. Extending this analysis to real CDS contracts that typically have multiple payment dates for the premium, and a time horizon greater than one year, is quite straightforward. The CDS premium or spread is calculated such that the present value of the expected premium payments equals the present value of the default probability weighted expected recovery over the time horizon of the contract. As mentioned before, the key drivers of value are the EDF credit measure, the LGD, and the market risk premium used to convert actual probabilities into risk-neutral probabilities.

Some modelers look at a cross-section of CDS spreads (or sometimes bond spreads) to back out parameters in a model of CDS value. As can be readily seen, extra assumptions must be made in order to "break apart" the multiplicative nature of the EL function. The equity-based default probability does not suffer from this convolution with LGD. A powerful combination from a modeling perspective is to estimate default probabilities from the equity market and combine these estimates with a cross-section of CDS data to estimate an implied market price of risk and implied LGDs. MKMV has successfully implemented this unified modeling approach to arrive at reliable estimates of each relevant driver of value. Interested readers should look to MKMV's Web site for more details of the research.

Equity-based default probability estimates can be a useful part of CDS analysis. This chapter discussed a three-step process

---

12 This transformation requires assumptions about investor's risk aversion and the behavior of the processes driving value. For an overview of the approaches used to model risk-neutral values, please see Jeffrey Bohn, "A Survey of Contingent-Claims Approaches to Risky Debt Valuation," *Journal of Risk Finance*, Vol. 1, No. 3. (Summer, 2000) pp. 53-78.

F I G U R E   7.18

Winstar Communications

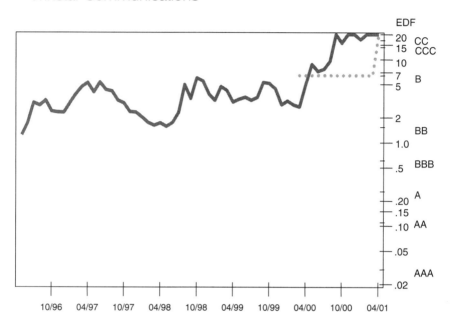

used to calculate MKMV's EDF™ credit measure, an example of an equity-based default probability:

- Estimate the market value and volatility of the firm's assets,
- Calculate the distance to default, the number of standard deviations the firm is away from default, and
- Scale the distance to default to an expected default frequency (EDF) using an empirical default distribution.

Because EDF credit measures are based on market prices, they are forward looking and reflect the current position in the credit cycle. They are a timely and reliable measure of credit quality. As a final example of the forward-looking strength of EDF values, Figure 7.18 shows Winstar Communications, which filed for bankruptcy in April of 2001. The first sign of a serious deterioration in the credit quality is in August 1998, when the EDF value jumps from 1.7% to 2.3% (BB to B). The EDF value climbed as high as 6% in October 1998, recovering a little as they secured additional financing before finally reaching 20% (D) in September 2000, eight months prior to filing for bankruptcy.

Equity-based measures of default such as the EDF credit measure can be productively combined with cross-sectional CDS market data to arrive at economically meaningful parameter estimates for assessing the relative value of CDS contracts. Even without sophisticated valuation models, equity-based default probabilities can augment general analysis of CDS exposures to minimize the risk of facing default as a protection seller and optimize the timing of buying protection on a deteriorating credit.

CHAPTER EXERCISES

1. Describe the three main elements that determine the default probability of a firm and indicate what each one measures.

2. How is asset risk measured? Given a firm with asset value of $70 billion and an asset volatility of 15%, how much asset value is added or subtracted for each one-standard-deviation move? Should a firm with high asset volatility seek to add or subtract leverage from its operations? Why?

3. Explain the six factors that determine default probability at a time period t. What occurs when the asset value of the firm declines below the default point?

4. Why is it inaccurate to average default rates over a long period of time? What can be done to prevent inaccuracies?

5. Assuming a loss given default of 25% and an EDF of 3%, what is the expected loss? What if the EDF rises to 5%? What if the recovery rate is 60% and the EDF is 4%?

6. How can an equity-based default probability be computed?

Portfolio Management of Default Risk

By Jeffrey Bohn[1]

INTRODUCTION

Portfolios of corporate liabilities tend to suffer from lack of diversification. Unfortunately, selling corporate liabilities can be difficult given the institutional constraints of portfolio holders and uneven liquidity for many corporate debt instruments. This limitation on selling corporate debt instruments makes active portfolio management difficult. With the advent of credit default swaps (CDS), the potential to achieve much better portfolio diversification is slowly being realized. The principles underlying portfolio analysis extend seamlessly to the modeling of CDS. In fact, corporate debt can be considered a combination of an otherwise default-risk-free security plus a short position (i.e., selling protection) in a CDS on the corporate obligor. The crux of credit portfolio analysis focuses on modeling CDS, whether explicitly or implicitly in the portfolio.

Holders of corporate liabilities tend to be banks, mutual funds, and pension funds. Recently credit hedge funds have entered the corporate debt market. These market participants tend to hold debt issued by obligors with relatively low levels of default risk. These same market participants are starting to include CDS on high-quality obligors in their portfolios. For the typical high-grade borrower, default risk is small, perhaps 1/10 of 1% per year. For the typical bank, borrower, this risk is about 1/2 of 1%.

Although these risks do not seem large, they are in fact highly significant. First, they can increase quickly and with little warning. Second, the margins in corporate lending are very tight, and even small miscalculations of default risks can undermine the profitability of lending or owning corporate bonds. But most importantly, many lenders are themselves borrowers, with high levels of leverage. Unexpected realizations of default risk have destabilized, decapitalized and destroyed lenders. Banks, finance companies, insurers, investment banks, lessors: none have escaped unscathed.

The systematic component of default risk cannot be hedged away, or "structured" away. The government cannot insure it away. It is a reflection of the substantial risk in companies' futures. CDS and other credit derivatives can be used to shift risk, but in the end, someone must bear this risk. It does not "net out" in the aggregate.

Although in general a poor investment strategy, it is possible to be rewarded for taking on large concentrations of risk in equities because these concentrations at times produce large returns. However, overwhelming evidence of the ineffectiveness of this *stock-picking* strategy has been available since the early 1970s and, as a result, the majority of equity investments are managed in diversified portfolios. Unlike equities, debt has no upside potential and thus the case for managing default risk in well-diversified portfolios is even more compelling. The limited upside potential of debt spreads means that there are no possible circumstances under which an investor or counterparty can be rewarded for taking on concentrations of default risk. Like other rare events with high costs, default risk can only be effectively managed in a portfolio. Default risk can be reduced and managed through diversification; those who can diversify default risk most effectively will ultimately own the exposure.

Every lender[2] knows the benefits of diversification. Every lender works to achieve these benefits. However, until recently lenders have been reluctant to, or unable to, implement systems for actually measuring the amount of diversification in a debt portfolio. Portfolios have "concentrations," which we see ex-post. Ex-ante, lenders must look to models and software to quantify

---

2 For the balance of this chapter, lenders should be interpreted broadly to include not just commercial banks, but also investors such as insurance companies, mutual funds, hedge funds, and pension funds that purchase corporate bonds, secondary market loans, and other structured corporate credit instruments.

concentrations. Until recently, these types of models have not been generally available. Thus it should not come as a surprise that there have been many unexpected default events in lenders' portfolios in the past.

Quantitative methods for portfolio analysis have developed since Markowitz's pioneering work in 1950. These methods have been applied successfully in a variety of areas of finance, notably to equity portfolios. These methods show the amount of risk reduction achievable through diversification. They measure the amount of risk contributed by an asset, or group of assets, to a portfolio. By extension, they also show the amount of diversification provided by a single asset or group of assets. The aim of these methods is to maximize the return to a portfolio while keeping the risk within acceptable bounds. This maximization requires a balancing of return to risk within the portfolio, asset by asset, group of assets by group of assets.

This logic can be illustrated by imagining that it was not the case. If a low-return-to-risk asset is swapped for a high-return-to-risk asset, then the portfolio's return can be improved with no addition to risk. The process is equilibrated by changes in risk. As an asset is swapped out of the portfolio, it changes from being a source of concentration to being a source of diversification, i.e., its risk contribution falls. The reverse applies as an asset is swapped into the portfolio. Thus the return-to-risk increases for the low-return asset and decreases for the high-return asset, until their return-to-risk ratios are equal. At that point, no further swap can raise return without also raising risk. This then characterizes the optimal portfolio or, equivalently, the optimal set of holdings.

This conceptual model applies to the default risk of debt and CDS as surely as it applies to equities. Equity practitioners, however, have used the last 25 years to develop techniques for measuring the asset attributes that are necessary for an actual portfolio management tool. The same development has not occurred for debt portfolios because of the greater analytical and empirical difficulties. In particular, it is necessary to quantify the level of default risk in a single asset, and to quantify the relationship between the default risks of each pair of assets in the portfolio.

In addition to knowing the default probability and loss given default (one minus the recovery given default), the portfolio management of default risk requires the measurement of default correlations. Correlations measure the degree to which the default risks of the various borrowers and counterparties in the portfolio are related. The elements of credit risk can therefore be grouped as follows:

Stand-Alone Risk

- Default probability, the probability that the counterparty or borrower will fail to service its obligations.
- Loss given default, the extent of the loss incurred in the event the borrower or counterparty defaults.
- Migration risk, the probability and value impact of changes in default probability.

Portfolio Risk

- Default correlations, the degree to which the default risks of the borrowers and counterparties in the portfolio are related.
- Exposure, the size, or proportion, of the portfolio exposed to the default risk of each counterparty and borrower.

Due to a variety of technical developments in finance, it has become both possible and feasible to make these measurements. MKMV has pioneered the development of these methods for the last 15 years in its practice with commercial banks and, more recently, with asset managers. The fruits of this development effort are several products designed to address the quantification and management of credit risk. As we have noted in Chapter 7, MKMV estimates an expected default frequency (EDF™) for firms with publicly traded equity and delivers this estimate via a PC-based viewer called Credit Monitor™ or an Internet-based viewer called CreditEdge™.[3] For firms without publicly traded equity, MKMV offers RiskCalc™, which also produces an EDF credit measure. MKMV's EDF values combined with facility-specific data can be used together with MKMV's Global Correlation Model™ and Portfolio Manager™ to analyze and manage portfolios of credit-risky assets. The result is that practical and conceptually sound

---

3 Both of these software products cover nearly 30,000 firms globally and come bundled with a variety of analysis tools.

methods exist for measuring actual diversification, and for determining portfolio holdings to minimize concentrations and maximize return in debt portfolios.

The methods underlying MKMV's products rely on a framework often called a "structural" approach to modeling default. This framework begins with economic explanations of default. The remainder of this paper provides an introduction to this approach and the implications for managing a portfolio of corporate liabilities. Note that analyzing CDS requires the same framework.

THE MODEL OF DEFAULT RISK

A corporation has fixed obligations. These may be no more than its trade obligations, although they could just as well include bank loans and public debt. At one time, there was no legal means to escape the fulfillment of such obligations; a defaulter fled or was jailed. Modern treatment allows the defaulter to escape the obligation but only by relinquishing the corporation's assets to the obligee. In other words, a firm owing a single creditor $75 million fulfills the obligation by either paying the $75 million or by transferring the corporation's assets to the lender.

Which action the borrower will take is an economic decision, and the economic answer is straightforward: If the corporate assets are worth more than $75 million, the borrower will meet the obligation. If they are worth less, the borrower will default. The critical point is that the action depends on the market value of assets; book or accounting value will not suffice. Note that the "option to default" is valuable. Without it, the corporation could be forced to raise additional capital with the benefit accruing not to its owners but instead to its prior lender.

A lender purchasing a corporation's note can be thought of as engaging in two transactions. In the first it is purchasing an "inescapable" debt obligation, i.e., one that cannot be defaulted on. In the second, it is selling a "put" option to the borrower that states that the lender will buy the corporation's assets for the amount of the note at the option of the borrower. In the event the assets turn out to be worth less than the amount of the note, the borrower "puts" the assets to the lender and uses the proceeds to pay the note.

The lender owns a risk-free note and is "short" the default option, which is the same as a CDS written on the borrower.

The probability of default is the same as the probability of the option being exercised. If the probability of default goes up, the value of the option goes up, and the value of the lender's position (because it is "short" the option) goes down.

The probability of exercising the default option can be determined by application of option valuation methods. Assume for a moment that the market value of the corporation's assets is known, as well as the volatility of that value. The volatility measures the propensity of the asset value to change within a given time period. This information determines the probability of default, given the corporation's obligations. For instance, if the current asset market value is $150 million and the corporation's debt is $75 million and is due in one year, then default will occur if the asset value turns out to be less than $75 million in one year. If the firm's asset volatility is 17% per year, then a fall in value from $150 million to $75 million is a three-standard-deviation event with a probability of 0.3%. Thus the firm has a default probability of 0.3% (17% of 150 is 25, which is the amount of a one-standard-deviation move; the probability calculation assumes that the assets have a lognormal distribution.)

The market value of the firm's assets in one year is unknown. Based on firm characteristics including past performance, the expected asset value is determined to be $150 million, with a standard deviation of $25 million. This information makes it possible to represent the range of possible asset values and their frequencies in Figure 8.1. The firm has obligations due in one year of $75 million. If the market asset value turns out to be less than $75 million, then the owners of the firm will prefer to default. If the asset value is greater than $75 million, then the owners will prefer to pay the debt, because they will retain the residual value. The shaded area thus represents the probability of default. It represents the frequency of outcomes where the asset value is less than $75 million.

The shape of the frequency distribution is often simply assumed, given the expected value and standard deviation. For many purposes this is satisfactory, but practical experience with default rates shows that this shape must be measured, rather than assumed, to obtain sufficiently precise estimated default rates.

Asset Market Value and Volatility

Just as the firm's default risk can be derived from the behavior of the firm's asset value and the level of its obligations, the firm's

F I G U R E   8.1

Future Firm Asset Value

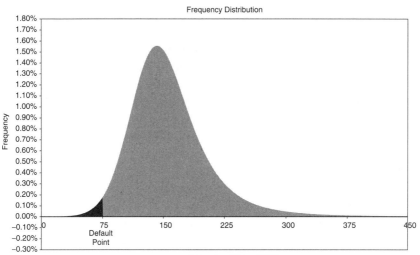

equity behavior can be similarly derived. The shareholders of the firm can be viewed as having a call option on the firm's asset value, where the exercise price is equal to the firm's obligations. If the market asset value exceeds the obligation amount at the maturity date, then the shareholders will exercise their option by paying off the obligation amount. If the asset value is less, they will prefer to default on the obligation and relinquish the remaining asset value to the lenders.

Using this framework, the equity value and volatility can be determined from the asset value, asset volatility, and the amount and maturity of obligations. What is actually more important is that the converse is also true: the asset value and volatility can be inferred from the equity value, equity volatility, and the amount and maturity of obligations. This process enables us to determine the market characteristics of a firm's assets from directly observable equity characteristics. (Readers should refer to Chapter 7 for more detail on how to implement this kind of model in practice.)

Knowing the market value and volatility of the borrower's assets is critical, as we have seen, to the determination of the probability of default. With it we can also determine the correlation of two firms' asset values. These correlations play an important role in the measurement of portfolio diversification.

The market value of assets changes unpredictably through time. The volatility in the historical time series is measured by the asset standard deviation, which was used in the previous illustration to describe the range of possible future asset values. The liabilities of the firm including equity represent a complete set of claims on all the cash flows produced by the assets. Thus the market value of the assets exactly equals the market value of the liabilities, including equity. As the market value of assets changes, the market value of liabilities changes, but the changes are not evenly apportioned across the liabilities due to differences in seniority.

The equity value changes close to dollar-for-dollar with the asset value. The vertical distance between the asset and equity values in Figure 8.2 is the market value of obligations senior to the equity ("debt"). The difference, i.e., the debt value, is shown below the axis. If the asset value falls enough, the probability of default on the debt increases and the market value of the debt also falls. A $1 fall in the asset value leads to perhaps a $0.10 fall in the debt value and a $0.90 fall in the equity value.

In percentage terms, the changes in the equity value are always larger than the changes in the asset value, because the equity value is a fraction of the total asset value. As the asset value, and thus equity value, falls, the equity volatility increases dramatically. The relationship between the asset and equity value is described by option theory. This theory makes it possible to infer

F I G U R E   8.2

Asset, Equity, and Debt Values

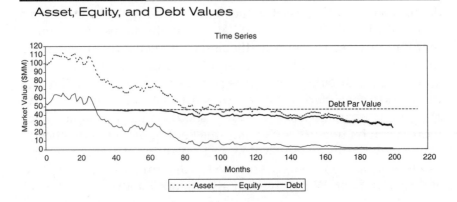

the asset value and volatility by knowing the level of fixed obligations and the equity value and volatility.

MEASUREMENT OF PORTFOLIO DIVERSIFICATION

Defaults translate into losses. The loss associated with a single default depends on the amount recovered. For the purposes of this exposition, we will assume that the recovery in the event of default is known, and that this recovery is net of the expenses of collection including the time value of the recovery process. Some CDS contracts are defining specific payments in the event of default, making this assumption even more appropriate. Thinking of the recovery as a percent of the face value of the loan, we can also specify the "loss given default" as one minus the expected recovery.

Using this structure, the expected loss for a single borrowing is the probability of default times the loss given default. Interestingly, the unexpected loss depends on the same variables as the expected loss. For a simple model of default or no-default, i.e., no modeling of credit migration, unexpected loss equals the loss given default times the square root of the product of the probability of default times one minus the probability of default. The unexpected loss represents the volatility, or standard deviation of loss. This approach raises the question of how to deal with instruments of different maturities. The analysis here uses a single time horizon for measuring risk. Establishing one horizon for analysis forms the basis of a framework for comparing the attractiveness of different types of credit exposures on the same scale. The risk at the horizon has two parts: the risk due to possible default, and the risk of loss of value due to credit deterioration. Instruments of the same borrower with different maturities (as long as the maturity is at or beyond the horizon) have the same default risk at the horizon, but the value risk (i.e., uncertainty around the value of the instrument at horizon) depends on the remaining time to maturity. The longer the remaining time, the greater the variation in value due to credit quality changes. (See Figure 8.3.)

For simplicity of presentation, the following analysis will assume that the maturity of all instruments is the same as the horizon. While this will eliminate maturity as an aspect of credit risk, it will not change the qualitative nature of any of the results.

F I G U R E   8.3

Expected and Unexpected Loss

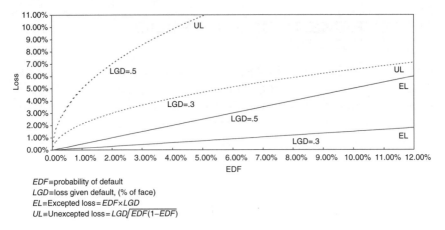

$EDF \equiv$ probability of default
$LGD \equiv$ loss given default, (% of face)
$EL \equiv$ Excepted loss $= EDF \times LGD$
$UL \equiv$ Unexcepted loss $= LGD\sqrt{EDF(1-EDF)}$

Modeling change in value at horizon requires a model of credit migration, substantially increasing the complexity of the calculations. Although maturity effects are important in practice, they are generally of lesser importance than the risk due to default.

Measuring the diversification of a portfolio means specifying the range and likelihood of possible losses associated with the portfolio. All else equal, a well-diversified portfolio is one that has a small likelihood of generating large losses. The average expected loss for a portfolio is the average of the expected losses of the assets in the portfolio. It is not a simple average but rather a weighted average, with the weights equal to each exposure amount as a percent of the total portfolio exposure.

It would be convenient if the volatility, or unexpected loss, of the portfolio were simply the weighted average of the unexpected losses of the individual assets, but it is not. The reason is that portfolio losses depend also on the relationship (correlation) between possible defaults.

A simple example illustrates this point. Consider an island on which it always rains on one side or the other in a given year, but never on both, with each side equally likely to receive rain. Consider two farms, one on each side of the island, each with debt on which they will default if it doesn't rain. A portfolio holding both loans in equal amounts, and nothing else, will have an expected default rate of 50%. Each borrowing will have an unexpected default rate of 50% (= $\sqrt{0.5 \times (1 - 0.5)}$). In other words, each of the portfolio assets is quite risky. But the portfolio as a whole has an unexpected loss rate of zero. The actual default rate and the expected default rate for the portfolio are identical. In each year, one and only one borrower will default, though which one is uncertain. There is a perfect negative correlation.

The alternative extreme is that it only rains half of the years on average, but when it rains, it always rains on both sides. This is perfect positive correlation; the farms will default in exactly the same years. Holding one loan is equivalent to holding both loans: there is no risk reduction from diversification.

An intermediate case is that raining on one farm makes it no more likely or less likely that it will rain on the other. The events of rainfall are independent. In this case, in one-fourth of the years both loans will default, in one-fourth neither will default, and one-half the time only one will default. There is now substantial diversification versus the perfect positive correlation case, because the likelihood of both defaulting is reduced by half.

Now let's extend this notion of diversification to the more general case of a portfolio with multiple risky securities. The portfolio loss measures can be calculated as follows:

$X_i \equiv$ face value of security i
$P_i \equiv$ price of security i (per \$1 of face value)
$V_p \equiv$ portfolio value = $P_1 X_1 + P_2 X_2 + \ldots + P_n X_n$
$w_i \equiv$ value proportion of security i in portfolio ("weight")
    $= P_i X_i / V_p$
$\rho_{ij} \equiv$ loss correlation between security i and security j
Note that $w_1 + w_2 + \cdots + w_n = 1$
$EL_i \equiv$ expected loss for security i
$EL_P \equiv$ portfolio expected loss = $w_1 EL_1 + w_2 EL_2 + \ldots w_n EL_n$
$UL_i \equiv$ unexpected loss for security i
$UL_p \equiv$ unexpected loss for portfolio

$$
= \sqrt{
\begin{aligned}
& w_1 w_1 UL_1 UL_1 \rho_{11} + w_1 w_2 UL_1 UL_2 \rho_{12} + \cdots + w_1 w_n UL_1 UL_n \rho_{1n} \\
& + w_2 w_1 UL_2 UL_1 \rho_{21} + w_2 w_2 UL_2 UL_2 \rho_{22} + \cdots + w_2 w_n UL_2 UL_n \rho_{2n} \\
& + \cdots + w_n w_1 UL_n UL_1 \rho_{n1} + w_n w_2 UL_n UL_2 \rho_{n2} + \cdots + w_n w_n UL_n UL_n \rho_{nn}
\end{aligned}
}
$$

Note that $\rho_{ij} = 1$ if $i = j$, and $\rho_{ij} = \rho_{ji}$ \hfill (8.1)

The portfolio expected loss is the weighted average of the expected losses of the individual securities, where the weights are the value proportions. On the other hand, the portfolio's unexpected loss is a more complex function of the ULs of the individual securities, the portfolio weights, and the pairwise loss correlations between securities.

In practice, actual defaults are positively, but not perfectly positively, correlated. Diversification, while not perfect, conveys significant benefits. Unfortunately, negative default correlations are rare to nonexistent. Calculating portfolio diversification means determining the portfolio's unexpected loss. To do this, default correlations and, ultimately, correlation in instrument values are required.

MODEL OF DEFAULT CORRELATION

Default correlation measures the strength of the default relationship between two borrowers. If there is no relationship, then the defaults are independent and the correlation is zero. In such a case, the probability of both borrowers being in default at the same time is the product of their individual probabilities of default. When two borrowers are correlated, this means that the probability of both defaulting at the same time is heightened, i.e., it is larger than it would be if they were completely independent. In fact, the correlation is just proportional to this difference. Thus, holding their individual default probabilities fixed, it is equivalent to say either that two borrowers are highly correlated or that they have a relatively high probability of defaulting in the same time period.

The basic default model says that the firm will default when its market asset value falls below the face value of obligations (the "default point"). This means that the joint probability of default is the likelihood of both firms' market asset values being below their respective default points in the same time period. This probability can be determined quite readily from knowing (i) the firms' current market asset values, (ii) their asset volatilities, and (iii) the correlation between the two firms' market asset values. In other words, the derivatives framework enables us to use the firms' asset correlation to obtain their default correlation.

This may not seem to be all that helpful, but in fact it is critically important to the empirical determination of default correlations. The correlation, for example, between equity returns, can be directly calculated because the histories of firms' stock returns are easily observable. Default correlations cannot be successfully measured from default experience. The historically observed joint frequency of default between two companies is usually zero. For instance, Exxon and Chevron have some chance of jointly defaulting, but nothing in their default history enables us to estimate the probability because neither has ever defaulted. Grouping firms enables us to estimate an average default correlation in the group using historical data, but the estimates so obtained are highly inaccurate.

In fact, no satisfactory procedure exists for directly estimating default correlations. Not surprisingly, this has been a major stumbling block to portfolio management of default risk. However, the derivatives approach enables us to measure the default correlation between two firms, using their asset correlations and their individual probabilities of default. The correlation between the two firms' asset values can be empirically measured from their equity values, as was described in the previous section.

Figure 8.4 illustrates the ranges of possible future asset values for two different firms. The two intersecting lines represent the default points for the two firms. For instance, if firm one's asset value ends up being below $180 million (the point represented by the vertical line), then firm one will default. The intersecting lines divide the range of possibilities into four regions. The upper right region represents those asset values for which neither firm one nor firm two will default. The lower left region represents those asset values for which both will default. The probabilities of all these

F I G U R E 8.4

Default and Nondefault Ranges

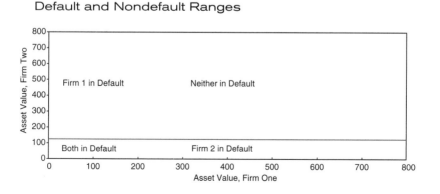

regions taken together must equal one. If the asset values of the two firms were independent, then the probabilities of the regions could be determined simply by multiplying the individual probabilities of default and nondefault for the two firms. For instance, suppose that firm one's default probability is 0.6% and firm two's is 0.3%. Then the probability of both defaulting, if they are independent, is the product of the default probabilities, or 0.0018%. If the two firms' asset values are positively correlated, then the probability of both asset values being high or low at the same time is higher than if they were independent, and the probability of one being high and the other low is lower. For instance, using the previous default probabilities, the probability of both defaulting might now be 0.01%, if their asset values are positively correlated.

By knowing the individual firms' default probabilities, and knowing the correlation of their asset values, the likelihood of both defaulting at the same time can be calculated. As noted in a previous box, the time series of a firm's asset values can be determined from its equity values. The correlation between two firms' asset values can be calculated from their respective time series.

We can calculate default correlation as follows:

$JDF \equiv$ joint default frequency of firm 1 and firm 2 i.e., actual probability of both firms defaulting together

$$\rho_D \equiv \text{default correlation for firm 1 and firm 2}$$
$$= \frac{JDF - EDF_1 EDF_2}{\sqrt{EDF_1(1 - EDF_1)EDF_2(1 - EDF_2)}} \qquad (8.2)$$

The numerator of this formula represents the difference of the actual probability of both firms defaulting and the probability of both defaulting if they were independent. Note that if the asset values are independent, then the default correlation is zero.

In practice, we extend this model to consider the correlation in the value of claims such as loans, bonds, and CDS within a portfolio. The default state corresponds with a particularly low value realization for the loan or bond issued by the defaulted firm. This extension requires estimation of the joint value distribution between each pair of credit-risky assets in the portfolio.[4] In this

---

4 For instance, MKMV's Portfolio Manager™ incorporates this richer approach to determine the value correlation among all securities in a portfolio.

way, the correlated credit migration over time can be captured to determine a more accurate measure of possible losses in the future.

MODEL OF VALUE CORRELATION

An important strength of the structural model of default presented here[5] is the ability to generalize relationships in a way to create a comprehensive credit portfolio model. In addition to the EDF values for each firm, the joint default frequency (JDF) must be calculated to determine a value correlation. In the context of the structural model explained above, the JDF can be calculated by focusing on the relationship between a firm's market asset value and its respective default point. EDF values embed this information on an individual firm level. The remaining piece of the puzzle is the correlation between each firm's market asset value.

Mathematically we can write down the following function for the JDF:

$N_2( )$ ≡ bivariate normal distribution function
$N^{-1}( )$ ≡ inverse normal distribution function
ρ_A ≡ correlation between firm 1's asset return
      and firm 2's asset return

$$JDF = N_2(N^{-1}(EDF_1), N^{-1}(EDF_2), \rho_A) \tag{8.3}$$

Estimating pairwise asset correlations for publicly traded firms can be done in a number of ways. One method would be to calculate a time series of asset values for each firm and then calculate a sample correlation between each pair of asset value series. While this method may seem reasonable in theory, in practice it is the least effective way to calculate correlations for credit portfolio modeling. We are most interested in the systematic comovement and work to estimate efficiently this comovement over a subsequent time horizon. Because the movement in a typical firm's asset value is mostly driven by factors idiosyncratic to that firm, sample correlations will reflect comovement that is unique to that sample period—not very useful for predicting an ex-ante correlation over a subsequent time horizon. Given the weakness in this approach (not to mention the problems associated with insufficient

---

5 This approach is implemented in MKMV technology.

observations needed to even calculate sample correlations), we turn to factor modeling to calculate correlations.

A factor model relates the systematic or nondiversifiable components of the economy that drive changes in asset value. For example, the entire economy may follow a business cycle, which affects most companies' prospects. The impact may differ from company to company, but they are affected nonetheless. Determining the sensitivity of changes in asset values to changes in a particular economic factor provides the basis for estimating asset correlation.

Changes in a firm's asset value constitute an asset value return or firm return. We can decompose this return as follows:

$$
\begin{bmatrix} Firm \\ Return \end{bmatrix} = \begin{bmatrix} Composite \\ Factor \\ Return \end{bmatrix} + \begin{bmatrix} Firm \\ Specific \\ Effects \end{bmatrix} \tag{8.4}
$$

The composite factor return proxies for the systematic risk factors in the economy. We can further decompose this composite factor return as follows:

$$
\begin{bmatrix} Composite \\ Factor \\ Return \end{bmatrix} = \begin{bmatrix} Composite \\ Factor \\ Returns \end{bmatrix} + \begin{bmatrix} Industry \\ Factor \\ Returns \end{bmatrix} \tag{8.5}
$$

$$
\begin{bmatrix} Country \\ Factor \\ Return \end{bmatrix} = \begin{bmatrix} Global \\ Economic \\ Effect \end{bmatrix} + \begin{bmatrix} Regional \\ Factor \\ Effect \end{bmatrix} + \begin{bmatrix} Sector \\ Factor \\ Effect \end{bmatrix} + \begin{bmatrix} Country \\ Specific \\ Effect \end{bmatrix} \tag{8.6}
$$

$$
\begin{bmatrix} Industry \\ Factor \\ Return \end{bmatrix} = \begin{bmatrix} Global \\ Economic \\ Effect \end{bmatrix} + \begin{bmatrix} Regional \\ Factor \\ Effect \end{bmatrix} + \begin{bmatrix} Sector \\ Factor \\ Effect \end{bmatrix} + \begin{bmatrix} Industry \\ Specific \\ Effect \end{bmatrix} \tag{8.7}
$$

Firm asset correlation can then be calculated from each firm's systematic or composite factor return. In this way, we relate the systematic component of changes in asset value, which produces a better estimate of future comovements in asset values. As an example of how to construct a usable factor model, we consider the MKMV Global Correlation Model, where industry and country indexes are produced from a global database of market asset values (estimated from the traded equity prices together with each firm's liability information) for nearly 30,000 publicly traded firms. These indexes are used to create a composite factor index for each firm depending on its country and industry classifications.

Mathematically, the following relationship is constructed:

$w_{kc} \equiv$ weight of firm k in country c
$w_{ki} \equiv$ weight of firm k in industry i

note that $\displaystyle\sum_{c=1}^{\bar{c}} w_{kc} = \sum_{i=1}^{\bar{i}} w_{ki} = 1$ where $\bar{c}$ is currently 45 countries

and $\bar{i}$ is 61 industries for MKMV's Global Correlation Model

$r_c \equiv$ return index for country c (estimated from publicly traded firms.)
$r_i \equiv$ return index for industry I (estimated from publicly traded firms.)
$\phi_k \equiv$ composite (custom) market factor index for firm k

$$\phi_k \equiv \sum_{c=1}^{\bar{c}} w_{kc} r_c + \sum_{i=1}^{\bar{i}} w_{ki} r_i$$

Once the custom index is calculated for a particular firm, the sensitivity (i.e., beta) to the market factors reflected in this index can be estimated. The relationship used for this estimation is written as follows:

$r_k \equiv$ return for firm k
$\beta_k \equiv$ beta for firm k
$\varepsilon_k \equiv$ firm-specific component of return for firm k
$r_k = \beta_k \phi_k + \varepsilon_k$

We can similarly estimate the sensitivity or beta ($\beta_{Country,Common\ Factor}$ and $\beta_{Industry,Common\ Factor}$) of countries and industries on factors we specify. The MKMV model uses two global factors, five regional factors, and seven sectoral factors; because industry and country-specific factors may exist (i.e.. those not linked through the 14 common factors), the model also uses country (45 countries) and industry (61 industries) specific factors. An example of calculating the sensitivity of firm k to a global factor is given as:

$$\beta_{kG} = \beta_k \left(\sum_{c=1}^{45} w_{kc} \beta_{cG} + \sum_{i=1}^{61} w_{ki} \beta_{iG} \right) \tag{8.8}$$

This calculation produces the parameters necessary to estimate the firm asset value correlation. We can develop this further:

$\sigma(j, k) \equiv$ covariance between firm j and firm k

$\rho_{jk} \equiv$ correlation between firm j's and firm k's asset value
returns

$\sigma_k \equiv$ standard deviation of firm k's asset value return

$$\sigma(j,k) = \sum_{G=1}^{2} \beta_{jG}\beta_{kG}\sigma_G^2 + \sum_{R=1}^{5} \beta_{jR}\beta_{kR}\sigma_R^2 + \sum_{S=1}^{7} \beta_{jS}\beta_{kS}\sigma_S^2$$
$$+ \sum_{i=1}^{61} \beta_{ji}\beta_{ki}\varepsilon_i^2 + \sum_{c=1}^{45} \beta_{jc}\beta_{kc}\varepsilon_c^2$$
(8.9)

$$\begin{bmatrix} Return \\ Covariance \\ j \ and \ k \end{bmatrix} = \begin{bmatrix} Global\,(G) \\ Economic \\ Factors \end{bmatrix} + \begin{bmatrix} Re\,gional\,(R) \\ Economic \\ Factors \end{bmatrix} + \begin{bmatrix} Industrial\,(S) \\ Sector \\ Factors \end{bmatrix}$$
$$+ \begin{bmatrix} Industry\,(i) \\ Specific \\ Factors \end{bmatrix} + \begin{bmatrix} Country\,(c) \\ Specific \\ Factors \end{bmatrix}$$
(8.10)

$$\begin{bmatrix} Return \\ Correlation \\ j \ and \ k \end{bmatrix} = \frac{\begin{bmatrix} Return \\ Covariance \\ j \ and \ k \end{bmatrix}}{\begin{bmatrix} Return \\ Volatility \ j \end{bmatrix}\begin{bmatrix} Return \\ Volatility \ k \end{bmatrix}}$$
(8.11)

$$\rho_{jk} = \frac{\sigma(j,k)}{\sigma_j \sigma_k}$$
(8.12)

The covariance calculation depends on the sensitivities or
betas ($\beta_{Company,Factor}$) for each firm combined with the factor vari-
ances (σ^2_{Factor}). To arrive at the correlation we must scale the covariance by the standard deviation of the returns as shown in the final
equation of the above group.

Simply said, the factor model focuses attention on the components driving comovements. These components can be separated into the effects listed above; however, the important aspect of this process is identifying the total systematic component. To the extent that it is correctly estimated, the subsequent decomposition into constituent effects is only necessary for gaining intuition behind the source of correlation between any two firms. This approach relies on the embedded systematic components reflected in the data on publicly traded firms around the world.

Returning to the JDF calculation, we combine this asset value correlation with the individual firm EDF values to arrive at a default correlation. Default correlation is sufficient if we do not model possible credit migration over our horizon of analysis. If we plan to consider the possibility of credit migration at horizon, we need to calculate the joint distribution of values among the loans made to the firms being analyzed. Explicitly calculating this relationship requires calculation of a double integral (over all possible firm asset values) for each pair of firms in the portfolio. For most sizable credit portfolios, this approach is cost prohibitive from a computational perspective. Instead, we can make use of the factor structure explained above to construct a Monte Carlo simulation, which draws the individual factors over and over again to determine the possible portfolio value realizations. Each of these portfolio value realizations embeds the loan value correlations since each loan value is calculated based on the relationship feeding back to each firm's asset value. These asset values derive from the sensitivity to each of the risk factors.

A simple example makes this process clearer: Assume we are analyzing a portfolio of three loans to three different companies. We determine that the asset values of company A and company B increase (decrease) whenever interest rates decline (rise). Company C is unaffected by changes in interest rates. In this economy, we have only one factor—interest rate movement. We then simulate this one factor. Whenever this interest rate factor is high, A's and B's asset values are small. These low asset values result in the loans to A and B being valued at a discount; C's loan value is unchanged, since C is not affected by the interest-rate factor. If the interest rate factor is low, A's and B's loans will be valued at a premium. The key to the correlation arises from the similar behavior in loan value whenever a particular factor level is drawn.

Clearly, the movement in the value of A's and B's loans are correlated, while C's loans are uncorrelated with the rest of the portfolio. The process of simulating different factor realizations generates a variety of portfolio value realizations. These value realizations can then be transformed into a loss distribution. The extent to which loan values move together links back to the sensitivities to the different risk factors in the factor model.

THE LIKELIHOOD OF LARGE LOSSES

We are all familiar with the "bell-shaped" or normal distribution. If portfolio losses had such a bell-shaped distribution, we could accurately specify the likelihood of large losses simply by knowing the expected and unexpected loss for the portfolio. The problem is that individual debt assets have very "skewed" loss probabilities. Most of the time the borrower does not default and the loss is zero. However, when default occurs, the loss is usually substantial. Given the positive correlation between defaults, this unevenness of loss never fully "smoothes out," even in very large portfolios. There is always a large probability of relatively small losses, and a small probability of rather large losses.

This "skewness" leads to an unintuitive result: a very high percentage of the time (around 80%), the actual losses will be less than the average loss. The reason is that the average is pulled upwards by the potential for large losses. There is a great danger of being "lulled" by a string of low losses into believing that the portfolio is more diversified than it actually is. Fortunately, the frequency distribution of portfolio losses can be determined using the information we have already discussed. Knowing this distribution for a given portfolio gives an alternative characterization of diversification:

- Portfolio A is better diversified than portfolio B if the probability of loss exceeding a given percent is smaller for A than for B, and both portfolios have the same expected loss.

Figure 8.5 contrasts the loan loss distribution for a portfolio with a bell-shaped loss distribution having the same expected loss and unexpected loss. There are two striking differences. The most obvious is that the actual loan loss distribution is asymmetric. There is a small probability of large losses and a large probability

F I G U R E   8.5

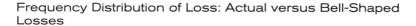

Frequency Distribution of Loss: Actual versus Bell-Shaped Losses

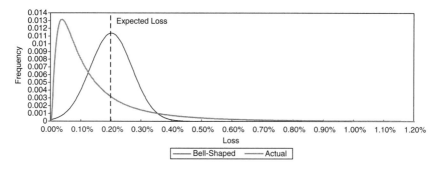

of small losses. If losses were determined as per the bell-shaped distribution, then losses would exceed the expected loss about half the time, and the other half of the time they would be less than the expected loss. For the actual loss distribution, realized losses will be less than the expected loss approximately 75% of the time. There is a significant likelihood that even a risky portfolio will generate consecutive years of low realized losses.

The second major difference is that the probability of very large losses approaches zero much more quickly for the bell-shaped distribution than for the skewed distribution. In fact, for a portfolio with a skewed loss distribution, there is an economically significant chance of realized losses that are six to eight standard deviations in excess of the expected loss. For the bell-shaped distribution, there is virtually no chance of a four-standard-deviation event occurring.

Figure 8.6 contrasts two loan loss distributions for different portfolios. The two portfolios have the same level of expected loss, but portfolio A has a higher unexpected loss. There is a significantly higher chance of incurring a large loss in portfolio A than in portfolio B. These probabilities can be seen by looking at the areas under the respective curves. For instance, the probability of a 4% loss in portfolio A is 0.1%, but the probability of a 4% loss in portfolio B is only 0.05%. The implication of this difference for the two portfolios in debt-rating terms is the difference between a single B rating and a single A rating. This view of diversification has an immediate concrete implication for capital adequacy.

F I G U R E   8.6

Frequency Distribution of Loss: Different Unexpected Losses

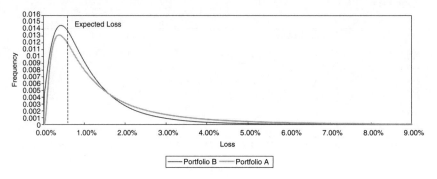

Given the frequency distribution of loss, we can determine the likelihood of losses, which exceed the amount of capital held against the portfolio. This probability can be set to the desired level by varying the amount of capital.

To illustrate how this can be done in practice, it is necessary to consider the market value, rather than the book value, of the portfolio. To do that, we need to be able to determine the market value of a security. Ideally, we want to use data from a deep and liquid market in the security we are modeling. In the case of most bonds and loans, the markets are typically neither deep nor liquid. The increasing liquidity in the CDS market provides a new, useful source of data regarding valuation of many corporate debt instruments. In any event, for most large portfolios of corporate debt, we must rely on models to determine a mark-to-market value. Let us consider the case of determining valuation of a loan.

VALUATION

Credit portfolio analysis requires a model for valuation. Tracking changes in a portfolio's market value is essential to managing a portfolio and evaluating a portfolio manager's performance. While an actual market price of a particular debt instrument or contract is always preferred at the starting date of analysis, a model is typically necessary for generating values conditional on simulated states of the world at the time horizon of analysis. When direct prices are not available, equity and CDS prices can be used to estimate the key drivers of value for any kind of credit-risky instrument. In particular, equity provides a "clean" (i.e., separated from loss given default and a market risk premium) estimate of a firm's default probability. CDS provides an estimate of risk-neutral expected loss; however, a model is needed to break apart the default probability, loss given default, and market premium that drives the expected loss.

In summary, the value of a credit-risky security requires specification of expected cash flows, a default probability, a loss given default, and a market risk premium. In the case of most cash instruments, the implicit default-risk-free security must also be considered. With this background, let's consider the process of modeling a security with credit risk in the context of a simple instrument: a loan.

The market value of a loan is simply the price for which it can be bought or sold. Although there is a loan sales market, loans by and large are not actively transacted for extended periods. The result is that current market prices do not exist for most loans. The objective of valuation is to determine what a loan should sell for, were it to trade. The value cannot be determined in the abstract or in some absolute sense, but only by comparison to the market prices of financial instruments that are traded. Valuation consists of extrapolating actual market prices to nontraded assets, based on the relationship between their characteristics. In the case of loans, the process involves consideration of the borrower's traded equity, CDS available on that borrower, and traded debt should it exist.

Bank assets have a variety of complexities: default risk, utilization, covenants, priority, and so forth. Many of these complexities can be viewed, and valued, as options belonging to the borrower or lender. For this exposition, one of the simplest cases will suffice, namely a fixed-term, fixed-rate corporate loan. If this loan were not subject to default risk, then it could be valued readily by comparison with the pricing on similar term AAA-rated notes. The level of default risk in AAA-rated notes is very small, making them a good market benchmark. On the other hand, Treasury notes, which literally have no default risk, are not as good a benchmark for corporate liabilities, due to persistent and unpredictable differences between corporate and government issues.

The so-called "pricing" on a loan is the set of fees and spreads that determines the promised cash flows between borrower and lender. This is the equivalent of the coupon rate on a bond.

The value of the loan is obtained by discounting the loan cash flows by an appropriate set of discount rates. The discount rates, in the absence of default risk, would simply differ by increments of term, according to the current term structure. In the presence of default risk, the discount rates must contain two additional elements. The first is the expected loss premium. This reflects an adjustment to the discount rate to account for the actuarial expectation of loss. It is based on the probability of default and the loss given default. The second is the market risk premium. This is compensation for the nondiversifiable loss risk in the loan. If the loan did not contain a risk premium, then on average it would only return the risk-free base rate. The key point is the qualifier: "on average." In years when default did not occur, the loan would return a little more due to the expected loss premium. However, in the event of default, it would return much less.

Because an investor could obtain the risk-free base rate not just "on average," but all the time, by buying the risk-free asset, the risky asset must provide additional compensatory return. This would not be the case if default risk were completely diversifiable, but (as we have discussed), it is not. The market will provide compensation for unavoidable risk bearing, i.e., the portion of the loan's loss risk that cannot be eliminated through diversification. The amount of nondiversifiable risk can be determined from knowing the borrower's probability of default and the risk characteristics of the borrower's assets. The market price for risk bearing can be determined from the equity, corporate debt, and CDS markets. This approach, based on option valuation methods, can be used to construct discount rates, specific to the borrower, which correctly account for both the time value of money and the expected and unexpected loss characteristics of the particular borrower.

In the case where a particular CDS can be considered comparable to the implicit CDS in a loan position, the CDS spread can be used to build an appropriate discount rate to arrive at the appropriate, risk-adjusted price of the loan. Unfortunately, the real world is not so simple. The loss given default assumptions are likely to be different between the loan and the CDS. Moreover, the pricing in the two markets may differ by a liquidity premium. Another possibility (although less defensible) is that the market risk premium differs in the loan and CDS markets. In order to resolve these issues and develop more confidence regarding a particular modeled price, we can use a model framework that economically relates each driver of value.

There are only two possible outcomes for a loan. Either it is repaid, or the borrower defaults. The loss distribution for a single loan is simply:

Event	Probability
Default	EDF
No default	1–EDF

In the event of default, we expected to lose a percentage of the face value of the loan equal to LGD. If the yield on the loan is Y and the risk-free base rate is R_f, then the return distribution can be characterized as follows:

Event	Probability	Return
Default	EDF	R_f–LGD
No default	1–EDF	Y

The expected return is the probability weighted average of the returns.

$$E(R) = EDF(R_f - LGD) + (1 - EDF)Y \qquad (8.13)$$

The required compensation for the actuarial risk of default is equal to $(LGD \times EDF)/(1 - EDF)$. This is called the expected loss premium. If the loan yield equaled the risk-free base rate plus the expected loss premium, then

$$Y = R_f + \frac{LGD \times EDF}{1 - EDF}, \text{ and} \qquad (8.14)$$

$$E(R) = EDF(R_f - LGD) + (1 - EDF)\left(R_f + \frac{LGD \times EDF}{(1 - EDF)} \right) \qquad (8.15)$$

$$E(R) = R_f \qquad (8.16)$$

The expected loss premium provides just enough additional return when the borrower does not default to compensate for the expected loss when the borrower does default.

The calculation above shows that if the only additional compensation were the expected loss premium, then the lender on average would receive only the risk-free base rate. It would be much better for the lender to just lend at the risk-free base, because it would get the same average return and would incur no default risk. There must be additional compensation for the fact that the realized return is risky even for a large, well-diversified portfolio of loans. That additional compensation is called the risk premium.

The required pricing on a loan is thus the risk-free base rate plus the expected loss premium plus the risk premium.

$$Y = R_f + \text{EL Premium} + \text{Risk Premium} \tag{8.17}$$

Subtracting the appropriate EL premium from the credit spread on debt securities or CDSs yields the market risk premium. If we think of the yield on a loan as being an average of these various discount rates (as "yield-to-maturity" is for a bond), then the value of the loan is simply its promised cash flows discounted at its yield. If the yield exceeds the loan rate, then the loan will be at a discount. An increase in the probability of default will push up the yield required in the market, and push down the price of the loan. Other factors remaining the same, loan value moves inversely to changes in default probability.

Combining data from equity, traded debt, and CDS markets, each driver of value can be estimated to provide a robust toolkit for assigning value to credit-risky exposures found in a credit portfolio. For example, default probabilities can be estimated out of the equity market, and LGD can be estimated based on corporate bond loss experience. These results can be combined with observed CDS spreads to estimate an implied market risk premium. The art lies in discovering which driver is best estimated in which market.

ECONOMIC CAPITAL AND FUND MANAGEMENT

We can consider an example of a bank by separating it into two parts: one part is the actual portfolio of assets; the second part is an amalgam of all other bank functions. Let us call the part containing the portfolio "the fund," and think of the fund as containing only a portfolio management function (i.e., no other bank functions). The fund is leveraged. It borrows from the rest of the bank at the appropriate market rate; we may think of it also as borrowing directly in the bond or money markets. The rest of the bank owns equity supporting the fund, although in principle some or all could be owned outside of the bank. In essence, the fund is an odd sort of leveraged money market fund. The fund's assets have a market value, either because the individual assets have actual market prices, or because we can value them as was discussed in the previous section.

The fund has fixed obligations, i.e., its borrowings. These borrowings also have determinable market values. The value of the fund's equity is exactly equal to the excess of the market value of its assets over the market value of its obligations. The economic capital of a bank is closely related to the market value of its equity. Rather than being the excess of the market value of assets over the market value of liabilities, economic capital is the excess of the market value of assets over the market value of liabilities, assuming the liabilities had no default risk. For a bank with low default risk, these values are virtually identical. However, for a distressed bank, economic capital can be zero or negative, whereas market equity is always positive. The "economic capital" fluctuates with the market value of assets. The fund can raise more equity or more debt and invest it in additional assets, or it can make payouts to debt or equity, reducing its assets.

The objective of fund management is to maximize the value of the fund's equity. In a hypothetical world of frictionless markets and common information, i.e., a world without institutional constraints, this would be achieved by:

- Purchasing assets at or below market; selling assets at or above market.

Regardless of circumstance, this is a desirable policy, and its implementation requires rigorous measurement of default risk, and pricing that by market standards at least compensates for the default risk. However, institutional constraints do exist, and markets are not frictionless nor information symmetrically dispersed. In fact, it is the existence of these market "imperfections" that makes intermediation a valuable service. There is likely no need for banks or mutual funds to exist in a world of perfect capital markets.

In practice, equity funding is "expensive." This may be because equity returns are taxed at the fund level, or because the lack of transparency of bank balance sheets imposes an additional "risk" cost (agency cost). The result is that banks feel constrained to use the minimal amount of capital consistent with maintaining their ability to freely access debt markets. For wholesale banks, that access is permitted only to banks with extremely low default probabilities (.15% or less per year).

Finally, the fund is an investment vehicle. In a world where transactions are costly, one of the fund's functions is to minimize those costs for final investors. It does this by providing competitive return for its risk. Failure to do this makes it a secondary rather than primary investment vehicle; in other words, if it is less than fully diversified, another layer of investment vehicles, and another round of transactions costs, are required to provide diversification to the investor.

Both of these considerations add two additional objectives:

- Obtain maximum diversification;
- Determine and maintain capital adequacy.

As previously discussed, capital adequacy can be determined by considering the frequency distribution of portfolio losses. Maintaining capital adequacy means that the desired leverage must be determined for each new asset as it is added to the portfolio. This leverage must be such as to leave the fund's overall default risk unchanged. Assets that, net of diversification, add more than average risk to the portfolio, must be financed (proportionately) with more equity and less debt than the existing portfolio.

Capital adequacy means using enough equity funding that the fund's default risk is acceptably low. A conventional measure is the actual or implied debt rating of the fund; the debt rating can be interpreted as corresponding to a probability of default. For instance, an AA-rated fund typically has a default probability less than 0.05%. The fund will default if it suffers losses that are large enough to eliminate the equity. Figure 8.7 shows the loss distribution of the fund's portfolio. For any given level of equity funding, it is possible to determine the probability of losses that would eliminate the equity. For instance, if this portfolio were 4% equity funded, then the probability of depleting the equity is 0.10%. This is equivalent to a single-A debt rating.

Maximum diversification means the lowest level of portfolio unexpected loss, conditional on a given level of expected return. Note that this is different than minimizing risk without regard to return. The latter can be accomplished by holding U.S. Treasuries. For each level of return, and for a given set of possible assets, there is a unique set of holdings that gives the minimum unexpected

FIGURE 8.7

Frequency Distribution of Loss: Capital Loss

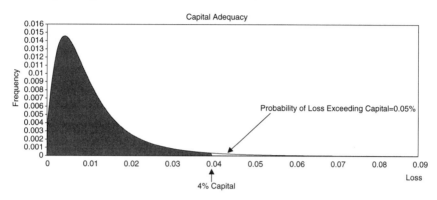

loss. When we depict the expected return and unexpected loss associated with each of these portfolios, the resulting graph is called the "efficient frontier." The process for determining how much "economic capital" (equity) to use in financing an asset, and the process for maximizing diversification, both require measuring how much risk an individual asset contributes to the portfolio, net of risk reduction due to diversification.

RISK CONTRIBUTION AND OPTIMAL DIVERSIFICATION

Diversification means that the risk in the portfolio is less than the average of each asset's stand-alone risk. Some part of each asset's stand-alone risk is diversified away in the portfolio. Thinking of it in this way, we can divide the stand-alone risk of an asset into the part that is diversified away and the part that remains. This latter part is the risk contribution of the asset to the portfolio; the risk of the portfolio is the holdings-weighted average of these risk contributions.

The residual risk contribution of an asset changes as the composition of the portfolio varies. In particular, as the holding of the asset increases, its risk contribution increases. The percentage of its stand-alone risk that is not being diversified away increases at the same time as the value weight of the asset in the portfolio increases.

Figure 8.8 shows the loss risk of a single asset. The total height of the bar represents the unexpected loss of the asset. The bottom

Loss in Portfolio

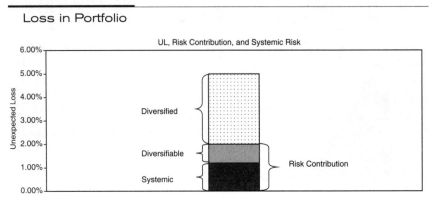

segment of the bar represents the portion of the unexpected loss that could not be eliminated through diversification even in the broadest possible portfolio. This is called the nondiversifiable, or systemic, risk of the asset. When one speaks of the "beta" of an asset, one is referring to this portion of an asset's risk. In the context of an actual portfolio, diversification will generally be less than optimal, and some portion of its risk that could be diversified away has not been. The second segment of the bar represents this portion. The sum of the bottom two segments is the risk contribution of the asset to the portfolio. It represents the risk that has not been diversified away in the portfolio. Some has not been diversified away because it cannot be (the systemic portion); some has not been diversified away because the portfolio is less than optimally diversified.

The portfolio's unexpected loss is simply the holdings-weighted average of the risk contributions of the individual assets. Risk contribution is the appropriate measure of the risk of an asset in a portfolio because it is net of the portion of risk that has been diversified away. As the holdings change, the risk contributions change. For instance, if the proportionate holding of this asset were increased in the portfolio, less of its risk would be diversified away, and the risk contribution would go up.

Systemic risk is measured relative to the whole market of risky assets. Risk contribution is specific to a particular portfolio: the particular set of assets and the particular proportions in which the assets are held. In a typical portfolio, there are assets whose returns are large relative to the amount of risk they contribute;

there are also assets whose returns are small relative to the amount of risk they contribute to the portfolio. These assets are mispriced relative to the portfolio in which they are being held.

In some cases, this "mispricing to portfolio" simply reflects that the assets are mispriced in the market, and it is ultimately fixed as the market price adjusts. More often, however, it reflects that the portfolio has too much or too little of the particular assets. If an asset that has too little return for its risk is partially swapped for an asset that is generously compensated for its risk, two things happen. First, the portfolio improves: without any increase in risk, the portfolio return improves. Second, as the holding of the former asset decreases, its risk contribution goes down; similarly, the risk contribution of the latter asset increases. As the risk contributions change, the return-to-risk ratios change for each asset. The former asset is no longer so underrewarded; the latter is no longer so overrewarded. Continuing the swap will continue to improve the portfolio until the return-to-risk ratios for each of the assets are brought into alignment with the overall portfolio. (See Figure 8.9.)

F I G U R E   8.9

Mispricing to Portfolio

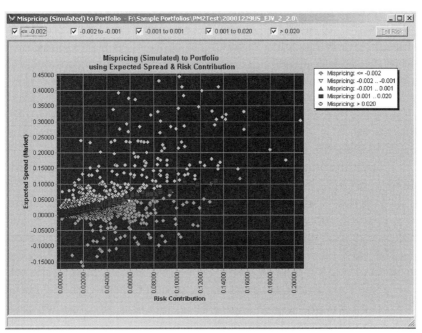

This process, applied to all assets in the portfolio, leads to the maximization of diversification for any given level of return. Thus, a key part of the portfolio management process is to measure the risk contribution of each asset and its return relative to that risk. An optimized portfolio will not contain the same amount of all assets; the holdings will be based on the risk contribution of each asset relative to its return. In fact, an optimized portfolio is one where all assets have the same return-to-risk ratio. Any deviation would imply the existence of a swap that could improve the overall portfolio. The availability of CDS now makes it easier for credit portfolio managers to find trades to improve their portfolios.

Swapping low return-to-risk assets for high return-to-risk assets optimizes a portfolio. To do this requires identifying which are the high and low return-to-risk assets.

Figure 8.10 (a) and (b), below, is taken from MKMV's Portfolio Manager software. It illustrates for a bond portfolio the return-to-risk characteristics of all the assets in the portfolio; the return to each asset is measured by its spread adjusted for expected loss, while the risk is measured by the risk contribution to the portfolio.

The assets represented by the (noninverted) triangles all have average return-to-risk ratios. One can think of this average return-to-risk ratio as defined by a line fit through the middle of the points on the graph. Assets lying above this average ratio level have high values; assets lying below it have low values. As the holding of a low return-to-risk asset is decreased, its risk contribution falls and its return-to-risk ratio improves. The reverse happens for high return-to-risk assets whose holdings are increased. This mechanism serves to move assets into the average range as the portfolio diversification is improved. No further improvement is possible when all assets lie within the band.

It is vitally important to note that the results of portfolio optimization depend on the set of potential assets that the fund can hold. With the availability of CDS, the set of diversifying exposures has increased substantially for holders of credit portfolios. In the final analysis, it will not make sense to maximize diversification over the existing set of assets in the portfolio without considering the effect of adding new assets into the portfolio. Because of the relatively low default correlations between most borrowers, the gains from broad diversification are substantial and do not decrease quickly as portfolio size increases.

F I G U R E   8.10 (a) and (b)

Risk versus Return

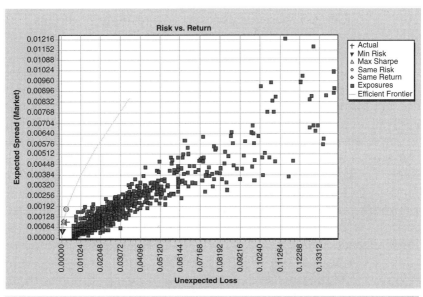

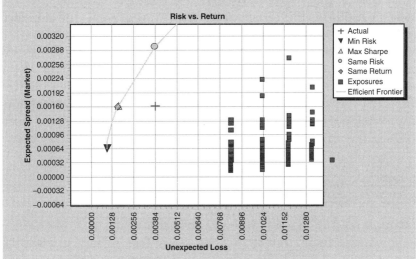

An equity mutual fund would be poorly diversified if it were limited to only holding those equities that it had underwritten itself. This is much more the case for debt portfolios because there are larger and more persistent benefits to diversification in debt than in equity. The implication is that funds will want to hold the broadest possible set of assets and must be prepared to buy them when it benefits the fund. The approach described here can be used to identify which credit exposures are desirable additions at which prices. Different holdings of assets in the portfolio result in portfolios with different risk and return characteristics. This is illustrated in Figure 8.10 (a) and (b), the latter being a rescaled version of the former.

The square points (■) represent the expected spread, unexpected loss pairs of individual assets. A portfolio that consisted 100% of a single asset would have the same risk and return as that asset. An actual portfolio constructed from these assets, depending on its proportions, will have a specific risk/return combination. The cross (✚) represents one such actual portfolio. Because the assets are positively correlated, all portfolios will have some risk. For a given level of return there must therefore be a portfolio with minimum but still positive risk. The diamond (◆) represents the portfolio with the same expected spread as the actual portfolio (✚) but the least possible risk. Similarly, there is an upward bound on achievable return at any level of risk. The portfolio represented by the gray circle (●) illustrates the maximal return portfolio with the same risk as the actual portfolio. The light line passing through these portfolios is the "efficient frontier." It represents the expected spread/UL values for those portfolios that have the smallest possible unexpected loss for a given level of expected spread. The unexpected loss of these portfolios lies far to the left of the ULs of the individual assets. This reflects the amount of risk that is eliminated through diversification. The inverted triangle (▼) is the global minimum risk portfolio. The triangle (▲) above it represents the portfolio on the efficient frontier with the highest return-to-risk ratio.

CREDIT DEFAULT SWAPS (CDS) AND CREDIT PORTFOLIOS

Throughout this chapter we have discussed CDSs in similar terms as bonds and loans. While a CDS does, in fact, behave in a similar fashion, several key differences associated with CDS modeling in a portfolio context should be emphasized. First, whether buying or selling protection, the credit risk of the counterparty may need to be considered. In many cases, counterparties to CDS contracts are high quality and have low default probabilities. However, large concentrations to the same set of high-quality counterparties may start adversely affecting the diversification of certain portfolios.

In the case of buying protection, the buyer is interested in both the default probability of the underlying obligor and the default probability of the counterparty. For portfolio risk modeling purposes, the important analytic is the joint default probability of the underlying obligor and the counterparty. This joint default probability will be a function of the individual default probabilities and the correlation between the underlying obligor and the counterparty. Note that buying protection is similar in form to shorting a loan or bond. While the value of the position may behave similarly to a short-loan or short-bond position, the presence of this joint default probability issue makes the CDS analysis a little more involved.

Some may argue that the joint default probability of a high-quality counterparty and a moderate- to high-quality underlying obligor is close enough to zero that it can be safely ignored. This argument neglects potential correlation effects that increase the size of the overall portfolio downside risk. Many portfolios held by financial institutions contain exposures both directly to the counterparties in the form of debt investments or credit lines and indirectly via positions in CDS contracted with the same counterparties. Properly accounting for this correlation may materially impact credit risk analysis of a portfolio. Said differently, the sheer size of exposures to a group of correlated, high-quality counterparties may result in higher probabilities of extreme portfolio losses.

This argument for ignoring counterparty risk also fails when economic conditions affecting a particular group of counterparties materially increases their risk. Recent experience in Japan demonstrates how once strong financial institutions may suddenly increase in riskiness, resulting in much higher joint default probabilities among the deteriorated counterparties and low-quality obligors. Frequent monitoring of the total risk exposure across a credit portfolio reduces the chance of facing a sudden increase in the joint default probabilities of counterparties and obligors. With suitable analytics, a warning system can be implemented to signal when to change counterparties for CDS.

In the case of selling protection, the seller, like the buyer, is interested in the default probability of the underlying obligor. The seller is also concerned with the default probability of the protection buyer because the periodic payment of CDS premiums are dependent on the health of the counterparty. Practically speaking, the amount of premiums is small relative to other types of exposures. If the protection buyer stops paying, the seller no longer has the obligation to deliver on the contract in the event of default. That said, the value of the contract will have changed given the elimination of the future cash flows when the protection buyer stops paying. Most portfolio managers can safely ignore this extra counterparty risk in the sense that the impact is small, but holders of large portfolios of CDS may want to consider modeling the behavior of protection buyers when they sell protection.

The other key difference with CDS contracts is the implementation of valuation models. Take care to understand the nature of the contract in terms of what is delivered in the event of default. For some contracts, a fixed amount is promised. For other contracts, an actual security—sometimes the cheapest to deliver—is promised. These characteristics should be reflected in the valuation models used for CDS.

Because a CDS contract is only a swap of premiums for an agreement to cover loss (in accordance with the agreement) in the event of default, one has to make an assumption regarding the implicit risk-free rate. Depending on whether the implicit risk-free rate is the U.S. Treasury curve, the dollar swap curve, or some other default-risk corporate borrowing curve (i.e., 0-EDF curve), the interpretation of the premium will change. This interpretation will influence estimates of the market risk premium as well as liquidity premiums.[6]

Credit portfolio management has two central features: the measurement of diversification at the portfolio level, and the measurement of how individual assets or groups of assets affect diversification. These measurements require estimates of (i) probabilities of default for each asset, (ii) expected recovery in the event of default for each asset, and (iii) default correlations between each pair of borrowers or obligors.

This chapter has described a consistent conceptual framework and actual methods for determining these quantities. The relevance and feasibility of the methods are best illustrated by simply noting that they are currently being used to assess credit portfolios in practice.

In particular, these methods enable the credit portfolio manager to assess:

---

6 Research at MKMV suggests that CDS premiums can be interpreted as implicit spreads over a corporate default-risk borrowing curve, which is 10 to 20 basis points below the dollar swap curve.

- The overall frequency distribution of loss associated with its portfolio;
- The risk and return contribution of individual assets or groups of assets;
- The risk/return characteristics of its existing portfolio and how to improve it;
- Overall economic capital adequacy;
- The economic capital required for new and existing assets;
- How to maximize diversification and minimize the use of economic capital.

In short, these new methods provide the means by which a portfolio manager can implement a rigorous program to manage its portfolio for maximum return while maintaining risk at a desirable level. With the availability of CDS, portfolio managers now have more ways to act on the results of the type of credit portfolio analysis outlined in this chapter.

CHAPTER EXERCISES

1. List and describe five elements of individual and portfolio credit risk.
2. Explain why the unexpected losses of a credit portfolio are not equal to the weighted average of the unexpected losses of each individual credit in the portfolio.
3. If the probabilities of default of Credit 1 and Credit 2 are 0.5% and 0.3%, respectively, and the correlation between the two is 0, what is the joint probability of default?
4. Why is estimating pairwise correlations through a sampling of asset time series not an optimal methodology? What approach might be preferable?
5. How might an institution compute the expected return on a loan or credit facility using EDF and loss given default?
6. Describe the key difference between evaluating a short position in a credit-risky bond and a long position in a CDS on the same risky bond.

CHAPTER 9

Ancillary Credit Risk Tools and Techniques

INTRODUCTION

In the last four chapters we discussed a variety of topics related to modeling of credit default risk and credit derivatives. These issues are of vital importance to intermediaries and end-users seeking to value their credit derivative positions properly. We now extend the quantitative theme by considering two other ancillary credit risk techniques—financial optimization/forecasting and ratings transitions. Both tools complement the credit risk management process by examining possible future states of a reference obligor's creditworthiness and should be considered by any institution involved in credit investment or risk management.

In this chapter we focus our attention on how institutions can project and manage the credit risks of individual and portfolio credit exposures using optimization. We then explore the process of developing ratings transitions and how these can be used to model credit risks. We supplement the discussion by including a brief review, in Appendix 1, of commercially available credit analytic packages.

OPTIMIZATION, FORECASTING, AND CREDIT RISK MANAGEMENT

We indicated in Chapter 1 that institutions should not enter into credit derivative transactions unless they have the ability to understand and manage the resulting risks prudently. This is especially vital for institutions that are in business to assume credit, market, liquidity, legal, and operational risks in exchange for a proper return. Banks, which specialize in originating, trading, and repackaging credit risks, are obviously at the forefront of this issue. They must be prepared to identify, measure, monitor and control risks and ensure a sufficiency of reserves and capital to protect against losses; compensation for these risks must be adequate. This is a challenging task in an environment characterized by competitive pressures, deregulation, and free flow of capital and information. As a result, banks can no longer be driven solely by relationship-based decisions; they must employ leading-edge analytics in order to identify areas of danger and opportunity within their credit businesses.

The effective credit risk management process incorporates future forecasts and downside scenarios affecting individual credits and broader portfolios and applies the results to risk-adjusted returns, credit reserves, loss provisions, and capital adequacy. For instance, forecasts can reveal potential areas of financial weakness within the operations of reference obligors, while scenario analysis can reveal previously unknown areas of credit risk concentration or potential credit problems.[1] Some banks already have an established history of using such tools to manage large and complex credits. Others have extended the process to include new forecasting and valuation techniques in order to more accurately predict expected defaults, recoveries, and enterprise values. Banks are discovering that building financial statement projections around a set of critical assumptions or value drivers with analytical sophistication can generate significant insights.

The U.S. Federal Reserve has noted that "formal presentation of financial projections or other forms of forward-looking analysis of the borrower are important in making explicit the conditions required for loan performance, and in communicating the vulnerabilities of the transaction to those responsible for approving

---

1 The Basel Committee has reinforced this notion explicitly, noting that "In the final analysis, banks should attempt to identify the types of situations, such as economic downturns (both in the whole economy or in particular sectors), higher than expected levels of delinquencies and defaults, or the combinations of credit and market events that could produce substantial losses or liquidity problems. Stress test analyses should also include contingency plans regarding actions management might take given certain scenarios."

loans."[2] Regulators require that every bank understand its customers' financial condition, ensure credits comply with existing covenants, verify that projected cash flows meet debt servicing requirements, affirm that collateral backing secured deals is adequate, and classify problem loans on a timely basis. Common problems affecting troubled banks include failing to properly evaluate and monitor borrowers, neglecting to obtain periodic financial information, and failing to stress test data using proper tools. These troubled banks may be unable to recognize early warning signs regarding deteriorating credit quality, thereby missing opportunities to work with borrowers to restructure credits in advance of default. Technology-driven financial forecasts, rather than single "what if" scenarios, can help characterize real-world events that might impair a loan, and form an essential part of advanced analysis that can be used to fulfill bank-driven and regulatory goals. These projections can be supplemented by statistical confidence levels related to the probability that a borrower's operating cash flow will fail to cover debt service and that its capital structure will prove inadequate. Rigorous forecasting tools are clearly central to initial approvals, establishment of adequate provisions and reserves, ongoing exposure monitoring, and credit risk mitigation via asset sales and credit derivatives hedging.

Borrowers raise cash through business activities, and via new financing from debt and equity sources (asset liquidations can generate cash as well, but are generally only of secondary importance and tend to be irregular). Internal payment of long-term credits is tied to historical and projected cash flow quality and cash flow magnitude. Historical cash flow analysis provides a record of past performance but leaves unanswered the question of whether a borrower will have enough cash flow to support future obligations. Gross operating cash flow is defined as net income plus noncash charges less noncash credits. If gross operating cash flow has historically consisted primarily of noncash items such as depreciation, deferred taxes, or asset write-downs, with only a small amount generated through income, the quality of the cash flow may be considered questionable and may ultimately prove insufficient to repay the liabilities. It is therefore imperative for a bank to identify the quality of a firm's cash flow. The magnitude of historical cash

---

2 Federal Reserve Board, Division Of Banking Supervision and Regulation, SR 00-7 (Sup)
  May 2, 2000, "Lending Standards For Commercial Loans."

flow relative to growth plans identifies a borrower's external financing requirements. The smaller the cash flow, the greater the debt load required to support long-term growth plans. If, for example, a borrower's operations are not producing enough cash flow to service outstanding loans, the firm's risk of defaulting rises. The bank must therefore determine why funds are being channeled into a company that cannot invest in productive assets capable of generating enough cash to repay debt. While historical examination of cash flows and loan repayment is an important element of credit analysis and management, it is not sufficient: tools are required to determine whether future earnings/cash flows will be sufficient to repay credits.

Applying formal forward-looking analyses, such as simulation-based optimization, can help an institution identify and manage overall portfolio risk and convince regulators of the existence of a rigorous credit process. Forward-looking analyses provide a potential solution for both large and small borrowers. Although it may be tempting to focus efforts primarily on large borrowers as a result of single exposure concerns, it is important to remember that small or middle-market borrowers may collectively comprise a significant portion of a bank's portfolio. We consider approaches to financial forecasting in the sections that follow.

A Simulation Approach to Financial Forecasting

Standard forecasting models are useful but are often burdened by the fact that they rely on single sets of assumptions, which usually lead to two static outcomes: base case and worst case. It is difficult to know which of a series of strategic options a borrower will pursue without analyzing differences in both the range and distribution of possible outcomes and the likely result associated with each option. Simulation processes emerge as potential tools to overcome the limitations of standard forecasting models.

A simulation is a computer-assisted extension of forecasting that can help answer a series of questions in a dynamic setting (e.g., "Will the borrower stay under budget if the bank finances the facility?," "What are the chances the project will finish on time and within budget?," "What are the probabilities that operating cash flow will cover debt service?," "Is multicollinearity a problem with the forecast?," and so forth). Monte Carlo simulation (MCS) is a practical implementation of the simulation process; it uses a random number generator to produce an entire range of outcomes and associated statistical confidence levels for multiple forecast runs. MCS solves problems involving elements of uncertainty that are too complex to be determined with standard modeling; importantly, it allows simultaneous manipulation of numerous variables, a significant benefit over standard forecasting frameworks.

Stochastic Optimization

Optimization procedures are used to identify optimum maximum or minimum values, subject to user-defined constraints. Current credit analysis optimization models are robust, solving problems with thousands of variables—which is especially relevant for complex project finance or restructuring deals. Any credit extension dependent on multiple variables and an objective function that needs to be maximized or minimized is a suitable candidate for a constrained or unconstrained optimization solution. Constraints are often part of the process. For example, a factory may be limited in size, or be able to produce only a certain amount of a given product per day; raw material may also be in short supply, working capital sources limited, and work-in-progress subject to labor-induced delays; capital costs might be constrained by systematic and unsystematic risk factors. Through optimization these (and other) constrained variables can be combined to produce maximum value within boundaries.

Deterministic optimization models cannot typically manage nonlinear problems (apart from those that can be expressed in "classical" mathematical programming form). Stochastic optimization models, in contrast, can accommodate nonlinear relationships based on equations used in mathematical programming formulations.[3] Ultimately, these models permit a more realistic representation of random variables. Consider a complex credit proposal where a bank is attempting to maximize an objective function over a feasible region; the proposal contains thousands of variables, so running sensitivities on each is unrealistic. Obtaining optimal values generally requires iterative or ad-hoc searching; this entails running a simulation for an initial set of values, analyzing the results,

---

3 In fact, the best stochastic models are extremely sophisticated, allowing users to incorporate other advanced features (e.g., table search, scatter search, neural networks).

changing one more or more values, rerunning the simulation, and repeating the process until a satisfactory solution is discovered. This process can quickly become tedious and complicated, even for small models. For instance, a simulation run may contain only two decision variables, but if each variable has 15 possible outcomes, each combination requires 225 simulation runs (15^2 alternatives). If each simulation takes only 1.7 seconds, then the entire process can be completed using two minutes of computer time. However, if the problem contains five decision variables, approximately 760,000 simulations (15^5 alternatives) are required; this is equal to five days of computer time. Any expansion to dozens or hundreds of variables expands the problem to dramatic proportions. However, a well-designed stochastic model can perform the task much more efficiently. Our case study on RI Furniture, which follows immediately below, illustrates the optimization process in greater detail.

Case Study: Optimizing RI Furniture's Credit Facility

RI Furniture, which started operations in 1986, manufactures a full line of indoor/outdoor furniture but is considering a restructuring of certain operating subsidiaries that represent approximately 65% of consolidated operations. ABC Bank is asked to approve a $3,410,000 loan facility for the firm and has been given the deterministic base case and conservative consolidating and consolidated projections (e.g., income statement, balance sheet, and cash flows). Operating profit margin distributions and investment ranges for each subsidiary are shown in Table 9.1.

TABLE 9.1

Product Line Assumptions

Product Line Assumptions	Distribution	Operating Profit Margin Range	Operating Profit Margin Most Likely
All-Weather Resin Wicker Sets	Triangular	5.5%–12.6%	11%
Commuter Mobile Office Furniture	Triangular	6.5%–8.7%	7.5%
Specialty Furniture	Triangular	0.5%–5.3%	4.7%
Custom-Built Furniture	Uniform	3.3%–6.6%	None

The Modeling Process   The deterministic forecasts given to ABC limits the variability of analysis outcomes, but it is difficult for the bank to easily identify which strategic option should be pursued if it cannot understand differences in the range/distribution of possible outcomes and the likely result associated with each option. Indeed, an overly aggressive restructuring program might reduce RI's credit-worthiness and increase default probabilities. In order to circumvent the problem associated with deterministic consolidating projections, bankers at ABC employ a stochastic model.[4] The model includes maximum/minimum and investment ranges supporting restructuring of each of RI's four product lines. The bankers develop, at a unit level, a probability distribution for each uncertain element in the forecast, establish an optimal funding array for the various business combinations, and hold cash flow volatility to acceptable levels in order to preserve the company's current credit rating. They then link the final optimization results to the consolidating/consolidated discounted cash flow (DCF) valuation module to determine postrestructuring equity values and probabilities that asset values will fall below debt values (e.g., an insolvency trigger, as described in Chapter 6).

The bankers first use the optimization model to create a run with a $3,410,000 investment constraint (i.e., the bank's facility cannot exceed $3,410,000); an additional run includes a constraint on the forecast variable's volatility.

The bank then uses the data from Tables 9.1 and 9.2 to develop the information illustrated in Figure 9.1. This reflects RI's original strategic restructuring plan, reworked into a stochastic model—but not yet optimized.

---

4 The model is based on OptQuest/Crystal Ball and McKinsey Discounted Cash Flow Valuation 2000.

T A B L E   9.2

Model Run: Investment Boundaries ($)

Product Line	Lower Bound	Upper Bound
All-Weather Resin Wicker Sets	1,000,000	1,250,000
Commuter Mobile Office Furniture	600,000	1,000,000
Specialty Furniture	570,000	1,100,000
Custom-Built Furniture	400,000	900,000

FIGURE 9.1

Stochastic Model

	B	C	D	E	F
1	**RI Furniture Co. Limited: Strategic Plan**				
2					
3		Annual	Lower	Upper	
4	Proposed New Product Lines	operating return	bound	bound	
5	All Weather Resin Wicker Sets	9.7%	$1,000,000	$1,250,000	
6	Commuter Mobile Office Furniture	7.6%	$600,000	$1,000,000	
7	Specialty Furniture	3.5%	$570,000	$1,100,000	
8	Custom Built Furniture	5.0%	$400,000	$900,000	
9					
10					
11		Amount		Constraint	
12	Decision variables	invested			
13	All Weather Resin Wicker Sets	$1,125,000		Decision Variables	
14	Commuter Mobile Office Furniture	$800,000		prior to optimization	
15	Specialty Furniture	$835,000			Total amount
16	Custom Built Furniture	$650,000			invested
17	Total expected return	$231,058		Objective	$3,410,000
18	(Annual operating return X Amount invested)				

FIGURE 9.2

Model Run: Optimization Results

	A	B	C	D	E	F
10						
11			Amount		Constraint	
12		Decision variables	invested			
13		All Weather Resin Wicker Sets	$1,247,100		Decision Variables	
14		Commuter Mobile Office Furniture	$993,671		prior to optimization	
15		Specialty Furniture	$570,000			Total amount
16		Custom Built Furniture	$598,998			invested
17		Total expected return	$245,757		Objective	$3,409,769
18		(Annual operating return X Amount invested)				
19						

The bankers then place a constraint on the investment/loan facility (i.e., All-Weather Resin Wicker Sets + Commuter Mobile Office Furniture + Specialty Furniture + Custom Built Furniture <=3410000). The results are depicted in Figure 9.2. Note that the investment falls within the constraint boundary, while expected return increases.

Simulation statistics reveal that the volatility of the expected return (which is the forecast variable), as measured by the standard deviation, is $20,000. This is an important result because the volatility of operating results affects the volatility of assets.[5] With the

---

5 For instance, Moody's KMV demonstrates that volatility measures the propensity of asset values to change within a given time period. This information determines the probability of default, given the corporation's obligations. Thus, if a company's current asset market value is $150 million and it has $75 million of one-year debt, default will occur if asset value falls below $75 million in one year.

results in hand, the bankers then discuss the first optimization run with management by focusing on maximum expected return, optimal investments/loan facility, and volatility of expected return. If volatility is unacceptable, the standard deviation must be reduced in order to preserve credit rating integrity. Assume that the bank requires a project standard deviation equal to, or less than, $17,800, as shown in Figure 9.3.

F I G U R E   9.3

Optimization Windows

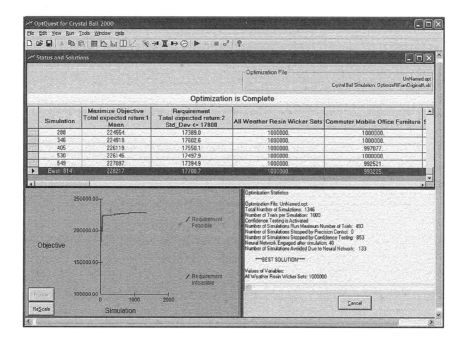

F I G U R E   9.4

Final Optimization Results

	B	C	D	E	F
10					
11		Amount		Constraint	
12	Decision variables	invested			
13	All Weather Resin Wicker Sets	$1,000,000		Decision Variables	
14	Commuter Mobile Office Furniture	$993,225		prior to optimization	
15	Specialty Furniture	$723,457			Total amount
16	Custom Built Furniture	$614,420			invested
17	Total expected return	$227,889		Objective	$3,331,102
18	(Annual operating return X Amount invested)				
19		Expected	Total		
20	Summary	Return	Investment	Standard Deviation	
21	Borrower's Original Projections	$231,058	$3,410,000	n/a	
22	Run One: Original Projections Optimized	$245,757	$3,409,769	$20,373	
23	Run Two: Project Volitility Constraint	$227,889	$3,331,102	$17,800	
24	Run Two: Project Volitility Actual			$17,701	
25	Expected Return and Loan Reduction	$17,868	$78,667		
26	(Bank Requirement: Reduce Project Risk)				
27					
28			Run One	Run Two	
29	Investment (Loan Amounts)	Original Strategy	Optimized; No	Optimized; Risk	
30		Not Optimized	Risk Constraint	Constraint	
31	All Weather Resin Wicker Sets	$1,125,000	$1,247,100	$1,000,000	
32	Commuter Mobile Office Furniture	$800,000	$993,671	$993,225	
33	Specialty Furniture	$835,000	$570,000	$723,457	
34	Custom Built Furniture	$650,000	$598,998	$614,420	
35	Total	$3,410,000	$3,409,769	$3,331,102	

This leads to the final optimization results illustrated in Figure 9.4.

Because the analysis was restricted to the unit level, the bankers must now link to the consolidating and consolidated DCF valuation framework. Consolidated discounted cash flow valuations provide a "going concern" value—the value driven by a company's future business activities. RI's value is determined by the present value of future cash flows for a specific forecast horizon (projection period) plus the present value of cash flows *beyond* the forecast horizon (residual or terminal value). In other words, RI's value depends on its cash flow potential and the risks associated with those future cash flows. These perceived risks help define the discounting factor used to measure cash flows in present value terms.

Cash flow depends on the economic outlook for the RI's products, current and future competition, sustainable competitive advantage, projected changes in demand, and the company's capacity to grow in light of its past financial and operating performance. RI's bankers examine a series of risk factors, including the company's financial condition, quality, magnitude, and volatility of cash flows, financial and operating leverage, and capacity to sustain operations on a profitable basis. The simulation shown in

Figure 9.4 produced an optimized result that reconciled the risk/reward agendas discussed earlier. The credit facility effectively declines to an optimized $3,331,102; because the firm requires less money, financial leverage declines.

This simple case study demonstrates how credit analytics that focus on stochastic financial forecasting can reveal possible credit strength/weakness of an obligor over time. Any institution seeking to add or hedge a particular reference credit using credit derivatives can benefit from the "forward-looking" nature of financial forecasts using stochastic optimization.

CREDIT RISK TRANSITIONS

Credit risk migrations, or rating transitions (we use the terms interchangeably), are a second major tool that can be used by institutions interested in tracing potential future states of creditworthiness and default. Ratings transition matrixes measure the probability of rating upgrades/downgrades over a particular time horizon. Assuming that rating transition rates are stable and follow a first-order Markov process, cumulative default rates can be projected over specific forecast horizons; transitions can also be constructed to produce default rates under stressed macroeconomic conditions.

Tracking such migrations can be used for different purposes. For instance,

- Bond investors may follow migrations because bond prices are impacted, positively or negatively, by ratings changes.
- Investors restricted to investing in investment-grade assets may use migrations to determine whether assets in their portfolios are approaching the sub-investment-grade category.
- High-yield investors that are hoping to capitalize on credit improvements may wish to employ migrations in their analytic assessment process.
- Banks that actively lend to different sectors of the rating spectrum can use migrations to estimate the direction of the credit portfolio, and the possible need for incremental risk reduction via credit derivative hedging or loan sales; they may also use migrations as a tool for managing credit reserve levels.

The essential conclusion is that transitions can be used as an additional tool in considering the future path of credit improvement or deterioration.

Methodologies

Transition matrixes measure probability-based upgrades and downgrades over specific time horizons. Rating agencies generally compute migrations over 1-, 5-, and 10-year horizons for industrial/ transportation companies, utilities, financial institutions, and sovereigns that have issued public long-term debt.

Various methods exist by which to compute transition matrixes. One approach focuses on static pools. Static pools are formed by grouping issuers by rating category at the beginning of each year of a multiyear study; each static pool is followed from that point forward. Issuers are assigned to one or more static pools, and when one defaults the default is assigned back to all of the static pools to which the issuer belongs. The static pool methodology is used in order to avoid certain pitfalls in estimating default rates, to ensure that default rates account for rating migration, and to allow defaults to be calculated across multiperiod time horizons. A variation on this approach applies an issuer's default against the issuer's initial rating—thus ignoring more recent rating changes. Another method computes default rates using the most recent year's default and rating data; this method can yield comparatively low default rates during periods of high rating activity, as prior year default activity is effectively ignored.[6] A further technique focuses on the implied senior unsecured rating of the issuer rather than the ratings of individual debt instruments floated by that issuer; transition matrixes are constructed in a similar fashion, but are considered "dynamic cohorts," changing when an issuer defaults or its ratings are otherwise withdrawn. As above, the first and last days of the year are used to construct the cohorts; the transitions thus express the ratio of issuers who

---

6 The pools can be considered static because membership remains constant over time. Each static pool can be interpreted as a buy-and-hold portfolio. Because errors are corrected with every new update, and because the criteria for inclusion or exclusion of companies in the default study is subject to minor revisions over time, it is not possible to compare static pools across different studies.

changed ratings to the total number of issuers that could have changed ratings.[7]

Though some differences in methodologies clearly exist, the versions used by the primary ratings agencies incorporate both seasoned and newly issued securities. This approach is thought to be appropriate for at least two major reasons: if an investor believes that current business conditions are similar to those of a previous year, it can consult directly with that year's cohorts to determine possible transition patterns; additionally, because very few issuers default early in their ratings history, lower default rates in periods of high or increasing ratings activity can be avoided.

Practical Application of Transition Rates

As we consider the applications of transitions, we begin with a review of global default experience based on S&P and Moody's statistics; this allows us to set the stage for practical interpretation and use of transitions, i.e., how the tool can be used as part of the credit risk management process (as in the CreditMetrics application and other analytical packages).

To begin, Table 9.3 highlights global average one-year transition rates from S&P (1981 to 2004).

Interpreting this data we note that, over the next 12 months, there is a 7.37% likelihood that an AAA credit will be downgraded to an AA, and a 5.27% likelihood that a BB will be upgraded to a BBB. Similarly, there is a 1.2% probability that a BB will default, a 5.7% probability that a B will default, and a 28.8% probability that a CCC will default.

Underpinning this table is a great deal of data regarding the composition of default probabilities and the potential movement of defaults over time; this includes data related to geographic mix, default experience by rating class, defaults by unit and amount, relation of defaults and economic factors, correlation of defaults

---

7 Several academic studies take a different approach to measuring and reporting ratings transitions, constructing transition matrixes, and assessing the changes from an initial bond rating. This approach argues that a distinction is important because of a seasoning effect that is observable only in the first years after issuance (e.g., as time passes, strong companies are able to call or repurchase their debt and refinance it with lower coupon issues. Thus the remaining pools of issuers naturally display higher default/transition rates).

T A B L E 9.3

S&P Global One Year Transition Rates, 1981–2004, %

From/ To	AAA	AA	A	BBB	BB	B	CCC/ C	D	NR
AAA	87.44	7.37	0.46	0.09	0.06	0.00	0.00	0.00	4.59
AA	0.60	86.65	7.78	0.58	0.06	0.11	0.02	0.01	4.21
A	0.05	2.05	86.96	5.50	0.43	0.16	0.03	0.04	4.79
BBB	0.02	0.21	3.85	84.13	4.39	0.77	0.19	0.29	6.14
BB	0.04	0.08	0.33	5.27	75.73	7.36	0.94	1.20	9.06
B	0.00	0.07	0.20	0.28	5.21	72.95	4.23	5.71	11.36
CCC/C	0.08	0.00	0.31	0.39	1.31	9.74	46.83	28.83	12.52

Source: S&P

and ratings, and so forth. Understanding the information that is embedded in such a matrix helps reinforce how the data can be used as a credit risk tool. We explore aspects of the data that implicitly or explicitly form part of the transition table.

10-Year Default Rates

The 10-year cumulative average default rates for seven rating categories are summarized in Figure 9.5. Not surprisingly, defaults rise

F I G U R E 9.5

10-Year Default Rates by Rating Category

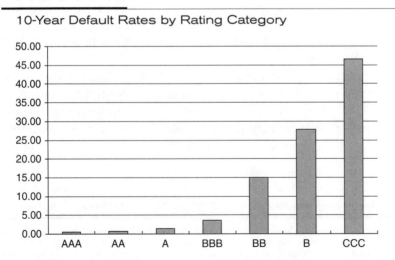

Source: S&P

steeply for speculative grade ratings (i.e., BB, B and CCC). Referring back to Table 9.3, we note that these three categories feature the highest probabilities of transitioning to default.

Defaults by Unit and Amount

Though the total amount of defaulted debt and the number of defaults in a given year tend to vary, Figure 9.6 demonstrates that they track each other to some degree. This makes conceptual sense, though in any given year variations can appear: one outsized default may be responsible for a large amount of defaulted debt relative to the number of defaults in that year (e.g., WorldCom), or many small defaults may raise the absolute number without materially increasing the amount of defaulted debt.

Default Ratios and Economic Conditions

Ratings are typically assigned by the rating agencies for the long term, with the objective of providing a rating that assesses the risk over industrial and economic cycles, rather than limiting the value of the rating to a shorter-term perspective. Not surprisingly, the default ratio for rated debt tends to rise significantly during recessionary periods. If an economic downturn lasts for several years, we might expect a greater amount of downgrade migrations into lower-rated categories.

F I G U R E 9.6

Rated Corporate Defaults by Unit and Amount

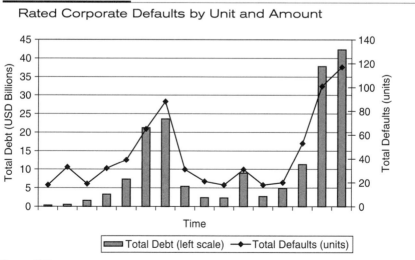

Source: S&P

Correlation of Ratings and Default Rates

Average cumulative default statistics demonstrate a strong correlation between credit quality and default probability; the lower the rating, the higher the probability of default. Though the ratings published by the agencies are sometimes criticized for lags, the data confirm, in general, the reliability and significance of the ratings. Table 9.4 illustrates that the lower a company's rating, the greater the default probability and the closer the default horizon. Conversely, the higher the rating, the lower and more distant the probability of default. For instance, while the average time to default for an AA-rated credit is 9.5 years, it is only 3.6 years for a B-rated credit. This suggests at least some degree of predictive power when considering default risk scenarios.

Anticipating Default Rates

Figure 9.7 presents possible relationships between the issuance of a high proportion of speculative-grade ratings versus the level of defaults (the solid line depicts speculative-grade ratings as a percent of the ratings universe, while the broken line shows the average level of defaults). A peak in speculative-grade debt ratings (as a proportion of all ratings) is followed by a peak in default rates three years later. Understanding such transition patterns and relationships can aid in the credit risk management process.

T A B L E 9.4

Time to Default

Original Rating	Avg. # of Years from Original Rating to Default
AAA	8.0
AA	9.5
A	8.5
BBB	6.5
BB	4.8
B	3.6
CCC	3.3

Source: S&P

FIGURE 9.7

Share of Speculative Ratings versus Default Rates (%)

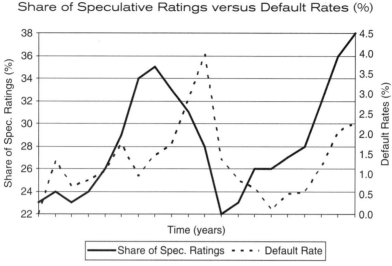

Source: S&P

Bank Loan Default Rates

Because banks loans are not actively traded instruments, long-term
default information (similar to that available) for bonds is not readily available. However, one study of bank loans and bonds
(Caouette, Altman & Narayanan) compares default rates over a
five-year period. Though some differences exist, default rates for
bank loans have generally been comparable to those of public
bonds. Armed with this type of information, it is possible to extend
the transition performance of long-term public debt to include privately arranged bank loan facilities. The average cumulative
default rates for bank loans and public bonds are summarized in
Table 9.5.

Recovery Rates on Corporate Debt

Rating agencies are still the primary suppliers of recovery data;
though stochastic recovery rate processes are developed and used
by some institutions, many continue to rely on rating agency data.
The recovery statistics in the table and figures below are derived
from Moody's annual study of default and recovery rates, in which

T A B L E 9.5

Comparing Bond and Bank Loan Five-Year Default Rates

Moody's Rating Category	Equivalent S&P Rating	Bank Loans	Bonds
Aaa	AAA	0.00	0.00
Aa	AA	0.00	0.00
A	A	0.12	0.05
Baa	BBB	0.04	0.54
Ba	BB	7.10	4.42
B	B	9.97	9.24
Caa	CCC	31.77	29.51

Source: Caouette, Altman & Narayanan.

the agency defines recovery value as the value of the debt in the secondary market one month after default.[8]

As we might expect, the seniority and security of a debt instrument have a dominant influence on the level of recovery. Normally, secured creditors are paid up to the amount of the value of their security (collateral); senior creditors and then junior/subordinated creditors follow them. Table 9.6 depicts both median and the average recovery values. While medians and averages are convenient indicators of recovery values, the standard deviation of recoveries is generally quite broad. Senior secured bank loans, for example, have an average recovery rate of 64%, but a standard deviation of 24%, meaning that recoveries for one standard deviation above and below the mean range from 88% to 40%. Consider, also, that the minimum recovery observed for senior secured bank loans was 5% and the maximum was 98%. An institution must therefore look beyond averages to the value of the security and the position of the debt in the capital structure of the company.

The average recovery values for different classes of debt are presented in Figure 9.8. Each column represents the average recovery

---

8 An alternate measure of recovery value attempts to follow a defaulted instrument through the restructuring, bankruptcy, and distressed exchange processes, discounting the payments received back to the point of default. This method introduces subjective factors, including estimates of the values of nonpublic debt and equity securities received in exchange for the debt and selection of an appropriate discount rate.

T A B L E 9.6

Recovery Statistics for Defaulted Corporate Debt (%)

Seniority/ Security	Median	Average	Standard Deviation	Minimum	Maximum
Senior Secured Bank Loans	72.0	64.0	24.4	5.0	98.0
Senior Unsecured Bank Loans	45.0	49.0	28.4	5.0	88.0
Senior Secured Bonds	53.8	52.6	24.6	1.6	103.0
Senior Unsecured Bonds	44.0	46.9	28.0	0.5	122.6
Senior Subordinated Bonds	29.0	34.7	24.6	0.5	123.0
Subordinated Bonds	28.5	31.6	21.2	0.5	102.5
Junior Subordinated Bonds	15.1	22.5	18.7	1.5	74.0

Source: Moody's

F I G U R E 9.8

Source: Moody's Average Recovery by Seniority/Security

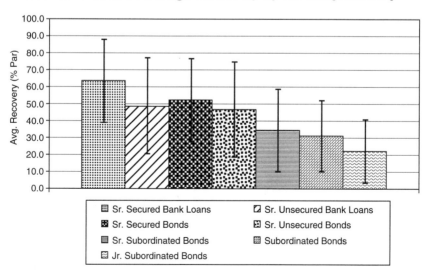

Note: Error Bars Show +1 and –1 Standard Deviation

Source: Moody's

value for a given class of debt. Superimposed on each column is an error bar, which reports one standard deviation above and below the average represented by the top of the column. For example, senior subordinated bonds (third column from the right) reflects mean recovery of 35% and +/− one standard deviation ranges of 59% and 10%.

The variability of recovery statistics can have a significant impact on potential loss levels. For instance, a $50 million senior unsecured bank loan with a mean recovery of 49% suggests a potential loss of $25.5 million; a maximum loss for the class of 95% yields a loss of $47.5 million.

Recovery values are also correlated with ratings. Figure 9.9 shows steadily declining recovery rates as the rating (at the time of default) declines; both mean and median values are included in the graph for comparison.

Loss Rates

The expected default rate and the expected recovery rate are used to determine the expected loss rate for a particular debt instrument or portfolio. The expected loss rate is calculated by multiplying the expected default probability and the expected loss given default;

FIGURE 9.9

Recovery Rates and Credit Ratings

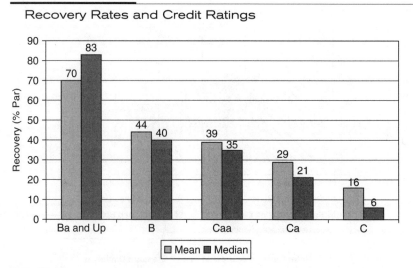

Source: Moody's

loss given default is simply (1 – recovery rate), e.g., a 70% recovery rate, is equivalent to a 30% loss given default. For instance, using the one-year BBB default rate of 0.22% and an average 70% recovery rate for securities rated above BB, the expected one-year loss rate is calculated as:

Expected loss = Expected default rate * loss given default

0.066% = 0.0022 * 0.30

Figure 9.10 shows expected average one-year credit loss rates by credit rating category (computed using data from Moody's average default rates and average recovery rates). Note once again the strong correlation between declining credit ratings and increasing expected loss rates, along with the dramatic shift in expected loss from investment grade to speculative grade (from Baa to Ba). These statistics are, of course, consistent with default probability transitions noted above.

With some background on ratings and default rates and how these form part of the ratings transition framework, we now consider how ratings transitions are used in practice by examining the CreditMetrics platform.

F I G U R E   9.10

One-Year Expected Loss Rates by Credit Rating

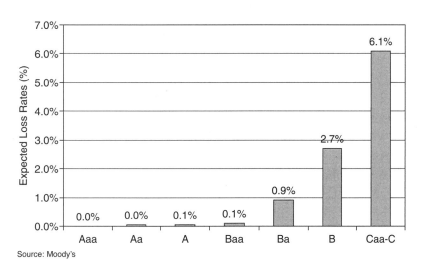

Source: Moody's

Applications in Practice: Credit Metrics

Risk management tools such as CreditMetrics use ratings migrations as a key input. CreditMetrics, originally developed by JP Morgan in 1997, models changes in portfolio value resulting from changes in credit quality. The platform builds on the concept that credit asset or portfolio values can be viewed not only in terms of default probabilities, but also in terms of changes in credit quality over periods (i.e., migrations); default is therefore a special-case credit phenomenon. For instance, starting from an initial risk rating position, a credit exposure included in the CreditMetrics portfolio can migrate to one of eight future states.

CreditMetrics incorporates information on individual credits, producing a distribution of portfolio values at some future fixed horizon. From this distribution, the model generates statistics that quantify the portfolio's absolute risk level, such as the standard deviation of value changes, or the worst-case loss for a given confidence level (e.g., 99%). While this provides a picture of a portfolio's total risk, exposures are also analyzed at a more granular level by considering the risk contribution of each exposure to the portfolio; this allows an institution to identify concentration risks or diversification opportunities, such as loan sales, acquisitions, securitizations, or credit derivative hedging—or to evaluate the impact of adding a new exposure.

General Structure

Estimating credit volatilities is challenging, as risk-rating migration and defaults occur relatively infrequently. Observing credit spreads or prices over a short historical period is unlikely to capture workable price volatilities associated with all possible changes in credit quality. To overcome this, the CreditMetrics methodology constructs the full process of possible credit quality changes; this is precisely equal to migration over time. The methodology is designed with three interlinking parts:

- The definition of the possible "states" for each obligor's credit quality and a description of how likely obligors are to be in any of these states at the horizon date.
- The interaction and correlation between credit migrations of different obligors.
- The revaluation of exposures in all possible credit states.

The first step in this process is to obtain a bond rating or risk grade. CreditMetrics determines the probabilities that the obligor will migrate to a particular state between a current and future period (horizon). The transition matrix provides probabilities of migration over the horizon for all of the system's states. The transition matrixes produced by the agencies can be applied to the CreditMetrics framework. However, while agency default rates are useful benchmarks for describing individual ratings categories, the use of average transition matrixes for credit portfolio modeling fails to capture the credit cycle; because agency matrixes represent averages over a long-term horizon, they fail to account for the current year's credit transitions. The CreditMetrics methodology addresses this by selecting smaller periods of the agency history and creating matrixes based on transitions in two or three increments (e.g., Table 9.7, which is Moody's equivalent of the S&P table presented above). It also explicitly models the relationship between transitions/defaults, and macroeconomic/industry variables, such as spread levels and economic growth.

Revaluation

After considering the migrations of individual credits, the model determines the value implied in the exposure's migration. Consider a Baa-rated, three-year, fixed 6% coupon bond, valued at par. Given a one-year horizon, the revaluation step consists of estimating the bond's value in one year under each possible rating transition. For the transition to default, CreditMetrics values the

T A B L E 9.7

Moody's One-Year Transition Matrix

	Aaa	Aa	A	Baa	Ba	B	Caa	D
Aaa	93.35%	5.94%	64.00%	0.00%	2.00%	0.00%	0.00%	0.02%
Aa	1.61%	90.53%	74.60%	0.26%	9.00%	0.01%	0.00%	0.04%
A	7.00%	2 28%	92.35%	4.63%	0.45%	12.00%	0.01%	0.09%
Baa	5.00%	0.26%	5.51%	88.46%	4.76%	71.00%	0.08%	0.15%
Ba	2.00%	0.05%	0.42%	5.16%	88.48%	5.91%	0.24%	1.29%
B	0.00%	0.40%	0.13%	0.54%	5.16%	84.22%	1.91%	6.81%
Caa	0.00%	0.00%	0.00%	0.62%	0.62%	4.08%	69.19%	24.06%

Source: Moody's

T A B L E 9.8

Values at Horizon for Three-Year 6% Baa bond

Rating at Horizon	Probability	Accrued Coupon	Bond Value	Bond plus Coupon
Aaa	0.05%	6.0%	100.4	106.4
Aa	0.26%	6.0%	100.3	106.3
A	5.51%	6.0%	100.1	106.1
Baa	88.48%	6.0%	100.0	106.0
Ba	4.76%	6.0%	98.5	104.5
B	0.71%	6.0%	96.2	102.2
Caa	0.08%	6.0%	93.3	99.3
D	0.15%	6.0%	40.1	46.1
		Mean	99.8	105.8
		Standard Dev.	2.36	2.36

Source: Moody's

bond given an estimate of the likely recovery value. Note that while public information is available, institutions may use their own recovery assumptions. For the nondefault states, Credit-Metrics obtains an estimate of a debt instrument's horizon value by using the term structure of bond spreads and risk-free interest rates. The end result reflects the values illustrated in Table 9.8—which includes a future rating at the horizon and the probability associated with that rating event, along with bond values in each state. This represents a practical, and useful, application of the transition process.

Building Correlations

The final step in the process involves construction of correlations between exposures. Identifying the exposure's risk contribution requires an estimate of correlations of credit quality changes between each pair of targeted references.

Several firms within the same industry can be downgraded simultaneously owing to systematic events (e.g., high fuel costs impacting airlines, poor real estate prices affecting local mortgage lenders, and so on). As obvious as these relationships may appear, deriving a meaningful estimate of corelationships is complex. Several methods can be considered, including:

- Uniform correlation: Setting correlations equal across all firms
- Bond spread correlations: Drawing correlations from bond prices
- Credit rating joint likelihood tables: Tabulating joint likelihood changes for two references together
- Equity price correlations: Extracting correlations from their stock prices
- Factor correlations: Deriving correlations from macrofactor models

CreditMetrics assumes changes in asset values reflected in equity prices produce credit migrations. The asset change distribution is then partitioned for each reference according to its transition probabilities. Figure 9.11 illustrates a Baa-rated obligor with default probability equal to 0.15%. In this example the default partition (which can be considered the obligor's liability level) is chosen as the point beyond which the 0.15% probability lies. The CCC partition is then chosen to match the obligor's probability of migrating to CCC, and so on; the results are shown in Table 9.9.

From this framework of individual exposure volatilities and pairwise correlations, CreditMetrics directly calculates the volatility for individual credit assets, a segment of the portfolio, or the

F I G U R E 9.11

Partition of Asset Change Distribution for a Baa Obligor

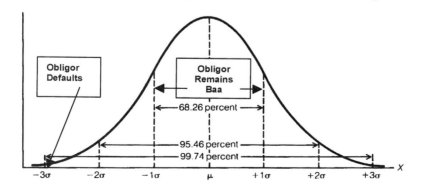

T A B L E 9.9

Baa Partition Results

Asset return	<–3.0	–3.0 to 2.8	–2.8 to –2.4	–2.4 to –1.6	–1.6 to 1.5	1.5 to 2.7	2.7 to 3.3	>3.3
New rating	Default	Caa	B	Ba	Baa	A	Aa	Aaa
Value	40.1	93.3	96.2	98.5	100.0	100.1	100.3	100.4

Source: Moody's

entire exposure portfolio. The resulting output can then be used for investment or risk management purposes.

CreditMetrics is just one example of how transitions can be used in assessing credit default risks. Various other commercial and proprietary platforms make similar use of transition matrixes to generate credit portfolio results. These can be, and in practice are, used by a broad base of intermediaries and end-users to help manage credit risks.

CHAPTER EXERCISES

1. Why would a bank extending a credit facility seek to optimize its credit decision? What goals is it attempting to achieve?
2. Why might a stochastic optimization process be considered more accurate than standard financial forecasting?
3. How many simulations would be required for an optimization routine based on 4 decision variables, each with 12 possible outcomes?
4. Describe four ways in which an intermediary or end-user can use ratings transitions as part of its credit derivate risk/investment management strategies.
5. Given a contract with a counterparty that features an expected default rate of 0.25% and a loss given default of 40%, what is the expected loss level?
6. Why might the standard deviation of recovery rates for a given year be particularly large for a specific class of debt?

7. Referring to Table 9.3, S&P one-year transition rates, speculate on why there is a 0.08% chance that a CCC-rated credit can migrate to AAA status.
8. What benefits do commercial transition-based applications such as CreditMetrics provide? What drawbacks must be considered?

PART 3

Regulatory, Control, and Legal Issues

CHAPTER 10

Credit Derivatives Documentation

INTRODUCTION

Proper dealing in credit derivatives requires effective legal, control, and settlements procedures. Legal documentation is at the center of control. Such documentation, which must have a legal basis in a local dealing jurisdiction, is designed to reflect the terms of trade between two counterparties and establishes the rights and definitions of each party. It is therefore essential in creating a secure dealing environment. Most derivatives documentation is contracted under the ISDA framework. Though other forms of documentation are employed (including, for example, the German Rahmenverstrag and the Association Française de Banque forms), these constitute a minority; accordingly, our focus in this chapter is on elements of the ISDA process.

ISDA, which was chartered in 1985, is the global trade association representing participants in the derivatives industry. The organization has routinely pioneered efforts to identify and reduce sources of risk in the derivatives and risk management business; notable accomplishments include:

- Developing the ISDA Master Agreement
- Publishing a wide range of related documentation materials covering a variety of derivative classes
- Obtaining legal opinions regarding the enforceability of netting and collateral arrangements

- Securing recognition of the risk-reducing effects of netting in determining capital requirements
- Promoting sound risk management practices
- Advancing the understanding and treatment of derivatives and risk management from both a public policy and regulatory capital perspective

These endeavors are consistent with its overall mission, which is to encourage the prudent and effective development of the OTC derivatives business by:

- Promoting practices conducive to the efficient conduct of the business, including the development and maintenance of derivatives documentation
- Promoting the establishment of sound risk management practices
- Fostering high standards of commercial conduct
- Advancing international public understanding of the business
- Educating members and others on legislative regulatory, legal, documentation, accounting, tax, operational, technological, and other issues affecting them

As a result of these efforts, the ISDA documentation framework has become the accepted industry standard for those dealing in the OTC derivatives market. In this chapter we consider the general ISDA documentation framework and the specific credit derivative confirmations and definitions that form part of the framework.

ISDA DOCUMENTATION FRAMEWORK

The general ISDA framework, which has been refined and expanded over the past two decades, is comprised of several components, any (or all) of which an institution may choose to use as part of its legal procedures:

- Master Agreement
  - □ Printed Form
  - □ Schedule
- Credit Support Documents
  - □ Credit Support Annex, Credit Support Deed
  - □ Margin Provisions

- Confirmations
  - Long Form
  - Short Form
- Definitions

The Master Agreement is comprised of the printed form, which is a multipage document of standard terms and conditions that is not intended to be altered by the two parties to the agreement, and the Schedule, which is the attachment that two parties negotiate and can enhance, alter, or customize at will (including inserting changes that alter the printed form). The Master Agreement serves as a mechanism to avoid separate, and lengthy, documentation of each individual transaction by establishing, and then repeatedly referencing, standard terms and conditions. The terms and conditions relate primarily to legal and credit issues. The 1992 Master Agreement, which replaced the 1987 agreement, was itself replaced in 2002 by a new version, which is 50% longer than the previous versions; the added material in the 2002 version is part of the industry's continued effort to clarify and standardize as much as possible within the legal environment, while retaining the flexibility to accommodate innovation.

The framework also allows for use of Credit Support Documents, which are intended primarily to establish credit arrangements between two parties (e.g., the need for one or both parties to post collateral, actions to be taken in the event certain credit exposure thresholds are breached or a ratings downgrade occurs, and so forth). The primary credit documents include the Credit Support Annex, the Credit Support Deed (used primarily under English law), and the 2001 Margin Provisions.

Confirmations, the third element of the framework, serve as evidence of individual transactions and can be negotiated in long form or short form. Long-form confirmations, as the name suggests, are detailed documents that contain all relevant aspects of the legal/credit terms of a transaction (much as the Master Agreement does) and are generally to be used when the product/market is relatively new and lacks dealing standards, or when the transaction is so customized that it requires specialized documentation. Short-form confirmations, in contrast, are relatively simple forms that serve primarily to document the economics of a new transaction; terms and conditions reference the Master Agreement and associated Definitions. Short forms are used when the market is standardized and mature and when product definitions are well established. Not surprisingly, the mechanism is efficient and reduces costs and operational errors.

Definitions are the last major component of the framework and serve to describe standard terms and provisions for different product/market segments. Definitions are introduced under ISDA sponsorship when a market has reached such a state of maturity that standardization is possible; standard Definitions have been issued for bullion derivatives (1997), government bond options (1997), Euro derivatives (1998), FX and currency options (1998), commodity derivatives (1993, 2005), equity derivatives (1996, 2002), and credit derivatives (1999, 2003). Short-form confirmations generally rely on, and reference, Definitions as part of the documentary process.

The general ISDA framework[1] is illustrated in Figure 10.1.

In the section that follows we briefly review certain clauses of interest that are contained within the Master Agreement; these should be read in conjunction with the detailed agreement and in relation to the specific 1999 and 2003 Credit Derivative Definitions described later in this chapter.

FIGURE 10.1

The General ISDA Documentation Framework

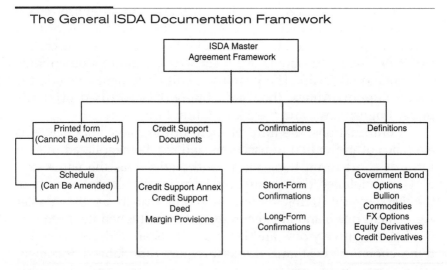

---

1 Note that the ISDA framework also includes certain bridges (cross agreements) and protocols (master change documents); we shall not consider them in further detail.

ISDA Master Agreement

The 2002 ISDA Master Agreement (Multicurrency Cross Border) updates the 1987 and 1992 documents, expanding the breadth of products covered (thus promoting cross-product netting), addressing new legal developments that have appeared over the past 15 years, and clarifying important aspects of preceding versions. Key sections of note include:

Section 2: Obligations

Section 2(a) indicates that each transaction confirmation dictates payment terms of both parties, along with the timing and the method of payment. This section, which allows for physical deliveries (e.g., bonds/loans for CDSs), clarifies that the payment obligations are subject to the condition that no event of counterparty default has occurred and that no early termination date has been designated.

Section 2(c) provides that payments may be netted, as long as they are due on the same date, are payable in the same currency, and pertain to the same transaction. Subparagraph (ii) of this section enables parties to elect the option of netting two or more transactions, provided that they occur on the same payment date and in the same currency.

Section 3: Representations

Section 3 allows both parties and any credit support provider (e.g., guarantor, letter of credit issuer) to make representations that are automatically replicated each time a new swap transaction is arranged. Any misrepresentation comprises an event of default that enables the nondefaulting party to terminate the swap agreement.

Subparagraph (a) contains basic representations that both parties declare, including those referencing:

- Status
- Powers
- Lack of violation or conflict
- Consents
- Binding obligations

Other subparagraphs contain representations about the absence of certain events of default and potential events of default, absence of litigation, and the accuracy of information identified in the schedule.

Section 4: Agreements

Section 4 contains a list of agreements that both parties are obligated to adhere to as long as either party has obligations under the agreement; this, in brief, includes the need for each party to:

- Furnish specified information
- Maintain dealing authorizations
- Comply with applicable laws
- Comply with tax agreements
- Pay stamp taxes/duties as applicable

Section 5: Events of Default and Termination Events

Section 5 contains a list of events that constitute an event of default or a termination event; note that these may be expanded or replaced by the credit derivative definitions cited below.

Section 5(a): Events of Default

- Failure to pay or deliver. This event applies to the failure of a party to make a scheduled payment or delivery under Section 2, three days after notice.
- Breach of agreement; repudiation of agreement. This can exist as an event of default only in limited circumstances and features a 30-day grace period following notice.
- Credit support default. This event provides that a credit support default can lead to an event of default under a derivative; it is not applicable if the derivative counterparty's obligation under the transaction is not supported by another entity (guarantor).
- Misrepresentation. This event applies to misrepresentation made by either party or its credit support provider.
- Default under specified transaction. This event provides that if a party defaults on its obligation under a specified

transaction, the nondefaulting party may elect to terminate the derivative.

- Cross default (obligation default). If specified in the schedule, this provision enables a party to declare the derivative to be in default if the other party or its credit support provider defaults on its obligation beyond an agreed threshold amount.
- Bankruptcy. This section applies to each party and any credit support provider and specifies that if one party is subject to a variety of events associated with bankruptcy or insolvency, the other party may declare the derivative in default.
- Merger without assumption. If a party consolidates/amalgamates or merges with, or into, another entity and the resulting entity fails to assume the obligations under the agreement or no longer benefits from a credit support document (guarantee), then the other party can terminate any transaction under the agreement.

Section 5(b): Termination Events   The following events constitute termination events under the Master Agreement:

- Illegality
- Force Majeure Event
- Tax Event
- Tax Event upon Merger
- Additional Termination Events

Each one of these events permits one of the parties to the transaction(s) to end the agreement and settle outstanding amounts due/payable.

Section 6: Early Termination; Closeout Netting

Section 6 represents the right to terminate following an event of default or termination. If either occurs, the nondefaulting/ affected party has the right to designate an early termination date (within 20 days of notice) in which the derivative(s) will terminate. Additionally, the parties have an opportunity to elect (in the Schedule) to have the derivative(s) terminate automatically and immediately upon the occurrence of certain events.

This automatic termination election is designed to allow the nondefaulting party to exercise its termination rights outside of insolvency proceedings. In other words, it enables an early termination date to occur prior to the filing of insolvency proceedings. Note that it may be disadvantageous to select the automatic early termination election for derivatives that benefit from a credit support provider. The immediate termination of the derivative may not provide sufficient time to access and benefit from the credit support. The section also provides details on the effect of designation, calculations on payment date, payments[2] on early termination (depending on whether early termination is via default or a termination event), and any setoff abilities. Closeout netting must be regarded as one of the chief benefits of the ISDA process as it allows an entire portfolio of transactions between two parties to be

---

2 For example, an ISDA Master Agreement may prescribe the method that the Calculation Agent should use to value the asset when dealer quotations are not available or are not used. The dealer price is generally determined either by referring to a market quotation source or by polling a group of dealers, and reflects changes in the credit profile of the reference obligor and reference asset. If it is not feasible to specify the method of valuation (such as default probabilities, or option pricing), an alternative might be to require the Calculation Agent to use a method of valuing the class of the referenced credit along with a detailed report outlining valuation methodology—formulas, assumptions, and models. If periodic valuations are required in the agreement, valuation methods should be consistent over the duration of the contract.

A Market Quotation is defined as a quotation from a leading dealer in the relevant market (selected by the nondefaulting party) for an amount that would be paid to the nondefaulting party or by the nondefaulting party in consideration of an agreement between the leading dealer and the nondefaulting party to enter into a transaction that would have the effect of preserving the economic equivalent of all payment or delivery obligations under the transactions. If more than three Market Quotations are provided, the Market Quotation is defined as the average of the remaining quotations after the highest and lowest are disregarded.

Section 6(e)(iv) of the ISDA Master Agreement supports the enforceability of the Market Quotation closeout valuation method. It states that the parties agree that, if Market Quotation applies, the amount recoverable under the ISDA Master Agreement on termination is a reasonable preestimate of loss and not a penalty. Further, such amount is payable for the loss of bargain and the loss of protection against future risks. Other than as specifically provided, neither party will be entitled to recover any additional damages as a consequence of such losses.

Loss is calculated by reference to the nondefaulting party's total losses and costs in connection with the ISDA Master Agreement as at the early termination date. It includes loss of bargain, cost of funding or, without duplication, loss or cost incurred as a result of its terminating, liquidating, obtaining or reestablishing any hedge or related trading position. It does not include legal fees. If Market Quotation has been specified but cannot be determined or would not produce a commercially reasonable result, then loss is deemed to apply with respect to that particular transaction.

condensed into a single net sum payable or receivable in the event of default. This eliminates the likelihood, at least in legal jurisdictions where netting is recognized, that a bankruptcy receiver will "cherry pick" only those contracts that have value to the defaulting party, while simultaneously dismissing those that are detrimental to the defaulting party.

Section 7: Transfer
Section 7 prevents both parties from transferring their obligations under the agreement to another party without the prior written consent of the other party.

Section 8: Contractual Currency
Section 8 indicates that payments under the agreement will be made in the relevant currency specified in the agreement for that payment (e.g., the "Contractual Currency"); in addition, it states that any shortfall or excess must be immediately rectified.

Other Sections
Sections 9 to 14 provide for rights and obligations with regard to multibranch dealings, expenses, and notices, and delineate governing law/jurisdiction and applicable definitions.

Credit Derivative Confirmations

Long-form confirmations are used for various classes of OTC derivatives, when a full Master Agreement has not been negotiated or the specific derivative product remains in a relatively nascent stage (i.e., it lacks standard terms and definitions).

As the credit derivative market began developing during the 1990s, ISDA published a standardized long-form confirmation providing a "menu" of choices for parties to use when structuring credit derivatives; the same form can still be used to document transactions. Parties using this mechanism can select from different types of credit events listed in the document, choose physical or cash settlement, and incorporate concepts such as materiality, payment default thresholds, and the use of public information to confirm the occurrence of a credit event. Other items can be included as required. The long-form confirmation can be used with an ISDA Master Agreement or as a separate, stand-alone contract.

The long-form confirmation for credit derivatives defines four significant terms:

- Reference Entity: the entity against which credit protection is bought or sold.
- Reference Obligation: the obligation of the Reference Entity used for determining the cash settlement amount in connection with a cash-settled trade.
- Obligation: the scope of a Reference Entity's liabilities that are covered by a Credit Event. An Obligation can be defined narrowly (e.g., obligations under a specified corporate bond issued by the Reference Entity) or broadly (e.g., any obligations of a Reference Entity).
- Credit Event: the specific event that can trigger action under a transaction. A Credit Event can occur with respect to the Reference Entity, or with respect to an Obligation of the Reference Entity (which may or may not be a specified Reference Obligation).

In order to avoid disputes and limit payment to true credit events, the confirmation permits the parties to require that the applicable credit event be publicly reported. The information does not need to prove the existence of the credit event. It needs only to reflect that a credit event has occurred. This concept also helps reduce sensitivities related to the disclosure of confidential, non-public information.

The confirmation also permits selection of materiality as an optional condition, allowing the parties to require a significant drop in the price of a Reference Obligation (price materiality) or a significant widening of the spread applicable to a reference obligation (spread materiality) before a payment is triggered. This concept serves to protect parties from nominal or technical, rather than "true" defaults.

In calculating the market value of the Reference Obligation for cash settlement, parties may specify one of a number of valuation methods, such as dealer quotations on a single day (market) or an average over some period (average market); they may also elect a quotation method (bid, offer, midmarket). The methods used to determine the amount of the payment triggered by the occurrence of a Credit Event can vary by transaction. For a cash-settled CDS, the cash settlement amount may be based on the difference between the specified value and the market value of the Reference Obligation at the time of settlement, or it may be a predetermined, fixed amount. For a physically settled CDS, the selling party may require the buyer to deliver a specific or general deliverable obligation, in a specified principal amount. Deliverable obligations can theoretically encompass a wide range of assets, including loans, bonds, and other contracts. Similar options can be selected for the other credit derivatives we have discussed in Part 1.

Credit Derivative Definitions, 1999 and 2003

Consistent with ISDA's policy of introducing definitions under the ISDA framework when a product/market reaches a sufficient state of maturity, Credit Derivative Definitions were introduced in 1999 and 2003 (along with a Restructuring amendment in 2001). We review several elements in this section.

1999 Definitions

In the aftermath of the financial market turmoil and defaults of 1997–1998 (e.g., Southeast Asian economies, Russia, Long-Term Capital Management), and in order to address some of the "subjectivity" that was entering the marketplace (e.g., interpretations related to credit events, deliverable obligations), ISDA sponsored the creation of Credit Derivative Definitions. The effort was also considered timely as the credit derivative market had reached a sufficient level of standardization to warrant the introduction of agreed terms and procedures. Ultimately, ISDA and the industry were (and are) interested in creating a "level playing field" for market participants. Accordingly, the 1999 Definitions were intended to ensure:

- Greater transparency by providing consistency and clarity in definitions and legal drafting.
- Availability of an objective assessment regarding the occurrence of a credit event (e.g., avoiding the possibility of technical defaults triggering credit derivative payouts).
- Clarity regarding the nature of a credit event, the classes of debt to which an event may apply, and the types of debt deliverable into physically settled transactions.

After circulating drafts for comments, ISDA published its first credit derivative definitions in 1999; key items included:

Credit Events   The credit event terms included under other aspects of the ISDA framework underwent significant changes:

- The Downgrade and Credit Event upon Merger clauses were removed and the Cross Default and Cross Acceleration clauses were renamed the Obligation Default and Obligation Acceleration clauses.
- The Failure to Pay clause was improved through the inclusion of a three-business-day grace period in order to minimize the likelihood of a technical default triggering action under a contract.
- The Restructuring definition (the most controversial element under the previous format as a result of subjective assessments) was clarified by setting forth a comprehensive, and objective, list of actions that might be considered to involve a restructuring; while not infinitely comprehensive, the list was considered a significant step forward.

The end result was the development of six credit events under the 1999 Definitions:

Bankruptcy: The 1999 Definition is identical to Section 5(a)(vii) of the ISDA Master Agreement and is drafted with sufficient scope to include trigger events related to bankruptcy or insolvency under English law and New York law, as well as the insolvency laws of other jurisdictions. In fact, the drafting is wide enough that it is conceivable that an action could be considered an act of bankruptcy even though the rating agencies may believe none has occurred (e.g., a meeting of shareholders to consider the filing of a liquidation petition).

Obligation Acceleration: The 1999 Definition is a subset of the Obligation Default discussed immediately following and covers any situation, other than Failure to Pay, where the obligation becomes due and payable as a result of a default by the reference entity—before the time when such an obligation would normally be considered due and payable. The definition contains a Default Requirement that sets a minimum threshold before which an acceleration is deemed to have occurred.

Obligation Default: The 1999 Definition covers a situation, other than Failure to Pay, where the Reference Obligation becomes capable of being due and payable as a result of a default by the reference entity—and before the time when such an obligation would normally be considered due and payable.

Failure to Pay: The 1999 Definition specifies that Failure to Pay is a failure by the Reference Entity to make any payments under one or more obligations, after taking account of specific grace periods; the clause covers situations where credit derivative guarantee payments are triggered.

Repudiation and Moratorium: The 1999 Definition addresses any instance where the reference entity or a governmental/sovereign authority disaffirms or challenges the validity of an obligation. A specific default threshold is also included.

Restructuring: The 1999 Definition covers events as a result of which the terms, agreed by the Reference Entity and the holders of the obligation, have become less favorable to the obligation holders than they would have otherwise been. These may include a reduction in the principal amount or interest payable under the obligation, postponement of a payment, change in the priority ranking of a payment, or change in the composition of a payment. A default threshold can also be specified for this clause. Note that the restructuring definition only applies in situations where the event results from deterioration in the creditworthiness/financial condition of the reference entity.

Obligations and Deliverable Obligations: Parties to a contract can choose from among various obligations that can trigger a credit event (e.g., "borrowed money"), and those that can be delivered under the physical settlement parameters (e.g., "bond or loan"). Parties must select one category and can then refine their selections by choosing certain characteristics that must apply (e.g., different currency obligations, no loan subparticipations, and so on).

Settlement Terms For physical settlement transactions, a "notice of intended physical settlement" must be filed; that is the buyer must inform the seller within 30 days of a credit event of its intent to deliver the Deliverable Obligations. If the notice is not delivered, no settlement will occur and the transaction terminates. The intent is to impose time constraints on the market in order to improve efficiencies and workouts.

Cash settlement has been expanded to accommodate instances where it is more difficult to obtain a market settlement quotation (e.g., emerging market bonds); parties can thus obtain a weighted average quote. If it is impossible to obtain quotes in a 14-day period, then the market value of the reference obligation will be deemed to be zero and the protection buyer receives a par payout.

2003 Definitions
The 1999 Definitions were seen as a significant step in improving the functioning of the market, and the core definitions remain in force to the present time. However, following a number of bankruptcies and failures between 2000 and 2002 (i.e., technology and telecom failures, Enron, WorldCom, the Argentine debt crisis), ISDA coordinated efforts to refine the definitions even further. In early 2002 enhancements to the core 1999 Definitions were circulated to the Market Practices Committee for comment; many of the resulting views were incorporated into the 2003 Definitions, key highlights of which we note immediately following.

Credit Events   Certain amendments were undertaken to the language related to bankruptcy, repudiation/moratorium, and restructuring. Restructuring, in particular, was altered to take account of contentious restructuring events (e.g., Marconi plc),[3] which roiled the markets. In particular, the Restructuring definition now includes four different options: trade without Restructuring; trade with "full" Restructuring, with no modification to the Deliverable Obligations; trade with "Modified Restructuring," which has been the North American norm since the publication of the Restructuring Supplement of 2001; and trade

---

3 The Marconi case serves as interesting case in restructuring. In 2002 the firm underwent a $4 billion workout and restructuring (agreeing with its creditors to replace outstanding debt with a combination of cash, equity, and bonds). This led to questions on whether a nonbinding agreement to restructure can be considered a credit event under ISDA's definitions. If a bank cannot settle credit derivatives when a company agrees to a nonbinding workout, the credit protection may expire too soon; if banks have to wait for the restructuring, the underlying debt might have to be exchanged for securities that may not be deliverable under a credit derivative (e.g., in the Marconi case, equity). ISDA has taken the view that a credit event is triggered if action is "in furtherance of an arrangement for the benefit of creditors, meaning action to avoid bankruptcy."

with "Modified Modified Restructuring," which is a new provision aimed primarily at the European marketplace.

Guarantees   The new definitions permit the transfer of risk on guaranteed obligations, so the obligations of a reference entity can include direction obligations, obligations of a "Downstream Affiliate" (e.g., Qualifying Affiliated Guarantee), or an obligation of a third party guaranteed by the reference entity (e.g., Qualifying Guarantee); the latter is only included if the parties make a specific reference in their confirmations.

Assignability   The new definitions permit novation of a credit derivative contract, a feature that was not previously permitted.

While these supplemental revisions provide further clarity to the original definitions, it is clear that the legal dimension of the marketplace will continue to evolve as further experience is gained with default and restructuring, and as new products are introduced by intermediaries. The process must therefore be regarded as dynamic and evolutionary, with any static review capturing only one time period in the process.

CHAPTER EXERCISES

1. Describe the major components of the ISDA documentation framework and the purpose each one serves.
2. Why would an institution choose to use a long-form, rather than short-form, confirmation in documenting its transactions with a counterparty?
3. What specific benefits accrue from the use of a closeout netting clause?
4. Why is the inclusion of guarantees in the 2003 Definitions as part of the risk transfer mechanism considered significant?

Regulatory and Control Issues

INTRODUCTION

The instruments considered in this text occupy an important position within the financial markets, serving as both risk-bearing instruments and risk management tools. Understanding how to properly manage credit derivatives from a control perspective is thus an important matter. Regulatory and control issues are of vital importance in the credit derivatives sector, particularly given the pace of growth and change that has occurred since the turn of the millennium. Experience gained with credit defaults and restructurings since the late 1990s has helped focus attention on a variety of control issues, including the need for a robust risk management framework and clarity in the legal drafting process. It has also revealed the importance of allocating an appropriate amount of capital in support of credit risk activities.

In this chapter we explore a series of control-related issues applicable to credit derivatives. We begin by considering the external control environment, focusing on regulatory issues (primarily for banks), including those set forth by the Bank for International Settlements (BIS) and bank supervisors. We then examine the internal control environment by considering institution-specific financial and risk management practices.

EXTERNAL CONTROL: REGULATORY ISSUES

Regulators have become more intimately involved with derivatives market regulation in recent years and have been active in shaping dimensions of the credit derivative market. In some instances regulators mandate specific risk and capital treatment of CDSs, credit options, and TRSs; in other cases they provide flexible guidelines regarding control procedures. Importantly, regulations or recommended behaviors are often developed in conjunction with industry practitioners in order to ensure relevance. There is some evidence to suggest that when practitioners view regulations as relevant and useful, they become more diligent in their application.

The BIS View of Credit Derivatives

The BIS issued its third consultative paper in April 2003 addressing derivative risk management and mitigation (including mitigation via credit derivatives); many of the suggested changes were incorporated in the final draft released in June 2004, and these now form part of the financial institution regulatory framework. The Basel II perspective on credit derivatives deals primarily with risk substitution, where the risk weight of the protection seller substitutes for the risk weight of the underlying credit-risky asset; that is, a protection buyer exchanges reference credit risk for counterparty risk.

The BIS indicates that a credit derivative must represent an express, unconditional, and irrevocable claim on the protection seller. It also specifies that any contract must feature:

- Objective and well-defined payouts:[1]
  - Failure to pay and analogous events with a grace period that is consistent with the grace period allowed the underlying credit
  - Bankruptcy, insolvency, or inability to pay the contracted amount, or admission in writing of inability to pay, and analogous events
  - Adverse restructuring of credit terms (i.e., forgiveness or postponement of principal, interest, or fees that results in

---

1 Note that the definitions do not correspond precisely with those used under ISDA guidelines (e.g., restructuring definitions are somewhat different).

a credit loss event, including charge-offs, specific provisions or other charges to income). Note that when restructuring is not included as a credit event, the amount of any risk-mitigating hedge is limited to 60%; in other words, 40% of the underlying exposure will be considered to be unprotected

- Limited asset mismatches (i.e., if the reference obligation and the underlying asset are different, they must still reference the same obligor, and the underlying obligation must rank *pari passu* or senior to the reference obligation).
- Synchronicity of maturity (i.e., in an event of default the credit derivative must not expire before the grace period).

Eligible protection sellers can include sovereign entities, public sector enterprises, banks, and securities firms with a lower risk weight than the counterparty, and other entities rated A– or better. As a general rule, no credit-protected exposure can lead to a higher capital requirement than an unprotected exposure (i.e., a position with credit protection cannot be treated worse from a capital perspective than one that lacks protection).

The *w* Factor

In framing its regulatory view, the BIS introduced the concept of the "*w* factor," which attempts to measure an obligor's unprotected risk. A credit derivative's (unadjusted) *w* factor is assumed to be 15%. The risk weight is measured through a weighted average of the risks of the obligor and the protection seller. In the instance of a fully protected exposure, the risk weight is given as:

$$r^* = w(r) + (1 - w)g \qquad (11.1)$$

where
- r^* is the adjusted risk weight
- w is the constant factor
- r is the risk weight of the obligor
- g is the risk weight of the protection seller.

For instance, if the protection seller's risk weight is 11% and the obligor's is 100%, the risk weight of a credit derivative-protected transaction is:

$$r^* = .15(1.00) + (1 - .15).11 = 24.4\%$$

This illustrates the benefit of the protection; rather than a 100% risk weight for capital purposes, the credit derivative contract lowers it to just under 25%.

Credit derivatives and CLNs may feature partially tranched risk protection (i.e., first loss, second loss, and subsequent losses protected under different contracts and parties). If a bank transfers junior risk and retains senior risk, the junior risk transfer is considered protected and the senior risk is considered unprotected, risk-adjusted at the weight applicable to the obligor. If the transferring bank retains junior risk and transfers senior risk, the junior risk is deducted from the capital of the protection seller. The risk weight for the protection buyer is based on the weighted average of the protection buyer's risk and the obligor's risk.

Application of Market Risk Capital Requirements to Credit Derivatives

In December 1995 the BIS Supervisors Committee approved an amendment (i.e., the market risk amendment) to the Basle Accord setting forth capital requirements for exposure to general market risk for all positions held in an institution's trading account (and for all foreign exchange and commodity positions, regardless of account location), as well as for specific risk of debt and equity positions held in the trading account. In addition, the amendment requires capital to cover counterparty credit exposure associated with OTC derivative positions (in accordance with the credit risk capital requirements set forth in the Basle Accord and implemented in the Federal Reserve's risk-based capital guidelines). The requirements of the U.S. rules implementing the market risk amendment became effective on a mandatory basis in 1998.[2]

---

2 The regulatory directives provide guidance on how credit derivatives held in the trading account should be treated under the market risk capital requirements by state member banks and bank holding companies. Specifically, the regulatory SR letter defines the risks to which credit derivative transactions are exposed and sets forth the risk-based capital requirements for each type of risk. In addition, the SR letter supplements SR letter 96-17 (GEN), dated August 12, 1996, which provides a detailed discussion of the more prevalent credit derivative structures and provides guidance on a number of supervisory issues pertaining to the use of credit derivatives, including the appropriate risk-based capital treatment for credit derivatives held in the banking book. The risk-based capital guidance set forth in SR letter 96-17 will continue to apply to credit derivatives held in the trading book of banks that have not implemented the market risk capital rule.

Credit derivative transactions held in the trading account are exposed to counterparty credit risk and general market risk; they are also exposed to the specific risk of the underlying reference obligation. The following defines each of the three risks as related to derivatives:

- General market risk—The risk arising from changes in the reference asset's value due to broad market movements (e.g., changes in the general level of interest rates)
- Specific risk—The risk arising from changes in the reference asset's value due to factors other than broad market movements (e.g., changes in the reference asset's credit risk)
- Counterparty credit risk—The risk arising from the possibility that the counterparty may default on amounts owed on a derivative transaction

General Market Risk   A banking organization subject to the market risk amendment must use internal models to measure its daily value-at-risk (VAR) for covered positions in the trading account (and for foreign exchange and commodity positions located in any account). General market risk capital charges for credit derivatives are calculated in the same manner as for cash market debt instruments.

Specific Risk   If a banking organization can demonstrate to regulators that its internal models accurately measure the specific risk of its equity and debt (including credit derivative) positions in the trading account, and this measure is included in its VAR-based capital charge, it can reduce or eliminate its specific risk capital charges (subject to the minimum specific risk charges prescribed in the amendment). Standard specific risk charges for credit derivatives may be calculated using the specific risk-weighting factors that apply to the referenced asset. Matched positions (i.e., those that represent a perfect match between the credit derivative and the underlying credit exposure) do not incur specific risk charges. In offsetting positions (i.e., those that represent a close, though not perfect, hedge), standard specific risk charges are applied only against the largest leg of the offsetting credit derivative and cash positions; that is, standard specific risk charges are not applied to each leg separately. Open positions (i.e., those that represent no effective hedge at all) attract the same standard specific risk charges as a cash position in the reference asset.

Counterparty Risk   Counterparty risk is calculated by combining the mark-to-market value of the credit derivative and an "add-on" factor representing potential future credit exposure. Under the Basle Accord (and the Federal Reserve's risk-based capital guidelines), the add-on factor is a specified percentage of notional amount, dependent on the type and maturity of the derivative transaction. In order to calculate a capital charge for counterparty risk, an appropriate add-on factor is needed. However, the matrix of add-on factors does not include a specific factor for credit or other derivatives for which the underlying transaction is a debt instrument. Based on an analysis of typical debt instruments underlying credit derivative transactions, regulators have determined that equity add-on factors can be used when the reference asset is an investment-grade instrument (or its bank-internal equivalent), or when the reference asset is unrated but secured by high-quality collateral; equity factors range from 6–10% based on maturities of one to five years. The commodity add-on factor can be used when the reference asset is rated below investment grade (or its bank-internal equivalent) or is unrated and unsecured; commodity factors range from 10–15% for maturities of one to five years.

As we have indicated above, the issue of whether a credit derivative is considered an eligible offset for purposes of risk-based capital depends upon the degree of credit protection provided. A relatively restrictive definition of a default event or a materiality threshold that requires a comparably high percentage of loss before payout may limit the amount of credit risk actually transferred in the transaction. If risk transfer is limited, the protection buyer cannot reduce the risk weight of the "protected" asset to the level of the counterparty/protection seller. Even if the transfer of credit risk is limited; however, the protection seller should still hold an appropriate level of capital against the underlying exposure while it is exposed to the credit risk of the reference asset. Note that the effectiveness of a credit derivative transaction is often subject to audit and regulatory requirements.[3]

Table 11.1 summarizes the three risk elements for each of the three defined position types. If risk exists, a capital charge is applied; if no risk exists, no capital charge is applied. It is clear from the table that all credit derivative positions create exposures to counterparties and, thus, have counterparty risk charges. In the case of matched positions only counterparty risk exists; the matched nature of the position eliminates the general market and specific risk of the reference asset. Not surprisingly, open and off-setting positions feature all three risk elements, but general market and specific risk are smaller in offsetting positions, as some degree of a market risk hedge actually exists.

TABLE 11.1

Credit and Market Risk Positions in Credit Derivatives

	Credit Risk	General Market Risk	Specific Market Risk
Open Position	Yes	Yes	Yes
Matched Position	Yes	No	No
Offsetting Position	Yes	Some	Some

---

3 For instance, the Federal Reserve indicates that the "guarantor" of a credit derivative should maintain capital against its exposure in the same manner as if it had exposure under other off-balance-sheet direct credit substitutes. Under FRB risk-based capital guidelines, 100% of the face amount of direct credit substitutes is assigned to the appropriate risk category. Credit derivative participants may also be exposed to credit risk of a counterparty, which can be measured in a manner similar to other derivatives, i.e., the current exposure (mark-to-market replacement cost) of the transaction plus an estimate of the potential future exposure of the transaction to market price changes.

The U.S. Bank Regulatory View
of Credit Derivatives

Like the BIS, U.S. banking regulators have attempted to create a framework for equitable treatment of credit derivatives. Regulators have agreed to recognize the benefits of credit derivatives for regulatory capital purposes if the contracts:

- Represent a direct claim on the protection provider
- Explicitly reference specific exposures (or classes thereof)
- Are evidenced in writing through a contract that is irrevocable by the guarantor
- Prohibit inclusion of a clause that would:
  - Allow the protection seller to unilaterally cancel the credit protection (other than in the event of nonpayment or other default by the protection buyer)
  - Increase the effective cost of credit protection as the credit quality of the underlying obligor deteriorates
- Are in force until the underlying obligation is satisfied in full (to the amount and tenor of the guarantee)
- Are legally enforceable against the seller in a jurisdiction where the guarantor has assets to attach

Regulators believe risk reduction benefits of conditional contracts (e.g., credit derivatives that do not adhere to the specifications above) are difficult to quantify as a result of their inherent uncertainties. Conditional contracts can be recognized when the banking organization is able to demonstrate that its assignment criteria fully reflects the reduction in credit risk arising from the conditionality, and that the contract provides a meaningful degree of credit protection.

In addition to the points mentioned above, certain additional criteria must be met in order for a credit derivative to be recognized for risk-based capital purposes. In particular, the following credit event definitions, which are similar to the BIS's own requirements, must be included as part of the contract:

- Failure to pay amounts due under the terms of the underlying obligation
- Bankruptcy, insolvency, or inability of the obligor to pay its debt

- Restructuring of the underlying obligation involving forgiveness or postponement of principal, interest, or fees, and which results in a credit loss.[4]

Regulators recognize credit derivative hedges for capital purposes only where the reference obligation on which the protection is based is the same as the underlying obligation.[5] Where credit derivatives do not match underlying exposures with regard to maturity, a special formula is applied:

$$P_a = P(t/T) \tag{11.2}$$

where

P_a is the value of the credit protection adjusted for maturity mismatch

P is the amount of the credit protection

t is the lesser of T and the remaining maturity of the hedge arrangement, expressed in years

T is the lesser of five and the remaining maturity of the underlying obligation, expressed in years

Regulators recognize credit derivatives that have a shorter maturity than the hedged obligation; however, a credit derivative with less than one year remaining until maturity that does not have a maturity that matches the underlying obligation is not recognized.

Regulators treat estimated average default (EAD) for derivative contracts included in the banking book or trading book in

---

4 With regard to restructuring events, there is a suggestion that a banking organization may not need to include restructuring credit events when it has complete control over the decision of whether or not a restructuring of the underlying obligation will occur. For instance, this would occur where the hedged obligation requires unanimous consent of the creditors for a restructuring. Regulators also have concerns that this approach could have the incidental effect of dictating terms in underlying obligations in ways that could diverge from creditors' business needs. There is also some question as to whether such clauses actually eliminate restructuring risk on the underlying obligation, particularly as many credit derivatives hedge only a small portion of a banking organization's exposure to the underlying obligation.

5 An exception occurs when the reference obligation ranks *pari passu* with, or is more junior than, the underlying obligation, and the underlying obligation and reference obligation share the same obligor and legally enforceable cross-default or cross-acceleration clauses are in place. Consistent with the BIS, U.S. bank regulators did not propose to recognize credit protection from TRSs in instances when the hedging bank records net payments received on the swap as net income but does not record offsetting deterioration in the value of the hedged obligation (either through reduction in fair value or by an addition to reserves).

accordance with the rules for calculating the credit equivalent amount for such contracts set forth under the general risk-based capital rules. Accordingly, when a banking organization buys or sells a credit derivative through its trading book, a counterparty credit risk capital charge is imposed based on the replacement cost plus add-on factors.[6]

Supervisory Guidance for Credit Derivatives

In reviewing credit derivatives, bank examiners consider the credit risk associated with the referenced asset as the primary risk, just as they do for loan participations or guarantees. A depository institution providing credit protection through a credit derivative carries the same credit risk exposure to the reference asset as if the asset were on its own balance sheet. This treatment applies when computing an institution's overall exposure to a reference credit for purposes of evaluating concentrations. In addition, depository institutions providing credit protection through a credit derivative should hold capital against the exposure to the reference asset. This broad principle holds for all credit derivatives but must be modified somewhat for credit derivative contracts that incorporate periodic payments for depreciation or appreciation (e.g., TRSs, spread options). For such contracts the institution can deduct the amount of depreciation paid to the beneficiary (net of any amounts paid by the beneficiary for appreciation) from the notional amount of the contract when determining the amount of reference exposure subject to a capital charge.

Note that in some cases the guarantor/seller and the beneficiary/ buyer are also exposed to the credit risk of the counterparty.

---

6 Regulators are still considering the levy of a counterparty credit risk charge on all credit derivatives that are marked-to-market, including those recorded in the banking book. Such a treatment would promote consistency with other OTC derivatives, which are assessed the same counterparty credit risk charge regardless of where they are booked. Furthermore, regulators note that, if credit derivatives booked in the banking book are not assessed a counterparty credit risk charge, banking organizations would be required to exclude these derivatives from the net current exposure to a counterparty for purposes of determining regulatory capital requirements. On balance, the regulators believe a better approach would be to align the net derivative exposure used for capital purposes with that used for internal risk management purposes. This approach would suggest imposing a counterparty risk charge on all credit derivative exposures that are marked to market, regardless of where they are booked.

For banks acting as dealers that have matching or offsetting positions, counterparty risk emerges as the primary risk exposure. In reviewing a credit derivative arranged by a financial institution as beneficiary, the examiner must review the organization's credit exposure to the guarantor/seller, as well as to the reference asset (if the beneficiary actually owns the asset). The degree to which a credit derivative transfers the credit risk of an underlying asset from the beneficiary to the guarantor may be uncertain or limited; the degree of risk transfer depends on the terms of the transaction. For example, some credit derivatives are structured so that a payout only occurs when a predefined credit event takes place. Some contracts require a payment only when a defined default event occurs and a predetermined materiality (or loss) threshold is exceeded. Default payments themselves may be based on an average of dealer prices for the reference asset during some period of time after default using a prespecified sampling procedure, or they may be specified in advance as a set percentage of the notional amount of the reference asset.

Examiners must ascertain whether the amount of credit protection a beneficiary/buyer receives by entering into a credit derivative is sufficient to warrant treatment of the derivative as a guarantee for regulatory capital purposes. Only arrangements that provide nearly complete credit protection to the underlying asset should be considered effective guarantees for purposes of asset classification and risk-based capital calculations. However, if the amount of credit risk transferred by the beneficiary is severely limited or uncertain, then the limited credit protection that the derivative provides the beneficiary should be disregarded.

Examiners should carefully review credit derivative transactions in which the reference asset is not identical to the asset actually owned by the beneficiary depository institution; the examiner must be satisfied that the reference asset is an appropriate proxy for the credit exposure the institution intends to offset. In making this determination, examiners should consider, among other factors, whether the obligor of the reference asset and owned asset are the same, and whether seniority in bankruptcy is identical.

An institution should not enter into credit derivative transactions unless its management has the ability to understand and manage the credit and other risks associated with these instruments in a safe and sound manner. Accordingly, examiners should determine the appropriateness of dealing in these contracts on an institution-by-institution basis. Such a determination should take into account management's expertise in evaluating credit derivatives, the adequacy of relevant control policies (including those outlined immediately following), and the quality of the institution's information systems and internal controls.

INTERNAL CONTROLS: RISK MANAGEMENT AND FINANCIAL CONTROLS

Institutions dealing with derivative products on a regular basis are generally aware of the need to build and maintain a proper internal control framework that permits prudent management of risks. Internal controls can take various forms but tend to relate primarily to credit and market risk management, independent financial valuation, and internal auditing. The combination of the three, working in a synchronous fashion, can create a more secure dealing environment, particularly when coupled with the legal controls described in Chapter 10.

Risk Management

Internal credit and market risk managers often serve as the "front line" of controls, enforcing a series of standards that are intended to keep a firm's risk operations in balance. Credit and market risk managers are involved in establishing limits and other controls for derivative businesses (including credit derivatives). These may also include formal "new product" reviews that examine the structural nuances and risks of new credit derivative products. Though the remit of most risk departments is often quite wide, we can summarize for our purposes a series of minimum risk controls that must be established.

Market Risks
The market risk framework requires:

- Identifying all market risks impacting credit derivative products; these may include
  □ Spread risk
  □ Correlation risk (both spread and default)

□ Volatility risk

□ Interest rate risk

□ Currency risk

- Quantifying all risks arising from the credit derivative trading business
- Establishing meaningful risk limits for the relevant market risk exposure classes in relation to the institution's stated risk tolerance level and the potential returns that can be earned
- Monitoring exposures on a continuous basis to ensure that exposures generated in the credit derivative business remain within limits, and making adjustments as necessary
- Considering new credit derivative products proposed by external parties or internal originators and ensuring that they meet the institution's risk criteria

Credit Risks

Similarly, the credit risk framework requires:

- Identifying all credit risks related to credit derivative products; these may include

□ Counterparty credit risk

□ Correlated credit risk

□ Default risk

- Quantifying all risks arising from the credit derivative business and establishing algorithms that demonstrate when credit derivatives serve to reduce, rather than increase, the institution's credit risk exposures; incorporating the hedge effects in decision making
- Establishing limits for the net credit exposures the institution is willing to assume, ensuring some relationship to the stated risk tolerance and the potential returns that can be earned
- Monitoring exposures on a continuous basis to ensure that exposures generated in the business remain within limits

These types of processes should be reviewed for efficacy on a regular basis (e.g., every year).

Internal Financial Controls

Internal financial controls exist in order to track and verify transactions that can impact a firm's balance sheet, income statement, and cash flow statement, including any credit derivative products forming part of a firm's operations. The duties of the financial professionals of a firm, with specific reference to credit derivative dealing, cross important boundaries that affect the front, mid-, and back-offices, as well as executive management and external regulators. In particular, minimum internal financial controls (that are independent of the business unit generating profit and loss (P&L)) should include:

- Ensuring that pricing feeds for credit derivatives come from an independent source that cannot be manipulated
- Establishing reserves for credit derivative positions that appear impaired (e.g., illiquid, close to default)
- Interpreting and implementing accounting policies related to the credit derivative dealing business, e.g., proper recognition of credit derivatives serving as hedges (with attendant reduction in capital charges)
- Making certain that the technology platform/trade entry screens include the entire population of daily dealings, in order to avoid any breaks/fails/settlement problems or financial fraud
- Reconciling daily trading activity in credit derivatives in order to generate a link to the firm's P&L and books and records
- Gathering independent pricing valuations of credit derivatives trading in the marketplace to ensure that the daily marking policy is equitable
- Creating independent risk management reports reflecting credit derivative activities; these may be applied to risk limits supplied by the market and credit risk management departments
- Preparing executive management/board level revenue and risk reporting to demonstrate the trends of the credit derivative business

These points are not, of course, exhaustive. Others can be incorporated in the process, particularly those that promote cooperating between risk management, treasury, and operations.

Internal Audit

Virtually all major institutions have some form of internal audit function to ensure the integrity of operations. The typical audit function examines business and control units on a regular cycle, testing activities against established policies and procedures to ensure proper compliance and control. Deficiencies, weakness, shortcomings, or other potential problems are flagged and elevated when internal auditors are performing their functions properly.

Given this function, it is clear that units that take or shed risk through credit derivatives should form part of the regular audit cycle. In addition, risk management and credit management units that promote the use of credit derivatives as part of the arsenal of risk management tools must be reviewed regularly. Auditors focusing on derivative books generally, and credit derivative books specifically, must ensure that the market and credit risk limits indicated immediately above are in force and effective in controlling exposures. Equally, they must verify the nature, quality, and accuracy of the pricing values/marks that the independent financial control units derive/supply for the computation of daily P&L, position tracking, and books and records reconciliation. Any discrepancies must, of course, be resolved as a matter of urgency.

Much of our discussion on the control and regulatory matters surrounding credit derivatives has been from the perspective of a bank or financial institution; this is logical because financial firms are the key originators, repackagers, traders, sellers, and users of the contracts. That said, nonbank financial institutions and corporates are also active in using credit derivatives, so some of the internal financial control and internal audit measures described above are readily applicable to their operations as well. Though a firm's processes may not be as extensive (given what is likely to be a much smaller scope of business), the same rationale and goals apply. It is also worth noting that in some cases an industry-specific regulator may impose additional constraints that dictate the level and complexity of business a firm can undertake.

Ultimately, financial and nonfinancial institutions that adhere to best practices established by regulators or their own boards of directors related to the entire range of internal controls will be well positioned to deal in credit derivatives. Such activities should, in turn, lead to additional growth and innovation in what is already a very vibrant marketplace.

CHAPTER EXERCISES

1. Distinguish between general market risk and specific market risk. Explain why regulators consider that an offsetting credit derivative position carries elements of general market risk and specific market risk.

2. Given a w factor of 15%, a risk weight of 18% on the seller of credit protection, and a 100% risk weight on the reference obligor, what is the average risk weight assignment to a credit derivative for capital purposes?

3. Under what circumstances should a regulator disallow hedge treatment for a credit derivative?

4. How might regulatory treatment for a credit derivative that allows for appreciation/depreciation rather than just pure default be adjusted?

5. Describe minimum standards of credit and market risk management that should be applied to credit derivatives dealing.

A Review of Commercial Credit Modeling Analytics

Credit modeling analytics are now commercially available to assist banks and other intermediaries and end-users in assessing their risks and exposures. These have become an essential element of credit risk quantification and management and can be applied equally to traditional credit assets, such as bonds and loans, and synthetic/derivatives assets, including credit derivatives, structured notes, and CDOs. In this appendix we consider the features of various credit analytic platforms in order to provide a sense of the tools that are available.

SAMPLE STANDARD AND POOR'S CREDIT ANALYTICS

CreditModel™

Industry- and region-specific credit scoring models are used to evaluate public and private firms with revenues in excess of $50 million. CreditModel™ allows a user to:

- Determine a credit score for a single company, or for all companies in a portfolio
- Screen new borrowers, customers, suppliers, or counter-parties by specific criteria
- Identify marginal credits that may require additional review
- Benchmark internal credit ratings against a globally recognized standard for which default rates are published; this

permits some degree of reconciliation between internal and external ratings/default probabilities
- Analyze credits for use in a securitization program
- Perform sensitivity analysis

Credit scores are represented by familiar S&P letter grade rating symbols (in lower case to indicate they are quantitatively derived estimates of S&P's credit ratings). Score reports also display default probabilities. Model inputs consist primarily of fundamental credit indicators such as interest coverage and cash flow/debt ratios; no market data is used. The variables with the most influence on the credit score are highlighted.

Default Filter™

Default Filter™ allows development, validation, and stress testing of default probability models based on an institution's own credit factors; the platform can be used by institutions that are in varying states of data collection and model development and includes:

- Data centralization and clearing tools
- Utilities to create homogeneous groups for modeling along with customization to accommodate regional and industry differences
- Model building based on a firm's proprietary credit factors
- Validation and stress testing components

CreditPro®

CreditPro® permits the creation of data tables extracted from S&P's proprietary database of historical ratings (in fact, the database of 9,000 obligors is the same one used by the agency in its annual long-term default study and corresponds to the migrations discussed in Chapter 9). The module computes, across time horizons, regions, and industries:

- Marginal and cumulative default rates
- Rating migration matrices
- Observed default correlations, conditional transition matrixes

LossStats™ Database

LossStats™ Database provides a comprehensive set of credit loss information created from information on more than 500 nonfinancial public and private U.S. companies that have defaulted since 1988 (including data on more than 2,000 defaulted bank loans and high-yield bonds). The database allows an institution to:

- Refine loss given default models
- Enhance the construction of structured vehicles through dynamic loss assumptions

Portfolio Risk Tracker

Portfolio Risk Tracker is S&P's portfolio risk model, allowing institutions to measure their risk and assess the risk contributions of individual credit facilities/transactions or subportfolios to total portfolio risk. The portfolio model is a transparent, multiasset platform (conventional products, structured products, emerging markets) that is built atop default probabilities, recovery rates, and correlations, allowing for:

- Dynamic modeling, allowing risk to be analyzed on a multiperiod basis
- Market and credit risk integration, enabling institutions to calculate their economic capital and perform risk assessments across the full range of risks they manage
- Default probability and recovery linkages
- Selection of default correlation sources, including equity-based, spread-based, and default-based measures

SAMPLE MOODY'S KMV CREDIT ANALYTICS

LossCalc™

The LossCalc application provides loss given default (LGD) estimates that take account of forward-looking indexes, including regularly updated industry recovery rates and median default probabilities, along with correlations between default risk and recoveries. The database is based on two decades of detailed market, fundamental, and security level recovery data (1,800 defaulted instruments, both rated and unrated) and can compute LGD for bonds, bank loans, and preferred stock. The platform calculates:

- Obligation-specific LGD estimates at default, and for one-year time horizons
- Explicit LGD confidence bands that measure uncertainty around the predictions
- Moving averages of normalized industry recoveries.
- Forward-looking median default rates
- Other factors, including Moody's Bankrupt Bond Index, trailing 12-month speculative grade average default rate, and changes in leading economic indicators
- Debt type and seniority for the transaction
- Firm leverage and the relative seniority of a debt transaction in the firm's capital structure

RiskAnalyst™

RiskAnalyst™ collects, analyzes, and stores financial statement data from multiple locations. The tool's centralized database is configurable, allowing inputs required by an internal rating system to be gathered and structured as needed. RiskAnalyst organizes data at both the borrower and portfolio levels, allowing for micro and macro analysis. The platform integrates with RiskCalc and CreditEdge to include private and public company EDF credit measures and permits:

- Collection, analysis, and organized storage of historical and projected financial statement data for standardized decision making in the risk analysis process
- Use of a centralized database repository for both single borrower and portfoliowide data, providing a transparent view of credit risk with the use of EDF credit measures

CreditEdge

CreditEdge is an investment decision tool that provides institutions with additional analysis of corporate credit risk. The platform allows

- Construction of client portfolios through more precise measurement of credit risk

- Highlighting of early warning credit risk changes
- Identification of relative value opportunities in the credit markets

RiskCalc

RiskCalc enables an institution to characterize the credit risk of thousands of private companies for easy monitoring of portfolio credit trends. RiskCalc is based on one of the largest private company databases—Moody's KMV CRD™ (Credit Research Database), with 7 million financial statements covering 1.5 million firms and 100,000 defaults. The platform computes:

- Forward-looking EDF credit measures that track changes in the economy and recognize unique industry differences
- Financial ratios and their individual contributions to risk
- Fundamental risk contributors
- "What-if" capability to examine the impact of new financial statements

The credit analytics sector has evolved dramatically over the past few years. Banks dealing with credit exposures in myriad forms now have a far better selection of analytical tools to help them quantify, optimize, and manage portfolios of loans, bonds, CDSs, credit spread options, TRSs, and other credit-risky assets. Each of these tools must, however, be considered in light of potential applications; some are relevant for microanalysis, others are macro-based; some favor traditional credit instruments, while others can accommodate synthetics.

Answers to Chapter Exercises

CHAPTER 1 EXERCISES

1. Describe the difference between unilateral and bilateral credit derivative contracts and give an example of each. Explain the impact of each one on intermediaries and end-users.

   Unilateral derivative contracts are those that require performance by only one of the two parties (i.e., the seller) once a premium/fee has been paid (i.e., by the buyer). Bilateral derivative contracts may require performance by either or both parties during the life of a transaction depending on the value of the contract. A credit spread option is an example of a unilateral contract, while a total return swap is an example of a bilateral contract. Unilateral contracts limit the downside of intermediaries and end-users to the premium/fee paid, while bilateral contracts have the potential of exposing either or both parties to downside risk. However, intermediaries and end-users need not pay a premium/fee for an on-market bilateral contract.

2. Explain how and why an investment fund might use credit derivative contracts.

   An investment fund may choose to use a credit derivative to assume particular credit risk exposures, e.g., creating a synthetic basket or portfolio of credit-risky assets. It may choose to do so in order to avoid taking physical possession of the credit assets (which would increase balance sheet footings) or having to fund them through outside sources.

3. Outline the types of risks a company might be exposed to and how they might be managed.

A company may be exposed to general business operating risks (inputs/outputs) as well as financial risks. General business risks are managed via hedging, investment, and capital allocation decisions and through strategic acquisitions and sourcing/distribution arrangements. Financial risks may include credit risk (risk of loss should a counterparty fail to perform on its contractual obligations), market risk (risk of loss should market variables move in an adverse fashion), liquidity risk (risk of loss should the company be unable to source sufficient cash to cover unexpected payments), legal risk (risk of loss arising from lack of proper legal documentation), and/or operational risk (risk of loss emanating from failures in standard business processes/infrastructure). Each one of these can be managed to varying degrees. For instance, credit and market risks can be reduced or hedged using financial derivatives (including credit derivatives), and by establishing internal risk limits that cap maximum exposure levels. Legal risks, in turn, can be managed by implementing appropriate legal documentation (including, for derivatives, ISDA Master Agreements). Operational risks can be managed by ensuring proper control procedures governing payments and settlements, and by implementing disaster recovery/redundancy plans.

4. Explain why the ability to separate credit risk exposure from a credit-risky asset is an important driver of credit derivatives market growth.

The ability to transfer credit risk exposures independent of the physical asset allows a hedger (e.g., a protection buyer) to preserve the appearance of a credit position while simultaneously shifting the risk to a third party (e.g., a protection seller). This can aid in the relationship management process. For instance, a bank may not want to be seen shifting its credit exposure to specific borrowers, as this may send a negative signal to both the borrowers and the marketplace; stripping off the exposure while retaining the physical loans eliminates the problem.

5. Discuss why legal and operational risks must be considered as part of the overall risk management framework. Give two examples of each type of risk as related to credit derivatives.

Legal and operational risks form part of the overall risk management framework, as each has the potential of generating losses for institutions that actively conduct financial operations. Examples of legal risks related to credit derivatives include outright lack of legal documentation and improperly defined events of default; either can lead to disputes and losses. Examples of operational risks include misdirected counterparty payments and collapse/failure of the credit derivative trading platform; either can, again, induce losses.

CHAPTER 2 EXERCISES

1. Explain how the asset swap arbitrage works and provide an example using the following instruments/rates:

   5-year fixed bond rate of 6%
   5-year FRN yield of LIBOR + 35 bps
   5-year swap rate of 5.50%

   The asset swap arbitrage works when an investor can create a synthetic floating-rate asset through a combination of a fixed-rate bond and an interest rate swap at yield levels that are more attractive than a straight investment in a floating-rate asset (or vice-versa in the case of a synthetic fixed-rate asset).

   In this example the investor can receive 6% by investing in the bond directly and can swap the fixed coupon for LIBOR flat in the swap market at a level of 5.50%; this allows it to create a synthetic floating-rate asset at a gross pickup of 50 bps. If it were to buy the FRN directly in the market and fund at LIBOR flat, it would earn 35 bps running; the synthetic asset swap arbitrage therefore yields an incremental yield of 15 bps running.

2. Describe how a bank or investor can obtain default protection by using an asset swap switch.

   An investor can contract to switch out of an asset swap package of a weaker credit reference in exchange for that of a stronger reference. As the weaker reference deteriorates into a state of financial distress, the investor has an effective put to its switch counterparty; in the extreme, as the reference defaults, the switch counterparty is obliged to accept the defaulted package. Naturally, the investor may have to pay a significant premium for this type of switch protection.

3. In what way is a CDS different than a conventional OTC swap contract? Describe a more appropriate analogy from the financial markets.

   A conventional OTC swap is a bilateral contract that calls for the exchange of periodic flows on a two-way basis. A CDS is not a swap in the conventional sense: it is a unilateral contract that involves only the contingent payment of a single flow if default occurs. The CDS is much closer in structure and function to a default option, which is a unilateral, single payment contract.

4. Name three factors that drive the price of a CDS and describe how each one influences price levels.

   The price of a CDS is influenced by the probability that the reference credit will default (the greater the probability, the higher the CDS price), the expected recovery rate (the higher the recovery rate, the lower the CDS price), and the correlation between the creditworthiness of the CDS counterparty and the reference credit (the higher the correlation, the lower the CDS price).

5. Explain why an unfunded TRS is similar to a synthetic financing.

   The total return receiver in an unfunded TRS uses no cash either to collateralize the transaction or purchase a securities portfolio (for the LIBOR stream), yet it obtains the economics of the reference security as if it had borrowed to purchase it; the LIBOR stream payable to the total return payer is akin to the financing cost on the transaction.

6. If an investor buys a 12-month credit spread call option on Company ABC's bond with a strike spread of 100 bps for a premium of 35 bps, what is the appropriate course of action if ABC's spread tightens to 50 bps? Widens to 150 bps? What is the breakeven level of the trade?

   *If the spread tightens to 50 bps, the investor should exercise the option for a net gain of 15 bps (e.g., 100 bps strike − 50 bps market − 35 bps premium) and a dollar equivalent gain of 15 bps * notional * duration. If it widens, the investor must allow it to expire unexercised, as the option is out-of-the-money. The breakeven level on the trade occurs at a spread level of 65 bps (e.g., 100 bps strike − 35 bps premium); each 1 bp tightening after 65 bps generates profit.*

7. Assume the following reference credit portfolio:

   Credit 1: $10 million notional, postdefault price 40
   Credit 2: $10 million notional, postdefault price 30
   Credit 3: $10 million notional, postdefault price 50
   Given a $30 million structure, how much will an investor receive?

   a. If Credit 2 defaults in a standard basket?

   The investor will receive $7 million, which is simply $10 million * (1 − 0.30)

   b. If Credit 2 defaults in a first-to-default basket?

   The investor will still receive $7 million, as only one credit has defaulted.

   c. If Credits 1 and 2 default in a first-to-default basket (in that order)?

   The investor will receive $6 million, which is $10 million * (1 − 0.40) for the first credit to default; the transaction then terminates, meaning no payment is due the investor on the second credit default.

   d. If Credit 3 defaults in a senior basket with a $5 million first-loss limit?

   The investor will receive no payout; the payout on a standard basket would be $5 million ($10 million * (1 − 0.50)), but the loss limit on the senior basket is set at $5 million.

   e. If Credit 1 defaults in a senior basket with a $5 million first-loss limit?

   The investor will receive a $1 million payout; the payout on a standard basket for Credit 1 is $6 million ($10 million * (1 − 0.40)) and the loss limit is $5 million, indicating a net payment of $1 million.

CHAPTER 3 EXERCISES

1. Describe four factors that drive CLN issuance and why each one is important.

   CLN issuance is driven by credit market access opportunities, customizable credit investment opportunities, transaction efficiencies, and synthetic replication possibilities. Credit market access is important, as it permits investors that are restricted from purchasing certain credit assets to do so; customization is important as investors can define, with significant specificity, the types of credit returns they seek; efficiencies are important, as they reduce administrative burdens and can lower transaction costs; and, synthetic replication is important as a limited supply of otherwise attractive credit investments can be expanded almost at will.

2. Consider a $100 million structured CLN on a reference credit trading at T+100 bps that pays 110% redemption when the spread is between T+90 bps and T+110 bps, and a reduced redemption of 1% for each basis point below T+90 bps or above T+110 bps. What will the dollar redemption value amount to if the reference credit trades at T+85 bps? At T+91 bps?

   At T+85 bps principal redemption declines by 5% points (e.g., 1% point for each basis point below the lower strike of 90 bps), to 105. At T+91 bps redemption remains at 110, as the credit spread is still within the defined band.

3. Describe the principal differences between standard CLNs and repackaged bonds.

   CLNs are often constructed using liabilities issued by high-rated corporates, sovereigns, and supranationals, while repackaged bonds tend to be created through SPEs or trusts. CLNs include packages of low-risk bonds and credit derivatives, while repackaged bonds are packages of credit-risky bonds and derivatives (often assuming the form of a securitized asset swap).

4. Describe how a TRS CLN can be structured to provide an investor with leveraged returns.

   An investor can purchase a note with an embedded TRS that features a notional principal amount that is greater than the issue size of the note. The increased notional generates a leveraged payment/risk, e.g., a $200 million TRS notional on a $100 million note issue creates 2:1 leverage.

5. Explain how an investor seeking a three-year Brazilian corporate credit exposure can use the CLN market to obtain its

desired risk/return profile when the market only features five-year corporate bonds.

The CLN can be structured with a TRS that references the five-year corporate bond, but with a specific transaction maturity of three years. At the maturity of the note, the underlying reference bond, with two years until maturity, can be liquidated in the market.

6. What minimum factors is a rating agency likely to require in a rated CDO?

   Rating agencies evaluating a CDO examine a transaction for structural/legal integrity, minimum levels of credit portfolio diversification, interest coverage, and overcollateralization, and maximum levels of credit concentration and correlation.

7. Explain how the two most common CDO "waterfall" tests work. Given an overcollateralization trigger of 105%, will the test pass or fail if the value of the collateral is 105, the principal for a mezzanine tranche is 50, and the principal of all tranches ranking senior is 55? What if the value of the collateral is 115?

   The two major most common "waterfall" tests are based on overcollateralization and interest coverage. Overcollateralization measures the degree to which the market value of the credit asset pool exceeds the value of outstanding liabilities. Interest coverage measures the degree to which pool cash flows are sufficient to service principal and interest obligations.

   At a trigger level of 105, the test will fail, as the overcollateralization test result is equal to 100%, or 5 points less than the minimum trigger level (e.g., 105/(50 + 55)). The test passes at 115, as the result is equal to 109.5%, or 4.5 points higher than the threshold (e.g., 115/(50 + 55)).

8. Compare and contrast the key features of cash, structured, and synthetic CDOs.

   All three CDOs use pooling of credit assets and tranching of liabilities in order to provide investors with specific credit-based returns associated with selected risk profiles. Cash CDOs are funded transactions that involve the physical transfer of credit assets from the sponsor to the SPE; they do not use credit derivatives. Structured CDOs are also funded but involve use of embedded credit derivatives to transfer risk; no physical transfer of assets occurs in a structured CDO. Synthetic CDOs are unfunded/partly funded deals that use only credit derivatives to transfer risk; like structured CDOs, they do not result in the physical transfer of assets.

9. Describe three ways in which CDS index tranches can be used to achieve specific risk or investment management goals.

An index swap can be used to acquire a diversified pool of standardized, liquid, credit risks by way of a single transaction (e.g., buying the swap/selling the protection). It can also be used to hedge a broad portfolio of credit risk (e.g., selling the swap/buying the protection). An index swap can also be used to structure relative value transactions, such as selling the broad index and buying a subindex (or vice-versa).

CHAPTER 4 EXERCISES

1. What minimum transactional requirements and end goals should be satisfied in order to increase participation in the credit derivative market?

In general, credit derivatives participation may increase if the market is perceived as transparent, efficient, liquid, legally clear/precise, and suitable (transactional requirements), and if it promotes market access, investment opportunities, and effective hedging (end goals). The absence of any of these may dissuade some institutions from participating.

2. Discuss how a fund might protect itself from concentrated credit risks using a combination of TRSs, CDSs, and credit spread options.

A fund can reduce concentrated credit risks in its portfolio by purchasing a series of CDSs or basket swaps (hedging), by buying TRSs on various reference credits (diversifying), and by buying credit spread put options on its existing portfolio (hedging).

3. Describe three ways in which a bank can use credit derivatives to improve/diversify its loan portfolio.

A bank can improve its loan portfolio by writing credit spread options on existing credits or new credits (e.g., a yield enhancement strategy), writing basket swaps and TRSs on new credits (e.g., a diversification strategy), or by purchasing basket swaps on existing credits (e.g., a hedging/credit substitution mechanism).

4. Assume a company has a $200 million dollar portfolio of accounts receivable (180-day maximum maturity) extended to a diverse base of institutional customers. Describe two credit derivative strategies that it can employ to protect against defaults in the receivables portfolio.

To hedge its receivables, the company can enter into a first-to-default basket swap comprised of its primary reference obligors (i.e., the largest and least creditworthy); the maturity of the basket swap can be synchronized to the 180-day time frame and renegotiated at each maturity date. The company can also purchase a standard basket swap that covers more than one default event; however, because the standard basket is more expensive than the first-to-default basket, the company would only select this strategy if it were concerned about the credit quality of several customers.

5. Assume a pension fund is attempting to capitalize on potential deterioration of a reference credit. To do so it decides to purchase a 12-month €10 million notional credit spread put with a strike spread of EURIBOR + 120 bps, for 30 bps of up-front premium. The put references a company's 10-year bond (current duration of seven years). What will the fund's gross and net payouts be in one year (when the duration of the reference bond is six years) if the reference spread widens to 160 bps? If it tightens to 100 bps? What is the breakeven spread level?

*The gross payout to the fund if the spread widens to 160 bps is €240,000, which is simply (€10 million * (0.0160 − 0.0120) * 6); the net payout is €210,000, which is the gross payout less €30,000 of premium.*
 The gross and net payouts to the fund if the spread tightens to 100 bps will be zero, as the option will be out-of-the-money.
The breakeven spread level is 150 bps (e.g., 120 bps + 30 bps).

CHAPTER 5 EXERCISES

1. Describe the relationship between covariance and correlation. If 2 reference credits have a default correlation coefficient of +0.7,

do we expect the likelihood of both defaulting to be greater or lesser than if the default correlation is –0.7?

Covariance measures the comovement of asset prices, i.e., the degree to which the two assets move together or separately. Correlation attempts to normalize the measurement of covariance through the introduction of a correlation coefficient, which is the covariance of asset prices divided by the standard deviation of each asset price; a positive correlation coefficient indicates they move in the same direction, a negative coefficient means they move in opposite directions. Accordingly, a default correlation coefficient of +0.7 reflects greater likelihood that two reference credits will default than one with a coefficient of –0.7 (which indicates precisely the opposite).

2. What is the main challenge an institution might face in attempting to estimate covariances? What alternatives exist?

The main challenge in covariance estimates relates to the large quantity of data required to produce meaningful results. For instance, an index with 2,000 constituents has more than two million parameters and requires at least 80 years of daily data to provide accurate covariance estimates. An alternative to this process is to use risk models that are built on the assumption that asset returns can be explained through a linear combination of factors (such as index returns, macroeconomic indicators, company characteristics, and so forth). Such models reduce the data requirement by a considerable amount.

3. Explain the steps involved in computing expected credit losses.

Expected credit losses can be determined by first computing the expected credit exposure of a contract; for static contracts such as loans this will be a fixed amount. For dynamic contracts such as derivatives, it will be a fluctuating amount that can be estimated by examining potential worst-case market movements related to the underlying derivative asset reference. It is then necessary to apply an estimated probability of default parameter to indicate the likelihood of counterparty default, and a recovery rate to indicate the size of the net loss (e.g., net loss given default). The three components yield an expected credit loss.

4. Describe the differences between systematic and idiosyncratic risks.

Systematic risk is the risk component in a multifactor risk model that can be explained by the model; all companies are exposed to some degree of systematic, or industrywide, risk. Idiosyncratic risk, in contrast, is a company-specific risk component that cannot be estimated by the model; it is a risk parameter that is unique to each individual company.

5. What result does a macroeconomic factor model attempt to produce? What advantages and disadvantages characterize this approach?

   A macroeconomic factor model attempts to explain the relationship between asset prices and risk through macro variables common to all companies (e.g., inflation, economic growth, interest rates, industrial production). The advantages of this approach relate to the availability of macro data and the intuitive linkage between economic factors and company performance. The main disadvantage relates to the sensitivity of the model to macro variable specification; this can lead to model error if not handled with accuracy.

6. In what ways is a cross-sectional model different from other multifactor models?

   A cross-sectional risk model relies on factors from a set of company-specific data (factor loadings) rather than actual sensitivities to factors, as is common in a standard multifactor model. This means that the model attempts to determine the relationship between asset prices (returns) and a set of factors specific to a company—rather than those common to all companies.

CHAPTER 6 EXERCISES

1. Using the basic CDS pricing framework, and assuming a recovery rate of 40% and the same interest rate structure for both the market and the model, establish the probabilities of default from the market CDS prices shown in the table below.

   The default and survival probabilities that agree with the new premiums are given as:

Recovery rate = 40%.

Period	Years	Futures/ Swap Prices	Discount Factors	Probability of Default	Probability of Survival	Denominator	Numerator	CDS Price
1	0.5	2.81	0.9861	0.0029	0.9971	0.491642	0.001716	0.0035
2	1	3.16	0.9694	0.0062	0.9909	0.971916	0.005322	0.0055
3	1.5	3.41	0.9505	0.0109	0.9800	1.437638	0.011538	0.0080
4	2	3.71	0.9289	0.0149	0.9651	1.885861	0.019842	0.0105
5	2.5	3.99	0.9054	0.0213	0.9438	2.313134	0.031413	0.0136
6	3	4.31	08789	0.0229	0.9209	2.717827	0.043490	0.0160
7	3.5	4.66	0.8493	0.0330	0.8879	3.094867	0.060305	0.0195
8	4	5.01	0.8175	0.0510	0.8369	3.436945	0.085320	0.0248
9	4.5	5.16	0.7916	0.0610	0.7759	3.744046	0.114293	0.0305
10	5	5.31	0.7652	0.0740	0.7019	4.012601	0.148269	0.0370

Period	Years	Market Rates
1	0.5	0.0035
2	1	0.0055
3	1.5	0.0080
4	2	0.0105
5	2.5	0.0136
6	3	0.0160
7	3.5	0.0195
8	4	0.0248
9	4.5	0.0305
10	5	0.0370

2. If the recovery rate were 45% rather than 40%, would an institution buy or sell protection at the CDS prices indicated above? Why?

A recovery rate of 45% suggests a better return in case of default, which would reduce the CDS premiums demanded. Accordingly, an institution would benefit from selling protection at the higher levels.

3. Why should a traded market reference approach to modeling not be regarded as a sufficient form of pricing on its own?

A traded market reference approach to credit derivative modeling implies that an institution is relying on third parties to supply pricing. While this approach can be helpful as an additional benchmarking tool, the approach places all valuation responsibility with external parties, which may be unsatisfactory from a governance perspective.

4. Why is the term structure of credit spreads not always upward sloping?

CCC-rated credits are the exception to the "upward-sloping" credit term structure rule. They feature downward-sloping term structures because the possibility of survival over the medium-term improves if a CCC-rated company can overcome short-term financial distress.

5. Given a 75 bp credit spread, a 4% risk-free rate, and a three-year time horizon, what is the future value of $1 on a continuously compounded basis? What is the implied probability of default assuming the same market data?

   Future value = exp((0.04 + .0075)*3) = $1.153153
   Implied probability of default = 1 – exp(–.0075*3) = .022249, or 2.225%

CHAPTER 7 EXERCISES

1. Describe the three main elements that determine the default probability of a firm and indicate what each one measures.

   The three main elements determining default probability include the value of a firm's assets (which measures the present value of the future free cash flows of the firm), asset risk (which measures the uncertainty regarding the firm's business and industry risks), and leverage (which measures the degree to which a firm uses liabilities in its capital structure to fund operations).

2. How is asset risk measured? Given a firm with asset value of $70 billion and an asset volatility of 15%, how much asset value is added or subtracted for each one-standard-deviation move? Should a firm with high asset volatility seek to add or subtract leverage from its operations? Why?

   Asset risk is commonly measured through asset volatility, an annualized standard deviation of the change in a company's asset value. Given $70 billion of asset value and 15% asset volatility, the one-standard-deviation range of asset values is $59.5 billion to $80.5 billion (e.g., +/– $10.5 billion). A firm with high asset volatility should generally seek to lower, rather than increase, its leverage. Leverage magnifies the effects of asset volatility, suggesting the prospects of increased financial distress may rise.

3. Explain the six factors that determine default probability at a time period t. What occurs when the asset value of the firm declines below the default point?

   Six key factors that determine default probability include a company's current asset value, the distribution of asset values at time t, the volatility of future assets at time t, the book value of liabilities, the expected growth rate in asset value to time t, and the length of the time period t. When a firm's asset value declines below the default point, its liabilities are greater than its assets, suggesting a state of insolvency.

4. Why is it inaccurate to average default rates over a long period of time? What can be done to prevent inaccuracies?

Because overall default rates can vary considerably over long periods of time (e.g., a doubling or tripling of defaults from peak to trough of a credit cycle), average default rates may overstate or understate true performance. A more accurate approach is to measure changes in default risk over time.

5. Assuming a loss given default of 25% and an EDF of 3%, what is the expected loss? What if the EDF rises to 5%? What if the recovery rate is 60% and the EDF is 4%?

Loss given default of 25% suggests a recovery rate of 75%. Thus, expected loss in the first instance is 0.75% (simply (1 − .75) ∗ (0.03)). If EDF rises to 5%, the expected loss is 1.25% (or (1 − .75) ∗ (0.05)). If the recovery rate is 60% and EDF is 4%, the expected loss is 1.6% (or (1 −.60) ∗ (0.04)).

6. How can an equity-based default probability be computed?

An equity-based default probability can be determined by estimating the market value and volatility of the firm's assets, calculating the number of standard deviations the firm is away from default, and then scaling this standard deviation "distance" using an empirical default distribution.

CHAPTER 8 EXERCISES

1. List and describe five elements of individual and portfolio credit risk.

Individual credit risk is influenced by default probability, or the likelihood that a counterparty will fail to perform on its obligations; migration risk, or the likelihood that a counterparty's probability of default will change and alter the value of its obligations; and loss given default, or the amount of loss that will occur, net of recoveries, in the event of counterparty default. Portfolio credit risk is impacted by default correlations, or the degree to which the default probabilities of

*various credit references/counterparties are related, and portfolio expo-
sure, or the amount of the portfolio exposed to default.*

2. Explain why the unexpected losses of a credit portfolio are not
   equal to the weighted average of the unexpected losses of each
   individual credit in the portfolio.

   *Unexpected losses cannot be added and averaged across an entire port-
   folio because losses depend on default correlations between credits in
   the portfolio. Although a portfolio's expected losses are equal to the
   weighted average of the expected losses, the unexpected loss computation relies on portfolio weights and pairwise loss correlations. Simply
   adding weighted averages may result on understatement or overstate-
   ment of losses.*

3. If the probabilities of default of Credit 1 and Credit 2 are 0.5%
   and 0.3%, respectively, and the correlation between the two is 0,
   what is the joint probability of default?

   *Because Credit 1 and Credit 2 default scenarios are independent (e.g.,
   correlation of 0), the joint default computation is simply 0.5%*0.3%,
   or 0.0015%.*

4. Why is estimating pairwise correlations through a sampling of
   asset time series not an optimal methodology? What approach
   might be preferable?

   *This method is generally not optimal because a firm's asset value is
   driven heavily by idiosyncratic factors, so sample correlations will
   reflect comovement unique to a particular sample period. This means
   the result will be of limited use in subsequent time horizons. To overcome this problem, it is often preferable to use a factor model, which
   focuses on the different components that drive asset comovements,
   including systematic variables.*

5. How might an institution compute the expected return on a loan
   or credit facility using EDF and loss given default?

   *An institution can set the expected return on the facility equal to the
   EDF * (risk-free base less the loss given default) and add to that
   (1 − EDF) * the yield on the loan. The combination produces the
   expected default/no default scenarios.*

6. Describe the key difference between evaluating a short position in a credit risky bond and a long position in a CDS on the same risky bond.

   The short position does not involve any counterparty performance; the CDS, which involves payment of a fee or premium in exchange for a compensatory payment should the risky-credit reference default, implies counterparty performance. Any modeling effort must therefore take account of the joint probability of default between the credit-risky reference and the counterparty.

CHAPTER 9 EXERCISES

1. Why would a bank extending a credit facility seek to optimize its credit decision? What goals is it attempting to achieve?

   Optimization can create a more rational credit decision than might otherwise be apparent through simple examination/stress-testing of single variables (i.e., the optimization might suggest a smaller or larger credit facility given a particular series of constraints). The ultimate goal is to maximize the level of return for a given amount of capital at risk, given a set of constraints.

2. Why might a stochastic optimization process be considered more accurate than standard financial forecasting?

   Stochastic optimization allows manipulation of multiple variables simultaneously through a Monte Carlo simulation process; this is generally seen as an improvement over standard deterministic forecasting, which is limited in its ability to handle multiple variables.

3. How many simulations would be required for an optimization routine based on 4 decision variables, each with 12 possible outcomes?

   An optimization routine would yield 12^4, or 20,736, possible outcomes.

4. Describe four ways in which an intermediary or end-user can use ratings transitions as part of its credit derivate risk/investment management strategies.

   Ratings transitions can be used for multiple purposes, including: tracking potential downgrades in order to avoid credit spread widening losses; tracking potential upgrades in order to capitalize on credit spread tightening gains; rebalancing a loan or bond investment portfolio to avoid impending concentrations in the subinvestment-grade sector; and, adjusting the level of credit reserves held against credits that may continue to migrate downwards (e.g., BB to B).

5. Given a contract with a counterparty that features an expected default rate of 0.25% and a loss given default of 40%, what is the expected loss level?

   *The expected loss is given as 0.25% * 40% = 0.10%.*

6. Why might the standard deviation of recovery rates for a given year be particularly large for a specific class of debt seniority?

   A single very large bankruptcy with very large or very small recovery values may be sufficient to skew the pool, introducing a larger standard deviation of recovery rates than might otherwise be expected.

7. Referring to Table 9.3, S&P one-year transition rates, speculate on why there is a 0.08% chance that a CCC-rated credit can be upgraded to AAA status.

   Because it is unlikely, in the normal course of business affairs, for a company to migrate from a CCC to an AAA in one year based solely on financial performance, the cause can be traced to an acquisition of the CCC credit by an AAA credit, which assumes responsibilities for all of the CCC credit's outstanding liabilities.

8. What benefits do commercial transition-based applications such as CreditMetrics provide? What drawbacks must be considered?

   Transition-based applications can provide useful insight into the credit risk profile of an entire portfolio as it evolves over time; this can give an institution a tool by which to identify credit investment opportunities or credit hedging requirements. Like other models, these platforms are based on a series of assumptions that have varying levels of reliability (e.g., assumptions regarding the computation of credit correlations, credit volatilities); care and conservatism are thus recommended.

CHAPTER 10 EXERCISES

1. Describe the major components of the ISDA documentation framework and the purpose each one serves.

   The ISDA framework is comprised of several different components, including: the Master Agreement (printed form and Schedule), which defines the standard and customized terms and conditions between two counterparties; the Credit Support Documents, which delineate any specific credit provisions between the two counterparties, including margining/collateral provisions, or downgrade events; Confirmations, including long- and short-form versions that record the specific details/valuations of individual trades; and, Definitions, which provide, for select products, standard legal and market definitions that can be used as a reference source by short-form confirmations.

2. Why would an institution choose to use a long-form, rather than short-form, confirmation in documenting its transactions with a counterparty?

   An institution would use a long-form confirmation when the market does not support standardized definitions, or if the terms of the transaction are so customized that significant enhancements/amendments are required.

3. What specific benefits accrue from the use of a closeout netting clause?

   Closeout netting permits a nondefaulting party to accelerate, and net down, all outstanding transactions governed by a Master Agreement upon the default of a counterparty. This permits all sums to be settled via a single payment/receipt, reducing or eliminating the potential for a negative legal judgment or a stay in bankruptcy.

4. Why is the inclusion of guarantees in the 2003 Definitions as part of the risk transfer mechanism considered significant?

   The inclusion is important because guarantees, though off balance sheet, represent liabilities of those issuing them, much as any other balance sheet debt item. This creates a more accurate and comprehensive definitional scope and ensures that any performance/nonperformance issues are treated consistently.

CHAPTER 11 EXERCISES

1. Distinguish between general market risk and specific market risk. Explain why regulators consider that an offsetting credit derivative position carries elements of general market risk and specific market risk.

   General market risk is the risk arising from broad, systemic market movements; Specific market risk, in contrast, is the risk arising from idiosyncratic, credit-specific, movements. Specific market risk is thus a more granular measure of exposure. An offsetting credit derivative position is considered to have elements of both general and specific market risk, as the position is not perfectly matched. Residual elements of risk exist, suggesting that general and specific market forces can still negatively impact the position (though not as much as in an open position). In general, specific risk capital charges are applied to the larger of the two exposure legs.

2. Given a w factor of 15%, a risk weight of 18% on the seller of credit protection, and a 100% risk weight on the reference obligor, what is the average risk weight assignment on a credit derivative for capital purposes?

   The average risk weight is given as: $0.15(1.00) + (1 - 0.15)(0.18)$ $= 0.15 + 0.153 = .303$, or 30.3%.

3. Under what circumstances should a regulator disallow hedge treatment for a credit derivative?

   A regulator should disallow hedge treatment for a credit derivative when it is ineffective in providing risk protection for the exposure being hedged. This may occur when the credit derivative contains an excess of basis risk, maturity mismatch, or when the default events governing the hedge and the underlying exposure can be triggered by different, and inconsistent, factors.

4. How might regulatory treatment for a credit derivative that allows for appreciation or depreciation rather than pure default be adjusted?

   Contracts involving appreciation/depreciation, such as TRSs, can be adjusted by deducting the amount of depreciation paid to the beneficiary (net of any amounts paid by the beneficiary for depreciation) from the notional amount of the contract.

5. Describe minimum standards of credit and market risk management that should be applied to credit derivatives dealing.

Institutions dealing actively in credit derivatives must create a credit and market risk management framework that includes a process to identify, quantify, manage, and report all risk exposures. The process must be sufficiently detailed to capture all potential risks, including spread, correlation, volatility, interest rate, currency, and counterparty risks. From a governance perspective the institution's directors and executives should establish relevant risk policies that create a framework, define an acceptable level of risk tolerance that relates risk capital allocations to potential returns, and monitor exposures on a regular basis to ensure continued compliance and comfort.

SELECTED REFERENCES

Acharya, V., Das, S., and R. Sundrama, "Pricing Credit Derivatives With Rating Transitions," *Financial Analysts Journal*, May/June 2002, Vol. 58, p. 28.

Aldred, C., "Regulators Eyeing Credit Hedge Coverage," *Business Insurance*, February 3, 2003, Vol. 37, p. 25.

Banks, E., 2002, *The Credit Risk of Complex Derivatives, 3rd Edition*, London, Palgrave.

Banks, E., and R., Dunn, 2003, *Practical Risk Management*, London: John Wiley and Sons.

Black, F., and M., Scholes, 1973, The Pricing of Options and Corporate Liabilities, *Journal of Political Economy*, 81, May-June.

Bodie, Z., Kane, A., and A. Marcus, 2005, *Investments, 6th Edition*. New York: McGraw-Hill Irwin.

Bollerslev, T., 1986. "Generalized Autoregressive Conditional Heteroskedasticity," *Journal of Econometrics*, 31, 307-27.

Bouteille, S., and W., Harwood, "Credit Derivatives and Corporates," *Business Credit*, June 2002, Vol. 104, p. 30.

Brennan, M. and E., Schwartz, 1980, "Analyzing Convertible Bonds," *Journal of Financial and Quantitative Analysis*, 15, pp. 907-929.

Burns, M., "Restructuring In, Says ISDA," *Investment Dealers' Digest*, January 13, 2003, p. 1.

Campbell, R., and R., Huisman, "Measuring Credit Spread Risk," *Journal of Portfolio Management*, Summer 2003. Vol. 29, Iss. 4; p. 121.

Caouette, J, Altman, E., and P. Narayanan, 1998, "Managing Credit Risk," *Financial Analysts Journal*, Vol. 54, No. 1.

Cathcart, L., and L., El-Jahel, "Multiple Defaults and Merton's Model," *Journal of Fixed Income*, June 2004, Vol. 14, Iss. 1; p. 60.

Chen, N., Roll, R., and S. Ross, 1986. "Economic Forces and the Stock Market," *Journal of Business*, July 1986.

Chen, R., and B., Sopranzetti, "The Valuation of Default-Triggered Credit Derivatives," *Journal of Financial and Quantitative Analysis*, June 2003, Vol. 38, Issue 2; p. 359.

Chorafas, D., 1999, *Credit Derivatives and the Management of Risk*: London: John Wiley and Sons.

Choudhry, M., 2004, *Structured Credit Products*, London: John Wiley and Sons.

Colter, A., "Credit Derivatives Lure Few Mutual Funds," *The Wall Street Journal*, January 21, 2002. p. 17.

Das, S., 1998, *Swap Derivatives and Financing, 2nd Edition*, Sydney: Law Book Company.

Das, S., 2000, *Credit Derivatives and Credit Linked Notes*, London: John Wiley and Sons.

Duffie, D., and Singleton, K., 1999, "Modeling Term Structures of Defaultable Bonds," *Review of Financial Studies*, Vol. 12.

Economist, "Rites of Passage; Credit Derivatives," January 12, 2002. Vol. 362, Iss. 8255; p. 78.

Elton, E.L., and M.J. Gruber, 1995. *Modern Portfolio Theory and Investment Analysis, 5th Ed.*, New York, John Wiley and Sons.

Engle, R.G, 1982. "Autoregressive Conditional Heteroskedasticity with Estimates of the Variance of United Kingdom Inflation," *Econometrica* 50, 987-1001.

Evans, N., " Peering Through Murky Waters," *Euromoney*, June 2002, p. 18.

Fama, E., and K., French, 1992. "The Cross Section of Variation in Expected Stock Returns," *Journal of Finance*.

Federal Reserve Board, Division of Banking Supervision and Regulation, 2000, SR 00-7 (Sup), "Lending Standards for Commercial Loans."

Glantz, M. 2003. *Managing Bank Risk*, Amsterdam: Elsevier.

Houweling, P., and T., Vorst, 2002, "An Empirical Comparison of Default Swap Pricing Models," Tinbergen Institute Discussion Papers, 02-004.

Hull, J. and A., White, 1995, "The Impact of Default Risk on the Prices of Options and Other Derivative Securities," *Journal of Banking and Finance*.

Hull, J., and A., White, 2000, "Valuing CDS I: No Counterparty Default Risk," *Journal of Derivatives*, Vol. 8, No. 1.

Ingersoll, J., 1987, *Theory of Financial Decision Making*, London: Rowan and Littlefield.

International Financial Law Review, "Marconi Reveals Shortcomings of Credit Swap Documents," IFLR, London, October 2002, Vol. 10, p. 3.

Jarrow, R., Turnbull, S., and D. Lando, 1997, "A Markov Model for the Term Structure of Credit Risk Spreads," *Review of Financial Studies*, Vol. 10, No. 2.

Kennedy, P., 1998. *A Guide to Econometrics, 4th Edition*, Cambridge, Mass: The MIT Press.

Kissell, R., and M., Glantz, 2003. *Optimal Trading Strategies*, New York: AMACOM, Inc.,

————. 2004, "A Practical Framework for Estimating Transaction Costs and Developing Optimal Trading Strategie to Achieve Best Execution," Elsevier Finance Research Letters.

Leland, H., 1994, "Bond Prices, Yield Spreads and Optimal Capital Structure with Default Risk," University of California Working Paper RPF-240.

Leland, H., and K., Toft, 1994, "Optimal Capital Structure, Endogenous Bankruptcy, and the Term Structure of Credit Spreads," *Journal of Finance*, Vol., No. 3.

Longstaff, F., and E., Scwhartz, 1995, "A Simple Approach to Valuing Risky Fixed and Floating Rate Debt," *Journal of Finance*.

Mackenze, M., "Credit Derivatives Survive a Series of Stress Tests," *The Wall Street Journal*, January 21, 2002, p.13.

Madan, D., and H., Unal, 1998, "Pricing the Risk of Default," *Derivatives Research*, Vol. 12.

Markowitz, H., 1952, "Portfolio Selection," *Journal of Finance*, 7 (1), 77-91.

McGinty, L., "Credit Index Products," *Global Investor*, December 2002, p. 15.

Merton, R., 1974, "On the Pricing of Corporate Debt,": *Journal of Finance*, Vol, 29, pp. 449-470.

Morris, J., "ISDA Upgrades Definitions," *Euromoney*, March 2003. p. 1.

Nelken, I., 1999, *Implementing Credit Derivatives*, New Jersey: Irwin.

Ong, M., 1999, *Internal Credit Risk Models*, London: Risk Books.

Poorman, F., "Credit Derivatives: An Overview for U.S. Banks," *Commercial Lending Review*, January 2003, Vol. 18, p.4.

Rizzi, J., "Risk Implications of Credit Derivative Instruments," *Commercial Lending Review*, July 2003, Vol. 18, p. 5.

Roll, R., and S. Ross. 1984. "The Arbitrage Pricing Theory Approach to Strategic Portfolio Planning." *Financial Analysts Journal*, May-June 1984.

Rutter, J., "Cutting Edge Credit," *Global Investor*, April 2002, p. 28.

Smithson, C., 1999, *Financial Risk Management, 3rd Edition*, New Jersey: Irwin.

Specht, B., "Synthetic Securitization Enters Next Generation," *Euromoney*, February 2001, p. 28.

Tavakoli, J., 2001, *Credit Derivatives and Synthetic Structures, 2nd edition*, New York: John Wiley and Sons.

INDEX

AAA
  bank, 109, 110
  credit, 267
  investors, 73
AAA/AA
  bank, 108, 111
  credit, 270
  investors, 79
  risks, 69
ABS markets, 80, 81
Absolute risk level, 276
Absorbing barrier model, 197
Active portfolio management, 217
Actuarial risk, 241
Addressing derivative risk management, 302
Agency default rates, 277
Agricultural portfolio, 104, 105
Amendment, market risk, 304, 305
Amortizing assets, 70
Ancillary credit risk techniques, 255
Ancillary credit risk tools, 255, 257, 259, 261, 263, 265, 267, 269, 271, 273, 275, 277, 279, 281
Anheuser-Busch's business risk, 186
Annual
  operating return, 262, 264
  probability, 204
Applicable credit event, 294
Applications, 3, 21, 53, 100–102, 107–111, 115–117, 130, 179, 213, 222, 267, 276, 278, 302, 304
Arbitrage CDOs, 67, 86, 87
ARCH models, 133, 134
Arranged bank loan facilities, 271
Assets, 26–30, 40, 54–60, 62–64, 78, 79, 81–83, 85–87, 123–126, 136–140, 185–190, 192–204, 219, 221–224, 242–248, 310, 311
  attributes, 219
  average, 126
  callability, 87
  changes, 245
  classes, 8, 26, 87
  classification, 311
  correlations, 228, 229
  coupons, 9, 41, 42, 113
  deteriorates, 18
  distribution, 196
  expropriation, 118
  issuers, 70
  liquidation, 19, 257
  liquidity, 28, 75, 167
    risk, 19
  management
    institutions, 67
  managers, 220

market value, 222, 262
pool, 64, 72–74, 78, 79, 85
  flows, 75
  high-grade, 77, 78
  high-yield, 77, 78
  portfolio, 71, 92
  price, 40
    postdefault, 40
  purchase, 86
  repackager, 62
  repackagings, 65
  return, 280
  risks, 186, 216
  sales, 257
  sizes, 187, 189
  substitution, 79, 84
  swap
    activity, 28
    arbitrage, 28
    bilateral default, 12
    coupon, 30
    strategy, 31
    switches, 6, 25, 26, 31, 50
    theme, 6
    referencing basis flows, 6
  swaptions, 6, 25, 26, 31
  time series, 253
  turnover, 84
  value
    correlation, 234, 235
    expected, 204, 222
    final, 194, 197
    path, 196, 202
    return, 232
    series, 231
  values, 86, 166, 185–187, 189–197, 199–201, 203, 204, 206–209, 216, 222–225, 229–232, 235, 261, 262, 279
    high, 194
  variance, 159, 204
  volatility, 18, 186–189, 192, 195, 196, 199–201, 204, 216, 222, 223, 228
  write-downs, 257
Asset-backed
  mechanism, 13
  security, 13
Asset/interest coverage ratios, 76
  approaches, 185
  changes, 224
  defaulted, 75, 93
  floating-rate, 9, 28
  individual, 226, 243, 245, 246, 252
  maturing, 86
  minus, 186
  multiple, 155
  physical, 13, 21, 88, 92
  pool, 75, 78, 85, 89
  protected, 306
  single, 219, 245
  structured, 66, 82
  synthetic, 11, 12, 28

underlying, 19, 27, 29, 31, 75, 91, 123, 176, 183, 192, 194, 199, 200, 311
Asset-specific return, 142
Asset-swapped basis, 32
Assumptions, 113, 138–141, 143, 148, 155, 163–165, 167, 169, 174, 177, 179, 197, 214, 225, 252
Average
  asset pool, 78
  cumulative default
    statistics, 270
  default
    correlation, 229
    rates, 209, 216
    return-to-risk ratios, 248
  risk, 244
    weight assignment, 316

Balance sheet
  assets, 13
Balanced portfolio, 104
Bank, 12–14, 17, 29–32, 34–36, 38, 39, 41, 42, 49, 50, 58, 59, 63–66, 100–108, 110–115, 163, 164, 217, 218, 242–244, 256–259
  assets, 239
  balance sheets, 243
  counterparty, 102, 117
  examiners, 310
  finances, 258
  functions, 242
  funds, 91
  issues, 13
  letters, 83
  loans, secured, 170, 272
  regulators, 309
  sponsor, 93
  supervisors, 301
Bankers, 124, 261–264
Banking
  book, 304, 309, 310
  buy-and-hold, 100
  organization, 305, 308–310
  problems, 17
  side, 146
Bankruptcy, 4, 33, 35, 56, 61, 79, 88, 108, 115, 137, 198, 207, 215, 216, 296, 298
  frequencies, 198
  protection, 185
  receiver, 293
  rules, 165
Bankruptcy-remote SPEs, 57
Bank-sponsored vehicles, 58
Basic default model, 228
Basket, first-to-default 43, 45, 51
Basket swaps, 9, 25, 42, 43, 46, 53, 60, 97, 102, 104–106, 116
BBB default risk, 111

BBB-rated
  credit, 102
  single obligor default risk, 74
Bilateral
  contract, 8, 17, 39
  credit, 23
Bond portfolio, 248
Bonds, 12, 13, 19, 31, 35, 41, 42,
  48, 50, 51, 54, 55, 61–65, 81,
  82, 88, 102, 171, 172, 273, 277,
  278
  bearer, 81, 82
  corporate, 69, 74, 166, 218
  emerging-market, 81, 87
  high-yield, 81, 85, 87
  public, 112, 168, 271
  subordinated, 166, 170,
    273, 274
  synthetic, 55, 62, 65, 66
Borrower defaults, 241
Business risk, 186, 187
Buy-and-hold portfolio, 266

Calculating default
  probabilities, 213
Calculating portfolio
  diversification, 228
Capital, 16, 17, 23, 26, 71, 86,
  104, 173, 197, 221, 238, 243,
  256, 301, 304, 307
  requirements, market risk, 304
  risk-based, 306
Cash
  flow
    model, 83
    structure, 84, 85
  flows, 9, 36, 40, 55, 56, 63, 67,
    71–74, 76, 79, 80, 84, 85,
    112, 170, 172, 257, 258, 264
  gross operating, 257
  market debt instruments,
    305
Cash-settled credit, 49
CCC-rated credits, 173, 281
CDOs, 13, 45, 46, 53, 66–70,
  72–80, 83, 84, 86–88,
  90–92, 95
  arbitrage, 72, 85, 87
  balance sheet, 66, 85, 86
  equity, 74
  funded, 87, 91
  high-yield, 72, 81, 82, 84
  investor, 45
  single tranche, 53, 92, 94
  standard, 13, 69, 71, 76
  structured, 13, 87–89, 91, 92
CDS, 7, 33–35, 41–43, 50, 51,
  60–62, 88–92, 103–106, 108,
  163, 164, 175–178, 183, 184,
  213, 214, 217–219, 239, 240,
  250–253
  contracts, 124, 183, 213, 216,
    225, 250, 252
  index default loss
    distribution, 94

markets, 109, 184, 213, 238,
  240, 242
premiums, 174, 176, 177, 179,
  214, 251, 252
prices, 177, 181, 205, 238
risk, 214
Changing portfolio credit
  quality, 73
Citibank, 57, 90
Classified assets, 17
CLNs, 11, 13, 53–58, 60, 61,
  87–90, 88, 93, 97, 100, 304
  sponsoring bank issues,
    13, 90
Collateral
  assets, 87
    high-quality, 13, 90
  portfolio/ 77, 78
  portfolios, 69
Collateralized debt obligation
  (CDO) structuring
  technology, 7
Combined default rate, 82
Commercial banks, 218, 220
Compaq Computer, 186–188
Compensatory payment, 7,
  10, 36, 43, 45, 46, 115,
  118, 169
Complete credit protection, 311
Comprehensive credit portfolio
  model, 231
Concentrated
  agricultural portfolio, 104
  credit risks, 119, 276
Concentrated portfolio, 107
Conditional contracts, 308
Constructing credit models, 213
Control
  minimum risk, 312
  risks, 256
Corporate
  assets, 221
  credit exposure, 96
  debt market, 217
  default-risk, 252
  defaults, 185
Correlated credit
  migration, 231
  risk, 313
Correlation, 10, 34, 36, 43, 78,
  85, 124, 125, 142, 146, 165,
  166, 223, 224, 228–232, 234,
  235, 251, 278
  relationships, 155
  risk, 312
Counterparty credit, 106
  exposure, 304
  limits, 54
Counterparty credit risk
  capital charge, 310
Coupons, 8, 29, 39, 42, 57, 60,
  62, 71, 82, 92, 93, 111, 112
  below–market, 71
Covariance matrix, 126, 127,
  135–137, 145, 146, 148, 156,
  158, 159

Credit, 3–5, 7–15, 17–23, 25, 26,
  34–36, 38, 39, 41–49, 51,
  56–61, 93–95, 97–102,
  111–119, 167–174, 302–312,
  314–316
  administration practices, 17
  analysis, 18, 258
    optimization models,
      259
  analytic packages, 255
  analytics, 101, 265
  assets, 12, 13, 58, 70–72, 90,
    101, 276, 279
  reference, 4, 17
  businesses, 256
  buyer, 10, 43
  correlations, 18, 42
  cycle, 209, 212, 215, 277
  deal, 107
  decision, 280
  default CLN, 60
  default
    contracts, 4, 119
    probabilities, 127
    put option, 33
    risks, 89, 255, 280
    swaps, 7, 25, 33–35, 183, 204,
      217, 250
  defaulting, 11, 44, 47
  defaults, 10, 62, 118, 173, 301
    reference, 4, 7, 10, 34, 44,
      47, 165
  derivate risk/investment
    management
    strategies, 280
  Credit derivatives, 3–5, 11,
    13–21, 23–26, 90, 97–99,
    101, 106, 107, 115, 116, 118,
    119, 285, 301, 302, 304, 305,
    307–312, 315, 316
    contracts, 3
    dealer, 35, 36, 116
    feature, 19
    hedge, 309
    hedging, 257
    market, 53, 97
    pricing, 174
    sector, 20, 301
    surfaces, 16
  deteriorates, 38, 42
    reference, 10, 11, 47
  deterioration, 4, 19, 29, 39,
    107, 225
  downgrades, 103, 123
  enhancements, 83
  events, 4, 12, 16, 20, 33,
    36, 37, 56, 58, 88, 169,
    293–298, 303
    defined, 33, 35, 58
  exposure
    concentrations, 103
    thresholds, 287
  exposures, 17, 54, 100, 101,
    104, 105, 107, 108, 117, 225,
    250, 276, 305, 306, 311
  facility, 253, 260, 265, 280

forward, 14, 48, 53
foundations, 17
guarantor, 4
guidelines, 57
hedge funds, 217
issuers, 34, 289
loss event, 303
losses, 17
  expected, 83, 129, 161
management units, 315
managers, 129
market
  data, 213
  risk premium, 213
markets, 7, 110, 183, 213
measure, 191, 215
migration, 225, 226, 235, 279
multiple reference, 10, 43
obligations, 115
  corporate, 13, 66
offsetting, 306, 316
originator, 76, 86
performance, 4, 62, 104, 109
portfolio
  analysis, 217, 238, 253
  management, 252
  results, 280
portfolios, 90, 105, 242, 248,
  250–253
product development, 53
products, 100
profile, 168, 292
protection, 56, 59, 93, 163, 298,
  303, 306, 308–311, 316
  buyer, 7
  seller, 7, 58
put, 48, 49
quality, 13, 35, 70, 73, 82, 83,
  86, 163, 207, 212, 215, 257,
  270, 276, 308
references, 6, 8, 20, 31, 37, 39,
  62, 101
reserves, 256
risk, 15–18, 22, 32, 33, 35, 36,
  42, 57, 83, 90, 91, 99–101,
  107, 128, 184, 220, 306–308,
  310, 311
  activities, 301
  analysis, 251
  assets, 92
  capital requirements set, 304
  concentration, 256
  control, 17
  correlation, 94
  counterparty, 305, 313
  exposure, 24, 62, 100, 128,
    129, 310
  framework, 313
  investment, 66
  limits, 315
Credit risk
  migrations, 257, 265
  portfolio, 92
  strength/weakness, 265
  structured, 12, 58
  structures, 168

substitutes, direct, 307
support, 288, 292
terms, 302
thresholds, 103
transitions, 277
volatilities, 18
weakness, 112
CreditEdge, 191, 220
Creditex, 15
CreditMetrics, 179, 276–281
  application, 267
  framework, 277
  methodology
    addresses, 277
    constructs, 276
  platform, 275
  portfolio, 276
  values, 277
Creditor banks, 64
Creditors, 108, 165, 173, 199,
  298, 309
Credit-protected exposure, 303
Creditrade, 15
Credit-risky
  asset class, 6
  assets, 11, 13, 19, 24, 42, 56, 58,
    63, 86, 108, 220, 230, 302
  bond, 5, 253
    price, 33
  exposures, 242
  instrument, 239
  issuers/borrowers, 53
  loans, 13
  references, 39
Creditworthiness, 4, 31, 255,
  261, 265, 297
Cross-default, 309
Cumulative
  average default rates, 268
  probabilities, 78, 173, 174
  five-year, 204
Customized
  credit, 99
    portfolios, 46
  credit-linked asset, 63
  portfolio, 46

Data, fundamental, 153
Dealer-quoted postdefault
  price, 88
Dealers, 34–37, 62, 163, 164, 168,
  292, 311
Debt, 4, 20, 35, 71, 190, 192–195,
  200, 204, 217–219, 222, 224,
  243, 244, 272, 298, 304, 305
  assets, 236
  defaulted, 269
  instrument, 238, 266, 272, 274,
    278, 306
  long-term, 204
  markets, 244
  obligations, 72, 73, 82
  portfolios, 218, 219, 221, 249
  service, 85, 257, 258
  values, 224, 261

Default, 33–36, 42–46, 60–62,
  78–81, 163–174, 176, 185, 186,
  188–191, 195–199, 202–205,
  207–213, 221–231, 240–242,
  265–272, 289–297
1-EDF, 241
approaches, 211
basket, 10, 25, 43
  swap, 43
conditions, 99
correlation
  coefficient, 160
  features, 79
  measures, 228
correlations, 79, 84, 160, 219,
  228–230, 235, 252
counterparty, 102, 289
credits, 43, 46, 79, 108
event, 44, 61, 114, 166, 306
expected, 78, 256
experience, 75, 82, 92, 229, 267
  global, 267
exposure, 35, 90, 109
features, 166
frequency, 198, 199
  expected, 167, 191, 197, 220
  joint, 230, 231
given, 34, 78, 79, 184, 213, 216,
  219, 225, 239, 240, 253, 274,
  275, 280
history, 198, 205, 208,
  210, 229
horizon, 270
instruments, 168
intensities, 166
levels, 164
loss data, 167
measurement, 197
measures, 205, 212
modeling, 164
obligor, 128, 129
option, 221, 222
partition, 279
payment, 61, 176, 177, 311
performance, 74, 87
point, 186–190, 196, 197, 199,
  203, 204, 206–208, 216,
  228, 229
respective, 228, 231
probabilities, 124, 164–167,
  169, 170, 174, 179, 183–186,
  189–191, 196–198, 201, 203,
  204, 213, 214, 216, 230,
  239, 251
  annual, 186, 188, 204
  cumulative 172, 204
  equity-based, 214–216
  joint, 164, 251
probability
  assessment, 108
  densities, 166
  method, 168
  transitions, 275
protection, 11, 13, 47, 50,
  62, 90
seller, 165

rates, 71, 78, 170, 190, 198, 203,
    208, 209, 222, 227, 265, 266,
    270, 271, 275
  cumulative, 171, 265, 271
  expected, 226, 227, 274,
    275, 280
  international, 198
  ratings, 168
  reference, 35, 93
  relationship, 228
  risk, 13, 65, 66, 73, 74, 99, 100,
    112, 113, 163, 174, 175, 190,
    191, 209, 213, 217–219,
    221–223, 225, 229, 239–245
  differences, 74
  scenarios, 270
  swaps, 7, 19, 91
    knock-in, 103
  technical, 4, 20
  threshold, 297
Defaulted
  credit, 93
  instrument, 272
  obligation, 108
Default-induced losses, 73
Defaulting, 82, 88, 160, 183, 204,
    227–230, 258
  party, 293
  references, 37
Default/no-default scenarios, 7
Default-related
  assumptions, 87
  losses, 79
Default/restructuring
  actions, 82
Defaults shift, 74
Default/transition rates, 267
Defined default event, 311
Definitions, credit event, 20,
    100, 308
Delayed portfolio ramp-up, 73
Derivative
  assets, 25
  contracts, 3, 5, 14, 17, 19, 20,
    23, 34, 36, 94, 165, 168, 299,
    309, 310
  counterparties, 104, 107
  market, 3, 11, 15, 16, 25, 47, 53,
    66, 97–101, 107, 119, 164,
    168, 169, 293, 295, 302
  reference/portfolio, 57
  risk, 22
  transactions, 17, 20, 54, 64,
    103, 104, 255, 304, 306, 307,
    311
Derivative-based structures, 13
Digital credit put option, 7
Discrete credits, 42
Distance-to-default, 188–191,
    198
  ratio, 213
Distressed
  bank, 243
    loans, 85
  loans, 80, 82
Distribution, asset change, 279

Diversification, 13, 44, 54, 59,
    70, 73, 78, 83, 84, 86,
    217–219, 226–228, 236, 237,
    244–246, 248–250, 252
Diversified
  asset pool, 75
  loan portfolio, 100
  portfolios, 42, 109, 111, 218
Dynamic credit exposure
  profiles, 103
Dynamic portfolios, 57

EDF credit measure, 191, 195,
    198, 199, 201, 203–205,
    207–209, 212–216, 220
EDF
  model, 205, 206
  values, 191, 197–199, 204, 205,
    207, 209, 211, 212, 215,
    220, 231
Effective
  credit risk management
    process, 256
  default
    measurement, 190
    protection, 50
  operational risk management
    controls, 21
  risk, 16
    management, 16
Efficient equity market, 206
Emerging-market CDOs, 83
Empirical default distribution
  mapping, 204
Equity, 70–75, 78, 84–86, 92, 98,
    99, 101, 127, 190–195,
    198–201, 218, 219, 224,
    238–240, 242–245, 249, 298
  add-on factors, 306
  funding, 243, 244
  higher-risk, 194
  holders, 79, 192–194
  investors, 72, 74, 78, 87, 95
  market, 184, 191, 207, 209,
    212–214, 242
  option, 110
  portfolios, 136, 219
  prices, 18, 164, 167, 183, 190,
    191, 212, 279
  risk, 71
    exposures, 123
  securities, 190, 193, 194, 272
  traded, 191, 220, 239
  tranche, 71–74, 80, 83, 84, 86,
    87, 89, 91, 94
  investors, 95
  value, 183, 194, 196, 201,
    206–208, 212, 223–225,
    229, 230
  volatility, 187, 201, 223, 224
Equity factors range, 306
Equity-based CDS price, 205
Equity-based default
  measure, 205
  probability estimates, 214

Equity-based EDF credit
  measure, 213
Equity-related cash flow, 71
Estimated
  asset volatility, 160
  average default, 309
  default
    experience, 74
    probabilities, 78
    rates, 222
Estimates, 68, 103, 123, 124, 129,
    136, 145, 146, 154, 155, 159,
    160, 163–165, 167, 213, 214,
    229, 231–234, 239, 278, 279
  covariance, 127, 130, 142
  incorrect, 124, 130, 183
  volatility, 130, 131
Estimating
  asset correlation, 232
  credit volatilities, 276
  default
    correlations, 229
    probability, 183
    rates, 266
  pairwise asset correlations, 231
European
  asset pools, 66
  credits, 108
  high-grade credits, 107
Events, 4, 20, 42, 61, 62, 66,
    79, 100, 118, 163, 164, 225,
    240, 241, 252, 289–291, 296,
    297, 302
  convertibility, 65
  termination, 290–292
Excess return model, 142
Exchange, 7, 8, 11, 29, 31, 33, 36,
    38, 39, 46, 56, 58, 60, 64, 65,
    69, 93, 94, 108–111
Exotic credit, 50
Expected credit
  default loss, 129
  exposure, 129
Expected
  default probability, 274
  loss premium, 240–242
Exposures, 12, 18, 33, 35, 41,
    49, 60, 106, 109, 112, 113,
    251, 276–278, 303, 304, 307,
    309, 310
  derivative, 106, 310
  primary, 18
Expropriation risk, 118
Extension risk characteristic, 92
External
  credit references, 57
  investors, 95
Extreme
  asset overvaluation, 173
  portfolio losses, 251

Factors, 15, 26, 28, 34, 51, 83,
    124, 138, 139, 144–146, 148,
    149, 152–155, 178–180, 183,
    235, 303

add-on, 306, 310
  discount, 175, 176
  explanatory, 154, 155
Fair price, 37, 38, 170
Fees, 5, 7, 10, 11, 13, 34, 35,
  43–45, 49, 56, 73, 74, 76, 87,
  90, 239, 302
Final investors, 244
Financial institutions, 14, 16, 17,
  36, 53, 57, 61, 68, 84, 99, 100,
  103, 203, 207, 209, 251, 315
Firm asset correlation, 232
First-to-default basket
  shares, 45
Five-year
  asset value, 204
  cumulative default
    probability, 204
Fixed
  asset, 28
  credit, 38
Fixed-rate bonds, 6, 26, 28,
  29, 31
Forecast correlation portfolio
  risk, 148
Forecasting
  default probabilities, 179
  models, standard, 258
Fund
  management, 242, 243
  manager, 108, 113
Fundamental asset swap
  packages, 27
Fundamental credit
  weakness, 116
Funded
  credit derivatives, 54
  synthetic CDOs, 91

GARCH
  models, 130, 134
  volatility model, 160
Generalized portfolio multi-
  index model, 151
Global
  credit, 25
  institutional investor
    networks, 66
  investors, 3
Group emerging-market
  assets, 83
Guaranteed credit default, 62
Guidelines, risk-based capital,
  304, 306

Hedge
  credit risk exposures, 14
  default risk, 60
  funds, 14, 40–42, 57, 69, 70,
    80, 86, 92, 107, 108, 110,
    111, 218
  risks, 65
Hedging risks, 92
High default correlation, 79

High-default-risk firms, 208
Higher-quality asset pools, 83
Higher-risk equity securities, 194
Higher-yielding assets, 69
Highest probabilities, 269
High-grade
  asset, 66
  buyers, 69
  bank loans, 87
  banks, 90
  credit risk portfolios, 92
High-quality
  assets, 91
  counterparties, 250, 251
High-rated FRNs asset, 26
High-return asset, 219
High-return-to-risk asset, 219
High-yield loans, 81, 101, 102
Historical default, 198
Horizon, 16, 100, 196, 204, 225,
  226, 235, 277, 278
Hypothetical portfolio, 73, 83

Implicit
  default-risk-free security, 239
  factor model, 154
  market price, 184
Implied
  asset
    value, 200
    volatility, 201
  default probabilities, 163
  forward credit, 60
  market
    price, 214
    risk premium, 242
Index, 36–38, 59, 94, 107, 138,
  148, 154, 233
  default losses, 94, 95
  defaults, 38
  model, single, 148, 149
Index-based multifactor
  model, 149
Industries, 4, 5, 18, 43, 70, 75,
  83, 88, 98, 100, 167, 187, 189,
  198, 232–234, 286, 287
Industry risk, 189
Initial
  portfolio, 69
  risk, 276
Institutional investors, 57,
  69, 70
Institutions, 14, 16–21, 26, 34,
  42, 54, 98, 100, 104, 130, 161,
  255, 256, 265, 271, 272,
  310–312
  corporate, 97, 98
  depository, 310
Instruments, 3, 5, 17, 19, 22, 48,
  53, 74, 168, 195, 225, 239,
  301, 311
Interest
  rate
    factor, 235
    risk, 60, 74, 81, 313

rates, 5, 6, 16, 18, 26, 28, 48,
  73, 75, 98, 151, 152, 166,
  201, 235, 305
  risk-free, 166, 200, 278
Intermediaries, 3, 6, 16, 17, 23,
  25, 26, 31, 32, 53, 54, 56, 57,
  99, 104, 255, 280, 299
Investment
  banks, 14, 80, 102, 103, 218
  credit-risky, 12, 58
  portfolios, 107
Investor-driven, 69
  capital markets, 5
Investor/intermediary goals, 69
Investors, 6, 12, 13, 26–32,
  49–51, 54, 56–66, 69–72, 74,
  76, 81, 82, 85, 86, 88–90,
  92–94, 99, 100, 171, 172
Issuer, 5, 12, 31, 54, 56, 57,
  59–62, 65, 79, 92, 102, 128,
  167, 266, 267
  defaults, 266
Issuer/asset repackager, 58
Issuers default, 267
Issuers/asset repackagers, 58

K-factor model, 140, 142, 147
Knockout credit option, 50

Legal/credit terms, 287
Lending, high-risk, 101
Leverage, 56, 60, 64, 73, 78,
  83, 186, 187, 189, 197, 203,
  218, 244
  factor, 60
Leveraged
  money market fund, 243
  portfolio, 64
Liabilities, 36, 44, 58, 70, 72, 79,
  86, 167, 185–187, 190–192,
  199–203, 224, 243, 257
  corporate, 166, 217, 221, 239
  total, 186, 201
Liquidity, 14, 17, 19, 20, 34, 37,
  53, 57, 66, 80, 85, 91, 92, 94,
  99, 107, 203
Loan portfolios, 103, 104, 119
Loans, 19, 20, 35, 41, 42, 50,
  80–82, 85–89, 101, 102,
  104–106, 128, 129, 225–227,
  230, 235, 236, 238–242, 250,
  251, 257, 258
Local credit risk, 67
Long credit, 17
  positions, 104
Long-dated credit asset, 64
Loss
  credit protection, 9, 40
  given default, 225
  risk, 240, 245
Losses, 16–21, 33, 45, 46, 78, 79,
  90, 91, 93, 94, 113, 114, 123,
  124, 225, 226, 236–240,
  244–246, 252, 253, 274, 275,
  292, 304

expected, 79, 83, 101, 213, 216, 225–228, 236, 237, 239, 241, 248, 274, 275
large, 21, 79, 236, 237
mark-to-market, 30, 102
potential, 20, 50, 119, 128, 129, 274
realized, 237
Low
asset
values, 194
result, 235
volatility, 187
default
rates, 266
risk, 243
probability event, 18
risk bond, 58
Low-default-risk firms, 208
Lower
asset values, 194
credit quality, 57
default
rates, 267
risk, 70
investor, 13
probability event, 45
quality assets, 83
risk weight, 303
Lower-rated fixed-rate bonds asset, 26

Macroeconomic
factors, 148, 152
models, 152, 153
Managed portfolio, 69
Manage/hedge portfolios, 42
Management process, credit risk, 255, 267, 270
Managers, credit portfolio, 248, 252
Managing default risk, 218
Market, 5–8, 14–16, 21, 22, 25, 26, 37–40, 92, 93, 99, 100, 116–118, 148, 149, 153, 154, 179, 190, 191, 206, 207, 242, 243, 297, 298
asset values, 222, 223, 228, 231, 233
bonds, 298
borrowers, 82
default instruments, 168
equity, 243
estimate, 168
events, 256
factors, 75, 233
fundamentals, 111
growth, 13, 15, 24
index, 148, 150
leverage, 201
movements, 148, 305
multiple, 191
net, 186, 187
opportunities, 68, 69, 86
participants, 14, 179, 217, 295

premium, 239
price changes, 307
prices, 12, 35, 164, 184, 190, 192, 193, 214, 215, 238–240, 243, 247
postdefault, 58, 75
secondary, 63, 64, 80, 111, 272
value, 40, 67, 71, 80, 84, 85, 185–189, 192–195, 197–200, 202, 221–224, 238, 239, 243, 294, 295, 298
value CDO, 84, 85
value structures, 84–86
Market-based
credit, 56
default information, 168
recovery price, 35
Market/credit default
elements, 58
Marketing loans, 104
Marketplace, 3, 16, 26, 29, 30, 36, 54, 99, 108, 154, 168, 295, 299
Market-related losses, 18
Market-traded contracts, 164
Mark-to-market exposure, 103
Match investor expectations, 72
Maturity, 8, 28, 34, 37, 40, 43, 60, 61, 64, 75, 99, 100, 113, 114, 223, 225, 306, 309
date, contracted, 29, 30
Maximum asset maturities, 83
Measure, distance-to-default, 189, 198
Measuring risk, 225
Mezzanine, index default losses, 94, 95
M-factor model, 152
Middle-market borrowers, 258
Minimizing risk, 244
Mispricing to portfolio, 247
Model
credit risks, 255
linking equity, 201
risk-neutral values, 214
Modeling
credit portfolio, 231, 277
default, 221
swaps, 163
Models, 73, 133, 134, 138, 139, 146–148, 151–153, 155, 163–169, 190, 191, 204–209, 218, 219, 225, 226, 230, 231, 238, 239, 260–262, 276, 277
base recovery rates, 167
cross-sectional, 153–155, 161
default, 197
equity, 201
factor, 140, 154, 164, 166, 232, 235, 236
fundamental, 153
option-pricing, 199
stochastic, 261, 262
structural, 183, 191, 231
valuation, 168, 184, 191, 216, 252

Moody's average default rates, 275
Moody's Investors Services, 170
Mortgage
banker, 207
loan
portfolios, 90
risk, 90
Multifactor
modeling approach, 154
models, 138, 139, 142, 143, 145, 146, 148, 153, 161
macroeconomic, 151, 152
risk models, 148
Multiple
credit
default events, 9
exposures, 42
references, 59
defaults, 77
reference assets, 107
Multiple-bank lenders, 88
Mutual funds, 107, 193, 217, 218, 243

Negative
default correlations, 228
Noncash credits, 257
Nondefault, 212, 229, 230
states, 278
Nondefaulting, 291
Nondiversifiable
risk, 240
Nontraded assets, 239
Notes, credit-linked, 11, 53
Notional portfolio, 93

Obligations, 4, 7, 10, 16, 20, 43, 45–48, 66, 88, 101, 107, 221–223, 289, 290, 293, 295–299
hedged, 309
underlying, 309
Obligor, 4, 16, 19, 43, 75, 78, 88, 91, 109, 111, 128, 165, 166, 251, 252, 279, 303, 304
credit ratings, 167
Optimal portfolio
liquidation strategies, 127
weights, 127
Option
to default, 221
premium, 30, 32
OTC credit derivatives, 15
Outsized default, 269

Package, asset swap, 6, 27, 29, 31
Parameters, estimated, 135, 138
Participants, 18, 26, 38, 97–99, 164, 285

Parties, 3, 4, 8, 12, 28, 29, 31, 33,
    39, 56, 72, 285, 287, 289–294,
    297–299, 304
  nondefaulting, 289, 291, 292
Payment, 4, 7, 8, 10, 11, 20, 28,
    33, 35, 38, 39, 42–44, 113,
    114, 117, 118, 163, 289,
    292–294, 297
  default, 33
    thresholds, 293
Pension funds, 14, 107, 108, 111,
    112, 119, 217, 218
Performing
  credits, 44
  value-at-risk analysis, 123
Physical
  probability, 184
  reference assets, 34
Political risk, 118
  insurance policy, 118
Pool, 13, 36, 37, 42, 66, 70, 71,
    74–83, 85, 86, 88, 90, 91, 95,
    108, 266, 267
Portfolio, 70, 72–74, 78–80,
    83–90, 103, 104, 126, 136,
    137, 193, 194, 217–221,
    226–228, 230, 235–238,
    244–248, 250, 251, 276
  analysis, 217, 219
  asset values, 123
  assets, 78, 227
  calculation, 79
  complexity, 75
  concentrations, 101
  construction, 78, 83
  correlation matrix, 147
  credit
    exposures, 255
    risk, 253
  defaults, 44
    reference, 88, 93
  diversification, 34, 85, 217,
    224, 225, 248
  downside risk, 251
  exposure, 93
  holdings, 221
  loss measures, 227
  losses, 226, 236, 244
Portfolio
  management
    expertise, 81
    function, 242
    process, 248
    tool, 219
  manager, 13, 69–71, 74–76,
    79, 81, 82, 85–87, 92, 123,
    142, 155, 220, 230, 238, 248,
    252, 253
    design, 85
    experience, 83
    performance, 84
    work, 70
  manager/team, 79
  optimal, 127, 219
  optimization, 127, 248
  optimized, 248

result, 250
return, 126, 247
risk, 126, 220, 258
  estimates, 142
  management, 17
  modeling purposes, 251
risk/return, 185
size, 248
swaps, 129
times, 85
value realizations, 235, 236
values, 123, 227, 276
Portfolio
  weights, 228
  well-diversified, 218,
    226, 242
Position/risk, 21
Postdefault, 36, 39, 58
  price, 7, 33, 43, 44, 46, 51, 94
  value, 12
Potential
  assets, 248
  credit problems, 256
  equity investors, 75
  maximum credit
    exposure, 103
  risk, 103
  secondary investors, 80
Preferred risk/return
    profiles, 69
Prevalent credit, 304
Price, 4, 9, 29, 34, 35, 38, 39, 41,
    42, 51, 102, 124, 125, 130,
    131, 168, 178–180, 190, 205,
    206, 241, 242
Price
  movement, 148, 152
  premium, 127, 128
  risk, 102
Pricing models, derivative, 164,
    165, 198
Primary
  credit documents, 287
  market transactions, 63
  risk, 310
    exposure, 311
Prior year default activity, 266
Probability, 79, 128–130,
    163–165, 169–176, 178–181,
    191, 201–204, 222–225,
    228–230, 236–238, 240–242,
    244, 251–253, 267, 277–279
  calculation, 222
  distribution, 190, 261
  implied, 108, 171, 181
  joint, 18, 228, 253
  reference credit, 34
  risk-neutral, 184, 214
  statistics, 171
  survival, 171, 174, 175
Problem assets, 17
Productive assets, 258
Professional portfolio
    managers, 79
Profile, extreme risk, 60
Project finance loans, 80, 82

Protection, 6, 12, 13, 37, 45, 56,
    60, 62, 90, 118, 176, 179, 181,
    207, 208, 251, 252, 303, 304
  buyer, 4, 20, 37, 38, 88, 94,
    165, 169, 251, 252, 298, 304,
    306, 308
  stops, 251, 252
  credit risk, 97
Providers, credit support,
    289, 292
Prudent
  risk constraints, 103
  risks, 70
Public credit markets, 116
Puttable asset swap
  functions, 29
  packages, 26

Quantitative credit risk analysis
    tools, 185
Quoted market prices, 108

Rate, 6, 26, 27, 74, 85, 172,
    195, 203
  risk-free base, 240–242
Rated credits, 170
Ratings, 43, 57, 83, 88, 103, 167,
    170, 210, 266, 268–271, 274,
    275, 278
Ratings-based default
    probability models, 167
Receivables portfolio, 100
Recoveries, 61, 93, 124, 163, 164,
    173, 174, 176, 183, 219, 225,
    256, 272–274
Reducing credit exposure, 106
Reference
  asset, 4, 8, 9, 12, 18, 32–34,
    36, 39, 40, 54, 58–60, 63,
    64, 76, 89, 169, 305–307,
    310, 311
  credit-risky, 3, 17
  price, 61
  trades, 61
Reference
  credit
    portfolio, 51
    risk exposures, 42
    trades, 96
    trading 96
  obligation, 7, 45, 88, 294, 295,
    297, 298, 305, 309
  portfolio, 46, 93
References, traded market,
    165, 168
Regulators, banking, 17, 308
Remarketable asset swap, 29
Repackaged
  bonds, 12, 53, 56, 62, 63, 96
  credit risk, 69, 256
Rescheduled bank loans, 64
Residual
  investor, 91
  risk contribution, 245

Restructuring
  credit events, 309
  risk, 309
Return, 17, 31, 64, 66, 72–74, 79,
    101, 102, 128, 138, 139, 172,
    173, 219, 232, 233, 240, 241,
    244, 247–249
  composite factor, 232
  expected, 126, 127, 130, 139,
    157, 202, 203, 241, 244, 245,
    253, 262–264
  index, 233
  total, 8, 39, 40, 58, 59,
    64–66, 113
Return-to-risk, 219
  assets
    characteristics, 248
    ratios, 219, 247, 248
    change, 247
Review credit, 311
Risk, 13, 16–21, 57, 58, 70, 73,
    74, 88–91, 94–96, 123, 124,
    127–130, 216–220, 225, 226,
    243–251, 302–305, 307,
    311, 312
  aversion, 214
  basis, 19, 75, 118
  calculations, 144
  capacity, 97, 109
    providers, 100
    users, 100
  capital
    charges, 305
    category, 307
  characteristics, 240
  charges, 305, 306
    counterparty, 307, 310
  contribution, 219, 245–248,
    276, 278
  contributions change, 246, 247
  control, 54
  convertibility, 65, 118
  counterparty, 17, 66, 306,
    307, 311
  currency, 37, 313
  decisions, 101, 123
  decomposition, 123, 148
  default/spread, 100
  economic, 9, 40
  elements, 307
  estimates, 123, 127, 130, 137
  exposures, 17, 86, 124
  factors, 235, 236, 264
  governance process, 103
  grade, 277
  idiosyncratic, 148, 159, 161
  junior, 304
  landscape, 124
  legal, 16, 20, 58, 83
  liquidity, 99
  management, 3, 21, 40, 53, 66,
    68, 123, 126, 130, 205, 255,
    312, 314, 315
    business, 285
    framework, 24
    practices, 301

  purposes, 155, 280, 310
  managers, 142, 146, 155, 159
  measures, 124
  modeling approach, 147
  models, 138, 149, 154
  operational, 16, 21, 24, 256
  operations, 312
  parameters, 16, 108
  premium, 73, 101, 167, 184,
    191, 240, 242
  prepayment, 82
  quantity, 148
  reduction, 17, 219, 227, 245
    benefits, 308
  stand-alone, 220, 245
  statistics, 123, 139
  substitution, 302
  systematic, 159
  transfer, 42, 69, 86, 87, 90,
    306, 311
    mechanism, 299
  weight, 302–304, 306, 316
  weighting, 91
Risk-adjusted
  calculations, 101
  price, 240
  rate, 17
Risk-based capital
  calculations, 311
  guidance set, 304
  purposes, 308
  requirements, 304
  rules, 310
  treatment, 304
Risk-bearing instruments, 301
Risk/capital motivations, 68
Risk-free
  asset, 240
  benchmark, 4, 8, 39, 47,
    60, 167
    fixed-rate, 11, 47
    rate, 39
  bonds, 11, 19, 56, 62, 172
  interest rate benchmark, 166
  investment, 172
  modeling, 166
  money market/Treasury
    bill, 111
  rate, 142, 171, 172, 181, 214
    implicit, 252
Riskiest component, 69
Risk-mitigating hedge, 303
Risk-neutral, 214, 239
Risk-rating migration, 276
Risk-return model, 148
Risk/return
  opportunities, 25
  parameters, 56
  profiles, 60, 96
Risk-weighting factors, 305

Sample correlations, 231, 232
Seasoned assets, 63
Secondary
  investors, 80

  market
    credit assets, 86
    loans, 218
Secured creditors, 272
Securities, 9, 13, 31, 39, 54–58,
    63, 64, 66, 75, 81–83, 86, 92,
    108, 227, 228, 238, 239, 272
  credit-risky, 12, 239
  reference, 4, 6, 60
Securitizations, credit portfolio,
    55, 56, 84
Senior
  creditors, 272
  index default losses, 94, 95
  investors, 76, 89
  risk, 304
  secured bank loans, 272
  tranche investors, 95
  risk position, 91
Short-term volatility, 159, 160
Simultaneous default, 36
Single
  credit/obligor, 79
  creditor, 221
  default, 225
    event, 45
  factor model, 149
  reference
    asset, 60
    credit, 109
Skewed loss probabilities, 236
Sovereign
  credits, 99
  risk, 118
Special-case credit
  phenomenon, 276
Sponsoring bank, 13, 86, 88,
    90, 93
Spread/default risk, 91
Standard
  asset swaps, 26
  bond portfolios, 92
  default CLN, 62
Statistical
  factor model, 154
  multifactor model, 155
Stochastic default intensities,
    166
Strategy, 47, 101, 102, 104–106,
    112, 113, 116, 117, 264
Structural credit risk
  modeling, 184
Structure, 7, 29, 31, 37, 38,
    43–45, 58–60, 62–65, 71,
    73–76, 78–81, 83–89, 91, 100,
    117, 166
  synthetic, 29, 31, 90, 92
  term, 48, 111, 167, 173, 181,
    191, 240, 278
  waterfall, 76, 77
Structured
  corporate credit
    instruments, 218
  credit
    assets, 54
    instruments, 5

debt securities, 53
finance
  assets, 73
  bonds, 81
  mortgage assets, 95
  notes/bonds, 81
Structured/synthetic
  credit, 25
Structuring credit
  derivatives, 293
Subordinated
  creditors, 272
  debt/equity hybrids, 71
  investors, 89
  risk, 69
  tranche investors, 78
Swap, 6, 26, 28–33, 64, 75, 87,
  166, 168, 219, 247, 248,
  252, 309
  bank, 27, 29, 32
  first-to-default, 45
  total return, 8, 17, 25, 39, 41,
  42, 113
Synthetic CDOs, 13, 66, 69, 81,
  87–92, 94, 96, 97
Synthetic credit, 25
  portfolio structures, 43
Synthetic
  credit risk exposure, 111
  short credit positions, 92
Synthetic/structured
  collateralized debt
  obligations, 11
Systematic risk factors, 232
Systemic risk, 246

Target portfolios, 13, 78, 88
Third-party
  credit borrower/issuer, 32
  investors, 86

Time
  horizon, 80, 205, 214, 231, 238,
  265, 266
  series model, 152
Tools
  credit risk, 9, 39, 268
  interest rate risk, 9, 39
  risk management, 276, 301, 315
Total asset
  value, 224
  volatility, 204
Trade, 14, 21, 26, 38, 50, 51, 55,
  61, 64, 86, 99, 110, 186, 239,
  248, 298
  credit, 26
Traded
  equity prices, 233
  firms, 231, 233, 235
Traditional credit-based
  banking, 5
Tranched risk protection, 304
Tranches, 13, 69–71, 73, 75,
  77, 78, 80, 83, 84, 87, 90,
  92–96, 167
  residual/equity, 69, 72, 74
Transaction risks, 17
Transactional
  requirements, 98, 99
  risks, 17
Transfer
  credit risk, 89
  risk, 90
Transferring
  bank, 304
  convertibility risk, 118
Transition
  matrixes measure
  probability-based
  upgrades, 266
  probabilities, 279
Transitions/defaults, 277

TRSs, 8, 9, 39–41, 53, 55, 58, 60,
  64, 66, 97, 100, 104, 119, 168,
  302, 309, 310
  funded, 9, 40
Two-factor model, 142

Unavoidable risk, 240
Unexpected default events, 219
Unilateral contract, 7, 9, 10, 17
Unprotected risk, 303
Unrelated reference credits, 44
Unsecured bank loan, 274
Unsystematic risk factors, 259
Up-front premium, 11, 41, 107,
  113, 119

Value
  correlation, 230, 231
  risk, 225
Value-at-risk, 127, 129, 130, 305
Valuing credit derivatives, 169
Vanilla credit, 49
Variance, 123, 125–127, 130, 131,
  133–135, 139, 142, 144, 146,
  158, 204
VK model, 191, 192, 199, 201
Volatile assets, 194
Volatility
  clustering, 131–133
  estimation models, 130
Volatility risk, 313

Weak reference credits, 36
Weighted average
  pool asset ratings, 83
  probability, 83
Widens, reference credit, 10, 11,
  49, 112

About the Authors

Erik Banks is chief risk officer at a multistrategy hedge fund and has been active in the banking sector for 20 years. Erik has held senior risk management positions at Merrill Lynch, XL Capital, and Citibank in New York, Tokyo, London, and Hong Kong, and has written 20 books on derivatives, risk, emerging markets, and merchant banking.

Morton Glantz is on the finance faculty of Fordham Graduate Business School in New York. He is widely published in financial journals and has authored a number of books, including *Optimal Trading Strategies, Managing Bank Risk, Scientific Financial Management,* and *Loan Risk Management.* He is also a financial advisor to government and business. Morton lives in the New York area with his wonderful, loving wife Maryann.

Paul Siegel is Chief Executive Officer of The Globecon Group, a specialized banking and financial services professional development, conference, and publishing firm operating in the capital markets, credit, risk, corporation finance, and wealth management markets. Paul holds a bachelor's degree in economics and a master's degree in business from the University of Pennsylvania and New York University, respectively. He lives in the New York area with his wife, Helen, and their two amazing children, Lexy and Sam.